Tom Davison

DECISION THEORY
AND HUMAN BEHAVIOR

DECISION THEORY AND HUMAN BEHAVIOR

Wayne Lee

JOHN WILEY & SONS, INC.

New York · London · Sydney · Toronto

PREFACE

This book is an introductory survey and evaluation of decision theory in psychology. Although many other books on decision theory exist, these books are either strictly or largely mathematical, and include little or no information on the behavior of real persons, or they deal with only a limited part of decision theory, for example, signal detection theory or game theory. In contrast, the present book emphasizes behavioral research and is reasonably comprehensive in its coverage; in particular, there are chapters devoted to subjective probability, utility, choosing between gambles, probability learning, signal detection theory, information processing in decision making, and game theory. Each chapter covers the relevant mathematical decision theory and surveys experimental results. The emphasis is on individual human behavior observed in a laboratory setting, not on real-life individual and organizational decision making.

This book does not attempt to survey the mathematics of decision theory in any substantial way. Only enough mathematics is presented to allow the reader to understand the basic principles and the experiments. The mathematical prerequisites are minimal. The reader should know the elements of probability theory and statistics. He should understand the analytic geometry of the straight line, and be able to solve for two unknowns from two linear equations. For Chapter 7, he must comprehend the idea of a probability density, and be familiar with the normal distribution. In brief, the mathematics in the book should be comprehensible to any graduate student or professional in the behavioral sciences, and to a large majority of juniors and seniors.

Most psychologists have very little understanding of decision theory. They think of it as mathematical and hard-nosed, and avoid it. That is unfortunate, for behavioral decision theory is well worth understanding, regardless of one's area of specialization. I hope that this book will make behavioral decision theory more accessible and comprehensible to professionals and students in all areas of psychology. People in many disciplines other than psychology per se are interested in human decision making. These disciplines include economics, sociology, political science, statistics, operations research, business administration, and human factors. Many texts in these fields discuss the decision making of some ideal person. But how do real people behave? The present book contains much information on this question that should interest students of the disciplines mentioned.

A reference list is given at the end of each chapter. Since the reference list is intended as a bibliography for the topics covered in the chapter, some citations, such as literary quotations, are given in footnotes. Otherwise, all chapter citations are given in the chapter reference list (which also may contain an occasional non-cited work). Certainly no chapter in the book covers all the relevant literature, nor is the reference list intended as a complete bibliography. Nonetheless, the referencing is substantial for most chapters.

I started this book while a member of the psychology faculty at the University of California in Berkeley and I completed it while employed in the Human Factors Research Department of Bell Telephone Laboratories in Holmdel, New Jersey. I am indebted to both institutions.

Duncan Luce read the entire manuscript with care, and is responsible for numerous improvements in both substance and style. I am also indebted to many other persons for assistance, encouragement, and suggestions. My sincere thanks goes to each of them. Only I, however, should be held responsible for the final contents.

Albany, California   WAYNE LEE
June 1971

CONTENTS

DECISION THEORY
AND HUMAN BEHAVIOR

CHAPTER 1

Rationality and Its Scientific Study

1.1 INTRODUCTION

Commentators on human conduct have attributed human choice to various bases, including instinct, id, altruism, reinforcement, blind passion, duty, wickedness, and moral uprightness. There is another possible basis of greater concern here: reason. Recent studies of decision theory in the behavioral sciences can be thought of as a continuation, using modern methods of scientific investigation, of the agelong quest of the social philosopher for an understanding of proper and actual human action in relation to reason.

Chapter 1 begins with a general discussion of the cultural background of "rational man." Next we consider the use of the term "rational" in decision theory. After discussion of some aspects of scientific investigation, we conclude with an overview of the role of decision theory in behavioral science.

1.2 RATIONALITY IN CULTURAL PERSPECTIVE

The role of reason in human affairs has been the subject of many of the most important philosophical debates throughout history. These debates have concerned the following issues: (1) To what extent can knowledge be gained from pure reason, and to what extent must it derive from experience? (2) To what extent can religious belief be founded on reason, and to what extent must it rest on faith and authority? (3) Will reason lead to virtuous behavior, or to selfishness and immorality? (4) Is the cultivation and application of reason a worthwhile endeavor for a person? (5) Is human behavior based on reason? Since decision theory concerns the use of reason in human decision making, we briefly discuss each of the five issues. The discussion here concerns the gen-

1

eral cultural background of decision theory. The technical background in probability theory and economics is discussed in Chapters 3 and 4.

Epistomological Rationalism

Epistomology is the philosophical study of the nature and origin of human knowledge. Epistomological rationalism, historically, was the doctrine that human knowledge could be derived on the basis of reason alone, using "self-evident" propositions and logical deduction. Philosophers adhering to this doctrine were called *rationalists.* Opposed to the rationalists were the *empiricists,* who held that, except for logical truths, experience was necessary to verify statements. The rationalist school can be traced to Plato: the empiricist school, although of ancient origin, became important much later with Bacon. These schools disputed vigorously until Hume leveled devastating criticisms at the extreme forms of rationalism.

Theological Rationalism

In religious thought, rationalism is opposed not to empiricism, but to revelation. The issue here is: are religious truths capable of being included in a rationalist theory, or must they be accepted on faith or authority? "Rationalism" in this context sometimes refers to epistemological rationalism, but at other times refers to the use of reason to investigate or justify religion, where "reason" includes the use of experience.

Rationalism has been present in varying degrees in Christian thought from the earliest times to the present. As a rule, the anti-rationalists have held the positions of authority in Christianity, and rationalist philosophers and theologians have had to tread very delicately to avoid condemnation. Still, some of the most prominent Churchmen were, and to this day are, rationalists. The Catholic Church has, since Medieval times, accepted the rationalist philosophy of St. Thomas; however, St. Thomas allowed that "authority" was the final arbiter in cases of conflict between reason and revelation. Reason has, for the most part, been accepted within religion only to the extent that it has confirmed religious authority.

Ethical Rationalism

Ethical rationalism is the doctrine that reason is the road to right action. It is not the same thing as religious rationalism, since it can be a secular philosophy as well as a religious one; however, ethical rationalism is typically part of any system of theological rationalism. According to ethical rationalism, right moral action results from knowledge and reason. If one wishes to find out what action is good, one must reason. With perfect knowledge, says the doctrine, one will naturally do the correct and moral thing; furthermore, moral action will result in happiness and the good life. This doctrine is hoary with age and great names, for example, Confucius, Socrates, Aristotle, the Stoics, and the Epicurians. The tradition has continued to present times, for example, in the person of Bertrand Russell.

A contrasting tradition asserts that the reasoning man will pursue his own ends at the expense of the social group. Skeptical pre-Socratic philosophers in Greece hypothesized that the gods were the invention of statesmen to frighten the populace away from self-interested, socially destructive behavior. Plato despaired, especially in his later years, that a society could be formed from a natural ethic, and he specified, in the utopian society portrayed in *The Laws*, inculcation of character-forming myths, state censorship, and persecution of heresy. The later Stoics believed that a natural ethic would be suitable only for the intellectual classes of a society and that religion was a necessary social force for the populace.

Self-interest seems naturally to be in logical contrast to social interest; however, many philosophers have taken pains to point out that these interests are not at variance with each other, or at least they need not be. Aristippus, in ancient Greece, suggested that even ostensibly social and self-disinterested acts are based on individual hope of pleasure or fear of pain. If public acts of benevolence bring social approval and cowardice in battle brings condemnation, then it is to a person's self-interest to be benevolent in his society and courageous in battle, even to the point of death.

Adam Smith, in the eighteenth century economic classic, *The Wealth of Nations,* portrayed man as acting in his self-interest in economic affairs, and yet argued that this implied no asocial result; on the contrary, man acting in his own self-interest also acts in society's interest. The man who is a skilled arrow maker can make the most profit from concentrating on arrow-making; yet, society benefits also by this self-interested specialization, since, *in toto,* more wealth will be created. Though he admitted that some selfish acts are detrimental to the public interest, Smith felt that any governmental attempts at regulation would do more public harm than that caused by the original detriment: the cure would be worse than the disease. Smith's moral justifications for self-interested economic behavior have lost much of their appeal, particularly since the Depression. We still hear, however, such sentiments as "What's good for General Motors is good for the country," which descend from Smith's rationalizations for the unregulated economy.

The eighteenth and nineteenth century utilitarians promoted a secular ethic which equated right action with that which resulted in the greatest happiness for the greatest number of people. Jeremy Bentham, one of the foremost utilitarians, reconciled self-interest and social interest by the workings of social, political, and theological *sanctions*. I act in the general good because it is in my self-interest to avoid social disapproval, arrest, and eternal punishment in hell. It is not just knowledge or reason *per se* that leads to moral action; within a proper framework of custom and law, however, self-interested behavior can be ethical.

Development in nineteenth century biology had profound effects on the discussions of natural ethics. The theory of evolution and natural selection led many thinkers to conclude that men were involved in a tooth-and-claw struggle with each other for survival. Moralists objected to the theory, in part, because of this view it presented of man against man. There were perhaps good reasons for these objections, since such thinking may have been partly responsible for tragic results by helping to rationalize Nazi amorality. Later writers in biology pointed out that the struggle for survival did not imply man against man, any more than it implied cell against cell in an individual, or bee against bee in a beehive. The society and the species can be the unit of selection as well as the individual, and thus there can be a common interest in cooperation.

The Value of Reason to the Individual

As we have seen, statesmen, churchmen, and moralists have often had serious reservations about rational man because of the difficulties he could create for them or for the social order. In addition, we find criticism of the life of reason as a goal for the individual. This has been expressed in various "back-to-nature" movements throughout history that have proclaimed that right action, happiness, and the good life are most apt to be attained by going back to a simpler life and avoiding the vanities of reason.

Although in *Proverbs* we are told "Happy is the man that findeth wisdom, and the man that getteth understanding,"[1] in *Ecclesiastes* we are told that ". . . in much wisdom is much grief: and he that increaseth knowledge increaseth sorrow."[2] The protagonist of the *Rubaiyat of Omar Khayyam* "Divorced old barren Reason from my Bed, And took the Daughter of the Vine to Spouse."[3]

A major theme of the eighteenth century Romantic movement in literature was the destructive effect on the human spirit of a too attentive use of reason. Faust is portrayed as disillusioned by his lifetime search for knowledge: a gentle young lady is much to be preferred. The English poet Wordsworth expressed a similar disillusionment with the reasoned life: communion with nature and acceptance of one's emotions were more important to him.

Rationality as a General Behavior Explanation

As we shall see, a good deal of the recent work in decision theory concerns the hypothesis that human behavior is, as a rule, rational. Examination of the opinions of the great thinkers of past ages reveals that, for the most part, no such hypothesis was entertained. The typical human action was supposed by the great thinkers in both Oriental and Western cultures to be based not on reason but on ignorance, superstition, or the passion of the moment, and the sorry state of civilization was traced to the sorry ways the typical man made

---

[1] *Proverbs*, iii, 13 (King James Version).
[2] *Ecclesiastes*, i, 18 (King James Version).
[3] *Rubaiyat of Omar Khayyam*, verse 55 (tr. by Edward Fitzgerald).

his choices. The common man's irrationality was the despair of great utopians like Confucius and Plato. Admirers of Socrates would hardly be apt to propose the hypothesis that human behavior is rational after Socrates was condemned by his fellow citizens as an enemy of the state.

The idea has been accepted that *some* men are rational, or largely so, at least for some class of decisions. Foremost among these is the *Self*. Complaints or conjectures about the irrationality of men, as far as I can judge, do not extend to be the one complaining. Those with views similar to the Self are, by implication, likewise absolved.

Philosophers such as Aristotle, Epicurus, Confucius, and the Stoics have described an ideal *philosophic man* who leads a placid life amid external turmoil by the application of reason to conduct. Such a philosopher, to the extent that he could follow his own ideals, might be considered a good approximation to rational man.

The rational man of decision theory can be traced to Man in the Marketplace, as presented by economic theorists. This *economic man* is the merchant pictured by Adam Smith; he is capable of seeing his own best economic interests and acting accordingly. Economic man's portrait is more clearly drawn in the classic summary of nineteenth century economic theory, the *Principles of Economics* by Alfred Marshall. Economic man is pictured as basing his economic actions and associations not on habit or custom, but on deliberate and knowledgeable reasoning about the possible results of his actions; his final choice is the course of action that can be expected to bring him maximum gain. Marshall clearly realized that this economic man was an ideal and not an exact description of economic behavior nor of behavior in general, but he thought that it was a close enough approximation for a limited sphere of man's decisions to allow the science of economics to utilize it. The term "economic man" is often used for the ideal rational man of decision theory, regardless of whether a business decision is involved.

Finally, with the development of modern science, we have that white-frocked rational ideal, *scientific man*. His conclusions, at least in his professional area, are supposedly based on fact and cold logic instead of his passions, desires, and prejudices. It can't be said, of course, that real scientists exactly match the ideal, but many scientists approach the ideal, in their professional areas, at least.

Throughout our lives we are admonished: "Use your head," "Think it through," "Be reasonable," "Let's try to be objective about this," etc. Yet when a person appears who approximates a rational ideal, is he applauded and admired? Often he is, yet we have reservations about him. Bertrand Russell noted of his eminent colleague, the philosopher Whitehead: "Socially he appeared kindly, rational and imperturbable, but he was not in fact imperturbable, and was certainly not that inhuman monster 'the rational man.' "[4] The "rational man"

---

[4] B. Russell, *The Autobiography of Bertrand Russell: 1872–1914*, Little, Brown, Boston, 1967, p. 203.

is often seen as cold-blooded, unemotional, unloving, and unlovable: in terms of a contemporary image, he has a computer for a brain.

Although most accounts of human behavior deny the general rationality of man, some writers have propounded a view that men, in general, act to advance to their own perceived best interests. Such a view sounds very much like a hypothesis of general rationality. Thomas Hobbes, for example, stated in *De Cive* that "everyone is compelled to seek what is good for him, and avoid what is bad for him by a necessity not less than that which compels the stone to fall downwards."[5]

Likewise, the utilitarian philosopher Jeremy Bentham, in *An Introduction to the Principles of Morals and Legislation* and *Deontology,* portrayed man as seeking to gain pleasure and avoid pain to the best of his ability. Bentham discussed a *hedonistic calculus,* which men supposedly apply to determine which decision to make. They choose the one which, according to the hedonistic calculus, will give the greatest happiness. In a sense, Hobbes and Bentham could be considered as proponents of the general rationality hypothesis. But they both only said that man *seeks* "happiness," not that his choices are actually the best for achieving "happiness."

It is often stated that Sigmund Freud demolished man's view of himself as a rational creature. Although there is, in a sense, some truth to the assertion, it is, I suspect, generally misunderstood. It certainly is not true that throughout history men of learning have generally considered human behavior to be based on "reason." It might be countered that "men of learning" are a small minority of "effete snobs," and that the masses of "real people" considered their own behavior to be based on reason. As I allowed previously, I expect that the Self usually had a Self-attributed rationality; the attribution of reason, however, did not extend to mankind, in general. For example, in the heyday of witchery and heresy, the behavior of many Others was perceived to be the result not of "reason," but of stubborness, wickedness, "error," possession by demons, etc. At least that would be my reading of history. Of course, our knowledge about history's "great silent majority" of illiterates is meager and secondhand.

What then, was the effect of Freud? Although he did not invent the idea of unconscious motivation, he did succeed in popularizing the notion among the educated classes in Western civilization. Assertions about human irrationality, when made in the context of Freudian theory, relate to the unconscious motivation of men. Freud and other psychoanalysts did not assert that only Others are unconsciously motivated—so is the Self. Freud's theory, then, requires the Self to accept its *own* irrationality, as well as the irrationality of others. This was his effect on man's view of mankind.

Freud's influence in this regard—though great—should not be overempha-

---

[5] T. Hobbes, *De Cive* (quoted from J. Cohen, *Humanistic Psychology,* Collier Books, New York, 1962, p. 24).

sized. As far as I can see, most Selves, today as before Freud, believe that they can give good and true reasons for their own behavior, whereas they perceive those who disagree with them to be "unreasonable," "illogical," etc., and even professional psychologists seem to be much more impressed with the lack of self-understanding in others than in themselves.

1.3 RATIONALITY IN DECISION THEORY

One trouble with the previous discussion, of course, is that the meaning of rationality (or reasonableness) is not at all clear. In the previous section "rationality" appeared to be used in several senses. In one sense, a rational man is one who does not lose his temper or get "carried away" by emotion. In another sense, a rational man is one who understands his own motivations. In an economic context, the rational man is one whose decisions are most favorable for producing profits. Many times, it seems, attributions of rationality or irrationality depend only on whether there is agreement with the Self, or a group of Selves holding the same viewpoint. Others who agree are "clearly" rational. Others who disagree are "clearly" irrational, unreasonable, etc. Finally, "rational man" has often been thought of as one having special methods or abilities to enable him to find truth that has escaped his fellow man. The methods have been called reasoning, logic, scientific method, etc.

In decision theory, the rational man is he who, when confronted with a decision situation, makes the choice (decision) that is best for him. This best decision is called a *rational* or *optimal* decision. We attempt no formal definition of the rational decision. Instead, we attempt to enlighten the reader about the concept of rationality in decision theory by listing and discussing some properties of a rational decision. The discussion is only introductory. For further clarification, it is necessary to read the succeeding chapters.

(*1*) *A rational decision is one* (*or more*) *of a specified set of possible decisions.* The basic idea of a "rational decision" is that it is, in some sense, a "best" or "optimal" decision. There may be more than one "best" decision if they are equally good, but an investigator cannot say that any decision is "best" unless he knows what the possible decisions are.

In laboratory studies of decision making, an experimental subject (*S*) is presented with a decision situation and told what his possible decisions can be. In actual human affairs, however, it is often not clear what the decision set is, either to a person or to an investigator of that person. The problem a person often has is to generate, i.e., think of, possible decisions which he can afterwards evaluate. Consider a committee of businessmen who have to decide on a location for a new manufacturing plant. At a given meeting of the committee there may be available a number of suggested plant sites, i.e., a decision set shared by the members and by a hypothetical investigator. The committee might pick one of these, satisfying standards of rationality so far as the investigator can tell.

But it is conceivable that there is a better plant site somewhere. Would it be rational to ignore such a possibility? If the committee knows that there are other possible plant sites that could be located by further searching, they could decide not to pick a plant site from the available set, but to search further. In a case like this, decision theory might still be applied if it had been agreed that "search further" was a possible decision, in addition to "buy plant site X." The problem of "deciding to search for more possible choices" is very important in real life, but is usually awkward for decision theory. In practice, Ss are given specified choice sets and are not required or expected to choose outside this set.

(2) *The rational decision depends on the decision principle employed by the investigator.* A decision principle is a rule for specifying which of the set of possible decisions is rational (or optimal). As we shall see in Chapter 2, there are a variety of *decision principles* or *criteria*. They can lead to conflicting specifications for the "rational decision." Thus, whether a decision is judged to be rational or not depends on the principle employed by the investigator. It is important, then, that the principle assumed for an investigation be clearly stated.

Oftentimes a decision, in foresight, could lead to one of several (or more) clearly distinguishable consequences. Sometimes the probabilities for these various results, contingent upon a decision, have well-known magnitudes, or at least calculable magnitudes that all expert probabilists would agree upon. If, for example, the decision involved placing a dollar bet in roulette, the probability for winning or losing could be determined by well-known methods. When such *objective probabilities* can be specified, it seems reasonable that these probabilities would bear on the rational decision, as, indeed, they do for some decision criteria. Such clear-cut probabilities are not available for most decisions men make. Nonetheless, some decision theorists feel that a probability-based criterion can still be employed by using a person's *subjective probabilities*. The theory and measurement of subjective probability are discussed in Chapter 3. For now, however, we can say that the subjective probabilities of two persons can differ, without either being "wrong."

Even if objective probabilities exist for a decision situation, a person may have subjective probabilities which differ from the objective ones. In such a case, a person may be "rational" with respect to his subjective probabilities but "nonrational" with respect to the objective probabilities. The usage of "rational" is not standard here; sometimes the person is required to use objective probabilities to be judged rational, and sometimes he is allowed to use subjective probabilities.

(3) *The rational decision for a decision situation may differ among persons.* One reason for this is, as noted, that subjective probabilities differ among people. Another reason is that people evaluate the possible consequences of a decision differently, and the rational decision is dependent on such evaluations. A very simple example: if the choice were between two phonograph records,

we could not require that the rational decision for all persons be one record or the other.

The value to a person of a particular consequence is called the *utility* of that consequence. (Utility theory and measurement is the topic of Chapter 4.) "Utility," in practice, reflects the *attractiveness* of a consequence to a person, as judged from foresight; this may differ from the contribution the consequence makes to the person's *welfare,* as judged by others or by himself in retrospect. Thus, to a drug addict, a shot of heroin would usually have a high "utility," and a rational decision (for him) would help him get it. The use of "rational" in such contexts is not usual, because people, in general, are reluctant to associate undesirable behavior (as seen by them) with reason. However, if "rational" were to be defined in terms of the desires others want a person to have, then the "rational" decision would depend on which "others" we pick. In any case, it does not seem sensible for the rational man to ignore his own desires in his decision making. This does not imply, of course, that he should ignore the wishes of other people altogether, for they will reward or punish him depending on his behavior.

(4) A rational decision is dependent on relevant information available to the person. We judge it not to be rational to ignore available information that is relevant to the decision, though for real-life situations particularly, the implications of such information for decision making are often not clear-cut. If a person were considering investing his money in stocks, for example, the "rational decision" should take account of relevant and available economic information. But the amount of relevant information would seem to be vast, if not limitless. The implications of much of it are not clearly understood by anyone. Who can say what the rational decision would be in the light of it? The concept of "availability" is likewise vague. Although we hardly could require rational man to take account of unavailable information in his decision making, in real life the availability of information is a matter of degree. Information in today's local newspaper is readily available. Information from a nonlocal newspaper of two year's ago is less readily available. Even "company secret" information, which might at first be thought of as "unavailable" to an outsider, might be obtained through espionage or bribery. The decision maker has to determine how much time, effort, and money to expend to obtain what information.

Laboratory studies provide a simpler setting. S is presented with information, the relevance of which is usually well understood by the investigator. In some experiments S is allowed the option of obtaining supplementary information, but, in analogy with real life, he must pay in proportion to the amount he wants (see Chapter 8).

Let us now compare and contrast the conception of the rational man in decision theory with other conceptions mentioned earlier. Decision theorists have been little concerned about outbursts of temper and other expressions of emotion. Rationality has been judged only in terms of the choices made, not in terms of the emotional concommitants of choice. Although, traditionally, the rational man has often been portrayed as one who carefully deliberates, and gives thoughtful and well-reasoned explanations for his beliefs or actions, decision theorists have been little interested in explanations; they have not cared much whether their Ss looked thoughtful while deciding, or whether they could give well-reasoned explanations for their decisions; they have not been concerned about the possible unconscious mechanisms behind the decisions. Rationality has been judged solely on the basis of the decisions made. In practice, the rational man of decision theory has been very closely related to the economic man who has tried to maximize profits. Decision theorists have been largely concerned with monetary rewards, although non-monetary rewards have not been neglected altogether.

We should not leave this section without mentioning the idea of *consistency* in decision making. Although the decision theory concept of rationality is usually described in terms of *best* decisions, in a sense, the best decision must be the one consistent with a person's preferences and beliefs. The interpretation of rationality in terms of consistency is considered further in Chapter 3.

For the moment we shall rest content with the concept of "rational decision." Of course, one rational decision does not make a rational man. A person's decision may be rational in one decision situation and nonrational in another. Presumably, the ideal rational man would be rational for all his decisions. Psychologists generally do not attempt to observe a wide class of decisions for a single person. Thus, we do not attempt to classify people as rational overall or not. Even for a particular decision situation it would be more useful to classify people on a continuum of "degree of rationality" rather than as "rational" or not. After all, it seems rather extreme to call a person "irrational" if he is not a perfect decision maker.

1.4   SOME ASPECTS OF SCIENTIFIC INVESTIGATION

We now consider some aspects of scientific investigation relating to studies in decision theory.

Models and Theories

Since we concern ourselves with decision *theory,* the meaning of "theory" is of some interest to us. A closely related and frequently used term is *model.* The distinctions between "theory" and "model" are not clear-cut in practice.

An area of scientific investigation can be divided into (1) the real-world objects and properties of these objects, (2) hypothetical constructs and rules for relating them, and (3) techniques for making observations on real-world objects and methods for deriving scale values for the observations. According to one usage, a *model* is domain (2) by itself, or part of domain (2). To test the empirical adequacy of the model, one must relate the model to the real world, domain (1), via observational and measurement techniques of domain (3). The three domains together, then, are said to constitute a theory. A theory can be rejected because of a failure of the model and the real world to correspond. A model, *per se,* can only be rejected on the grounds of logical inconsistency, but as part of a theory it can be rejected on empirical grounds. The foregoing usage of "model" and "theory" occurs, within psychology, in Torgerson's (1958) book, *Theory and Methods of Scaling.*

Other authors use "model" and "theory" in a quite different way. "Theory," for these authors, is a rather vague term referring to a set of concepts, methods, and findings associated with some approach to a science. A "model" is a special case of a theory, typically an application of the theory to a particular situation using rather specific assumptions allowed, but not required, by the theory. With this usage, a "model" can be subjected to an empirical test, and confirmed or disproved; however, disproof of the model does not entail disproof of the theory, since other models for the same situation would be possible based on the same theory. This usage of "model" and "theory" is exemplified by Atkinson, Bower, and Crothers (1965) in their book on mathematical learning theory.

The usage of "model" and "theory" in the decision theory literature is not standardized. Although it is not uncommon for authors to reject "decision theory" on the basis of evidence, "decision theory" lives on in different versions (models). Thus, as it has turned out in practice, "decision theory" is not a specific scientific system capable of being confirmed or disproved. It is a collection of concepts, methods, and findings based on the idea of rational decision making. Specific models for human choice arising out of decision theory, however, can be subjected to empirical test and confirmed or disproved. Such usage corresponds to the second definition for "theory" and "model." We shall not attempt, however, to maintain purity and consistency in the usage of these terms throughout the book, but rather will follow whichever terminology seems to be more natural and conventional for the topic under consideration.

Measurement and Scale Type

"Measurement" usually refers to the assignment of a quantity to represent the degree to which some object or event is characterized by some attribute. The development of accurate and reliable measurement methods has been important in all fields of science, and decision theory is no exception. Of particular importance for measurement in decision theory is the concept of *scale type.* Scale type concerns the degree of arbitrariness in the numbers a measurement method produces. For example, the number representing the temperature just cold enough to freeze water is often stated to be 32°F. But 32 is arbitrary since other numbers can be used to represent the same temperature, for example, 0°C.

Measurement methods are classified according to the degree of arbitrariness in the measures. The degree of arbitrariness is expressed in terms of the mathematical transformations allowed on a set of measures. If there is no arbitrariness, we speak of an *absolute scale*. An example is the number of objects, as determined by counting. If the arbitrariness is restricted to multiplication by any positive constant, we speak of a *ratio scale*. An example is "weight." A series of objects measured in pounds could be measured in ounces by multiplying each pound measure by 16. If the degree of arbitrariness is restricted to any positive linear transformation, we speak of an *interval scale*. A positive linear transformation has the form $y = ax + b$, where y represents a new measure, and x represents the corresponding original measure. a is a positive constant and b is a constant not restricted in sign. Temperature is usually measured on an interval scale; to go from the centigrade scale x to the fahrenheit scale y we use the positive linear transformation, $y = (9/5) x + 32$. If the degree of arbitrariness is restricted only to any positive monotonic transformation, we speak of an *ordinal scale*. A positive monotonic transformation requires that for any $x_2 - x_1 > 0$, we must have the corresponding $y_2 - y_1 > 0$. There are other scale types, but let us limit our discussion to these four: absolute, ratio, interval, and ordinal.

There is not a one-to-one relationship between an attribute and the scale type for its measurement. Scale type depends upon the operations employed in making the measurements. Thus, the heights of persons can be measured with a ruler, yielding ratio scale measures. But if the persons were ranked in height, we could obtain only ordinal scale measurement of height.

The four scale types mentioned allow, in order, an ever greater range of transformations. The class of positive monotonic transformations includes positive linear transformations as a subclass. The class of positive linear transformations includes multiplication by a positive constant (*similarity transformation*) as a subclass, and the *identity transformation* "allowed" for the absolute scale is a special case of the similarity transformation when the constant for multiplication is 1. To say, then, that an ordinal scale allows any positive monotonic transformation does not mean that the other transformations are not allowed—they are, as special cases. Likewise, interval scale measures can receive similarity transformations. It's just that ordinal scales can be transformed in more ways than interval scales can, and interval scales can be transformed in more ways than ratio scales can.

The four scale types can be usefully discussed in terms of what remains *invariant* (unchanged) when allowable transformations are applied. For the ordinal scale, the transformations allowed leave the ordering of objects measured invariant. Thus, if heights of persons were measured on an ordinal scale, new scale values obtained from any allowable transformation would have the same ordering. For an interval scale, allowable transformations not only leave ordering invariant, but also leave the ratio of distances invariant; i.e., $(y_2 - y_1)/(y_4 - y_3) = (x_2 - x_1)/(x_4 - x_3)$, regardless of the values chosen for a and b in the positive linear transformation. For a ratio scale, allowable transformations maintain the preceding two invariances, and, in addition, maintain the ratio between any two measures on a scale invariant; i.e., $y_2/y_1 = x_2/x_1$ regardless of the constant of multiplication chosen. For the absolute scale, measures cannot be changed, thus the preceding three invariances are maintained; absolute value of a measurement remains invariant as well.

The theory of scale type contains ambiguities and has been the subject of considerable controversy. For more extensive and elaborate discussions of scale type see Stevens (1951), Torgerson (1958), Luce (1959), Suppes and Zinnes (1963), Adams, Fagot, and Robinson (1965), and Pfanzagl (1968).

Evaluation and Comparison of Scientific Theories

Psychology is rife with theories, and it is often difficult to know what stance to take in regard to them. Is one theory correct, and, if so, must the others be rejected? Or can more than one theory be maintained? On what grounds can any theory be accepted or rejected? In particular, how is a "decision theory" in psychology to be evaluated vis-á-vis other extant theories? Some relationships between decision theory and other psychological theories are discussed in Chapter 10. At present we discuss only general considerations for the comparison of theories (where "theory" sometimes refers to a general approach, and sometimes to testable models).

A number of criteria have been discussed for the evaluation of theories, including accuracy of predictions, simplicity, usefulness, stimulation of research, and generality.

A scientific theory is expected to generate predictions which can be judged as to accuracy through observation of real-world phenomena. (These predictions might come from a "model" based on a "theory," rather from the "theory" per se.) Perfect accuracy is not required of a theory. Physicists, for example, cannot predict perfectly the way a ball will drop through the air. For one thing, the effects of air currents cannot be precisely accounted for. (Of course, under some highly controlled conditions, physicists can make extremely accurate predictions.) Nonetheless, some "reasonable" degree of accuracy in making predictions is expected of an acceptable theory.

Simplicity has a number of aspects, including the number of theoretical terms and the complexity of their relations. Of two theories making the same predictions, the one with fewer and more simply related terms would be preferred. It must be admitted, however, that the notion of "simplicity" is ambiguous and complicated, so it may be hard to state which of two theories is more simple.

A theory can be useful in many ways: in dollars and cents to a business man, but also in ideas and relations to a scientist whose job is to find such ideas and relationships. Naturally, all else equal, the more accurate and simpler theories are the more useful ones.

It is often said that a theory is good if it stimulates research, even if the theory is eventually rejected. The research so stimulated produces new empirical knowledge and provokes scientists to formulate improved theory, if such be needed.

"Generality" refers to the breadth of phenomena covered by a theory. If other things are equal, the wider the range of observations with which a theory can deal, the more impressive and acceptable it is. A theory may be very general, however, without being useful and without making accurate predictions. Psychology abounds with very general statements of principle which have not been proved to have much predictive power.

In some cases theories are compared for the purpose of accepting one and rejecting another. But two theories might be *complementary* rather than *competitive;* that is, they might concern different phenomena, so that one would not wish to eliminate either. Two theories are competitive when they make different predictions about the same phenomena. Even between competitive theories in psychology, however, a comparison will not typically cause rejection of the theory with the poorer predictions. There are many reasons for this: (a) It may be possible to bolster the poorer theory by revision. (b) There may be many comparisons between the theories, with some predictions favoring one theory and some favoring the other. One cannot simply accept the theory with the greatest number of superior predictions, if only for the reason that not all predictions have equal importance. (c) The poorer theory may be valuable in dealing with another set of variables which the better theory makes no reference to at all; i.e., the theories are in part complementary. (d) The theory making the better predictions may require more predictor observations, or different ones that would not necessarily be available nor convenient to obtain. Thus, in some cases, the more poorly predicting theory, according to the comparison, might be superior for some uses because it operates with fewer or more convenient predictors.

Tautologies in Science

Although the term tautology is used with a number of meanings, I shall use it to refer to a scientific assertion that is inherently unsusceptible to refutation. In other words, a tautological assertion cannot be refuted by empirical observations regardless of what the observations are.

Tautologies may be acceptable within a science, but it seems to me that scientists should at least distinguish between factual discoveries and tautologies. It is not always obvious, however, that one is dealing with a tautology; an assertion may be testable in one context and interpretation, but tautological in another context and interpretation. Many of the so-called laws of science would appear to be tautologies, at least in some contexts, yet expositions of these laws present them as empirical or theoretical discoveries.

Consider Ohm's law, which states that voltage equals current times resistance: $V = I \cdot R$. It is very easy to memorize this law and repeat it, but it is less easy to understand its meaning. What is resistance? Commonly resistance is determined by measuring voltage across and current through a resistor. Then the resistance R is determined as $R = V/I$. But if $R = V/I$, it is tautologically true that $V = R \cdot I$, thus Ohm's law would hold regardless of the nature of reality. But the law is usually taken to mean that R (i.e., V/I) is constant as the current through a resistor changes. In this sense, the law is testable, but unfortunately it is not exactly true—and hence it is no "law." For though V/I may be very nearly constant for a constant temperature of the resistor and for a given range of voltages, it certainly does not remain constant without these restrictions. Certainly, the ratio V/I is not constant for a light bulb: the ratio is lower when the light is first turned on and higher when the bulb becomes hotter. By stipulating various restrictions to the law, such gross discrepancies as those that occur in the case of the light bulb can be avoided. Whether one ends up with an approximation, a law, or a tautology can only be determined by examining the final system.

A similar discussion could be carried through for Newton's second law, force equals mass times acceleration, $f = m \cdot a$. One can learn to parrot this law very easily, but to understand it is difficult. Common sense would lead us to believe that this law could be disconfirmed, since there are three quantities which might or might not, *a priori,* have such a relation. However, the tautological character of the equation is indicated by the fact that Newtonian mechanics can be set up without any term "force" whatsoever (Frank, 1955).

Psychology would appear to abound with tautological assertions, though, indeed, because of the variations and ambiguities of exposition, many of the fundamental assertions of important theories are difficult to analyze. Decision theory also includes these difficulties. A fundamental assertion that "man chooses rationally (optimally)" may be taken to be true by tautology; this was essentially the approach taken by Jeremy Bentham. Or, the statement may be considered to be false, based on many experiments which we shall examine in later chapters. Yet, when it is taken to be false, another psychologist can (and typically does) assert that conditions were somehow improper, or that the definition of the rational decision was faulty. (Somewhat analogous would be the various restrictions and reservations that could be brought forth if someone asserted that Ohm's law was factually false.)

1.5 DECISION THEORY IN BEHAVIORAL SCIENCE

Decision theory is not exclusively a psychological discipline. It was developed first by mathematicians and economists. When we speak of decision theory in psychology, it is well to distinguish between several uses of the term and to differentiate these uses from "decision theory" in mathematics and economics. In this regard, we refer to *behavioral, economic,* and *mathematical decision theories.*

Behavioral decision theory has largely been concerned with the hypothesis of general rationality plus the related peripheralia used to formulate and test the hypothesis. Behavioral decision theory, like other theories of behavior, aspires to give an accounting and explanation of human behavior—in particular of human decisions, but the meaning of "decision" is so vague that clear-cut boundaries for the applicability of decision theory cannot be stated.

A distinction is often made between *normative* and *descriptive* decision theory. Normative decision theory is said to concern the choices that a rational man *should* make in a given situation, regardless of the choices that real men actually make. Descriptive theory is said to concern the choices real people actually make, regardless of the choices they should make. In practice, the distinction between normative and descriptive theories often becomes blurred. After all, the hypothesis of general rationality states that men *do* make the decisions they *should* make. If this is the case, normative and descriptive theories merge into one.

In practice, what happens is this: A normative model is proposed for some decision situation. Then naturalistic or experimental observation of actual human choices reveals a discrepancy between normative and actual behavior. Instead of leaving it at that, many investigators feel impelled to bring normative theory and observed behavior into better agreement. The problem is attacked from both ends. It is hypothesized that the instructions or other conditions of the experiment are somehow faulty: they are not credible to S, or they are insufficiently informative, or they ask too much of S, or whatnot. New experimental conditions are then proposed which are supposed to lead S to choose more rationally. The normative theory is likewise adjusted. As we have seen, in defining the "rational choice" one has a goodly number of options. One can see whether alternative interpretations of "rational" correspond better to the observed behavior. Are the assumptions of the normative model valid for S? Does he perhaps have other utilities (goals) he is trying to maximize that are ignored in the model? Perhaps other utilities and other measures of utility should be employed in the normative model. Does the normative model assume an ability to process information beyond actual human capacity? We don't expect rationals Ss to have perfect perception, memory, and calculational abilities, so perhaps the normative model can be "degraded" to correspond to limited capacities of real Ss. In brief, attempts are made to align rational and actual human choice. "Normative" models are revised with a view toward making them more "descriptive." Since the revisions are motivated as much or more by a desire to attain descriptive accuracy as by clearer understanding of what S "should" do, it is difficult to fit such revised models neatly into normative or descriptive categories.

In reference to the activities of investigators in aligning normative theory and observed behavior, we shall say that the investigators are attempting to *rationalize* the decision making of men. "Rationalize" here refers to the dictionary meaning "to make rational." It does not refer to the psychoanalytically-derived "rationalize," meaning to give a superficially plausible but false explanation for one's own behavior.

Economists have been less concerned than psychologists with rationalizing observed human behavior and more concerned with choices that should be made to maximize profit or utility. Mathematicians, likewise, have usually been little concerned with explaining actual human choice. They have been more concerned with the mathematical theory of rational decision making, and more generally, with the development of the mathematics of extrema.

It should be pointed out that the boundaries of behavioral, economic, and mathematical decision theories are vague. These three fields certainly have considerable overlap. Likewise the boundaries of these fields relative to psychology, economics, and mathematics, respectively, are vague. A topic discussed under the heading of "decision theory" is probably not the exclusive concern of "decision theory."

Oftentimes people inquire about the practical applications of decision theory. What good is it? Can it be used to improve one's decisions? In a sense, the use of mathematical decision theory as the basis of a behavioral theory constitutes an application of decision theory. Inquiries about applied decision theory, however, are directed to the value of decision theory in such areas as business, military, and personal decision making. We comment briefly on such practical applications of decision theory in Section 10.3. For the most part, however, this book is not concerned with "practical" applications. Instead, it concerns the use of decision theory in conceptualizing and understanding human behavior.

Chapter 2 is an introduction to the mathematical elements of decision theory, including decision principles. Chapter 3 deals with the elements of mathematical probability, the philosophy of probability, and the measurement of subjective probability. Chapter 4 focuses on the theory and measurement of utility. Chapter 5 reviews empirical studies of human behavior in choosing between gambles, and discusses various concepts that have been used in attempting to account for such behavior and Chapter 6 reviews the so-called "probability learning" literature—literature on the prediction of uncertain events. Chapter 7 discusses "signal detection theory," i.e., the use of decision theory in psychophysics. Chapter 8 is concerned with the utilization of information in decision making and Chapter 9 with decision making when the consequence depends on the decisions of several participants. This area is usually called game theory. The final chapter contains both a discussion of decision theory as it relates to some other psychological theories, and a discussion of applied decision theory.

REFERENCES

Adams, E. W., Fagot, R. F., & Robinson, R. E. "A theory of appropriate statistics," *Psychometrika* (1965), **30,** 99–127.

Atkinson, R. C., Bower, G. H., & Crothers, E. J. *An Introduction to Mathematical Learning Theory.* New York: Wiley, 1965.

Bentham, J. *Deontology,* arranged and ed. by J. Bowring, 2 vols. London: Longman, 1834.

Bentham, J. *An Introduction to the Principles of Morals and Legislation.* Oxford: The Clarendon Press, 1876 (reprint of 1823 edition).

Frank, P. "Foundations of Physics," in O. Neurath, R. Carnap, & C. Morris (eds.), *International Encyclopedia of Unified Science,* Vol. I. Chicago: University of Chicago, 1955, pp. 423–504.

Luce, R. D. "On the possible psychophysical laws," *Psychological Review* (1959), **66,** 81–95.

Marshall, A. *Principles of Economics* (8th ed.), London: Macmillan, 1920.

Pfanzagl, J. *Theory of Measurement.* New York: Wiley, 1968.

Stevens, S. S. "Mathematics, Measurement, and Psychophysics," in S. S. Stevens (ed.), *Handbook of Experimental Psychology.* New York: Wiley 1951, pp. 1–49.

Suppes, P. *Introduction to Logic.* Princeton, N.J.: Van Nostrand, 1957.

Suppes, P., & Zinnes, J. L. "Basic Measurement Theory," in R. D. Luce, R. R. Bush, & E. Galanter (eds.), *Handbook of Mathematical Psychology,* Vol. I. New York: Wiley, 1963, pp. 1–76.

Torgerson, W. S. *Theory and Methods of Scaling.* New York: Wiley, 1958.

CHAPTER 2

Elements of Mathematical Decision Theory

2.1 INTRODUCTION

The present chapter presents the elements of mathematical decision theory. In particular, we discuss the formalization of decision situations, the distinctions between different decision situations, and proposed rules (*decision principles*) for rational decision making.

Game theory (or *theory of games*) is often used as a synonym for decision theory, so the present chapter might be said to concern the elements of game theory. The term "theory of games," however, is often reserved for decision situations involving more than one person. Most of this book concerns situations involving just one decision maker, i.e., *individual decision making*. Only Chapter 9 is devoted to the more general case of N-person decision making. The material of the present chapter is basic to both individual and N-person decision making.

It would be well to state explicitly that the "theory of games" is not particularly concerned with those recreational activities called "games." Such recreational games are not excluded from the theory, however, for they involve players in decision situations. But the "theory of games" cannot tell a player how to proceed in most games, for the games are too complex. It would avail a chess player nothing to study the theory of games.

Since there has been a best-selling book of psychology by Berne (1967) called *Games People Play,* perhaps it is worthwhile to mention that the theory of games of concern to us has very little connection with Berne's "transactional game analysis." In addition, one should distinguish between the theory of games and military, management, and political games played on computers (see Section 10.3).

2.2 THE PARTICIPANTS

We begin by assuming that each of two persons makes a decision and that these decisions determine a *consequence*. In game theory the persons are called *players,* but in decision theory more generally they are also given other designations, for example *decision makers* or *actors*. In some contexts the player is taken to be a conglomerate interest such as a corporation or a nation, but in this book the player is almost always an individual—ideal or real. Let the players be denoted by P^A and P^B. Our discussion throughout this book will concentrate on P^A, whom we designate the *protagonist*. P^B is variously called the *coplayer, competitor,* or *opponent*. When, in a psychological experiment, the roles of P^A and P^B are taken by real persons, we typically employ the usual designation *subjects* (abbreviated Ss). Our present assumption of two persons allows us to discuss the elements of two-person game theory. But we can also discuss individual decision making by interpreting P^B not as a person, but as *nature*. The weather condition today or the random result from throwing a die can be thought of as the "decision" of "nature." Generally speaking, "nature" is used to refer to a set of possible events, one of which occurs, when this event is not perceived to be the choice of a "person." It is, of course, assumed that the occurring event has, together with P^A's choice, an important bearing on the consequence; otherwise, nature would not be included in the formalization of the decision situation. As we shall see, analysis of a decision situation is very much affected by whether P^B is a rational, self-seeking actor or a disinterested "nature."

2.3 THE NORMAL FORM GAME

Let the possible decisions for P^A be $a_1, a_2, \ldots, a_i, \ldots, a_m$, and let the possible decisions for P^B be $b_1, b_2, \ldots, b_j, \ldots, b_n$. P^A can choose any one (and only one) of m possibilities, and P^B can choose any one (and only one) of n possibilities. It is usually assumed that each possible decision could be readily chosen with equal ease. If, for example, a basketball team needs two points to win with 5 seconds left in the game, can we say that a_1 means "shoot a basket," a_2 means "throw the ball out of bounds," etc.? Hardly. For the player with the ball cannot readily choose to "shoot a basket." We could, however, let a_1 be, "attempt to shoot a basket." Of course, "attempting to shoot a basket" may take more effort than "attempting to throw the ball out of bounds." Such differences in effort or pain in expressing the choice ("carrying out the decision") could be formalized as part of the consequence rather than part of the deciding. But the experiments we discuss do not require such an adjustment—ostensibly, at least.

There is, of course, an important distinction between a possible decision and the specific decision chosen by P^A on a particular trial. There are no well-established terminological practices recognizing this distinction. In reference to the a_i's as potential choices for P^A, we use the terms *options* or *alternatives*. When we speak of P^A's *decision, choice,* or *act,* we refer to the result of the act of choosing, i.e., to a particular single a_i chosen, such as a_2. In speaking of *possible, available,* or *potential* decisions, choices, or acts, however, we refer to options.

The term *strategy* is used in a variety of ways. Sometimes it is used as a synonym for "option" or "decision." Frequently "strategy" implies a plan for making a "final decision." If, for example, an option has the form of a plan for making different "final actions" depending on various possible contingencies, it might be called a strategy. "Strategy" is also used as a synonym for decision principle, which is a rule for selecting among the options.

When P^B is interpreted as "nature," the "options" are usually called *states of nature, states of the world,* or, in some contexts, *hypotheses.* Nature's choice is then called the *true state of nature, true state of the world, true hypothesis,* or, more commonly, the *outcome.* A joint decision is designated by the form $a_i b_j$. "Joint" by no means implies concurrence or cooperation between the players. It

TABLE 2.1
A Game Matrix

	b_1	b_2	b_3
a_1	o_{11}	o_{12}	o_{13}
a_2	o_{21}	o_{22}	o_{23}
a_3	o_{31}	o_{32}	o_{33}

is simply used to refer to the options or decisions of both players. The state of affairs resulting from the joint decision is called the *consequence.*[1] A consequence is usually given a verbal description such as "P^A receives \$1 from P^B." The consequence resulting from the joint decision $a_i b_j$ is designated o_{ij}.

There are $m \cdot n$ possible joint decisions and a like number of (possible) consequences. The possible decisions for P^A and P^B together with the contingent consequences can be listed in a *game matrix,* as illustrated in Table 2.1.

Generally speaking, it would be desirable for P^A to know P^B's decision before

---

[1] What is called the "consequence" in this book is often called the "outcome" in other expositions, for example, in Luce & Raiffa (1957). However, "outcome" is commonly used in probability theory to refer to the result of a "probability experiment," for example, "heads" resulting from a coin-flip. We use "outcome" in this sense, but also in the broader sense of the "true state of nature" in a decision situation. Our use of "consequence" agrees with Savage (1954).

committing himself, or vice versa. We assume, however, that both P^A and P^B must commit themselves to their respective decisions without prior knowledge of the other player's choice. Our formalization describes the so-called *normal form* for a game. Since for so many actual decision situations the players alternate moves (they do not decide concurrently), the normal form assumptions might appear to restrict severely the applicability of our theory. It can be shown, however, that a game described in terms of alternating moves between players, i.e., a game in *extensive form*, can be put into a normal form representation. Roughly speaking, a normal form "decision" for a game of chess, for example, would be very detailed strategy or plan for dealing with any contingency which might arise. Once the two players had independently chosen their strategies, a referee could play the game without the players and determine the consequence. As a practical matter, however, the number and complexity of the "decisions" for a normal form chess game would be so great that they could never be written out or individually compared.

In spite of such practical difficulties, the normal form game has theoretical generality. This, I suppose, partly justifies the almost exclusive use of normal form game in experimental work. (But S is typically required to choose from only two or three possibilities—hardly realistic.)

The mathematical analysis for rational decision making requires that the consequences be evaluated quantitatively for each person (but not for "nature"). For this chapter and for most of decision theory, it is assumed that the value of a consequence to a person can represented by a single number, called a *utility*. (But multidimensional utilities are sometimes considered: see Section 4.7.) The theory and measurement of utility is treated in Chapter 4. For now we simply assume that such numbers are available. The *utility matrix* is similar to the game matrix, except that utilities are entered in the table instead of consequences. The utilities of a consequence for two persons, P^A and P^B, will, in general, differ, so there must be two utilities for each consequence. The utility for P^A for consequence o_{ij} is designated $u_{ij}{}^A$, and the utility for P^B is designated $u_{ij}{}^B$. Table 2.2 illustrates the utility matrix. For individual decision making, a cell of the table would require only one entry, $u_{ij}{}^A$, since nature is presumed not to evaluate the consequences nor to "choose" in accordance with such values.

TABLE 2.2
A Utility Matrix

	b_1	b_2	b_3
a_1	$u_{11}{}^A,\ u_{11}{}^B$	$u_{12}{}^A,\ u_{12}{}^B$	$u_{13}{}^A,\ u_{13}{}^B$
a_2	$u_{21}{}^A,\ u_{21}{}^B$	$u_{22}{}^A,\ u_{22}{}^B$	$u_{23}{}^A,\ u_{23}{}^B$
a_3	$u_{31}{}^A,\ u_{31}{}^B$	$u_{32}{}^A,\ u_{32}{}^B$	$u_{33}{}^A,\ u_{33}{}^B$

For individual decision making, then, the superscript is unnecessary and the designation u_{ij} can be used.

Oftentimes the numbers entered in a "utility matrix" are not strictly justified in terms of utility theory. For example, the entries are often amounts of money which a player will receive or lose, depending on the consequence. But the value to a person of an amount of money is usually thought not to be exactly represented by the quantity of money per se (see Chapter 4). Amount of money is often used, however, in place of utility, since it is readily known and may be assumed to approximate utility for the range of money involved. Sometimes, in psychology experiments, Ss are rewarded with points, and the number of points is taken to approximate utility. Although it is often convenient to use such approximate measures for utility, it would be just as well to avoid calling such approximations "utilities." Therefore, we use the more general term, *payoff matrix*. The entries of a payoff matrix may be utilities or only an admittedly approximate substitute. Likewise, we use the symbolism v_{ij} for the value of a consequence; a "value" may be a utility or only an admittedly approximate substitute. ("Value" is also used, as is common in mathematics, for a quantity that a variable has assumed; for example, we might say, "if x has the value 5, ...") As we shall discover in Chapter 4, the proper techniques for the measurement of utility are not well-established (indeed, the whole concept of "utility" is open to question). Thus even when we use "utilities" instead of "values," it does not imply that we really have the proper numbers to use for decision theory. It only means that an attempt was made, based on some current theory for utility measurement, to represent the values of a person more adequately than money or points does.

2.4 CONDITIONS OF PLAY

We say that the protagonist makes his decision under one of several *conditions: certainty, rational competition, risk,* and *ignorance.*[2]

Certainty

The protagonist is said to make his decision under the condition of certainty if there is only one consequence possible for each of P^A's options. The condition is represented by a game matrix having only one column; i.e., P^B has, in effect, only one possible choice. The only decision criterion proposed for this condition is for P^A to choose the decision with the most preferred consequence (greatest utility).

The condition of certainty plays only a relatively small role in mathematical decision theory, since (for unidimensional utilities) the decision criterion is so simple. Nonetheless, a good deal of human choice takes place under the condi-

---

[2] This differs from the rather familiar breakdown used by Luce & Raiffa (1957, p. 13): certainty, risk, and uncertainty.

tion of "certainty," and these choice situations interest psychologists considerably. *Ss* are often required to state which of a set of objects they would prefer, provided they could have any one they desire. Pollsters, for example, ask *Ss* which of two candidates they prefer. Consumer researchers ask *Ss* which of a group of products they prefer.

"Certainty" is a mathematical abstraction. Real-life decisions, even those characterized by the "condition of certainty," involve uncertainty. For example, if our protagonist is in a restaurant and must choose his entree from the menu, the decision situation would typically be characterized as "choice under certainty." Let us say the protagonist prefers chicken to roast beef or halibut. The tastiness of P^A's order must have some uncertainty about it, the moreso if P^A is eating at the restaurant for the first time. In fact, it might be that if P^A could sample the three possibilities he might change his preference. The uncertainty associated with the value of a consequence is not limited to the "condition of certainty."

Rational Competition

P^A is said to make his decision under the condition of rational competition if P^B is a "rational" being who is free to and will adopt whichever strategy that self-interest can justify. In mathematical decision theory, it is assumed that any decision strategy acceptable to a fully rational protagonist would be equally apparent and acceptable to his rational competitor. The decision criterion recommended reflects this assumption. In a real-life two-person game it may be incorrect to assume that the *S* in the role of P^B is such a rational competitor. (Some evidence is presented in Chapter 9.) Nonetheless, a real person may be more like a rational competitor than like "nature."

Risk

The protagonist is said to make his decision under the condition of risk if he is "aware" of the probabilities for the various possible choices by P^B. The co-player in the condition of risk is usually interpreted as "nature" rather than as a "rational opponent."

When the condition of risk exists, each of P^A's options can be interpreted as a *gamble* (or *bet,* or *lottery*), since in decision theory a gamble is defined to be a choice for which the probabilities of the possible consequences are known (or at least calculable). The possible choices in gambling games such as roulette have payoffs (consequences) with known probabilities, and thus are "gambles" in the sense of decision theory. But the term "gamble" is not restricted to "gambling games." For example, business, military, and everyday individual decisions are often interpreted as gambles (see Section 5.9). It may be that the probabilities for many such situations cannot be calculated objectively from the mathematical theory of probability. In such circumstances it may be said that the protagonist has "subjective probabilities" for the various consequences. A discussion of objective and subjective probabilities is provided in Chapter 3. For now let us simply say that different individuals may have different subjective probabilities for the same events; furthermore, some authorities—in particular, the "Bayesians" (see Chapter 8)—consider subjective probabilities to be available for any set of possible outcomes. Therefore, these authorities view all decision making as occurring under the condition of risk, and all decisions as gambles (except, possibly, for the condition of certainty).

Ignorance

The protagonist is said to make his decision under the condition of ignorance if he recognizes the possibility of more than one consequence for a decision, but is completely ignorant concerning which consequence might occur; he has no reason to think that it will be determined by the choice of a rational co-player, nor does he have any basis for judging outcome probabilities. In brief, the protagonist knows that his decision can have any one of several possible consequences, but that is as much as can be said.

General

The four conditions mentioned are ideals. A real-life decision situation might not fit into any category very neatly. For example, as noted, one could question the characterization of any decision situation as one of certainty. The presence of a real person as P^B doesn't assure the condition of rational competition, for a real person may not choose according to any recognized rational principle. On the other hand, the condition of rational competition might hold for an impersonal P^B, for example, a computer programmed to play rationally. Many real-life decision conditions would appear to be intermediate between "risk" and "ignorance." A real protagonist might feel very uneasy about stating or assigning exact probabilities for a set of possible outcomes. Yet the condition of ignorance would appear not to apply, because the person has some ideas about the relative probabilities of the outcomes. We discuss such "rough," or "ambiguous" probabilities in Section 5.4.

2.5 PURE AND MIXED STRATEGIES

We have discussed the decision problem up to now as if P^A had to decide which single a_i to choose. As we shall see, however, a rather different approach is sometimes recommended to P^A: namely, to let a random mechanism determine which option to choose. For example, P^A might plan to choose a_1 if a flipped coin lands heads and a_3 if it lands tails. This represents a (*randomized*) *mixed strategy*.

More generally, a mixed strategy consists of a subset of the original set of options plus a specification for the probability of choice for each option in the subset. Such a strategy is, in general, designated $(p_1a_1, p_2a_2, \ldots, p_ma_m)$. For the case mentioned above the designation would be $(\frac{1}{2}a_1, \frac{1}{2}a_3)$; the options with probabilities of zero are not included. It is assumed that P^A specifies the probabilities for his mixed strategy (including probabilities of zero), but once these are specified, he exercises no further control over the pure strategy to which he is finally committed—it is instead determined by some random mechanism with corresponding probabilities.

In comparison with the mixed strategies, the original options a_1, a_2, . . . are called *pure strategies*. Although we formerly let a_i designate an arbitrary pure strategy, when considering mixed strategies we shall let a_i designate an arbitrary strategy from the entire set of pure and mixed strategies.

By considering all possible mixed strategies, P^A has an infinite number of possible strategies to choose among; for with even only two pure strategies, there are an infinite number of values for p_1. But isn't it hopeless to try to choose among an infinite set of possibilities? Well, for one thing, mixed strategies need not always be considered. For many circumstances it is known that no possible mixed strategy can be better than an available pure strategy, so the mixed strategies can be ignored. Where they are required, however, the value of a mixed strategy varies regularly with the p's; this simplifies the problem considerably.

Intuitively, the idea of a randomized strategy may seem peculiar. Choosing an option on the basis of a random result might seem credible if P^A were perplexed about what decision to make: "What the heck, I might as well flip a coin to decide." But as a rational approach to decision making, it is a little hard to swallow. We expect our political and business leaders to try, at least, to make the "best decision." The Secretary of Defense might have a hard time explaining why some military decision was made by "throwing dice" or some computerized equivalent. A mathematical justification for mixed strategies is given in Section 2.9. For now let it be said that randomized strategies are seldom defended except for the condition of rational competition. Roughly speaking, they are a protection against an ability by the rational competitor to "read" P^A's intentions. A real-life analogue of a randomized strategy is the "mixing" of plays by an astute quarterback to keep the opponents "off balance."

In some situations it may be recommended that P^A mix his choices, i.e., change them from trial to trial, but that he do this in a systematic rather than a random manner. In particular, P^A might do well to alternate his decisions in coordination with coplayer P^B. Then the successive joint decisions might be a_1b_1, a_2b_2, a_1b_1, a_2b_2, etc. This is called a *correlated* or *coordinated mixed strategy*. It can sometimes be justified for so-called negotiable games (Chapter 9).

2.6 THE STRATEGY SET GRAPH

The pure and randomized mixed strategies for a two-person game can be illustrated on a *strategy set graph*. A payoff matrix and its strategy set graph are shown in Figure 2.1. Each point on the graph represents a possible strategy—

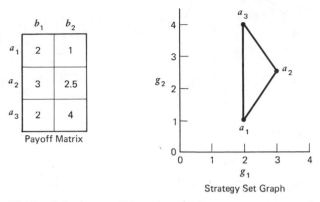

Figure 2.1. A payoff matrix and its strategy set graph. The strategy set consists of points on the boundary and within the boundary.

pure or mixed—for P^A. The abscissa gives the expected payoff to P^A for a strategy (point) if P^B chooses b_1, and the ordinate gives the expected payoff to P^A if P^B chooses b_2. The two expected payoffs are designated g_1 and g_2.

An expected payoff is the mean payoff per trial resulting if many, many trials were conducted. For g_1 it is assumed that b_1 would be played for each of these trials, and for g_2, b_2. For a pure strategy, the expected payoff would be given by an entry in the payoff matrix. Each trial would yield P^A the same payoff (for constant P^A strategy and constant b_j). For example, a_1 would always yield P^A 2 against b_1. For a randomized strategy, say $(\frac{1}{2} a_1, \frac{1}{2} a_2)$, the payoff on a trial (against b_1, say) could be either 2 or 3. The g_1 for that strategy would be an average of the possible payoffs weighted according to the probability of occurrence. In this case $g_1 = 2.5$. (The concept of expected payoff is discussed in more detail in Section 2.8.)

The point for each of the three pure strategies is shown in Figure 2.1. The strategies possible by mixing any two pure strategies are represented by the points on the straight line between those two pure strategies. Any point within the triangle formed by the three pure strategies represents at least one available strategy, and all available randomized strategies lie on or within the triangle.

The entire set of strategies available to P^A, pure and mixed, is said to be a *convex set,* meaning that for any two strategies on the graph, all points on the straight line connecting them are also in the set. The set of available pure and mixed strategies always forms a convex set regardless of the number of options available to P^A (or P^B) and regardless of the payoffs for the different consequences. The set need not appear triangular on the strategy set graph. Some other convex sets are shown in Figure 2.2(a). These represent possible payoff matrices. Figure 2.2(b) illustrates some nonconvex sets.

If P^B has more than two options, the strategy set graph cannot be illustrated in two dimensions, since a dimension is required for each b_j. For three options,

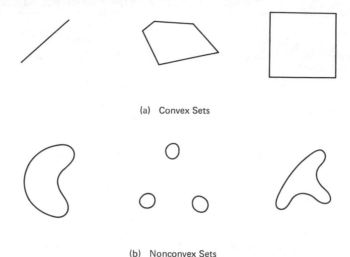

(a) Convex Sets

(b) Nonconvex Sets

Figure 2.2. (a) Three convex sets. (b) Three nonconvex sets.

the set of pure and randomized strategies for P^A can be imagined as a solid, three-dimensional object. The imagination begins to boggle at the mention of more than three dimensions, but mathematically, at least, it is possible to discuss the strategy set for P^A as an n-dimensional convex body if P^B has n pure strategies available. For illustrative purposes, we largely confine P^B's options to two in the present chapter.

2.7 ADMISSIBLE STRATEGIES AND THE DOMINANCE PRINCIPLE

If strategy a_i' yields P^A a higher payoff than strategy a_i for at least one of the opponent's (nature's) options, and a payoff equally high or higher for all other b_j's a_i' is said to (*weakly*) *dominate* a_i. *Strong dominance* is said to hold if the payoff for a_i' is higher for *every* b_j. When used without qualification, "dominance" is to be interpreted in the weak sense allowing—but not requiring—equality between the payoffs for a_i' and a_i for at least one of the b_j's. Strong dominance is a special case of (weak) dominance; i.e., if a_i' strongly dominates a_i, then, it must (weakly) dominate a_i as well (but the converse is not *necessarily* true).

Dominance is readily illustrated on a strategy set graph. We adopt the convention that the direction "up" on the graph is "north," "right" is "east," etc. If a_i' lies to the northeast (or due north, or due east) of a_i on the strategy set graph, then a_i' dominates a_i. (If we say northeast, but disallow due north and due east, strong dominance holds.) Figure 2.3 illustrates the four pure strategies of a payoff matrix: a_1 dominates a_3 and a_4; a_3 dominates a_4; a_2 dominates a_4. (Both a_1 and a_2 strongly dominate a_4.)

The concept of dominance applies to mixed as well as to pure strategies. Furthermore, we can speak of a mixed strategy dominating a pure strategy or vice versa. "Dominance" likewise applies when P^B has more than two options, though the concept "northeast" would become "more positive on each dimension."

All strategies in a set which are not dominated by any other strategy in the set are said to be *admissible*. Admissible strategies can exist only on the northeast boundary of a strategy set graph, since only these points fail to have other points northeast of them. The admissible segment of the boundary can be localized by moving a horizontal line southward from above the strategy set until it contacts the set, and moving a vertical line westward until it makes contact. The admissible strategies form the strategy set boundary connecting the two admissible strategies in contact with the lines. This concept is illustrated in Figure 2.4 for the strategy set of Figure 2.3, now including randomized strategies as well. The horizontal line contacts the set at a single, admissible point. The vertical line contacts the set along a segment of the boundary, but only the northernmost point of that segment is admissible. The admissible segment of the strategy set is shown by a heavy line. The admissible segment is a straight line in Figure 2.4, but it may consist of a number of straight line segments. (A continuous curvature for any portion of the strategy set boundary implies infinitely many pure strategies. We assume a finite number.)

The *dominance principle* is our first proposed rule for selecting a rational strategy. It states that the rational strategy must be admissible, i.e., undominated.

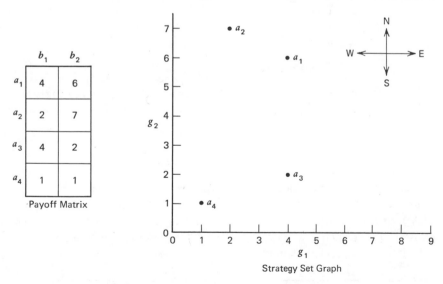

Figure 2.3. The pure strategies of the payoff matrix are shown on a strategy set graph. The dominance relations between these strategies are discussed in the text.

This rule seems compelling, since for any possible inadmissible strategy, an alternative admissible strategy could be proposed yielding P^A a higher payoff regardless of the choice by P^B. Nonetheless, the dominance principle is insufficient for specifying a choice in our example, for a_1, a_2, and all possible randomized mixes of them are admissible, and the dominance principle makes no distinctions between them.

The dominance principle is also referred to as the *sure-thing principle*. However, the "sure-thing principle" associated with Savage (1954) is somewhat different. See Savage (pp. 22–26) or Adams (1960, pp. 232–233).

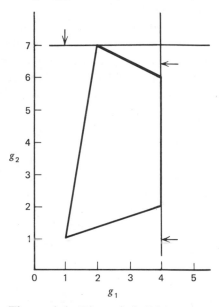

Figure 2.4. The admissible segment of the strategy set graph is shown by a heavy line. It was determined by moving a horizontal line south from above and a vertical line left (west) from the right (east).

2.8 THE EXPECTED VALUE PRINCIPLE

The most prominent and widely advocated rule for decision making is the *expected value principle,* also known as the *Bayes principle.*[3] The expected value (EV) principle asserts that an option with maximum expected value should be chosen. The principle is applied only to the condition of risk, for in order to calculate the expected values for P^A's options, the probabilities for the states

---

[3] The Bayes principle is to be distinguished from Bayes' formula (Section 3.2) and Bayesian statistics (Section 8.9). Bayesian statistics, however, includes use of the Bayes principle and Bayes' formula.

of nature must be available to P^A. As noted in Section 2.4, however, some authorities are willing to interpret almost any decision situation as a condition of risk, so for them the maximum expected value principle is universally applicable.

For the condition of risk, a probability p_j is specified for each b_j. The expected value[4] for an option a_i is

$$\mathrm{EV}_i = p_1 v_{i1} + p_2 v_{i2} + \cdots + p_j v_{ij} + \cdots + p_n v_{in}$$

$$= \sum_{j=1}^{n} p_j v_{ij} \qquad (2.1)$$

According to the EV principle P^A should compare the EV_i's and choose the a_i with the largest EV_i. In case of a tie for the largest EV between two or more options, the principle allows P^A to choose any of the tied options. Although a randomized mixed strategy may have an EV as large as an optimal a_i, it can never have a larger EV. Therefore, P^A can ignore the possible mixed strategies and choose among the available pure strategies.

For the condition of risk, each pure strategy a_i is by definition a gamble (Section 2.4). The expected payoff of a gamble (option) can be throught of as the mean payoff to P^A if he chose that gamble and received a payoff for a very large (ideally, an infinite) number of trials. It may be that one cannot "expect" to receive exactly the "expected payoff" for any single trial. For example, if P^A chose a gamble with $p_1 = 1/3$, $p_2 = 2/3$, $v_1 = 1$, and $v_2 = -1$, the expected payoff would be $-1/3$, yet on a single trial P^A must receive either 1 or -1; he cannot receive $-1/3$.

The EV principle accords with the dominance principle; that is, the optimal strategy specified by the EV principle is always admissible. The particular admissible strategy chosen, however, depends on the values of the p_j's. Indeed, one can specify p_j's to make any admissible strategy optimal by the EV principle. In other words, the set of admissible strategies and the set of possibly optimal strategies by the EV principle are identical.

The EV principle actually consists of a family of principles which differ according to the interpretation of the values and the probabilities in Equation 2.1. Roughly speaking, the values may be either "objective" or "subjective," and the probabilities may likewise be "objective" or "subjective." Objective value is usually interpreted as amount of money or some other commodity. Utility is the name given to subjective value. Likewise, as noted in Section 2.4, the probability of an outcome may be an objective or a subjective quantity peculiar to a particular decision maker. These distinctions lead to a four-way breakdown of expected payoff. Designations and abbreviations for the four principles or

---

[4] "Expected value" is a central concept in probability theory, where it is perhaps more often called the *expectation*. In probability theory, the "value" of "expected value" need not refer to desirability, but to any quantity, and therefore expected value could as well be called the expected quantity (of a variable).

TABLE 2.3
A Family of Expected Payoff Principles (or Models)

Probabilities   Payoffs

	Objective	Subjective
Objective	Objectively Expected Value (OEV)	Expected Utility (EU)
Subjective	Subjectively Expected Value (SEV)	Subjectively Expected Utility (SEU)

models are given in Table 2.3. Edwards (1955) gave a similar breakdown, but he called the OEV model the EV (expected value) model. However, "expected value" is a general term in probability theory that is not usually restricted to objective probabilities and values. Therefore, we reserve expected value (expected payoff) for general use, for reference to the family of principles, and coin OEV for more specific use. A commonly used synonym for objectively expected value is *actuarial value*. Edwards' breakdown lists SEM (subjectively expected money) in place of our SEV. We list SEV, since objective measures of value other than money might be employed. In decision theory, the term "value" is often used in contradistinction to utility to refer to objective quantities. The terminology and abbreviations of Table 2.3 reflect this usage. In this book, however, value (v) is a general designation which may refer to utility. Just as we have used the abbreviation EV_i to refer to the expected value of option a_i, we use the abbreviations OEV_i, EU_i, SEV_i, and SEU_i when we wish to be more specific.

The OEV principle was proposed in the early days of probability theory, but it was seen even then to be untenable (see Section 4.5). It was replaced with the EU principle, which has remained prominent to this day. The SEU principle became important during the present century. The SEV principle has been of lesser importance, but it has its place; in particular, an advocate of the SEU principle might allow that monetary values could sometimes be employed, in which case the SEU principle reduces to the SEV principle.

2.9   THE MAXIMIN PRINCIPLE

For each possible choice the protagonist (P^A) could make, there is at least one worst consequence, i.e., one with the smallest payoff. This worst consequence is called the *security level* for the choice. (For mixed strategies, the security level is the worst *expected* payoff.) According to the *maximin principle,* P^A should choose the option with the largest security level; i.e., P^A should choose the option that *maxi*mizes the *mini*mum payoff.

Although we could ignore mixed strategies when solving a decision problem with the EV principle, we cannot ignore them for the maximin principle, because a mixed strategy may have a security level (a smallest *expected* payoff) larger than that for any pure strategy. Henceforth, unless we specifically note, we assume that the solution is to be chosen from the entire strategy set. Otherwise, we speak of the *pure strategy maximin principle*. Even if the solution is chosen from the entire strategy set, however, it does not imply that the solution must be a mixed strategy: it could be pure or mixed.

The maximin principle is often called, instead, the *minimax* principle because statisticians, especially, enter losses into the payoff matrices, so that the larger the entry, the less desirable the consequence. In that case, P^A attempts to *mini*mize his *max*imum losses. The principles are equivalent, however.

As with the EV principle, more than one option can be specified as optimal by the maximin principle, since two or more options can have equally high security levels. If only one option is optimal, it is admissible. If more than one option is optimal, at least one of these options must be admissible, but among these options there may be dominated strategies (not strongly dominated strategies, however).

Let us, as is sometimes done, further restrict the maximin principle solution to admissible strategies. At least one admissible maximin solution can be found for any payoff matrix. Since, as previously noted, the admissible strategy set is the same as the set of possible EV solutions, the maximin solution must be one of the possible EV solutions. But whereas, the EV solution that obtains depends on the p_j's as well as on the payoff matrix, the maximin solution depends only on the payoff matrix, and, indeed, does not require that p_j's be specified.

The maximin strategy has been defended both for games against nature and for games against persons. For the condition of ignorance the EV principle cannot be employed because probabilities are not specified, but the maximin principle can provide a solution. Of course, some authorities would deny that a true "condition of ignorance" exists, so the preceding argument in favor of the maximin principle would be inapplicable. It is sometimes argued that the maximin principle is worthy because it is conservative—it protects the protagonist in case the choices by P^B are particularly unfavorable to P^A. But good reasons are seldom advanced for assuming that P^B's choices would tend to be particularly unfavorable, except in the context of zero-sum games with rational competition.

Literally, "zero-sum" means that the payoffs for P^A and P^B for each consequence sum to zero. If P^A receives \$1 for o_{ij}, P^B loses \$1 for the same consequence. In a more general sense, zero-sum means that an improvement for one player in going from one consequence to another implies a proportional deterioration in the position of the other player. In a zero-sum game the interests of the players are strictly opposed, so that whatever one player gets must come

TABLE 2.4
A Zero-Sum Payoff Matrix

(a)

	b_1	b_2
a_1	2, -2	4, -4
a_2	-8, 8	3, -3
a_3	1, -1	6, -6
a_4	-3, 3	-1, 1

(b)

	b_1	b_2
a_1	2	4
a_2	-8	3
a_3	1	6
a_4	-3	-1

at the expense of his opponent. Most real-life games are probably not well characterized as zero-sum. For example, in the "game" of nuclear war both players would prefer the consequence "stalemate" to the consequence "mutual annihilation." Nonetheless, the zero-sum formulation can perhaps represent situations where the consequence implies a win for one party and a loss of comparable magnitude to the other party. Gambling between friends may be approximately zero-sum (it usually is literally zero-sum in dollars, but not in utilities, perhaps). Chess or checkers might be considered as approximately zero-sum.

Although the payoffs for the players in a "zero-sum game" need not literally sum to zero, it is convenient for exposition to assume that they do. Table 2.4(a) illustrates a zero-sum payoff matrix with the payoffs for both players entered. Table 2.4(b) illustrates the abbreviated form of the matrix, which is conventional. Only the payoffs for P^A are entered; the entries for P^B can be omitted since they are known to be the negatives of the entries for P^A. Henceforth we use only the abbreviated form for zero-sum matrices.

The entries of the abbreviated matrix can be considered to be the losses for P^B as well as the gains for P^A. Because of this, some authors refer to the "maximin" strategy for P^A, but the "minimax" strategy for P^B. This book, however, uses "maximin" for both players.

We were saying that good reasons could be advanced for employing a maximin solution for zero-sum games with rational competition. The maximin solution for this case was presented by John von Neumann and Oskar Morgenstern in their epochal *Theory of Games and Economic Behavior* (first published in 1944). This book established the theory of games (in the more restricted sense) and presented a monumental new theory of utility (Section 4.1).

The theory of games attempts to specify a rational strategy for each of the rational players. It is assumed that each player knows the payoff matrix entries and each knows that his coplayer is equally rational. Thus, each player must consider that any strategy he can justify on rational grounds will be anticipated by his coplayer, who will try to take advantage of such insight in planning his own strategy. For some zero-sum payoff matrices the theory of games recommends that the players use a pure maximin strategy. For other matrices a mixed maximin strategy is recommended.

It is very easy to tell if a pure strategy solution is acceptable. Find the pure maximin strategy for each player, say a_i and b_j. Given that the players were to choose a_i and b_j, find the worst consequence possible for P^A and the worst consequence possible for P^B. If the worst consequence for both is the same o_{ij}, then the solution is a_i for P^A and b_j for P^B. Consequence o_{ij}, under such circumstances, is called a *saddle point* of the matrix. We illustrate.

In Table 2.5(a), the pure maximin strategy for P^A is a_2, yielding him at worst 4 (consequence o_{21}). The pure maximin strategy for P^B is b_1, yielding him at worst -4 (consequence o_{21} also; recall that P^B's payoffs are the negatives of those listed). Consequence o_{21} is a saddle point and the solution for the game is a_2b_1.

A matrix may have more than one saddle point. A player can choose any of his saddle point strategies (though we assume he will not choose a dominated strategy). All such strategies yield both players the same payoffs.

In Table 2.5(b), the pure maximin strategy for P^A is a_2, yielding him at worst 2 (consequence o_{22}). The pure maximin strategy for P^B is b_1, yielding him at worst -4 (consequence o_{21}). The worst consequences for P^A and P^B when each plays his pure maximin strategy differ (o_{22} and o_{21}). The matrix has no saddle point, and the strategy pair a_2b_2 is not recommended by the theory of games.

The difficulty with a_2b_2 is not hard to discern. As we said, both players are assumed to be equally rational. If P^A can justify a_2 to himself, then P^B can forsee P^A's conclusion. Anticipating a_2, P^B would do best to choose b_2, since he would then get -2. P^A, however, being as rational as P^B, can anticipate P^B's choice, and therefore is motivated to choose a_1 and get 8, whereupon P^B is motivated to choose b_3 to get 5, etc., in a never ending cycle.

Such cyclical reasoning does not arise when there is a saddle point, as in Table 2.5(a). As we noted, the pure maximin strategies are a_2 and b_1. Even if P^A anticipates b_1, however, he has no motivation to change his choice from

TABLE 2.5
Two Payoff Matrices

	(a)				(b)		
	b_1	b_2	b_3		b_1	b_2	b_3
a_1	-2	8	-5	a_1	-2	8	-5
a_2	4	6	7	a_2	4	2	7

a_2, since a change would lower his payoff. Likewise, P^B would have no motivation to change his choice if he anticipates a_2.

If neither player would be motivated to alter his choice from $a_i b_j$, knowing his opponent's choice and being assured the opponent would not alter his choice, then $a_i b_j$ is an *equilibrium pair*. Saddle point strategies always form an equilibrium pair. When there is no saddle point, a mixed strategy equilibrium pair can always be found, namely, the mixed maximin strategies. The idea of equilibrium is vital to the justification of the maximin solution to zero-sum games between rational players, for without equilibrium it would be difficult to justify having a rational player settle on a particular strategy.

Now let us derive the mixed strategy solution for the matrix of Table 2.5(b). The solution is not hard to find when there are only two a_i's. With only two a_i's, all mixed strategies available to P^A must be of the form $(p_1 a_1, p_2 a_2)$, where p_1 and p_2, in this context, are p_i's, not p_j's. Since $p_2 = 1 - p_1$, any available randomized strategy can be specified by giving p_1.

Let the expected value of a strategy to P^A, conditional on the choice of b_j, be symbolized g_j, as before. Then

$$
\begin{aligned}
g_j &= p_1 v_{1j} + p_2 v_{2j} \\
&= p_1 v_{1j} + (1 - p_1) v_{2j} \\
&= p_1 (v_{1j} - v_{2j}) + v_{2j}
\end{aligned}
\tag{2.2}
$$

Equation 2.2 shows that for a given payoff matrix, g_j is a straight line function of p_1. The three g_j lines for the matrix of Table 2.5(b) are plotted in Figure 2.5.

For any mixed strategy (i.e., for any p_1), there is a lowest EV to P^A across the three b_j's. When p_1 is small, this lowest EV is given by b_2; for intermediate p_1's it is given by b_1, and for the higher p_1 values it is given by b_3. The lowest EV as a function of p_1 is shown in Figure 2.5 as a heavier line. It gives the lowest possible EV for P^A for any of his strategies. These are his *mixed strategy security levels*. The arrow points out where P^A can have the largest security level. The corresponding p_1 can be read on the abscissa below.

An analytic solution for p_1 can be found, once we know that the solution occurs where $g_1 = g_2$, for from Equation 2.2 we can then write:

$$
p_1 (v_{11} - v_{21}) + v_{21} = p_1 (v_{12} - v_{22}) + v_{22}
$$

With specified v's, this equation has one unknown, p_1, which we calculate to be $p_1 = 1/6$. With p_1 known, we can calculate the expected value of the game to P^A (from the equation for g_1 or g_2) to be 3. The same type of graphical and analytical treatment is possible for the saddle point matrix. The security level contour would be highest for $p_1 = 0$, i.e., for pure strategy a_2.

What should P^B's strategy be? From Figure 2.5 we can infer that it must be of the form $(p_1 b_1, p_2 b_2)$, since only b_1 and b_2 can keep P^A's payoff as small as possible, and for a zero-sum game P^B's payoff relates inversely to P^A's. (p_1 and p_2 are now p_j's.) Since we now have only a single variable to consider, namely,

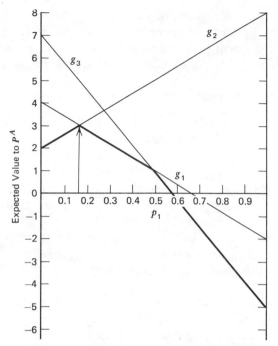

Figure 2.5. Line g_j gives the expected value to P^A of mixed strategy (p_1a_1, p_2a_2) if P^B chooses b_j. The graphs are for the payoff matrix of Table 2.5(b). The heavy lower contour gives P^A's mixed strategy security level as a function of p_1. The arrow shows where the security level is maximum; the corresponding p_1 is the maximin strategy.

p_1, we can proceed for P^B just as we did for P^A (but we must use the negatives of the matrix entries for P^B's values).

We leave this calculation to the reader, who should find that the expected value of the game for P^B is the negative of P^A's value.

The maximin strategies for P^A and P^B always form an equilibrium pair (for zero-sum games), so even if a player anticipates his opponent's maximin strategy, he has no motivation to deviate from his own maximin strategy. Of course, when we come down to it, P^A must play a_1 or a_2, and P^B must play b_1 or b_2. But since the choices are made randomly, a player cannot anticipate his opponent's choice of a pure strategy with assurance. By assuming his opponent to be rational, however, he can anticipate the probabilities.

The calculation of maximin strategies becomes complicated except for very small payoff matrices. Computations are usually performed on a computer. Solutions to so-called *linear programming*[5] problems involve the same sort of compu-

---

[5] Vajda (1960) and Glicksman (1963) relate linear programming and game theory at an elementary level.

tations, so the same computer programs can be used. Before concluding that he can't solve a matrix by the methods we have presented, however, the reader should eliminate all dominated pure strategies for both players from the payoff matrix. The solution to the reduced matrix is valid for the original matrix.

2.10 OTHER DECISION PRINCIPLES

The EV and maximin principles are the most important decision principles (ignoring the rather inconclusive dominance principle). No other principles are widely discussed and used. Therefore, we shall not spend much time with any others.

The so-called *Laplace principle* recommends that if P^A has no reason to believe that any state of nature is more probable than any other, he should choose the option with the highest mean payoff. This is equivalent to the EV principle with equal subjective probabilities for the states of nature. The recommendation to assign equal probabilities to the states of nature for the condition of ignorance was widely accepted in the early days of probability theory. It is known as the *principle of insufficient reason* (or the *principle of indifference*). This principle fell into disrepute due to its subjectivity, but something very much like it has arisen anew as part of the so-called Bayesian movement in statistics (Section 8.9). But equal probabilities arising from ignorance may have different implications for decision making than equal probabilities based on knowledge (see Section 5.4).

Another decision principle often mentioned is the *minimax regret principle*. A quantity called "regret" can be calculated for each player for each consequence. The *regret* for P^A for consequence o_{ij} is the difference between the maximum possible payoff to P^A, given b_j, and the payoff given $a_i b_j$. A payoff matrix and its associated regret matrix are shown in Table 2.6.

The regret for consequence o_{11} (3) was obtained by subtracting the payoff for o_{11}, 7, from the maximum possible payoff given b_1, namely, 10. The name "regret" is attached to this quantity because once P^A found out that P^B chose b_1, he would "regret" that he hadn't chosen a_3, which would have been best for

TABLE 2.6
A Payoff Matrix and Its Regret Matrix

	Payoff Matrix				Regret Matrix		
	b_1	b_2	b_3		b_1	b_2	b_3
a_1	7	3	5	a_1	3	5	0
a_2	-2	8	-4	a_2	12	0	9
a_3	10	-5	0	a_3	0	13	5

him. The amount of "regret," common sense tells us, would relate to the difference between P^A's payoff for his choice, a_1, say, and the payoff he might have obtained. Of course, if P^A chooses the option that would give him maximum payoff, conditional on b_j, his regret would be zero. Due to the manner of defining regret, at least one cell in each column of the regret matrix must be zero, and the remaining cells must be positive. (However, the regrets for P^B would be based on *row* maximum payoffs, so each row would have at least one zero entry, but not necessarily each column).

The name "regret" is not always applied to the quantities we have calculated. Instead, "loss" or "risk" is sometimes used; since these terms have other common uses in decision theory, we use "regret."

The *minimax regret principle* requires that P^A choose an option that *mini*mizes the *maxi*mum regrets; i.e., for each available strategy there is a maximum regret (an expected regret for mixed strategies), and P^A should choose the option with the smallest of these maxima. The solution can be found by taking the negatives of the entries of the regret matrix, treating these entries as "payoffs," and finding the maximin "payoff," as explained in Section 2.9.

The minimax regret principle fails to exhibit "independence from irrelevant alternatives," by which is meant that addition of a new, non-optimal option to a payoff matrix may cause the originally optimal option to become non-optimal. For example, suppose P^A is offered chicken or steak and prefers steak. But then he is told that fish is also available, and he replies, "In that case, I'll have chicken." The intuitive feeling of most people is that a decision principle should exhibit independence from irrelevant alternatives, i.e., P^A should stick with his steak, even if he finds out that fish is available; if he wants to change his mind, it should only be to choose fish. The EV and maximin principles do exhibit such independence.

Since there is a regret analogue to the maximin principle, cannot there be an EV analogue to consider as well? Yes, indeed. We could propose that P^A choose the option with the smallest expected regret. Such a principle, however, is entirely equivalent to the EV principle, so there is no point in considering it separately. The option with the largest EV also has the smallest expected regret. What's more, the magnitude of the difference in the expected regrets between any two options equals the difference in EV, though the sign differs.

2.11 SUMMARY

Chapter 2 has presented the elements of mathematical decision theory. We have concentrated on the normal form of the "game," which requires that each player make his choice before learning the coplayer's choice. Our main aim has been to state decision principles (criteria), i.e., rules for selecting a decision on a rational basis. We have considered the possibilities that the "other person" in a "game" be either a human being or an abstract "nature."

Several such rules were described. The most prominent is the EV (expected value) principle, which requires choice of the option with the highest EV. The EV of an option is a probability-weighted sum of the payoffs. Since probabilities and payoffs can be objective or subjective, the EV principle is actually a family of principles. If one insists on using objective probabilities, the EV principle cannot be applied to the many situations lacking known, objective probabilities. Some authorities propose that subjective probabilities can be used universally.

The maximin principle does not require specification of probabilities for the b_j's. It requires that P^A choose the option with the largest security level. Although with specified probabilities, the EV solution can always be found from among the available pure strategies, the maximin solution may be either a pure or a mixed strategy. The maximin principle can best be justified for zero-sum games against a rational opponent, but some proponents of the principle feel that its applicability ranges beyond that context.

Although other decision principles have been suggested, the EV and maximin principles have received the widest support and investigation. Both principles lead to admissible solutions; by one interpretation, they do not so much conflict as differ in their applicability.

REFERENCES

Adams, E. W. "Survey of Bernoullian Utility Theory," in H. Solomon (ed.), *Mathematical Thinking in the Measurement of Behavior.* Glencoe, Ill.: The Free Press, 1960, pp. 151–268.

Berne, E. *Games People Play.* New York: Grove Press, 1967.

Edwards, W. "The Prediction of Decisions among Bets," *Journal of Experimental Psychology* (1955), **50**, 201–214.

Glicksman, A. M. *Linear Programming and the Theory of Games.* New York: Wiley, 1963.

Luce, R. D., & Raiffa, H. *Games and Decisions.* New York: Wiley, 1957.

Raiffa, H. *Decision Analysis.* Reading, Mass.: Addison-Wesley, 1968.

Savage, L. J. *The Foundations of Statistics.* New York: Wiley, 1954.

Vajda, S. *An Introduction to Linear Programming and the Theory of Games.* New York: 1960.

von Neumann, J., & Morgenstern, O. *Theory of Games and Economic Behavior* (3rd ed.), Princeton, N. J.: Princeton University Press, 1953.

CHAPTER 3

Probability Theory and Subjective Probability

3.1 INTRODUCTION

Consider some event that may happen in the future. You are not sure that it will happen, nor are you sure that it will not happen. Of two possible events, you may feel that one event is more likely to occur than the other. Such "partial beliefs," or "possibilities," constitute an extremely important part of our lives. We continually consider such possibilities and the effects they could have on us. We have seen that rational choice depends on the probabilities of various "states of nature, " and in many cases such probabilites will have to be a matter of personal judgment. These probabilities based on the beliefs of persons are called *subjective probabilities* or *psychological probabilities*.

The ancient Greek philospher Democritus asserted that "chance" is simply a name for our ignorance of causes. The French mathematician Pierre Simon de Laplace (1749–1827) held a similar view, based on the philosophical doctrine of determinism. According to determinism, all future happenings, including the outcomes of coin-flips, dice-throws, etc., develop from and are already determined by current conditions; it is only our limitations in comprehending current conditions and the laws of nature that prevent us from predicting all future outcomes perfectly.

Philosophical determinism does not currently hold sway.[1] Nonetheless, it is

---

[1] To a large extent, the uncertainty principle of quantum mechanics is responsible for the current unpopularity of determinism. The uncertainty (or indeterminancy) principle asserts that there are fundamental limitations in the accuracy of simultaneous measurement of the momentum and position of a particle (for example, an electron or photon). In spite of this principle, however, the issue of determinism in physics is still open (Lindsay, 1968).

clear enough that for many common uses of "probability," the uncertainty implied by the term relates to our ignorance rather than to any inherent indeterminancy of the facts. For example, we speak of the probability that a human fetus is male as being about $1/2$; yet, in fact, the fetus is already either male or female.

A person who would accept a probability statement about the sex of a fetus might object to probability statements concerning other outcomes which have already occurred. For example, can we still speak of the probability of heads in a coin-flip as being $1/2$ if the coin has already been flipped and lies unobserved beneath someone's hand? What about my belief that the St. Louis Cardinals won the National League Pennant in 1947. Can I state a subjective probability for this belief (which, as it turns out, was mistaken—it was 1946), or is it improper to speak of probability in relation to established fact? In the present book we follow those theorists who interpret probability with respect to an individual's knowledge and ignorance. Therefore, we are willing to speak of the "probabilities" of past events as well as of future events.

The distinctions between *objective* and *subjective* probabilities have been a source of agitation and confusion in probability theory for a long time, and the last word has not yet been spoken. In the early days of systematization of probability, authorities such as Jacques Bernoulli (1654-1705) and Laplace spoke of probability as "degree of belief," so it seemed that the theory they developed had to do with the beliefs of individuals, i.e., with subjective probabilities. "Objective probabilities" are supposedly independent of any belief that a person might have, and if a person changed his beliefs, this would not change any probability under discussion. If the probability that a die will come up an ace is $1/6$, then it is $1/6$ regardless of my beliefs on the matter. A large part of the confusion seems to have come about because probability theory was (and often is) discussed in terms of beliefs, and thus it sounded as if the theory dealt with beliefs (i.e., with real people). A close reading of these theories, however, indicates that they actually dealt with consistent, logically related beliefs—not with the actual beliefs of people. The experts allow that the study of actual beliefs is a legitimate concern of psychology, but that the body of work developed over the past several centuries known as probability theory does not concern actual beliefs.

In the present book we cannot deal exclusively with logicomathematical probability theory, nor with subjective probability (individual beliefs)—we have to consider both. Naturally, as psychologists we are interested in the beliefs of real people, whether they are consistent or rational or whatever. But we must also concern ourselves with the logical aspects of probability theory because here we might find simple models for relating beliefs in some situations, and because investigation of behavioral decision theory includes inquiry into logical or rational belief, as well as into actual and inconsistent belief.

We begin with a presentation of the elements of mathematical probability theory. Next we consider the various theories dealing with the meaning and measurement of "probability." Although the elements of mathematical probability theory are not disputed, the meaning and measurement of probability are subject to considerable controversy. Next we consider methods commonly employed to measure subjective probabilities of real persons, as well as some empirical findings based on these methods. We conclude with a discussion of the perception of chance and luck in everyday life.

3.2 ELEMENTS OF MATHEMATICAL PROBABILITY THEORY

Sample Points, Sample Space, and Events

Our treatment in this section is limited to *discrete* probability theory; i.e., we assume that the *outcome* of a so-called *experimental trial* (or *experiment*) is the occurrence of exactly one of a set of finite and perfectly discriminable possibilities. Each such possibility is called a *sample point* (or *point*), and the collection of all possibilities under consideration is called a *sample space* (or *space*). For example, the "experiment" might consist of drawing a card at random[2] from a shuffled deck of 52 playing cards. Each of the 52 cards is a possible draw, so each is a "sample point."

An *event* is a set of sample points. An event is said to occur if any of the sample points in the set occurs. For example, the suit spade is an event consisting of 13 sample points. We say that a spade occurs, or that the *outcome* is a spade, regardless of which of these sample points occurs. The term "event" may be used for a set of size one, i.e., for a single sample point, or for the set of all sample points, i.e., the entire sample space.

Each sample point is included in more than one event. For example, the point "king of spades" is part of the event "spade" and part of the event "king." In fact, it is the only point that these two events (sets) have in common. Although only one sample point can occur in one experimental trial, many events can occur in one trial—all those events containing the sample point which occurs.

Two or more events in a space are *disjoint* if no point in the space is a member of more than one of the events, i.e., if no two of the events have a point in common. At most one of a set of disjoint events can occur in one experimental trial. The "states of nature" in a decision situation are presumed to be disjoint. Disjoint events are also called *mutually exclusive events* (or *exclusive events*).

---

[2] "Random" sometimes, as here, implies that the method of determining the outcome gives each sample point equal probability. More generally, "random" is used synonymously with "probabilistic," without requiring equal probabilities.

Combining Events

Let E symbolize an arbitrary event in some sample space under consideration, and let E' symbolize another arbitrary event. $E \cup E'$, the *union* of E and E', is the event composed of all sample points in E or E' (or both). The union of events "spade" and "king" is composed of 16 sample points—the 13 spades plus the three non-spade kings. The union of J events is symbolized $\cup_{j=1}^{J} E_j$. It consists of all sample points in the J events.

If the union of a set of events under consideration contains all the points in the sample space, that set of events is said to be *exhaustive*. The set of events "spade," "heart," "diamond," and "club" is exhaustive, because these events include every possible card (point). Since the four events are also exclusive, we speak of an *exclusive, exhaustive set of events*. The states of nature in a decision situation are assumed to be exclusive, exhaustive events.

$E \cap E'$, the *intersection* of events E and E', is the event composed of points common to E and E'. The intersection of the events "spade" and "king" is "the king of spades." The intersection of J events is symbolized $\cap_{j=1}^{J} E_j$. It is the event consisting of points common to all J E_j's. There may be no points common to two or more E_j's, in which case the intersection is sometimes said to be the "empty set," or just "empty."

Fundamental Properties of Probabilities

Let $p(E)$ be the probability of event E. The following fundamental properties for probabilities are typically presented:[3]

(1) $0 \leq p(E) \leq 1$, for each possible E in the space.

(2) The probability for the event containing all the sample points in the space is 1.

(3) $p\left(\bigcup_{j=1}^{J} E_j\right) = \sum_{j=1}^{J} p(E_j)$, for sets of disjoint E_j's.

Property (1) says that the probability for any event in the space is no less than 0 and no greater than 1. Property (2) says there is a probability of 1 that some sample point will occur. We associate a probability of 1 with certainty, so this property says that one of the sample points must (is assumed to) occur. Otherwise, the theorems of probability are not applicable. If our space is heads and tails for a coin flip, the theorems of probability only hold assuming heads or tails must occur. If the coin lands on edge or is lost in a drain, the theorems are inapplicable. (In practice, one might void such an unexpected result and conduct a new experimental trial.)

---

[3] In different presentations of mathematical probability, these "properties" appear variously as assumptions, conventions, and theorems. We simply call them "properties" of probabilities.

Property (3) says that the probability of the event derived from the union of disjoint events is the sum of the probabilities for these disjoint events. Consider the disjoint events "spade" and "heart"; their union is the event "spade or heart." If $p(\text{spade}) = \frac{1}{4}$, and $p(\text{heart}) = \frac{1}{4}$, then $p(\text{spade or heart}) = \frac{1}{4} + \frac{1}{4} = \frac{1}{2}$. But "spade" and "king" are not disjoint events, and $p(\text{spade}) + p(\text{king}) \neq p(\text{spade or king})$.

Note that these properties do not reveal the quantitative value for the probability of any sample point. How are such quantities to be determined? It has been usual since the early days of probability theory for probabilists to assume that all sample points in a space have equal probabilities. Once this has been assumed, it follows from the properties above that if there are N sample points, the probability for an event consisting of only a single point is $1/N$, and that the probability of an event consisting of n sample points is n/N. These assumptions are generally readily accepted for drawing cards from decks and balls from urns, for flipping coins, and for roulette and dice games; but such an approach to quantifying the probabilities is often not applicable, since the set of possibilities cannot be broken down into a set of (apparently) equally probable events. Most spaces of interest in human decision making cannot be so analyzed.

Independent Events and Conditional Probabilities

For convenience let $E \cap E'$ be symbolized $E\,E'$. Two events E and E' are, by definition, *independent* if and only if

$$p(E\,E') = p(E) \cdot p(E') \tag{3.1}$$

To exemplify use of this definition, let E be "spade" and E' be "king." The intersection is "spade and king," i.e., the "king of spades," which, assuming equal probabilities for the 52 points, has a probability of $1/52$. Also, $p(E) \cdot p(E') = (1/13)(1/4) = 1/52$. Therefore "spade" and "king" are independent. Spade and heart are not independent. Their intersection is the empty set, which has a probability of 0. Yet $p(\text{spade}) \cdot p(\text{heart}) = (1/13)(1/13)$, which is not 0. Although strictly speaking, independence is defined by Equation 3.1, it often happens in practice that independence is accepted on intuitive grounds, and use of the product rule (Equation 3.1) is then justified by the independence presumed to exist between events.

Let $p(E|E')$ be the *conditional probability of event E (given event E')*. By definition,

$$p(E|E') = \frac{p(E\,E')}{p(E')}, \tag{3.2}$$

provided $p(E') \neq 0$.

The *absolute*, or *unconditional probability* $p(E)$ equals the conditional probability $p(E|E')$ if and only if E and E' are independent. To see this, substitute

$p(E)$ for $p(E|E')$ in Equation 3.2, obtaining

$$p(E) = \frac{p(E\ E')}{p(E')}$$

Multiply both sides by $p(E')$ to obtain

$$p(E) \cdot p(E') = p(E\ E'),$$

which is the condition for independence for E and E'.

The conditional probability $p(E|E')$ can be thought of as the probability for E if the sample point occurring on a trial is known to be from E', but is otherwise unidentified. In essence, the points comprising E' form a new sample space, and probabilities conditional on E' have the same properties as absolute probabilities, except that they relate to this new sample space which is a subset of the original space. To say that E and E' are independent is to say that the probability of E is the same in the original space and in the reduced (conditional) space defined by E'. The probability of king is $1/13$. The probability of king is also $1/13$ in the reduced space of spade cards only. King and spade are independent.

Multiple Trials

Many probability problems concern not a single experimental trial, but a series of them. We are not just concerned about the probability for heads for a coin-flip. We are also concerned about the probability of getting seven heads for a series of ten coin-flips. So far we have only talked about probabilities in relation to single trials; however, each possible result for a series of trials can be conceived as a *compound sample point* in a *compound sample space*. For example, if one flips a coin and throws a die, these two trials can be conceived as a compound trial having one of 12 possible outcomes (2 outcomes for the coin times 6 outcomes for the die). The *compound event* "heads" has six compound sample points. In the compound space, one can apply the properties, definitions, and formulas that have been given for single trials. The compound space for ten coin-flips has 2^{10} points. "Seven heads" is an event in the space.

The concept of "independence" is often applied to trials as well as to events. Thus, we say that the coin-flip and die-throw trials are independent. Mathematically, independent trials are defined by probabilities in the compound space. In practice, one often makes the intuitive judgment that the outcome for one trial is independent of (not influenced by) the outcome of the other trial. This judgment is then used to justify application of the "product rule" between component space probabilities, for example, $p(\text{heads}) \cdot p(\text{one pip}) = 1/2 \cdot 1/6$, which is equivalent to treating heads and one pip as independent events in the compound space.

Bayes' Formula

Bayes' formula (Bayes' rule)[4] is one of the most important equations in decision theory. It concerns the effect of relevant data (information, observations) on the probabilities of a number n of possible circumstances. In terms of probability theory, these n possible circumstances form a set of exclusive, exhaustive events. In practice, these events are often called hypotheses and are symbolized H_j. They are often identified with "states of nature," which, as we noted, likewise form a set of exclusive, exhaustive events. One hypothesis is "true" and the rest are false (one state of nature occurs, the rest do not). The true hypothesis is not known; instead, each H_j has a probability.

Instead of accepting these probabilities as final and making a decision on the basis of them, it is sometimes possible to collect data bearing on these hypotheses. Ideally, these data would indicate which single hypothesis is true. Oftentimes, however, the data will be suggestive but not conclusive; they will only allow modification of the original, *prior* probabilities to new, *posterior* probabilities.[5]

Let D symbolize the data (event) observed, and let $p(D|H_j)$ be the conditional probability that D would occur given that H_j were true. In the context of Bayes' formula, $p(D|H_j)$ is called a *likelihood*. We assume that the likelihoods are known for each H_j for each possible D. By our assumptions, the absolute probability of D, $p(D)$, can be calculated thusly:

$$p(D) = \sum_{j=1}^{n} p(D|H_j) \cdot p(H_j) \qquad (3.3)$$

Our purpose is to calculate $p(H_j|D)$, the posterior probability of H_j conditional on observation of the data D. By Equation 3.2 we write

$$p(H_j|D) = \frac{p(H_jD)}{p(D)} \qquad (3.4)$$

Given the likelihoods and the prior probabilities, we can calculate $p(D)$ with Equation 3.3. We next have to calculate $p(H_jD)$. But by Equation 3.2 we can write

$$p(D|H_j) = \frac{p(DH_j)}{p(H_j)} \qquad (3.5)$$

---

[4] Named after the English clergyman and mathematician, Thomas Bayes (1702–1761). Bayes did not present Bayes' formula in the form familiar to contemporary scientists (Equation 3.7), but he apparently understood how to make the same calculation.
[5] Prior probabilities are often called *a priori* probabilities. Posterior probabilities are often called *a posteriori* probabilities.

Event DH_j is the same as event H_jD (the intersection is the same regardless of the order of writing), so by multiplying Equation 3.5 by $p(H_j)$ and rearranging we obtain

$$p(H_jD) = p(D|H_j) \cdot p(H_j) \tag{3.6}$$

By substituting the $p(H_jD)$ of Equation 3.6 and the $p(D)$ of Equation 3.3 into Equation 3.4, we obtain the usual form of *Bayes' formula:*

$$p(H_j|D) = \frac{p(D|H_j) \cdot p(H_j)}{\sum\limits_{j=1}^{n} p(D|H_j) \cdot p(H_j)} \tag{3.7}$$

We limit our presentation in this section to derivation of the formula. We shall have a good deal more to say about the use and interpretation of this formula in subsequent sections and chapters.

3.3 INTERPRETATIONS OF PROBABILITY

The major controversies of probability theory do not concern the mathematical properties of probabilities, as presented in the previous section. Instead, they concern the interpretation of "probability" and the determination of the probabilities of real events. Most current texts on probability *assume* equally probable sample points; in other words, the approach is "if the sample points are equally probable, such and such assertions about probabilities follow."

But what if the assumption is wrong. Then the deductions must be wrong. It would be well, therefore, for real-world concerns, to be able to determine if probabilities are equal for all sample points. But how can this be done? We could flip a coin many times to see if heads and tails come up equally often. But we really wouldn't expect them to come up with equal frequency, even if the probabilities were equal. And, indeed, actual experiments of this sort often suggest that the probabilities for heads and tails are not *exactly* equal. The equality assumption for other commonly discussed spaces, such as die faces, seems likewise to be inexact.

Many uses of the term "probability" don't appear to be amenable to a sample space approach at all. For example, a person might speak of the probability of life on Mars. What is the sample space here? If the space consists only of "life on Mars" and "no life on Mars," very few people would want to assign equal probabilities to these points. It certainly does not seem possible to do so on the basis of "symmetry." We can't observe results for many trials, either, as we can with a coin. In fact it would be pointless to do so, since one (valid) observation would obviate a probability statement.

Is a statement concerning the probability of life on Mars, then, meaningless? Or is the probability of a different sort than the kind we see discussed in the typical probability text? These are issues concerning which the various "schools of probability theory" debate.

The three major schools (theories) of probability which have contended in recent decades are the *frequency* (or *objective,* or *empirical*), the *logical* (or *necessary*), and the *personalistic.* The approach to probability of eighteenth century probabilists such as J. Bernoulli, Laplace, and Bayes is called the *classical* school. Although the classical school contained the seeds of the other schools, it is not, per se, a current contender.

Some authorities hold that all probability statements are subject to a single interpretation (frequency, logical, *or* personalistic). This is called the *identity* conception of probability. Others hold that one interpretation may be correct for some probability statements, whereas other statements are subject to an alternative interpretation. This is the *disparity* conception. Carnap (1962), for example, uses "probability$_1$" for "logical" probabilities and "probability$_2$" for "frequency" probabilities.

Classical Probability

A Philosophical Essay on Probabilities by Pierre Simon de Laplace is an interesting and readily available source document for classical probability. Laplace discussed probability in terms of human belief, but it seems clear that he referred to ideal rather than actual human belief.

According to Laplace, "the theory of chance consists in reducing all the events of the same kind to a certain number of cases equally possible, that is to say, to such as we may be equally undecided about in regard to their existence, and in determining the number of cases favorable to the event whose probability is sought." (Laplace, 1951, p. 6) "Cases favorable to the event," are, in our previous terminology, simply those sample points ("cases") comprising the event. Laplace then states that the probability of an event is the ratio of the number of favorable cases to that of all cases possible. His approach to probability, in this respect, hardly differs from most textbook treatments in recent decades.

Laplace was, philosophically, a determinist, and thought that events were "probable" only in view of human ignorance, but the theory of probability cannot in general be said to concern situations of complete ignorance. Rather, "Probability is relative, in part to this ignorance, in part to our knowledge." (Laplace, 1951, p. 6) For example, the laws of probability concerning dice depend on the *knowledge* that each face of the die is equally likely to occur and that the outcomes on each of two dice are independent.

An important feature of the classical school was acceptance of the *principle of indifference* (also known as the *principle of insufficient reason,* or the *principle of equal distribution of ignorance*). According to the principle of indifference if a person has no reason to consider any one event more likely than any of the others, then all events should be considered equally probable. The principle was used to provide the prior probabilities needed for use of Bayes' formula (Equation 3.7).

The principle came under attack by nineteenth century frequentists, who viewed it as too subjective for scientific purposes. Although the principle was discredited by the attack, something rather similar to it has recently been revived by the personal probabilists.

Frequency School

The *frequency* (or *objective,* or *empirical*) concept of probability can be traced to ancient times, but precise formalization of frequency theory came as part of a reaction to the classical school. The first full-fledged treatment of frequency theory appeared in *The Logic of Chance* (1st ed. 1866) by John Venn.[6] Probability was defined as the limiting value of a relative frequency as the number of cases increased indefinitely. More current versions of frequency theory appear in von Mises (1939) and Reichenbach (1949).

Objections have been raised to the frequency view on several counts. First, although this school likes to think of itself as empirically oriented and scientific, there can be no empirical confirmation of a statement about the limit of an infinite series. It is impossible to observe such a series in reality, and therefore to confirm the statement. Is a statement of probability then meaningless? The reply might be that a (necessarily limited) empirical series could not precisely confirm a probability statement, but could give evidence for or against it. Against this it might be countered that no definite acceptance or rejection could be made. Consider the proposition that the probability of heads when tossing a coin is 1/2. Then in a thousand tosses, it is *possible* to get any number of heads, from zero to one thousand, even if the proposition is true. No finite series, however long, can establish that the proposition is true or false, and we still are left with the question of the meaningfulness and empirical orientation of this approach. The reply by (some) frequentists is that of course one can't confirm the proposition without any doubt whatsoever, but one can provide degrees of confirmation. One is apt to believe the statement in the above experiment of 1000 trials if the number of heads comes out 491, but to reject it if the result comes out 821 heads. Current methods of statistical inference proceed pretty much along this line of reasoning. Statistical techniques of estimation and hypothesis testing are interpreted as giving no guarantee of certitude, but rather reasonable conclusions based on the evidence.

A second objection to the frequency position is that it cannot deal with the important class of probability statements referring to unique events. Consider

---

[6] Kyburg and Smokler (1964) have prepared a book of selected readings in subjective probability theory, including a selection by Venn.

two such statements:

(1) The probability of rain tomorrow in San Francisco is 3/5.
(2) Caesar probably sired Brutus.

Now statement (1) refers to a particular day and place. It will rain or it will not.[7] How can the statement that the probability is 3/5 be verified? How can we count the relative number of rainy to total days when there is only one day. Of course, if it rains, we have the ratio $1/1 = 1$, and if it doesn't, the ratio $0/1 = 0$. Does this mean we could have confirmed statement (1) only if the probability had been 1 or 0? Is the statement meaningless? Intuitively, we think not. The frequentist reply might be that the statement is meaningful in the frequency sense, but it is an elliptical form of the statement that (1′) The relative frequency (probability) of rain in San Francisco for those days following days when the conditions were (approximately) like those today has been 3/5. There are, of course, some problems here in specifying which other days had conditions like those of today, since we can observe conditions so discriminately that there would be no such other similar days.

Some frequentists might say that statement (2) is meaningless or that it refers to a kind of probability different from the one used in science, and that this kind of probability is too vague for scientific purposes. Reichenbach is one of the few frequentists who attempt to give such historical statements frequency interpretations. The interpretation is similar to the interpretation of (1). One considers the class of such statements made under similar circumstances. Needless to say, the difficulties here are more formidable than in (1). In the first place, it is not all clear what statements should be included in a class. In the second place, it is not clear, if one had such a class, what the frequency of true statements would be, since, presumably, the truth of many of the statements would, like statement (2), be unknown.

Logical or Necessary School

The logical school of probability is usually traced to *A Treatise on Probability* (1921) by English economist John Maynard Keynes (1883–1946). Adherents of the logical school emphasize the development of probability within a logical system of assumptions and inferences. The basic difference between traditional deductive logic and probability theory, or inductive logic, is that propositions in deductive logic are treated as true or false (or sometimes meaningless), whereas propositions in a system of inductive logic may be said to be only probable. Keynes asserted that, strictly speaking, all propositions are true or false,

---

[7] Strictly speaking, the statement is open to question. For a "few drops" might fall on part of the city and it is not clear that such a slight and limited downfall would be interpreted as "rain in San Francisco." I suppose the weather bureau has some objective standards for "rain" or "no rain," and we take the bureau's judgment as the final authority.

but that we speak of them as probable in relation to the evidence which we have with respect to them. For example, the proposition that "it will rain tomorrow in San Francisco" is actually either true or false, since it will or will not rain, but in relation to our present evidence the proposition has a probability. There is no fixed correct probability that it will rain; the probability can differ depending on the evidence available.

Keynes was critical of Venn's frequency theory because Venn's analysis only applied to series or classes in relation to which one can speak of relative frequency. Keynes felt that other kinds of probability statements were subject to logical analysis as well, and he attempted to develop a theory of probabilistic reasoning that could encompass a greater range of propositions than Venn's frequency theory. As we have noted, however, subsequent frequentists have attempted to broaden the applicability of frequency theory. Keynes recognized that such extensions might be attempted, but doubted that his criticisms could be met without severe complications of the theory.

Although Keynes rejected frequency theory, he, too, objected to the principle of indifference of the classical school. His objections, however, related not to the principle's lack of objectivity, but to the logical inconsistencies to which it can lead.

Personalistic (Subjective) School

The main source in English on the personalistic (or subjective) theory of probability is Leonard Savage's *The Foundations of Statistics* (1954). Savage states that the theory is derived mainly from the work of Bruno de Finetti, whose own publications are largely in Italian and French (but see de Finetti, 1951, 1964). A comparable but independent treatment of probability had been presented earlier by Ramsey (1931) in 1926. The personalistic viewpoint did not have an important impact on probabilists until quite recently, but during the last decade it has been the subject of considerable controversy. Nonetheless, many of its basic ideas are not recent. The personalistic school has blended important ideas from the classical and logical schools with modern utility theory. The mixture has proved potent enough to challenge the rather casually accepted frequency point of view held by most statisticians over the past century. Personalistic probability theory applied to statistics is called *Bayesian statistics*. (We discuss Bayesian statistics in Chapter 8.)

The terminology of personal probability theory, like that of classical theory, suggests that the theory concerns the beliefs of people, i.e., real people. This is perhaps unfortunate, for the theory does not basically pertain to real persons any more than classical probability theory did. The term "personal probability" is actually not often used in connection with measured probabilities of real persons. Instead the term "subjective probability" is used, or, less often, "psychological probability." However, "subjective probability" is frequently used as a synonym for the "personal probability" of an ideal person, so terminology is not a reliable basis for distinguishing between discussions of real and ideal persons. Nonetheless, we shall, in this book, try to use "personal probability" and "subjective probability" in relation to ideal and real people, respectively.

Personalists view probability as a degree of belief of an ideal person who is perfectly consistent in his beliefs. This contrasts with frequency theory but accords with logical theory. Since probability is degree of belief, and therefore subjective, personal probabilists do not share the objection of the frequentists to the subjectivity of prior probability estimates in applications of Bayes' formula. In fact, personal probability theory has stimulated intensified interest in Bayes' formula and its applications.

Has personal probability theory, then, re-established the principle of indifference? Sort of, but not exactly. As we saw, personal probabilists are not bothered by charges of subjectivity, so they could not reject the principle of indifference on that account. On the other hand, they really have no need to defend the principle against charges of vagueness and inconsistency. As long as a person's probabilities are consistent, he is not required to invoke a principle of indifference as justification.

Let us consider an objection that Keynes presented to the principle of indifference, and show how personal probability theory can avoid the difficulty. Keynes imagined a man who inhabits an unknown country. Assuming ignorance of populations and areas, he is, by the principle of indifference, equally likely to inhabit the British Isles as France. But he is also equally likely to inhabit Ireland (part of the British Isles) as France, and equally likely to inhabit Great Britain as France. These statements, however, are inconsistent, for the last two equalities imply that he is twice as likely to inhabit the British Isles as France, contradicting the stated equality. More generally, the difficulty is that a possible outcome may be subdivided, and application of the principle of indifference to the new sample space is inconsistent with the original application. It is often not clear why one subdivision should be preferred to another.

Personal probability theory does not provide the proper breakdown of the sample space. But an ideal person of the theory is required to be consistent. He need not judge a man equally likely to inhabit France or the British Isles, even if he can think of or give no reason for believing one possibility to be more likely than the other; but if he does judge them equally likely, he may not go on to hold inconsistent beliefs.

Well, then, what should the relative probabilities be? There is no particular correct value. There can be more than one set of consistent probabilities, or, in effect, more than one ideal person. Even though the persons differ in their personal probabilities, each is equally "correct." This differs from the frequency theory view that an event has a real, "objective" probability, even if it cannot be known exactly.

The acceptance of different probability values for different (ideal) persons is the most salient feature distinguishing personal probability theory from logical probability theory. It is typical for expositions of logical probability theory to state something like "upon evidence e, there is only one probability of h, which is logically entailed by e, and no other probability of h can be accepted," whereas the personalistic theory would state that different people can have differing personal probabilities, and both can be "right."

This distinction between the two schools becomes ambiguous, however, upon closer examination. Over the years, many theorists have asserted that the correct value of probability is dependent upon the information available, and that two persons with different information could reasonably hold different views on the probability of an event. Laplace, for example, said that "In things which are only probable the difference of the data, which each man has in regard to them, is one of the principal causes of the diversity of opinions which prevail in regard to the same objects." (Laplace, 1951, p. 8) He gives an example of three urns, one having black balls, and the other two having white balls; the probability that a ball from the third urn is black is demanded. With no knowledge, the probability is 1/3, but if it is known that the first urn contains white balls, the probability is 1/2. Keynes recognized that individual beliefs may differ even within his system, for it is only the relations between the premises and the conclusions that are irrefutable. If different persons have different premises, or in other words, different evidence, then they would be expected to have different probabilities.

Another noteworthy distinction between the personal and logical schools is the intimate relationship between personal probability theory and decision making. Logical probabilists have not had much to say about the role of probability in decision making,[8] whereas Savage (pp. 27–28) considers that probabilities can be meaningfully expressed only in the context of decisions on which they bear. The ideal man of Savage's theory prefers the alternative with the largest subjectively expected utility (SEU). (There are other, lesser known personalistic theories, however, in which decision making is not basic; we shall not be concerned with these.)

It should be pointed out that, as much as the personal and logical theories oppose frequency theory, neither theory holds data on relative frequencies of events, where available, to be irrelevant. Quite the contrary. Such data constitute evidence, and the implications of evidence for probability values is central for both theories. As we noted in connection with Bayes' formula, evidence (data) can lead to alterations in the probabilities of events (hypotheses). The ideal person of personalistic theory is supposed to use observed frequencies to revise his probabilities. As more and more such data are observed, the current probabilities generally come to relate more and more to the data observed, and less and less to the original probabilities. Although several (ideal) persons may begin

---

[8] Carnap (1962, p. xv), a proponent of logical probability, has come to favor defining logical probability in relation to decision making.

with rather different prior probabilities, they will generally come to have very similar probabilities if they both receive a considerable amount of common frequency data. It is mostly with respect to "initial" probabilities and small amounts of data that the ideal persons can differ substantially.

Theory and Practice

Although on the surface the contending schools of probability sound quite different, upon closer examination, and considering the variations within a school, the distinctions between them become blurred. Certainly they cannot be differentiated according to their rejection or acceptance of the fundamental mathematical properties of probabilities, for they all concur about these. The properties and formulas of Section 3.2 are not under contention. All schools try to present "logical" and "consistent" theories of probabilities, and all schools recognize that sufficient amounts of frequency data can largely determine what a probability value should be. Furthermore, application of Bayes' formula and the decision-theoretic point of view are accepted by expert advocates of all three schools, though not to the same extent.

Because of the similarities between schools, it has frequently been stated that the controversies between them are of little interest or import to practical scientists (Savage, 1954, p. 1; Carnap, 1962, p. 191), or that the "publicity" given to such discussions has created the "erroneous impression" that "essential disagreement can exist among mathematicians" (Feller, 1950, p. 6). During the past decade, however, the publicity has increased considerably, and it is now far from clear that the controversies lack practical import or that the differences between viewpoints of "mathematicians" are not of general concern. Savage (1962, p. 9), by the way, reversed his original belief that personal probability theory did not suggest changes in statistical practice, swept along, as it were, by his own current.

How can the theory of personal probability affect practice? Well, for one thing, it appears that if the theory is accepted, measured subjective probabilities, even when such probabilities cannot be justified objectively, could be given respectful consideration by men of science. One could employ such probabilities in decision making without fear that the brethren of pure science will charge one with witchcraft.

How to measure subjective probabilities? That we take up in the succeeding section. For now, however, assume that such methods exist, or can be found. We have stated that personal probability theory concerns ideal, not real, persons, who have perfectly consistent probabilities. If, as we would suspect, the subjective probabilities of real persons are not consistent, personal probability theory cannot justify use of such measures in decision making; personal probabilities are consistent, and measured "subjective probabilites" of real persons, if not consistent, should be no more acceptable to personalists as probabilities than to objectivists. So what would a personalist recommend in the face of such inconsistency? The person should make adjustments so that he will be consistent. The personalists would hope that the person would be willing to do this, once his inconsistency is pointed out to him. There are many different adjustments adequate to bring about consistency; the personalist could offer no advice on which of these a person should choose (Savage, 1954, p. 59).

The preceding paragraphs concern normative applications of personal probability theory. The theory has also been of considerable influence in relation to descriptive application. Considerable effort has been expended to determine whether the SEU model or some variant of it can describe actual human behavior (see Chapters 4 and 5). Interpretation of such efforts naturally will be affected by one's interpretation of probability. If one feels that there are objective probabilities which should, ideally, apply for decision making, one would be less apt to interpret SEU-consistent behavior as rational than if one accepted personal probability theory.

3.4 METHODS FOR MEASURING SUBJECTIVE PROBABILITY

There are two general approaches to the measurement of subjective probability. One is to interrogate S more or less directly concerning his belief-strengths for various events (or propositions). The second is to observe or inquire concerning S's preferences between possible "decisions," and to infer therefrom what his subjective probabilities might reasonably be.[9]

Direct Methods

There are a variety of direct methods. The boldest approach, perhaps, is simply to ask S what his probabilities are for a series of events, and require him to state a series of numbers between 0 and 1. Alternatively, the response need not be the probability required per se, but rather a response that can be simply translated into the required probability. For example, S might be required to divide a line into two parts corresponding to the relative probabilities of two disjoint events. Then, assuming that the events are exhaustive, the experimenter can calculate the probabilities from the two lengths. The technique might utilize pencil and paper or a slider. A similar technique requires S to pile poker chips into piles proportional to event probabilities. Possible variants of the technique are endless.

S might be required to state the *odds* favoring one event over another. Instead of asking S for the probability of rain tomorrow, we might ask him for the odds favoring rain (event E_1). His reply might be "three to one." The odds for E_1

---

[9] Savage (1954, p. 28) refers to the *direct* and *behavioral* methods of interrogation, respectively; however, his "behavioral" class, is, perhaps, less inclusive than our "indirect class."

over E_2 is interpreted as the ratio of probabilities $p(E_1)/p(E_2)$. Given the odds, if E_1 and E_2 are exclusive, exhaustive events,

$$p(E_1) = \frac{\text{odds } (E_1/E_2)}{\text{odds } (E_1/E_2) + 1},$$ (3.8)

or, for our example,

$$p(E_1) = \frac{3/1}{3/1 + 1} = \frac{3}{4}$$

When S divides a line, he could be thinking in terms of "odds" rather than "probabilities," per se.

Not all queries about probability need result in a number between 0 and 1, i.e., a *quantitative probability*. The experimenter may instead only require S to order the probabilities, i.e., to state the relative magnitudes. The result is *qualitative probability*.[10] Various experimental techniques may be employed to derive an ordering. S may be requested to report the relative subjective probabilities for pairs of events, or he may be required to rank the subjective probabilities for a set of events. *Confidence ratings* are typically taken by the method of single stimuli, i.e., S gives his "confidence" that his response on a trial is correct without explicit comparison with other trials. The confidence rating may be a quantitative probability, but often the response is on an ordinal verbal scale such as "certain I was correct," "think I was correct," "more likely correct than incorrect," etc. Responses with the same confidence ratings are taken to have the same subjective probabilities.

The direct methods of subjective probability measurement have been used by psychologists for many decades. And even earlier yet, Jeremy Bentham proposed that jury witnesses mark degree of certainty on a scale (Keynes, 1921, p. 20); perhaps one day they will.

Indirect Methods

Although application of the indirect methods to subjective probability measurement is fairly recent, the idea can be traced to the classical era. Thomas Bayes considered the expected value (expectation) of a gamble to be primitive, i.e., immediately and readily apprehensible, and defined probability in terms of it. (By contrast, the direct methods take probability, or at least relative probabilities, to be primitive.) According to Bayes (1763), "The *probability of any event* is the ratio between the value at which an expectation depending upon the happening of an event ought to be computed, and the value of the thing expected upon its happening."

---

[10] Keynes (1921) believed that all logical probabilities need not be comparable, so that one could aspire, in general, only to find partial orderings. According to Jeffreys (1961, p. vi), Keynes came to accept complete ordering; Good (1965, p. 7), however, disputes this.

What is the value at which the expectation of an event ought to be computed? Suppose P^A has an opportunity to accept a gamble paying $100 if it rains tomorrow, but nothing otherwise. Alternatively, he could accept a sum of cash without contingencies. If the sum of cash were too small, P^A would prefer to take his chances for the $100. If the sum of cash became large enough (but less than $100), P^A would presumably prefer the cash, rather than take his chances on receiving nothing. Ideally, we can conceive of an amount of cash which P^A finds equally attractive as the gamble. Call this an *indifference offer*. Ideally, for larger cash amounts P^A would prefer the cash, and for smaller amounts, the gamble. Ignoring for now the methodological difficulties, assume that the indifference offer has been found. Then it can be taken as the value of the expectation, the quantity we desired. Let this quantity be symbolized EV (expected value).

According to Bayes, the probability p of rain could then be computed as

$$p = \frac{EV}{100} \tag{3.9}$$

If P^A is indifferent for $68, $p = 0.68$; if he is indifferent at $10, $p = 0.10$. Equation (3.9) can be derived from the formula for the EV of the gamble:

$$EV = p \cdot 100 + (1 - p)0$$

More generally, if v_1 and v_2 are the values of the consequences associated with p and $1 - p$,

$$p = \frac{EV - v_2}{v_1 - v_2} \tag{3.10}$$

Our discussion has concerned an attractive gamble, i.e., one the P^A would rather accept than not. If the gamble were unattractive, the indifference offer would be negative, i.e., P^A would be indifferent between accepting the gamble and *paying out* an amount of cash.

Instead of requiring S to choose between a cash value and a gamble, P^A might be asked to *bid* for the gamble. Of course P^A would prefer to pay less than the indifference offer for a desirable gamble if he could. A number of techniques have been used to prevent Ss from offering spuriously low bids. One technique is to *auction* off the gamble to a group of Ss. Rather than see another person receive the gamble, an S should be willing to bid any amount up to or including his indifference offer. In practice, the selling price of a gamble is treated as the indifference offer for the buyer. The auction technique was used by Preston and Baratta (1948) in, apparently, the first experimental measurement of subjective probability based on inference from EV.

Lichtenstein (1965) used an alternate method of getting "honest" bids from single Ss (i.e., not in the group context of the auction). She only accepted a random two-thirds of the bids, explaining to S that rejected offers were un-acceptably low compared to group norms.

A direct estimate of subjective probability might, in a sense, be thought of as a decision. The decision alternatives are the numbers between 0 and 1. Toda (1963) has discussed decision situations requiring such an "estimation decision" for which expected value to S is maximal only if his response is his subjective probability. This contrasts with the direct estimation technique per se, which levys no explicit penalty for an erroneous report.

The techniques for indirect assessment of probabilities discussed so far have assumed, at a minimum, the validity of the SEV model (Section 2.8) for human decision making. If, as is commonly thought, utility cannot be accurately repre-sented by amount of money, the measurement techniques must be subject to unknown errors. By assuming instead, the validity of the SEU model, different indirect techniques would be required for subjective probability measurement. SEU-based measurement of probability is discussed in Section 4.3.

A simple method for qualitative comparison of two probabilities can be given which is acceptable for either the SEV or SEU model. Suppose we wish to know for which event S has a higher subjective probability: rain tomorrow, or no rain tomorrow. We ask S to predict whether or not it will rain, stipulating the following conditions: if it rains and he so predicted, he receives \$1; or, if it does not rain and he so predicted, he receives \$1; if his prediction is wrong he receives nothing. Then by either the SEV or SEU model S should predict the event with the higher subjective probability.

Comparison of Methods

Savage (1954, pp. 27–28) gives the following argument in favor of indirect ("behavioral") assessment of probabilities over the direct methods. As given, the argument concerns qualitative probability, but a similar argument could be given for quantitative probability. "In the first place, many doubt that the con-cept 'more probable to me than' is an intuitive one, open to no ambiguity and yet admitting no further analysis. Even if the concept were so completely in-tuitive, which might justify direct interrogation as a subject worthy of some psy-chological study, what could such interrogation have to do with the behavior of a person in the face of uncertainty, except of course for his verbal behavior under interrogation? If the state of mind in question is not capable of manifest-ing itself in some sort of extraverbal behavior, it is extraneous to our main inter-est. If, on the other hand, it does manifest itself through more material behavior, that should, at least in principle, imply the possibility of testing whether a person holds one event to be more probable than another, by some behavior expressing, and giving meaning to, his judgment."

Savage's distinction between stated and implied probabilities is analogous to a distinction between stated and behaviorally implied attitudes that has con-cerned attitude measurers. A white mother who has always paid lip service to racial liberalism might be extremely distressed if her daughter married a black man. Assessment of attitudes via the lip service would clearly be inadequate.

Although there is evidence that different methods of measuring subjective probabilities can give differing results, it is not altogether clear that the indirect methods of measurement are to be preferred. The validity of such methods depends on the validity of some model, which, in practice, has been the SEV or SEU model. But these models are not entirely accurate (see Chapter 5). Furthermore, the indirect methods, particularly those relating to the SEU model, are time consuming and complicated to apply, whereas the direct methods are quite simple and quick. The upshot is that psychologists have used the direct methods much more often than the indirect methods, and they seldom discuss or concern themselves with the issues raised by Savage.

Of the various direct methods, which one or ones are to be preferred? Although some evidence pertinent to this question is available, further research is required before a reasonably complete answer can be forthcoming. That answer could be of considerable practical importance.

3.5   SOME EMPIRICAL STUDIES AND RESULTS

We now consider some empiricial studies of subjective probability. Our purpose is to present some of the variables, methods, and results that have interested psychologists. Other chapters contain related material. Some cross-referencing is provided as we proceed.

In many studies of subjective probability, the experimenter reports a comparison between the measured subjective probabilities and "true," "objective," or "conventional" probabilities. The "objective" probability for heads in a coin-flip is typically taken to be 1/2, though, indeed there is not sufficient "objective" evidence to establish the exact quantity. For this reason, such "objective" probabilities are sometimes said, instead, to be *conventional* probabilities, in that the probability assigned is the "usual" one. As noted previously, such "conventional" probabilities are not available for many events, so a comparison of subjective probabilities with them is not possible.

Prediction and Estimation of a Binary Series

Suppose a series of independent experimental trials is conducted on a sample space with two exclusive, exhaustive events. On each trial S is to predict which event will occur. Then he observes the trial outcome. S's prediction might be thought of as a qualitative probability judgment concerning which of the two events has a higher probability.[11] Since the probability of each event is constant over trials, it might be thought that S would make the same prediction on each

---

[11] S is typically allowed no "equally likely" response. It is possible, then, for prediction of E_1 or E_2 to represent not a difference in subjective probability, but an equality.

trial, at least after having some experience observing outcomes. Actually, however, over a succession of trials Ss typically vary their predictions between the events. Although prediction proportions are dependent on various experimental variables, a common finding is that the mean proportion of predictions across Ss for an event is approximately equal to the objective probability for that event, a phenomenon known as *probability matching*.

One should take care to avoid interpreting the prediction proportion as a subjective probability. If the subjective probability for E_1 on each trial is 0.75, the choice proportion would not be 0.75—presumably it would be 1.0, as it would be for any subjective probability greater than 0.5. If a payoff is given for a correct prediction (and nothing for an incorrect one), the prediction task ostensibly gives indirect measures of qualitative probability. Although payoffs increase the number of predictions of the more frequent event, S still predicts both events over a series of trials. There is a very large literature on the prediction of a binary event and related experiments. We consider the topic in greater detail in Chapter 6.

Systematic Over- and Under-Estimation

It is often found that when the quantitative subjective probabilities for events with a range of objective probabilities are determined with the same Ss, the average subjective probabilities for the lower probability events are larger than the objective probabilities, whereas the average subjective probabilities for the higher probability events are smaller than the objective probabilities. There is, then, an intermediate point where subjective and objective probabilities are equal—the *indifference point*. The situation is illustrated in Figure 3.1.

We speak of the Ss' "over-" and "under-estimations" of probabilities, assuming that probability estimations (direct subjective probability measurements) should, in some ideal sense, equal the "objective" probabilities. The over-under effect has been found with direct assessment for many tasks, for example: estimation of relative letter frequencies of the English Language (Attneave, 1953); estimation of the number of blue balls to be drawn from an urn containing blue and yellow balls, when the urn composition and total number of balls to be drawn is given (Cohen, 1960, p. 136); estimation of success probability by bus drivers in attempting to drive a bus through two posts without touching them (Cohen, Dearnaley, & Hansel, 1956b); and estimations of the answers to simple probability theory problems by college students (Howard, 1963). The over-under effect has also been found with indirect assessment (Preston & Baratta, 1948; Sprowls, 1953; Mosteller & Nogee, 1951; Griffith, 1949). Occasionally, the effect is absent (Mosteller & Nogee, 1951, for one group of Ss; Robinson, 1964).

The over- and under-estimations are not limited to probability judgments. The "central tendency" of judgments is a well-known psychophysical finding for all kinds of judgment continua. In Chapter 8 the phenomenon is discussed

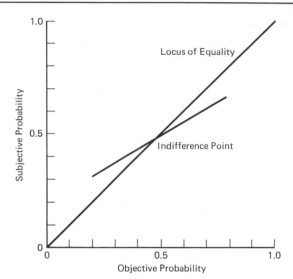

Figure 3.1. Illustration of the customary central tendency effect. The "locus of equality" is the graph which would result if subjective probability equalled objective probability. The location of the indifference point and magnitudes of estimation errors were chosen arbitrarily. They actually vary depending on experimental conditions.

in terms of Bayesian information processing; S is conceived to weigh current probabilistic (or other) judgmental evidence with prior probabilities derived from previous trials and pre-experimental experience. The influence of the priors, which reflect the whole range of objective conditions, produces a "central tendency" in the judgments. Interpretation of the phenomenon in Bayesian terms does not imply that human judgments accord with the judgments a mathematician might predict with Bayes' formula. Human beings might be thought of as imperfect Bayesian information processors.

Confidence and Response Quality

There are many kinds of psychological experiments which require S to give a series of responses, each of which can be scored by the experimenter as "right" or "wrong." With each response S can be required to give a verbal or quantitative confidence rating indicating how sure he feels that he made the right response on that trial. It has been found for numerous experiments that if one tabulates the responses according to the level of confidence indicated, the higher the confidence level, the greater the percentage of correct responses. This has been found for a wide variety of tasks in which S is unable to perform perfectly, including psychophysical paired comparison and category judgment tasks, multiple-choice tests, recognition and free recall memory tests, and, in general, wherever such confidence ratings have been taken (Johnson, 1955, Ch. 10; Adams & Adams, 1961; Swets, 1964).

Response Time and Confidence

It has been generally found that *S* responds faster when he is quite certain that his response is correct than when he is in doubt. For example, when the task for each *S* was to predict whether he could throw a ball through a gap or not, *S*s took about 2 seconds to decide when chances of success and failure appeared to be about equal, but only 1 second when either success *or* failure appeared to be certain (Cohen, Hansel, & Walker, 1960). The relationship between response time and confidence has been recognized for many years, and there have been attempts to describe the relationship mathematically, but no firm conclusion has resulted (Seward, 1928; Volkmann, 1934).

The Sum of Subjective Probabilities

In mathematical probability theory, the sum of the probabilities for a set of mutually exclusive and exhaustive events equals 1. Do subjective probabilities likewise sum to 1? Cohen, Dearnaley, and Hansel (1965a, 1957) had children in age groups 9–10 and 13–14 estimate the number of successes or number of failures out of N trials for throwing a ball through an opening. Different but comparable groups of children made the success and failure estimates to assure that the second estimate would not simply be derived from the first by subtraction. The subjective probability for success (or failure) was calculated as the estimated number of successes (or failures) divided by the number of imaginary trials. When the number of imaginary trials offered was five, the subjective probabilities for success and failure summed to about 1. However, the sum exceeded 1 if only one trial were offered, and was less than one for more than five imaginary trials, particularly for the more difficult conditions. As the number of imaginary trials increased, the subjective probabilities for both success and failure decreased. The subjective probabilities for the older children summed more nearly to 1 than those for the younger children for a large number of imaginary trials (100 or 1000).

The failure of subjective probabilities to sum consistently to 1 is very troublesome. Of course, as noted, some direct measurement techniques such as odds estimations assure that the sum is 1.

Chance Versus Skill

S seems to think of probabilities in different ways—even if he attaches the same number to them—depending on whether he perceives the outcome to be based on his own skilled performance or on entirely "chance" factors over which he has no control. If *S* attempts to hit a target with a dart, his success or failure depends on his skill. But we believe that only "chance," not skill, affects the outcome in roulette. The distinctions between chance and skill situations are not entirely clear-cut. Believers in psychokinesis, for example, would perceive the outcome in roulette to be skill-related. On the other hand, some persons might attribute their failures in, say, an athletic event to "bad luck" rather than to deficiency in skill.

A fairly large number of studies have investigated the difference between chance- and skill-related events. In one (Cohen & Hansel, 1959), S was offered a choice between two situations having ostensibly the same probability of success. Success in each case required both success on a skill task and a chance task. Ss preferred the situation in which the skilled act was difficult and the chance event highly probable, rather than the other way around. In other words, S preferred the difficult (improbable) component of a skill-chance combination to be skill, over which they felt they have some control.

In an imaginary skill situation requiring both S and an imaginary partner to hit a target, however, S did not prefer to take the major portion of the risk unto himself; instead, he chose to equalize the probabilities of success for himself and his partner (Brim & Koenig, 1959).

Multiplicative Probability

We noted in Section 3.2 that for two independent trials, the probability of a compound event is the product of component probabilities. But is this true for subjective probabilities? The question can be answered by measuring component subjective probabilities and then the compound subjective probability to see if they relate by multiplication.

John Cohen and his associates have found that for students of ages 12-15, the subjective probability of the compound event was higher than the product of component subjective probabilities. The discrepancy was much greater when both component trials were chance rather than both skill. The skill-chance condition resembled the skill-skill condition (Cohen, Dearnaley, & Hansel, 1958b; Cohen & Hansel, 1958). Undergraduate students were able to combine probabilities in the chance-skill condition without mean overestimation of the compound probability (Cohen, Dearnaley, & Hansel, 1958a). It seems as if some of the younger students were subjectively averaging the components instead of multiplying; or, they viewed a condition requiring two independent successes from three jars as if one success from six jars were required.

General

What can we conclude about the relationship between measured subjective probability and probability theory? First, subjective probabilities do not in general equal the objective, or conventional, probabilities that mathematicians assign to events. Nonetheless, there is often a fairly good correspondence between the two, and in some circumstances subjective probabilities closely approximate objective ones. Second, subjective probabilities are not, in general, consistent.

The subjective probabilities of exclusive, exhaustive events need not sum to 1, nor does the multiplication rule for independent events always hold. Third, subjective probabilities tend to become more nearly consistent as a person develops mentally from childhood through adolescence.

The failure of subjective probabilities to equal objective ones is not, per se, unsettling from the viewpoint of personal probability theory. The inconsistency of subjective probabilities, though, is a serious matter. Strictly speaking, these quantities which we call "subjective probabilities" have no theoretical justification for being called "probabilities" at all, for even personal probabilists require that "probabilities" be consistent. They are measures obtained from Ss, and we call them "subjective probabilities," but if they are not consistent, one cannot resort to personal probability theory to justify the label or to defend their use in practical applications requiring input of probabilities.

It may be that research will result in training procedures, instructions, and measurement techniques leading to highly consistent subjective probability measures. This will be necessary if personal probability theory is really to concern probabilities of persons, and even then the concern will be limited to measures based on those procedures, instructions, and techniques.

There has been some discussion of developing a probability theory not requiring summation of exclusive, exhaustive events in a space to 1, or to any other constant. Instead, the sum would depend on the particular set of exclusive, exhaustive events chosen (Edwards, 1962). It has been suggested that such a *non-additive probability theory* might be helpful for modeling subjective probabilities, and might be required in a general theory of rationality. For the foreseeable future, however, theorists and experimentalists will most likely shun the added complexity and aesthetic unattractiveness of non-additive probabilities.

3.6 THE PERCEPTION OF CHANCE AND LUCK IN EVERYDAY LIFE

Man is not content to merely observe the panorama of events occurring around him; he desires to understand and control these events. To this end he has developed superstition, religion, and science. The idea of "chance" is also important in this regard, for "chance" can serve as a catchall cause to "explain" whatever happenings that elude other conventional explanations. When something good happens to someone for which we have no convenient alternative explanation, we refer to his "good luck," when we might instead admit our lack of understanding.

For some theologians and believers, "chance" is rejected as a "cause" for anything, since God determines all. "The lot is cast into the lap; but the whole disposing thereof is of the Lord."[12] This view resembles the determinism of

---

[12] *Proverbs*, xvi, 33 (King James Version).

Laplace, except that "God" instead of the "Laws of Nature" is seen as all-determining.

According to another view, God or another supernatural power doesn't routinely determine chance outcomes, but can be induced to by supplication. The ancient Greeks had a goddess of chance, Tyche, who was worshipped throughout the Hellenistic world. John Wesley, the founder of Methodism, "cast lots" (drew one of several written messages out of a hat) to determine whether to marry, accepting the result as "Thy will." But a "bad lot" might be attributed to insufficient prayer and might be rejected (David, 1962). Besides prayer, superstitious incantations have commonly been used to influence "chance" outcomes. And according to the doctrine of psychokinesis, "will power" can affect random outcomes.

Quite apart from divine interference, supersititious incantations, or will power, we seem to feel that "chance" should favor the superior man. In a western movie, the cowboy hero never loses at poker; if the outlaw gets four queens, we can be sure the hero will get four kings—and without cheating, too. If our hero did not win, our estimation of him would decrease even though objectively we have to realize that getting four kings has nothing to do with any of his qualities.

Some people other than heroes are perceived to be lucky. Just as "chance" is a catchall "cause" to explain any happening we can't think of any other cause for, "lucky" is a catchall trait to explain the good things that happen to a person when we cannot—or would rather not—attribute the success to conventional traits such as intelligence or diligence.

The oilmen of Texas agree that when the great oil strikes were being made which established today's fortunes, there was no science or savvy determining which men made it. It was simply luck—not divine intercession, or the result of incantations. This sounds quite in line with a scientific view—until we look at who is lucky. It's not just anybody who is lucky, but certain persons who have "more luck" than others. Here is an oilman explaining what makes for success in the business: "Every once in a while, young fellows come in to see me and ask my advice about going into the oil business. I never know just what to tell them, but I always get around to one thing: I ask them if they're lucky. Do they like to gamble? Are they good poker players? And how's their luck generally? If they like to gamble and if they're lucky, they'll probably do all right in the oil business." (Bainbridge, 1963, p. 89) Now a scientist might say someone who wins a big lottery is "lucky," but he wouldn't be referring to a trait of the person, as the oilman was. It would simply be another way of stating that the person won a long shot.

For more on chance and luck in everyday life, see *Behaviour in Uncertainty* by John Cohen (1964) and *Games, Gods and Gambling* by F. N. David (1962).

3.7 SUMMARY

The typical mathematical presentation of discrete probability theory begins by assuming a sample space of equally probable sample points. An event consists of a set of sample points. Disjoint events have no common sample points. Two events are independent if the probability of their intersection (common points) equals the product of the event probabilities. Probabilities conditional on an event E can be thought of as probabilities defined in the reduced sample space E. Bayes' formula (Equation 3.7) allows calculation of posterior probabilities for a set of exclusive, exhaustive events (hypotheses), given relevant data, prior probabilities, and likelihoods.

The strictly mathematical aspects of probability theory are not the subject of controversy between the schools of probability. The controversies concern, instead, the meaning, measurement, and scope of "probability." "Frequency theory" interprets a probability to be basically a relative frequency; "logical theory" interprets "probability" to be a degree of credibility of an event implied by the evidence, logically consistent with other event probabilites; personal probability theory is particularly characterized by the acceptance of differing probabilities by different "persons" for the same event. Upon closer examination, the differences between the schools become blurred.

Acceptance of the personal probability viewpoint could have important practical implications by legitimatizing measured probabilities of real persons. Such legitimation, however, requires that a real person's "subjective probabilities" be consistent, since personal probability theory makes no provision for inconsistent ones.

There have been two general approaches to the measurement of subjective probabilities: direct interrogation and indirect inference from decisions. The direct methods are simpler and have been used for most of the subjective probability measurements to date. The theoretical appeal of the indirect methods is countered by skepticism concerning the accuracy of the decision models they assume. The "subjective probabilities" of real persons are not consistent, so personal probability theory cannot legitimatize these measurements. Hopefully, techniques for deriving consistent subjective probabilities can be devised.

To some philosophers, "chance" has meant ignorance of the causes of actually determinate events. Although philosphical determinism does not currently hold sway, it seems clear enough that many probability judgments are indeed a matter of our current information rather than "true chance," as when we say that the probability that a fetus is male is about $1/2$.

Whereas some religiously-inclined persons have argued that God determines all, others have believed that supernatural influences on "chance" events appear only in answer to supplication. Supersititious incantations and will-power have also been considered efficacious in influencing chance events. "Chance" is used generally as a catchall cause and "lucky" as a catchall trait to explain happenings lacking alternative conventional "explanations."

REFERENCES

Adams, J. K., & Adams, P. A. "Realism of Confidence Judgments," *Psychological Review* (1961), **68,** 33–45.

Attneave, F. "Psychological Probability as a Function of Experienced Frequency," *Journal of Experimental Psychology* (1953), **46,** 81–86.

Bainbridge, J. *The Super-Americans.* New York: New American Library, 1963.

Bayes, T. "An Essay towards Solving a Problem in the Doctrine of Chances," *Philosophical Transactions of the Royal Society* (1763), **53,** 370–418. Reprinted in *Biometrika* (1958), **45,** 293–315.

Brim, O. G., Jr., & Koenig, F. W. "Two Aspects of Subjective Probability among College Students," *Journal of Communication* (1959), **9,** 19–26.

Carnap, R. *Logical Foundations of Probability,* 2nd ed. Chicago: University of Chicago, 1962.

Cohen, J. *Chance, Skill, and Luck.* Baltimore: Penguin, 1960.

Cohen, J. *Behavior in Uncertainty.* New York: Basic Books, 1964.

Cohen, J., Dearnaley, E. J., & Hansel, C. E. M. "The Addition of Subjective Probabilities, "*Acta Psychologica* (1956a), **12,** 371–380.

Cohen, J., Dearnaley, E. J., & Hansel, C. E. M. "Risk and Hazard," *Operational Research Quarterly* (1956b), **7,** 67–82.

Cohen, J., Dearnaley, E. J., & Hansel, C. E. M. "Measures of Subjective Probability," *British Journal of Psychology* (1957), **48,** 271–275.

Cohen, J., Dearnaley, E. J., & Hansel, C. E. M. "Skill and Chance," *British Journal of Psychology* (1958a), **49,** 319–323.

Cohen, J., Dearnaley, E. J., & Hansel, C. E. M. "The Mutual Effect of Two Uncertainties," *Durham Research Review* (1958b), **2,** 215–222.

Cohen, J., & Hansel, C. E. M. "The Nature of Decisions in Gambling," *Acta Psychologica* (1958), **13,** 357–370.

Cohen, J., & Hansel, C. E. M. "Preferences for Different Combinations of Chance and Gambling," *Nature* (1959), **183,** 841–842.

Cohen, J., Hansel, C. E. M., & Walker, D. B. "The Time Taken to Decide as a Measure of Subjective Probability," *Acta Psychologica* (1960), **17,** 177–183.

David, F. N. *Games, Gods and Gambling.* New York: Hafner, 1962.

De Finetti, B. "Recent Suggestions for the Reconciliations of Theories of Probability," in J. Neyman (ed.), *Proceedings of the Second Berkeley Symposium on Mathematical Statistics and Probability.* Berkeley, Calif: University of California, 1951, pp. 217–226.

De Finetti, B. "Foresight: Its Logical Laws, Its Subjective Sources," translated by H. E. Kyburg, Jr., in H. E. Kyburg, Jr. & H. E. Smokler (eds.), *Studies in Subjective Probability.* New York: Wiley, 1964, pp. 93–158.

Edwards, W. "Subjective Probabilities Inferred from Decisions," *Psychological Review* (1962), **69,** 109–135.

Feller, W. *An Introduction to Probability Theory and Its Applications.* Vol. 1. New York: Wiley, 1950.

Good, I. J., *The Estimation of Probabilities*. Cambridge, Mass.: M.I.T. Press, 1965.

Griffith, R. M. "Odds Adjustments by American Horse-Race Bettors," *American Journal of Psychology* (1949), **62,** 290–294.

Howard, T. C. "The Relation between Psychological and Mathematical Probability," *American Journal of Psychology* (1963), **76,** 335.

Jeffreys, H. *Theory of Probability,* 3rd ed. Oxford: Oxford University Press, 1961.

Johnson, D. M. *The Psychology of Thought and Judgment*. New York: Harper, 1955.

Keynes, J. M. *A Treatise on Probability*. London: Macmillan, 1921. Reprinted by Harper, 1962.

Kyburg, H. E., Jr., & Smokler, H. E. (eds.) *Studies in Subjective Probability*. New York: Wiley, 1964.

Laplace, P. S. *A Philosophical Essay on Probabilities*. Translated by F. W. Truscott and F. L. Emory. New York: Dover, 1951.

Lichtenstein, S. "Bases for Preferences among Three-Outcome Bets," *Journal of Experimental Psychology* (1965), **69,** 162–169.

Lindsay, R. B. "Physics—To What Extent Is It Deterministic?" *American Scientist* (1968), **56,** 93–111.

Mosteller, F., & Nogee, P. "An Experimental Measurement of Utility," *Journal of Political Economy* (1951), **59,** 371–404.

Preston, M. G., & Baratta, P. "An Experimental Study of the Auction-Value of an Uncertain Outcome," *American Journal of Psychology* (1948), **61,** 183–193.

Ramsey, F. P. *The Foundations of Mathematics*. New York: Harcourt Brace, 1931.

Reichenbach, H. *The Theory of Probability*. Translated by E. H. Hutton and M. Reichenbach. Berkeley and Los Angeles: University of California, 1949. German edition, 1935.

Robinson, G. H. "Continuous Estimation of a Time-Varying Probability," *Ergonomics* (1964), **7,** 7–21.

Savage, L. J. *The Foundations of Statistics*. New York: Wiley, 1954.

Seward, G. H. "Recognition Time as a Measure of Confidence," *Archives of Psychology* (1928), **16,** No. 99.

Sprowls, R. C. "Psychological-Mathematical Probability in Relationships of Lottery Gambles," *American Journal of Psychology* (1953), **66,** 126–130.

Swets, J. A. (ed.) *Signal Detection and Recognition by Human Observers*. New York: Wiley, 1964.

Toda, M. *Measurement of Subjective Probability Distribution*. State College, Pa.: Division of Mathematical Psychology, Reprint No. 3, 1963.

Venn, J. *The Logic of Chance,* 3rd ed. London: Macmillan, 1888 (1st ed., 1866).

Volkmann, J. "The Relation of Time of Judgment to Certainty of Judgment," *Psychological Bulletin* (1934), **31,** 672–673.

von Mises, R. *Probability, Statistics, and Truth*. Translated by J. Neyman, D. Sholl, & E. Rabinowitsch. New York: Macmillan, 1939 (1st German ed., 1928).

CHAPTER 4

Utility Theory

In Chapter 2 we assumed that consequences (or "entities") could, somehow, be assigned numerical values, called "utilities," which would reflect the subjective values of the consequences to our protagonist, P^A. In the present chapter we investigate how such assignments might be made and interpreted.

4.1 VON NEUMANN-MORGENSTERN UTILITY THEORY

Interest in the theory and measurement of utility has a substantial history, largely within economics. Many economists during the nineteenth century hoped to base economic science on the preferences of individual consumers, and to this end they felt that it was necessary to be able to measure the utility to a consumer of a commodity or *commodity bundle* (group of commodities). However, there was no consensus concerning the measurability of utility. It was generally agreed that individuals could rank-order preferences; this ordering could provide ordinal utility, i.e., measurement of utility on an ordinal scale. No agreement was reached, however, on a method for determining *cardinal utility,* i.e., intervale-scale utility.[1] Finally, through the early decades of the present century, controversy over this question abated because most economists became convinced that the main body of their work did not depend on the cardinal measurability of utility. (See Stigler (1950) and Edwards (1954) for a review of this issue.)

Interest in cardinal utility was revived in the 1940's by John von Neumann and Oskar Morgenstern, who included a theory of cardinal utility in their book, *The Theory of Games and Economic Behavior*. The cardinal utility theory of von Neumann and Morgenstern related to a theory of choices between gambles, i.e., so-called risky choices. Previous economic work had been largely concerned

---

[1] Section 1.4 contains an introductory discussion of scale type.

with choice under the condition of certainty—hence the difference in the type of utility measurement required.

We abbreviate "von Neumann and Morgenstern" as N–M. N–M presented an axiomatic treatment of utility; i.e., they assumed that preferences between gambles obey a set of assumptions (axioms). They then proved that given the assumptions, interval-scale numbers can be assigned to consequences and gambles derived therefrom.

N–M Axiom System

Symbolism:

$\{o_1, o_2, \ldots, o_r\}$; A set of possible consequences (or entities, as N–M call them).

p; Any probability, $0 < p < 1$.[2]

$o_i, o_j, \ldots$; Arbitrary members of the set of consequences. When we consider compound gambles, o_i, o_j, etc. will also be used to designate arbitrary gambles which, in the final analysis, have $o_1, o_2, \ldots$ as possible consequences.

$[po_i, (1 - p)o_j]$; A gamble, which, if chosen, yields consequence o_i with probability p and consequence o_j with probability $1 - p$.

$\succ$; Preference: $o_i \succ o_j$ means that o_i is preferred to o_j. (Also denoted $o_j \prec o_i$.)

$\sim$; Indifference: $o_i \sim o_j$ means that P^A is indifferent between o_i and o_j.

N–M postulate the following axioms for some individual P^A.

Axiom (1).

For any two entities in the set, exactly one of the following three relations holds: $o_i \succ o_j$, $o_j \succ o_i$, or $o_i \sim o_j$.

Axiom (2).

If $o_i \succ o_j$, and if $o_j \succ o_k$, then $o_i \succ o_k$.

Comments:

This property of preferences is called *transitivity*. Finally, numbers will be assigned to the consequences to represent relative desirability of the consequences; since numbers are transitive (i.e., if $x > y$, and $y > z$, then $x > z$), preferences must also be transitive if they are to be represented by the numbers.

Axiom (3a).

If $o_i \succ o_j$, then $o_i \succ [po_i, (1 - p)o_j]$.

Axiom (3b).

If $o_i \prec o_j$, then $o_i \prec [po_i, (1 - p)o_j]$.

---

[2] Although probabilities may equal 0 or 1, when $p = 1$ a gamble reduces to a certain consequence, and when a consequence has $p = 0$, it may be eliminated from a gamble altogether.

Comments:

In other words, axiom (3a) says that P^A prefers a sure thing, o_i, to a gamble that could give him o_i *at best,* and might give him a less valued consequence, o_j. Axiom (3b) says that P^A prefers a gamble that could give him o_i *at worst,* and possibly could give him the preferable o_j, to the sure thing, o_i. These preferences are to hold for any p, $0 < p < 1$.

> *Axiom (4a).*

If $o_i > o_j > o_k$, then there exists a p such that $[po_i, (1-p)o_k] < o_j$.

> *Axiom (4b).*

If $o_i > o_j > o_k$, then there exists a p such that $[po_i, (1-p)o_k] > o_j$.

> *Comments:*

Axiom (4) states that in a choice between a sure thing (i.e., o_j) and a gamble involving consequences more and less desirable than o_j, a value of p exists such that the sure thing is preferred, and a value of p exists such that the gamble is preferred. Presumably, if one makes p smaller and smaller (but $p > 0$ always), one makes the import of o_i in the gamble less and less, so that one approaches a choice between o_j and o_k. Similarly, by making p larger and larger (but $p < 1$ always), the import of o_k in the gamble becomes less and less, so that one approaches a choice between o_i and o_j.

> *Axiom (5).*

$$[po_i, (1-p)o_j] \sim [(1-p)o_j, po_i].$$

> *Comments:*

The order in which the constituents of a gamble are listed does not affect preference.

> *Axiom (6).*

$$[p[p'o_i, (1-p')o_j], (1-p)o_j] \sim [p''o_i, (1-p'')o_j], \text{ where } p'' = pp'.$$

> *Comments:*

A "consequence" of a gamble may itself be a gamble $\left(\text{i.e., } [p'o_i, (1-p')o_j]\right)$; in which case, if the consequence with probability p occurred, P^A would receive o_i (with probability p') or o_j (with probability $(1-p')$). The events with probabilities p and p' are assumed to be independent, and thus the situation may be reduced to a "normal" form $[p''o_i, (1-p'')o_j]$, where p'', the probability for consequence o_i, equals pp', the probability of the joint occurrence of two independent events (see Section 3.2). The axiom states that the form of the gamble, "normal" or compound, has no effect on preference.

Implications of the Axioms

N–M show that these axioms imply the following series of conclusions:

(1) It is possible to assign a single real number to each entity in the set of possible consequences; the number for each entity is called its *utility.*
(2) With these numbers, one can calculate expected utility for any possible choice considered by the axioms.

(3) The choice pair member with the higher expected utility is the one preferred by P^A; P^A is indifferent between choice pairs with equal expected utilities.
(4) The set of numbers assigned as utilities is not unique; other sets may be substituted for the "original" set if and only if the "new utilities" for the entities, $u'(o_i)$, relate to the "old utilities," $u(o_i)$, by a positive linear transformation, i.e., if $u'(o_i) = au(o_i) + b$, where a and b are real numbers, constant as i changes, and $a > 0$.

interval scale of msmt.

(5) The relative magnitudes of the "expected values" of the alternatives with the "new utilities" agrees exactly with the relative magnitudes with the "old utilities."
(6) Such agreement would not obtain, in general, if order-preserving but nonlinear transformations were performed on the "original" utilities. Therefore, this more general class of transformations is not allowed, and therefore we do not have *ordinal* utility—we have *cardinal* (interval-scale) utility.

It is important to note the order of this train of thought. P^A's preferences logically antedate the existence of utilities. Thus, one must be wary of saying that "P^A prefers a_1 to a_2 *because* a_1 has a higher expected utility." Preference, in the axioms, is a primitive notion; it is presumed to exist between gambles, and there is no implication that calculations of expected utility lie behind P^A's preferences. To avoid circumlocutions, we shall often speak of P^A choosing "in accordance with expected utility theory," or some such; the reader should realize at such times that there need be no implication that P^A is aware of utilities and expected utilities—he need only "know what he likes." On the other hand, do not assume that our protagonist, P^A, will never make explicit calculations of expected utility. Such calculations are sometimes recommended for normative purposes. We shall never assume, however, that P^A actually makes calculations—in his head or on paper—unless we say so.

The "utility theory" of N–M is not, as a mathematical opus, open to empirical test. There is no question that the numbers (utilities) can be found such that P^A's preferences can be interpreted in terms of the relative expected utilities of the choices, providing that the axioms accurately represent the structure of preferences for P^A. But we can ask whether the axioms do indeed represent the structure of preferences for real persons, and therefore whether N–M utility theory is applicable to real human preferences. It is actually impossible to test the axioms in their entirety for a particular person and a finite set of entities, since the axioms make assertions about the preferences for an infinite set of alternatives. Consider, for example, axiom (3a); for just two entities, o_i and o_j, P^A would have to be offered an infinite number of choices, since the axiom is proposed for every p, $0 < p < 1$. It would not prove that the axiom is true to demonstrate that it is true for, say, 16 values of p—it would only suggest that axiom (3a) were true.

In spite of the impossibility of a complete test, N–M theory can be subjected to a limited empirical test; after all, one might at least demonstrate the inadequacy of the axioms by offering P^A a finite set of choices, even though one cannot thereby fully demonstrate the adequacy of the axioms. Before becoming involved with empirical testing, however, let us consider some *a priori* criticisms that have been leveled against the axioms viewed as assertions about actual human choices.

It has often been noted that N–M theory takes probabilities for granted. The p values of the theory are "objective" probabilities, whereas, as we saw in Chapter 3, subjective probabilities, insofar as they can be measured, may often depart from the objective ones. In view of this, one would tend to be skeptical of the correspondence of N–M axioms with human choice.

It is part of the folklore of gambling that some people sometimes gamble "for the sake of gambling"; this could affect the preference between alternative possible choices. Suppose, for example, that P^A were offered a choice between a sure thing (receive o_i for sure) and a gamble with the same expected utility. Then, if there were a so-called "utility of gambling" in addition to the utility of the entities, P^A would prefer the gamble to the sure thing. Such a utility of gambling might be exhibited in a failure of axioms (3), (4), and (6) (the latter because P^A might prefer the compound gamble to the simple one). The question of attraction for risk *per se* will be taken up at greater length in Chapter 5.

The axioms imply perfect sensitivity and consistency of human preferences. Axiom (1), for example, says that *exactly* one of the following relations holds: $o_i > o_j$, $o_j > o_i$, or $o_i \sim o_j$. Realistically, when consequences are valued about equally, does not a person believe he prefers o_i one moment, o_j the next moment, and shortly thereafter believe he cannot make up his mind, i.e., he is indifferent? If so, it cannot be said that exactly one of the three relations holds—unless, perhaps, one were referring to a moment in time. But then one withdraws the axiom from any possible empirical test, since a person can hardly demonstrate preference inconsistency in a "moment."

4.2   THE MOSTELLER-NOGEE UTILITY MEASUREMENT

Frederick Mosteller and Philip Nogee (1951) set out to:

(1) observe the betting behavior of real Ss for real money in a laboratory situation;

(2) construct a *utility curve* for each S relating measured utility to amount of money; and

(3) determine whether predictions of gambling behavior based on these utilities curves were useful.

Their work was inspired by Friedman and Savage (1948), whose assumptions about utility were based on N–M.

Ss were offered a series of gambles, each of which they could accept or refuse. If S refused, he neither won nor lost any money. If he accepted, he had to put up 5¢; then dice were thrown, and with probability p he won an amount x¢ (and kept his 5¢); with probability $1 - p$ he lost his 5¢. According to the expected utility formulations of choice, indifference between accepting and refusing to bet can be interpreted as equality between the expected utility of betting and not betting, or, if x_o cents is the offered winning amount which results in such indifference,

$$pu(x_o) + (1 - p) \cdot u(-5) = u(0) \qquad (4.1)$$

According to the theory of cardinal utility, we can arbitrarily pick two numbers to represent the utilities for two entities, as long as the larger number is assigned to the preferred one of the two entities. Since there are an infinity of possible positive linear transformations, there are an infinity of possible numerical assignments for the utilities of a set of entities; according to N–M theory, there is no basis for preferring one to another. The two arbitrary utility assignments merely determine which of the infinite number of possible representations will be employed.

Mosteller and Nogee made the following arbitrary assignments:

$$u(0) = 0 \text{ utiles}$$
$$u(-5) = -1 \text{ utile}$$

A *utile* is the unit of the utility scale, one utile representing, in this case, the utility difference between −5¢ and 0¢.

Upon entering these assignments in Equation (4.1) one can derive

$$u(x_o) = \frac{1 - p}{p} \qquad (4.2)$$

Since equality in utility corresponds to indifference between choices, if one could find the monetary value x_o for which an S was indifferent between the alternatives of accepting or rejecting an offer, the utility for that x_o would be $(1 - p)/p$. For different p's there would be different x_o's, and thus one could find the utilities for various amounts of money. This is the essence of the procedure employed by Mosteller and Nogee. Literally, the procedure does not determine the utility values for given amounts of money, since a utility value is strictly determined by p, which is specified by the experimenter. Literally, the procedure determines the amount of money which has a specified utility, $(1 - p)/p$.

So far so good. But is there such a value of x_o, and how can it be found? First, it seems reasonable that one could bring P^A to prefer to accept the gamble for any given p by specifying a large enough winning amount (designate such an amount x_h). After all, if need be, x could be, in principle, \$5, \$10, \$100, \$1000, or even larger yet. P^A could lose at most a nickel on a trial. (The Ss were screened to eliminate anyone who had moral scruples against gambling *per se,* but no such Ss were found.) On the other hand, a value of x low enough, x_l, could be found to lead P^A to prefer *not* to gamble on that trial (x might be 0¢, for example, in which case by gambling P^A would at best gain nothing and could possibly lose 5¢). It seems reasonable to believe that by starting at x_l and increasing x on successive trials to x_h that gambling should be increasingly attractive, and that at an intermediate value of x an x_o value should exist.

The experience of psychologists with physical stimuli suggested that one could not simply ask P^A whether he was indifferent between the two choices and expect him to respond positively if and only if $x = x_0$, since Ss might indicate indifference for a range of x values and might respond probabilistically (inconsistently) to successive presentations of the same options. Actually, N–M utility theory assumes that P^A has consistent, not probabilistic preferences between options. Nonetheless, believing that probabilistic preferences would obtain, N–M used a psychophysical method designed to find a probabilistic indifference point—the *method of constant stimuli* (Woodworth & Schlosberg, 1954, Chapter 8). The method requires P^A to state whether he prefers a standard stimulus (not gambling) or a stimulus which varies in value from trial to trial—the offered gamble with different x values. Then the percentage of times P^A accepts the gamble is plotted against x. The indifference point x_o is

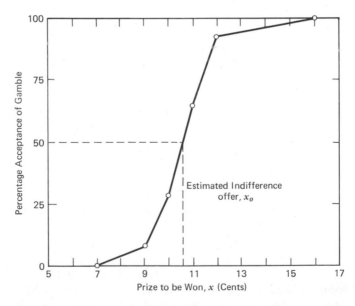

Figure 4.1 Percentage acceptance of the gamble as a function of winning amount of the gamble, for one S and one probability of winning. x_o, the indifference offer, was estimated as the offer corresponding to 50% acceptance. (After Mosteller and Nogee, 1951.)

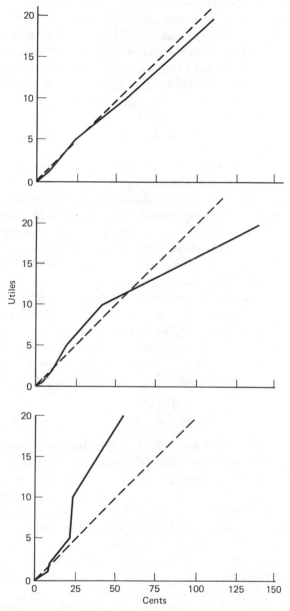

Figure 4.2. The measured utility functions for three Ss. The dotted lines represent the functions that would obtain if Ss preferred the choice with the higher OEV, i.e., if the gamble with prize x_0 had an OEV of 0ϕ. (After Mosteller and Nogee, 1951.)

the estimated x value which would lead P^A to choose the gamble on 50 percent of the trials (and refuse it on 50 percent of the trials).

Indeed, the Ss' choices were probabilistic. Figure 4.1 illustrates the results from one S for one p value. From different curves for different p values, a set of indifference points were found for each S to correspond to the specified u values. Then a utility curve was plotted for each S giving u as a function of x. The curves for three Ss are shown in Figure 4.2. Note that particularly for bets with the lower probabilities of winning (higher u values), there was a considerable difference between Ss in the size of the offered prize required for indifference.

Mosteller and Nogee constructed other gambles and predicted Ss' choices from their utility curves and the expected utility rule. Given the inconsistency of choice previously noted, they did not expect the predictions to hold exactly. They did find, however, that the higher the expected utility of a bet, the greater was the probability that S would choose it. Predictions based on expected utility were more accurate than predictions based on actuarial value.

Since the method of utility measurement assumed, like N–M, that Ss accurately utilized objective probabilities, considerable interest attaches to the method of presenting probabilities to the Ss. Mosteller and Nogee used a variation of poker dice. The events were the possible outcomes from throwing five dice. Outcomes were valued comparably to the ranking of hands in poker: five of a kind, four of a kind, full house, three of a kind, two pairs, one pair, no pairs. A gamble presented to P^A consisted of a "hand" to be beaten and an amount of money to be won, for example,

44441

$10.00::5¢

which meant that if the offer were accepted, the dice would be thrown, and if a better hand than 44441 appeared (for example, 55551, or 22222), P^A would win $10.00; if the hand did not beat 44441, P^A would lose 5¢. As stated, P^A could refuse to accept the gamble altogether. Ss were given a sheet of paper containing the odds for winning each hand, and in addition were given instruction on the calculation of those odds and experience in rolling the dice. Obviously, it was not simply assumed that Ss intuitively knew the odds for an offered hand. It did not appear that Ss used the stated odds to calculate expected money and to choose accordingly.

4.3   MEASUREMENT OF UTILITY ASSUMING SUBJECTIVE PROBABILITIES

If it is necessary to measure subjective value, i.e., utility, to understand choice between gambles, then why can it be assumed that subjective probability need not be measured, but can be assumed to equal objective probability? After all,

Preston and Baratta (1948, see Section 3.4) used a procedure similar to Mosteller and Nogee's, but measured subjective probability while assuming that value to P^A could be represented by amount of money. At least one of these approaches must be wrong. If P^A's choices reflect both subjective values and subjective probabilities, and if both kinds of subjective quantities differ from the corresponding objective ones, then both measurement procedures must be invalid.

This suggests that a theory of choice between gambles which incorporates both utility and subjective probability would be worth considering. Such a theory would have P^A preferring the gamble with the higher *subjectively expected utility* (SEU), i.e., the expected utilities calculated with subjective probabilities. Then a reasonable goal would be to develop a measurement procedure which allows both utility and subjective probability to be measured.

Ramsey's Theory

The outline of such a procedure was proposed in 1926 by Frank Ramsey (1931). Mosteller and Nogee became aware of Ramsey's work only after they had initiated their own work. The method requires, first of all, an event ("proposition") which has a subjective probability of $1/2$. Let o_iEo_j mean that P^A receives o_i if event E occurs, but receives o_j if event E does not occur. Provided that P^A prefers one of (o_i, o_j) to the other, event E has a subjective probability of $1/2$ if and only if $o_iEo_j \sim o_jEo_i$. This condition can be explained easily in terms of the SEU model. The postulated indifference can be translated into the equality of SEU's,

$$pu_i + (1 - p)u_j = pu_j + (1 - p)u_i, \tag{4.3}$$

where p is the subjective probability of E. Rearrangement of Equation 4.3 yields

$$p(u_i - u_j) = (1 - p)(u_i - u_j),$$

and if $u_i \neq u_j$, as postulated, then we must have $p = 1 - p$, or $p = 1/2$.[3]

Let us denote an event whose subjective probability is $1/2$ as E^*. Once such an event has been found, a method is available to compare utility intervals. Suppose $o_iE^*o_j \sim o_kE^*o_l$. This implies, by Ramsey's axioms, that $u_i + u_j = u_k + u_l$ or, $u_i - u_l = u_k - u_j$. Thus, the postulated indifference establishes the equality of two intervals. Since equality of intervals (plus order of preference) can be maintained by transformations of utilities by a positive linear transformation, but not by a larger class of transformations, utility is established on an interval scale. In contrast with the procedure of Mosteller and Nogee, which employs a range of probabilities, Ramsey's procedure only requires an event with a subjective probability of $1/2$.

Next Ramsey considered the measurement of subjective probability for other

---

[3] This assumes additive probability theory (see Section 3.5).

events by using the measured utilities. Suppose the player is indifferent between a sure thing o_j and a gamble. Then $u_j = pu_i + (1 - p)u_k$, and since the utilities have, by presumption, already been measured, the equation can be solved for p:

$$p = \frac{u_j - u_k}{u_i - u_k}$$

Ramsey's essay attracted little attention in its day. Von Neumann and Morgenstern did not refer to Ramsey, but during the ensuing resurgence of interest in utility theory, Ramsey's essay was "discovered."

The Davidson, Suppes, and Siegel Utility Measurement

Basing their work on Ramsey's ideas, Davidson, Suppes, and Siegel (1957)[4] (D–S–S) developed axioms and experimental procedures for the measurement of utility and subjective probability. They called their theory *finitistic* because the axioms for utility measurement refer to only a finite number of choices; as we noted, the N–M axioms refer to an infinite number of choices.

The measurement procedure requires that one begin by postulating the existence of a finite number of entities equally spaced in utility. D–S–S postulated six such entities, which they labeled *f, c, a, b, d,* and *g* from lowest utility to highest. Let us call the set of six entities having these utilities the measurement set. The entities having these utilities are unknown initially. One must have a larger, ordered, known set of entities to present to P^A. One need not know the utilities for this set (initially, at least); however, the differences in utility between successive members should be small (though the differences need not be equal). "Amount of money in cents" was used for this set. One can arbitrarily assign utility values to two members of the known set, as explained in Section 4.2, so D–S–S let $-4\cent$ have a utility of -1, and $+6\cent$ a utility of $+1$. The situation may be summarized as follows:

Utility Scale

Entity	f	c	a	b	d	g
Utility	-5	-3	-1	$+1$	$+3$	$+5$
Cents	?	?	$-4\cent$	$+6\cent$	?	?

The entities are equally spaced in utility by assumption. Two members of the known set were assigned utility values arbitrarily. The equal-spacing and ordering assumptions then determined that the remaining entities have utilities of -5, -3, etc. It remains to determine the number of cents whose utilities equal -5, -3, $+3$, and $+5$; i.e., the entities *f, c, d,* and *g* must be identified.

This "backwards" procedure goes against our intuitive notion that utility mea-

---

[4] Related theoretical papers preceded this publication: Davidson, McKinsey, & Suppes (1955); Davidson & Suppes (1956).

surement should start with entities whose utilities we wish to know and should determine these utilities. Note, however, that a "backwards" procedure of beginning with the utilities and finding the entities was also employed by Mosteller and Nogee. Both procedures result in the construction of a scale relating utility and amount of money. Once such a scale is found (for a given S), one can estimate the utilities for any intermediate amounts of money by interpolation. Note that both procedures require that a set of entities closely spaced in utility be available; one cannot simply start out with an arbitrary set of entities whose utilities are of interest.

D–S–S next required an event E^* with a subjective probability of 1/2. We noted that if $o_iEo_j \sim o_jEo_i$ (when o_i and o_j are not equally desirable), then E is E^*. As we mentioned, however, one cannot simply ask P^A if he is indifferent between two gambles. Recall that Mosteller and Nogee wished to find an x_o which would yield indifference, so they varied x, noted the choice percentage for each x, and interpolated at 50 percent. The analogous procedure would require some set of events closely spaced and ordered in subjective probability. The event yielding 50 percent choice would be E^*. However, probabilistic responding observed by Mosteller and Nogee was not typical for the Ss of D–S–S.[5] Thus, a different but similar approach was required.

Suppose P^A were offered the following symmetric payoff matrix:

	heads	tails
a_1: "heads"	5¢	−3¢
a_2: "tails"	−3¢	5¢

If the subjective p(heads) were slightly higher than 1/2, P^A would prefer a_1, since $SEU_1 > SEU_2$. But then if the payoff matrix were changed to

	heads	tails
a_1	5¢	−3¢
a_2	−3¢	6¢

a_2 should be preferred. If the increase in the winning amount for a_2 cannot tilt the preference to a_2, it must mean that subjective p(heads) is notably greater than 1/2. If subjective p(heads) were only slightly smaller than 1/2, an increase in the winning amount for a_1 should tilt the preference from a_2 to a_1. In general terms, if the preference for a symmetric payoff matrix could be reversed by a 1¢ change increasing the attractiveness of the other option, the two events involved were taken to have subjective probabilities close enough to 1/2 to be used as E^* in subsequent research.

---

[5] We cannot be sure what caused the difference. However, D–S–S used a simple event (in contrast to the poker dice), collected all data for an S in a single session (rather than in many sessions over weeks), and used bets with generally smaller amounts of money, thereby making the 1¢ increments in x more impressive (D–S–S, 1957, p. 41).

D–S–S tried a number of events with objective probability of 1/2, such as heads, odd on a die, and matching of two coins, but these events did not have subjective probabilities of 1/2. Finally, however, they made a special die which met the condition. The die had one nonsense syllable (for example, ZOJ) engraved on three faces, and another nonsense syllable (for example, ZEJ) engraved on the other three sides. For all 19 Ss, the die met the condition.

Next, P^A was offered a series of choices between gambles based on E^*; these choices determined the amount of money to be associated with entities f, c, d, and g. Because a is located midway between c and b in utility, the theory requires that $aE^*a \sim bE^*c$, but an offer slightly less than c (c_l) would produce $aE^*a > bE^*c_l$; an offer slightly higher than c (c_h) would produce $bE^*c_h > aE^*a$. (Note that aE^*a is actually a sure thing; by choosing this "gamble," P^A would receive payoff a regardless of the random outcome.) P^A was offered a choice between aE^*a and bE^*x, where x was a variable, integral number of cents. Initial x offers were low so that P^A preferred aE^*a, but the x offers were increased cent by cent until P^A changed his preference to bE^*x. The x value just before change of preference was c_l, whereas the value just after change of preference was c_h. Thus we can conclude that $c_l \leq c \leq c_h$, where $c_h - c_l = 1 \cancel{c}$, but it cannot be said exactly where in the interval c occurs. D–S–S let it go at that. They gave interval limits for c, and this was true for other unknowns as well.

Once the limits for c are determined, one determines limits for d. Because of the assumed equal distances between the entities, the theory requires that $bE^*a \sim dE^*c$. One could substitute x for d and find the values just before and after preference change, as before, except that c is not known exactly, as a and b are. Only the limits of c are known. The values of x for change in preference must, then, be noted for two different entries for c, c_l and c_h. For each of c_l and c_h an upper and lower limit for d can be found. The larger of the upper limits is taken as d_h and the smaller of the lower limits is taken as d_l. The range for the limits of d can be no smaller and may be larger than the limits for c. The limits for f are found similarly from the theoretical indifference, $dE^*f \sim bE^*c$, and then the limits for g are found from $gE^*f \sim aE^*b$. Unhappily, each successive stage allows larger and larger possible limits. Once limits are obtained for all entities, certain tests of self-consistency are possible based on theoretical indifference relations not previously employed, for example,

$$aE^*c \sim bE^*f \qquad \text{to check } c \text{ limits}$$
$$dE^*c \sim gE^*f \qquad \text{to check } c \text{ limits}$$
$$aE^*d \sim gE^*c \qquad \text{to find } a \text{ limits}$$
$$bE^*d \sim gE^*a \qquad \text{to find } b \text{ limits.}$$

If the axioms are adequate to describe human choice, c limits determined from different indifference relations should be consistent, i.e., they must have a common region. Likewise, for the other entities.

For the procedure just described, P^A viewed the successive options and made his successive choices without any die-throwing. After his choices had all been made the die was thrown once for each choice and the winnings and losses were tabulated. This technique was mentioned in Mosteller and Nogee, but was not used by them. Its purpose is to eliminate any possible effects on preference of the results of previous trials.

For 15 of 19 Ss the behavior was consistent and utility functions could be constructed. The functions were double-valued since they showed the upper and lower limits. The functions for three Ss are shown in Figure 4.3. Three Ss had

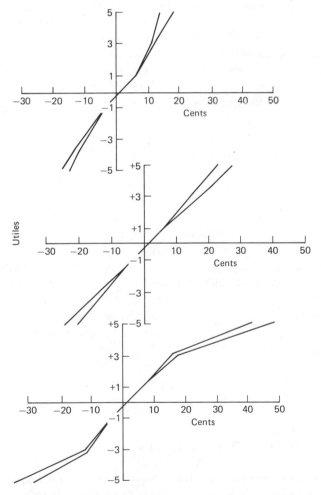

Figure 4.3. The measured utility functions for three Ss in the D–S–S experiment. The method provides utility intervals (literally, cents intervals for given utilities) rather than point estimates. (After Davidson, Suppes, and Siegel, 1957.)

curves consistent with the expected money hypothesis. (The center graph of Figure 4.3 is for one of these.) The authors concluded that, all in all, the similarity between their results and Mosteller and Nogee's was "fairly striking." The utility curves for some Ss were re-determined after a period of a few days to several weeks. The stability of the curves over this period of time seemed highly satisfactory.

After the utility curves were found, it was possible to measure the subjective probabilities for arbitrary events. In Section 3.4 we discussed the indirect method of measuring subjective probability—inference from observed preferences between gambles. D–S–S used the indirect approach: they assumed the validity of the SEU model, and inferred subjective probabilities from observed choices. As in the case of utility measurement, however, the method of D–S–S provided subjective probability limits for an event rather than a point estimate. D–S–S used a special die with four faces (two other faces had been rounded). Each face had a different nonsense syllable printed on it, and each had an objective probability of $1/4$. Subjective probabilities were measured for seven Ss, each of whom had been consistent during utility measurement. For two Ss the subjective probabilities varied between the faces. For four of the remaining five Ss, the upper bound for subjective probability was smaller than the objective probability of $1/4$.

Several related methods for utility measurement have been published. Like the D–S–S method, they all require P^A to choose between gambles with two equiprobable outcomes. Unlike the Mosteller and Nogee and D–S–S methods discussed above, however, these methods do not attempt to find gambles between which P^A is indifferent; rather they accept as basic data the stated preferences of Ss between gambles. They thereby avoid the requirement of a closely spaced and ordered set of possible consequences. On the debit side, however, these methods constitute a clear retreat from the aspiration to measure utility at full interval-scale strength. The measures are subject to a larger class of transformations than the linear class. The measurement is stronger than ordinal-scale, however; i.e., not all positive monotonic transformations are allowable. Some references for these methods are: Davidson, Suppes, and Siegel (1957, Chapter 3), Suppes and Walsh (1959), Siegel (1956), Hurst and Siegel (1956), and Coombs and Komorita (1958).

4.4   DIRECT ESTIMATES OF UTILITY

In Section 3.4 we observed that there are two general methods for the measurement of subjective probability: (1) the *indirect* method, which requires only that S state preferences between gambles, and (2) the *direct* method, which requires that S relate his subjective probability directly. A similar dichotomy occurs for utility measurement. We have been discussing indirect methods for utility measurement. But might it not be possible that Ss could relate their utilities for different entities via direct judgments?

Over the years a number of economic theorists (for example, Bentham, Gossen, and Fisher) have suggested that utility could be measured by direct comparison of the pleasures produced by two commodities. One commodity was to be the unit of measurement to measure the other(s). Pareto pointed out that if *differences* in values could be subjectively compared, then utility could be determined to within a linear transformation (i.e., cardinal scale measurement). But Pareto doubted that Ss were capable of such judgments (Stigler, 1950).

More recently, S. S. Stevens (1959) argued in favor of direct scaling methods for utility measurement. Stevens has long argued for direct techniques for the scaling of the usual psychophysical continua such as loudness and brightness. The direct methods in psychophysics were contrasted with the jnd (just-noticeable-difference) methods, used by Fechner and Thurstone, which indirectly relate distance between stimuli to the percentage of times they are confused with one another. For utility measurement, however, "indirect" methods are primarily those based on choices between gambles.

The particular direct methods Stevens advocates for psychophysical measurement are the *magnitude* and *ratio* methods. The magnitude estimation method requires S to state numbers for each stimulus of a series such that the numbers reflect the subjective magnitudes of the stimuli. The ratio estimation method requires S to state numbers reflecting the magnitude ratios for pairs of stimuli. There are also magnitude and ratio *production* methods, requiring S to choose the stimulus giving a required magnitude or ratio. Stevens has found that these methods yield approximate power functions relating subjective intensity (ψ) and physical energy (ϕ) for a wide variety of stimulus continua.[6] If k_1 and n are constants, the power function is

$$\psi = k_1 \phi^n \tag{4.4}$$

Stevens' findings contrast with the tradition based on the methods and theory of Fechner that the functions are logarithmic, i.e., that

$$\psi = k_2 \log \frac{\phi}{\phi_0} \tag{4.5}$$

where k_2 is a constant, and ϕ_0 is the stimulus intensity at "threshold."

There are two basic questions concerning the use of ratio and magnitude methods for utility scaling: (1) can Ss use these methods, and (2) are the results valid? Concerning the former, will not Ss' responses be dominated by the actual numerical amounts of money? If they are told that $100 equals 100 utiles, and asked, "$200 equals how many utiles?," will they not respond,

---

[6] ψ is the Greek letter psi; ϕ is the Greek letter phi.

"200"? If so, the results would have utility linearly related to money, a result that could hardly be accepted considering the method.

Galanter (1962) required Ss to name the quantity of money that would bring twice as much happiness as a stated amount. Ss consistently protested about the impossibility of making such judgments, but they were prodded into making them nonetheless. The power function fitted to the results had an exponent (n) of 0.43.

Although this one experiment is hardly conclusive, let us consider the second question—are the results valid? "Validity" has various interpretations. Certainly Stevens has presented no axiomatics for choice, if that is what one requires for validity. However, if the directly measured utility values proved to be useful in predicting Ss' choices most psychologists would, I believe, be tolerant of his methods.

Besides scaling money, Galanter scaled subjective probability of different events, and then constructed gambles based on these events. Ss' choices were predicted from the SEU rule. Predictions based on the power utility function were superior to predictions based on logarithmic or linear utility functions. It would appear, then, that the direct scaling methods deserve consideration.

If one is going to delve into traditional psychophysical scaling methods to measure utility, one need hardly stop with the magnitude and ratio methods. After all, a wide variety of scaling techniques are available which, psychologists believe, can result in at least interval-scale measurement. Gulliksen (1956), for one, is willing to measure "utility" with the Thurstone method of paired comparisons. This method requires only that S compare two consequences for desirability; however, the scaling method requires probabilistic responding; thus, it could hardly work for scaling money.

4.5   SHAPE OF THE UTILITY FUNCTION

The St. Petersburg Paradox and Bernoulli's Utility Function

A famous eighteenth century contribution to decision theory and utility theory was Daniel Bernoulli's (1964) solution to the so-called *St. Petersburg paradox.* The paradox purported to show that people do not, in general, choose the gamble with the higher objectively expected value, nor would it be reasonable to do so. The demonstration consisted of a hypothetical game played by "Peter" and "Paul." Peter tosses a coin as many times as necessary to get a head; when the first head appears he stops. He agrees to give Paul one ducat (or let us say $1) if the first head appears at the first toss, $2 if the first head appears at the second toss, $4 if at the third, and, in general, double for each additional trial (2^{n-1} if the first head appears on the nth trial). The objectively expected value to Paul can be calculated from the standard formula defining expected value, $EV = \Sigma_i p_i v_i$ (which, you will recall, we interpreted as a mean of a possible distribution of values on different trials). Actually there would be an infinite number of terms in the sum since there is some possibility that the first head will not appear until trial n, regardless of the size of n. The probabilities may be very, very small for large n's, but the payoff to Paul would be very, very large should such events happen, so these terms for large n cannot be ignored. Assuming that the tosses are independent, the probability that the first head appears on the nth trial means the probability of the sequence $tttt \cdots th$, which, for independent events, is given simply by multiplication (see Section 3.2) and is $p(t)p(t)p(t)p(t) \cdots p(t)p(h) = (\frac{1}{2})^n$. Thus, the expected value equals

$$\sum_{n=1}^{\infty} \left(\frac{1}{2}\right)^n 2^{n-1} = \sum_{n=1}^{\infty} \left(\frac{1}{2}\right)^n \left(\frac{1}{2}\right)^{-(n-1)} = \sum_{n=1}^{\infty} \left(\frac{1}{2}\right)^1$$

$$= \frac{1}{2} + \frac{1}{2} + \frac{1}{2} + \cdots + \frac{1}{2} + \cdots = \infty$$

(The following algebraic properties were used: $x^n = (1/x)^{-n}$, and $x^a x^b = x^{a+b}$.)

In brief, the expected value to Paul of the game is infinite. If people value choices according to the expected value, then Paul should be willing to pay Peter any amount for the chance to play the game, for no matter how much he offers to pay Peter, the game should be worth more to him. Therefore, Paul should be willing to sign over all his possessions plus his future earning power and all inheritances and gifts for the chance at one play of the game. But no one is actually willing to do this, be they probabilists who understand the infinite expectation of the game, or laymen who evaluate the game intuitively. Paul should be willing to pay *some* entry fee to play the game, however, since he is certain to get $1, and is "likely" to get more from the game. How much would you be willing to pay to play?

Bernoulli suggested that people do not maximize expected value in the sense of expected amount of some commodity, but maximize "moral expectation," which today we would call expected utility. Let Δu be the increase in utility contingent upon an increase of Δx in commodity x. Bernoulli proposed that the increase in utility contingent upon the increase in x is inversely proportional to the amount of commodity already available; i.e.,

$$\Delta u = k_2 \frac{\Delta x}{x},$$

where k_2 is a constant. This assumption implies that the utility function must be logarithmic, i.e., that the function relating utility and amount of commodity has the form proposed by Fechner for subjective intensity in psychophysics (Equation 4.5). The correspondence is not fortuitous, since Fechner's psychophysics was based on Bernoulli's utility theory.

If utilities from the logarithmic function are substituted for amounts of money, the expected value, i.e., expected utility, of the St. Petersburg game becomes finite. Viewed in terms of expected utility it is only reasonable that a person should limit the price he is willing to pay to enter the game. This does not, of course, *prove* that the utility function is logarithmic or that people always choose the alternative with the higher expected utility.

The logarithmic function is not the only one that has been proposed for the utility of money, nor the only one which would give a finite expected utility in the St. Petersburg game. Bernoulli pointed out that Gabriel Cramer, a distinguished mathematician, had independently noted that if "moral expectation" (utility) were proportional to the square root of money, the game would have a finite expected value. The square root function suggested by Cramer is a power function (Equation 4.4) with exponent $n = 0.5$:

$$\psi = k_1 \phi^{0.5},$$

where ψ is utility and ϕ is the amount of money. It is curious that the exponent found by Galanter (1962) in his empirical measurement was not far from this—0.43.

The Friedman-Savage Utility Function

Authorities since the time of D. Bernoulli and Bentham have generally supposed that the utility function is concave downward, i.e., that the marginal utility Δu for a unit increment in the amount of a commodity becomes less and less for larger and larger amounts of a commodity. Either the logarithmic function of Bernoulli or the power function of Cramer and Stevens would be consistent with decreasing marginal utility. N–M utility theory makes no assertions about the shape of the utility function; the utility function *could* have any shape and still be consistent with N–M theory. (The same would be true of Ramsey's theory.)

Friedman and Savage (1948) addressed themselves to the following question: What must the shape of a utility function be (if one can exist) for a person who:

(1) obeys N–M axioms, i.e., behaves according to the maximum expected utility principle,
(2) participates in gambling games (such as roulette and craps), and
(3) buys insurance?

Although exact data are not available, there are many people who participate in gambling games, and many who buy insurance, and thus we may presume that there exist a large number of people who do both. The gambling game requires P^A to *forsake a sure thing* (neither gain nor loss) in order to enter a risky situation that may involve a loss (his stake) or a gain, whereas insurance buying requires P^A to *forsake a risky situation* that could involve a large loss or zero loss by paying a sure thing (the premium). It is curious that with both gambling and insurance buying P^A takes the choice with the *lower* expected monetary (actuarial) value.[7] Preference for the choice with the lower actuarial value is not, per se, inconsistent with expected utility theory; however, it is not obvious that both gambling and insurance-buying can be consistent with the expected utility theory. Friedman and Savage (1948) showed that if the utility curve had the proper shape, consistency would be possible.

Vickrey (1945) had noted that a utility curve concave upward could explain gambling in terms of EU, though the upward curvature disagreed with the conventional hypothesis. Friedman and Savage, however, accepted the upward curvature for one segment of the utility curve. Let us see how upward curvature can rationalize acceptance of a gamble with negative OEV. Suppose that by "staking" 40 (dollars, say) P^A can win 100 with probability 1/4. The objectively expected value for gambling, OEV_g, is,

$$OEV_g = \frac{1}{4} 100 + \frac{3}{4} (-40) = 25 - 30 = -5$$

This compares with an OEV of 0 for refusing to accept the gamble. Now suppose the utility function given in Figure 4.4 obtains (solid line). Then

$$EU_g = \frac{1}{4} 25 + \frac{3}{4} (-8) = 6\frac{1}{4} - 6 = \frac{1}{4},$$

which compares with an EU of 0 for not gambling. Thus the EU principle requires that P^A accept the gamble, even though it has a negative OEV. If the utility function were linear ($u'(100) = 20$), the EU principle would agree with the OEV principle. The discrepancy comes about because of the increment in utility of winning of the upward curved utility function over the linear function, $u(100) - u'(100)$. This enhances the first, positive term of EU_g. The same analysis would apply if a smoothed utility curve were drawn through the three points of the function considered.

A similar analysis for insurance can be given, but for insurance the utility function must be concave downward. Suppose that a premium of 30 (dollars) protects P^A against a possible loss of 100; i.e., if the destruction of property takes place, the insurance company will make good the loss, so that P^A is only out his premium. If he does not insure, he might sustain the loss of 100 (with probability of, say, 1/4), but has no loss with probability 3/4. He would, naturally prefer to have no loss and pay no premium, but by paying no premium he may sustain a large loss.

The OEV with insurance would simply be the premium, −30. The OEV

---

[7] In 1967, American motorists paid $10.6 billion in premiums and got back $6.4 billion in payments (*New York Times,* Oct. 14, 1968, pg. 1).

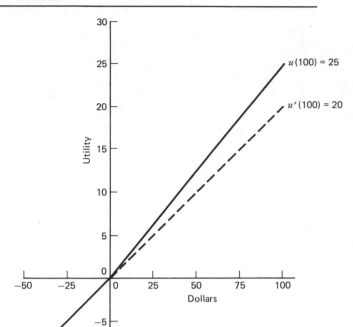

Figure 4.4. The solid line represents a hypothetical utility function that would rationalize, in EU terms, acceptance of a gamble with negative OEV. The dotted line is a straight-line continuation of the initial, lower segment.

without the insurance would be

$$\mathrm{OEV}_{i'} = \frac{1}{4}(-100) + \frac{3}{4}0 = -25$$

Thus the OEV principle would specify that no insurance be bought. Suppose, however, that the utility curve of Figure 4.5 obtained. Then,

$$\mathrm{EU}_i = -6$$

$$\mathrm{EU}_{i'} = \frac{1}{4}(-25) = -6\frac{1}{4}$$

Thus the EU principle would specify that insurance be bought. The change from the OEV result was due to the displacement of $u(-100) = -25$ down from the utility for a linear function $u'(-100) = -20$. In other words, the possible loss is worse in subjective terms than in economic terms, and thus protection from that loss is more important when viewed in subjective terms than in objective terms. The same analysis would apply if a smoothed curve had been drawn.

Thus, insurance buying against the OEV principle but consistent with the EU principle can be explained in terms of a utility curve concave downward, whereas gambling in opposition to the OEV principle can be explained in terms of a utility curve concave upward. Friedman and Savage put the two segments together to get a curve explaining both gambling and insurance buying by the same P^A. Such a curve is shown in Figure 4.6. The far upper region of the curve had to revert to the concave downward form to explain the fact that lotteries typically have more than one prize. (See Friedman and Savage for the analysis. The final segment also circumvents the St. Petersburg paradox.)

The Markowitz Utility Function

The utility curve of Friedman and Savage is supposed to be constant regardless of changes in the economic fortunes of P^A. If P^A became very wealthy (through an inheritance or whatnot), then his position would move up on the utility curve; if he became poor, his position would move down. (The same applies for Bernoulli's curve.)

Harry Markowitz (1955) noted that this would imply that people who were rich enough or poor enough would not gamble for moderately large prizes, since such gambles would pertain to portions of the utility curve with downward concave curvature. Actually, however, there are avid gamblers in all economic classes. Markowitz suggested that there should be a utility function for each individual in which the position of the inflection points would be relative to the *customary wealth* of the individual.

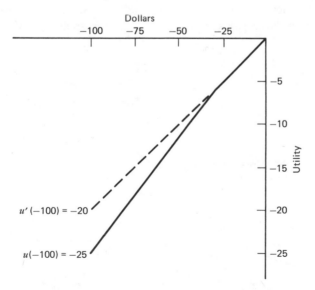

Figure 4.5. The solid line represents a hypothetical utility function that would rationalize, in EU terms, buying insurance even though expected monetary loss without insurance is less than the cost of the insurance.

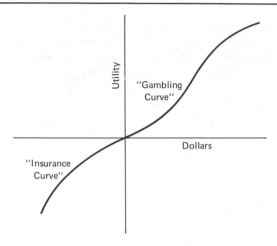

Figure 4.6. The general shape of the utility function for money proposed by Friedman and Savage (1948). The lowest section, concave downward, rationalizes insurance buying, and the middle section, concave upward, rationalizes gambling.

Figure 4.7 illustrates the curve proposed by Markowitz. The "customary wealth" is zero on the abscissa and ordinate. Gains in wealth from the customary position are positive and losses are negative. Both a rich man and a poor man would "customarily" be at zero utility, and thus both could be induced to gamble by the upward concave curvature for moderate gains. (The downward concave curvature for very large gains limits the size of the stakes P^A would be willing

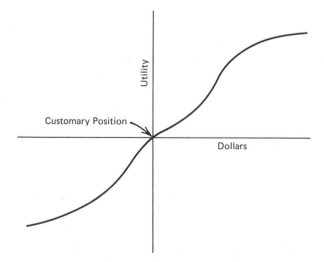

Figure 4.7. The general shape for the utility function for money proposed by Markowitz (1955).

to put up.) The meaning of "moderate" might differ for a rich and poor man. Markowitz added an upward concave section at the lower end of the curve since, presumably, beyond some point one becomes relatively numbed to further losses.

The meaning of "customary wealth" is far from clear. Is one always at "zero utility" regardless of gains and losses? Markowitz assumed that sudden, windfall changes in financial position are not immediately incorporated into "customary wealth." A winner at gambling might rise on the curve to the point where he no longer can be induced to gamble (though others "don't know when to quit"), whereas a loser might wish to continue gambling.

The amount of money equivalent to zero utility is arbitrary for N–M and Ramsey interval-scale utility theories. If there is a "natural" zero point for an "interval scale," it is a ratio scale. Discussions of ratio-scale utility typically take the "customary wealth" of an individual to be such a natural zero point.

4.6 INTRANSITIVITY AND STOCHASTIC UTILITY THEORY

The N–M axioms (Section 4.1) postulate the consistency (Axiom 1) and transitivity (Axiom 2) of preferences. Factually speaking, however, human preferences often are neither consistent nor transitive. Of course, one cannot dispute that the preferences of an individual may be consistent and transitive for some *moment* in time. As a practical matter, however, the relevant empirical observations require P^A to make a series of choices over some time period, and even when the circumstances relating to the choices are kept ostensibly the same, inconsistency and intransitivity are often observed. Recall, for example, that Mosteller and Nogee's Ss chose inconsistently.

Some authors have attempted to develop a theory of choice and utility that would incorporate choice inconsistency. Such a theory might be more adequate than N–M theory descriptively, though the normative appeal would be less. Such *stochastic utility theories* start by assuming that one alternative is preferred to another probabilistically rather than consistently. Consider the following definitions from Davidson and Marshak (1959), showing how the concepts of preference and transitivity are altered in a stochastic theory:

1. $p(o_i, o_j) = p(o_i > o_j)$ $[p(o_i, o_j) + p(o_j, o_i) = 1]$
2. o_i is *absolutely preferred* to o_j if and only if $p(o_i, o_j) = 1$.
3. o_i is *stochastically preferred* to o_j if and only if $1 > p(o_i, o_j) > 1/2$.
4. o_i is *stochastically indifferent* to o_j if and only if $p(o_i, o_j) = 1/2$.
5. o_j is the *stochastic midpoint* between o_i and o_k if and only if $p(o_i, o_j) = p(o_j, o_k)$.
6. *Weak stochastic transitivity* for o_i, o_j, and o_k is said to hold when: if $p(o_i, o_j) \geq 1/2$ and $p(o_j, o_k) \geq 1/2$, then $p(o_i, o_k) \geq 1/2$.
7. *Strong stochastic transitivity* for o_i, o_j, o_k is said to hold when: if $p(o_i, o_j) \geq 1/2$ and $p(o_j, o_k) \geq 1/2$, then $p(o_i, o_k) \geq$ maximum of $[p(o_i, o_j), p(o_j, o_k)]$.

The aspiration of Davidson and Marshak (1959) was to have meaningful assignments of "utilities" to "entities" in spite of the choice inconsistency. They envisaged a probabilistic ordering of consequences; the higher an entity is in the ordering, the more alternative entities there are to which it is stochastically preferred. They defined a real-valued function u to be a utility function if and only if for each o_i, o_j, o_k, and o_l in the set of entities,

$$p(o_i, o_j) \geq p(o_k, o_l) \text{ if and only if } u(o_i) - u(o_j) \geq u(o_k) - u(o_l)$$

In essence, Davidson and Marshak have it that equal choice probabilities relate to equal utility d.fferences. This measurement principle is well-known in psychophysics, having originated with Fechner.

We shall not enter into a detailed discussion of stochastic utility theory and the variations thereof. The mathematical theory has been worked out rather extensively and elegantly; a fine summary may be found in Luce and Suppes (1965). The experimental results are less appealing. Although some ingenious efforts have gone into the testing of stochastic theories, it is difficult to gain a firm opinion concerning the adequacy of the various models. It appears, however, that experimenters who test their own theories generally find the results more encouraging than experimenters who test the theories of others.

We consider briefly some work designed to test the existence of weak stochastic transitivity, since such transitivity is so generally required by stochastic utility theories. It is possible for stochastic transitivity to hold and yet for a triad of preferences to show intransitivity; for example, the preferences for P^A on three successive trials could be $o_i > o_j$, $o_j > o_k$, and $o_k > o_i$, even though stochastic transitivity held. The existence, then, of a triad of strictly intransitive pairwise preferences in S's data does not confirm the failure to stochastic transitivity. It must be demonstrated that the observed intransitivities are not the result of transitive stochastic preferences.

No one, apparently, argues that people *always* fail to satisfy stochastic transitivity. Instead, the question is, under what conditions do people fail to satisfy stochastic transitivity?

May (1954) had college students choose between various hypothetical marriage partners. The different prospects differed in intelligence (very intelligent, intelligent, fairly intelligent, looks (very good looking, good looking, plain) and wealth (rich, well off, poor). Ss had only slight inconsistency for pairwise choices, but 17 of 62 Ss had an intransitive preference pattern.[8]

---

[8] Davis (1958) noted that two of eight possible sets of pairwise preferences for three entities are intransitive. Since about the same proportion, 1/4, of May's Ss had intransitive choices, Davis suggested that choices were randomly made and that no consistent intransitivity occurred. However, random choice is not consistent with the fact that all of May's intransitive Ss had the same pattern of pairwise preferences—none had the opposite preferences, which would also give an intransitive pattern.

TABLE 4.1
**Scores of Three Prospective Marriage Partners on Intelligence, Looks and
Wealth**

	Intelligence	Looks	Wealth
o_i	1	3	2
o_j	2	1	3
o_k	3	2	1

May could explain the systematic intransitivities in his data by assuming
that an intransitive S preferred the prospective partner who was higher than
the alternative on two of the three dimensions. Let the highest level of any
of three dimensions be 1, the second highest 2, and the lowest 3. Then Table
4.1 describes three prospects, $o_i, o_j,$ and o_k: $o_i > o_j$ because o_i is superior in
intelligence and wealth; $o_j > o_k$ because o_j is superior in intelligence and looks;
$o_k > o_i$ because o_k is superior in looks and wealth.

May's analysis is patterned after the so-called "paradox of voting," which
was known as far back as 1882 (Arrow, 1963, p. 3). Instead of three attributes,
let there be three voters, and let Table 4.1 give the rank preferences of these
voters for candidates $o_i, o_j,$ and o_k. Then let a fourth person act as elector and
decide on the preferred candidate on the basis of majority vote. Two voters
prefer o_i to o_j, so it would appear that o_i is a more satisfactory candidate than
o_j; but $o_j > o_k$, and $o_k > o_i$. Voting can produce an intransitive community
preference pattern among candidates. It should be clear that with such intransitivities, one cannot assign single numbers (utilities) to the entities whose
magnitudes can reflect preferences. Although stochastic utility theory may give
a satisfactory accounting of intransitivities found in some preference data, it
cannot explain such systematic intransitivities as just described.

Tversky (1969) has provided a choice model different from May's for producing consistent intransitivities—one also based on multi-attribute entities.
Tversky also provided an experimental demonstration of intransitivity. Intransitivity is not compatible with choice models based on unidimensional
utilities. (Unidimensional utility theory requires that the subjective value of a
possible consequence be given by a single number). Multidimensional utility
theory—the topic for the next section—allows a consequence to be evaluated
with more than one number. Some, but not all, multidimensional utility
theories yield intransitive preference patterns.

4.7 MULTIDIMENSIONAL UTILITY THEORY

A "consequence" might consist of "components" in several senses:

(1) As we have noted (Section 4.1), a "consequence" might be a gamble,
which may be said to have as components the possible "true consequences" that

P^A might finally receive with the gamble. This possibility is incorporated into N–M theory and is not of special concern in multidimensional utility theory. The following two cases are of special concern, however:

(2) The "consequence" might be a *commodity bundle* having physically distinguishable components; for example, the consequence might be a "candy bar and a book."

(3) The consequence might not have physical components, but might have several attributes; for example, the prospective marriage partners in Section 4.6 differed in intelligence, beauty, and wealth.

We might refer to a consequence with components as a *compound consequence*. Although N–M and Ramsey's theories can assign utilities to the *compound consequences* in all three cases, providing the axioms apply, separate numerical assignments for components are made only for case (1). The question then arises, could separate *component utilities* be assigned to the components or attributes, and could such component utilities be related to a single-valued *compound utility* for the compound consequence? On the other hand, might one have meaningful component utilities, but no single-valued compound utility? As we shall see, both possibilities occur; they are the concern of *multidimensional utility theory*.

Additive Utility Theory

Economists have long been concerned with the utility for a community bundle in relation to component utilities. For simplicity, they often assumed that an *additive model* held. Suppose the bundles have two components. Let o_i, o_j, o_k, . . . be the possible "first" components, and o_p, o_q, o_r, . . . be the possible "second" components. Then a compound consequence is denoted, for example, (o_j, o_r). The additive model states that the utility of the compound equals the sum of the component utilities; i.e.,

$$u(o_i, o_p) = u(o_i) + u(o_p) \tag{4.6}$$

for all compounds that could be constructed from the given components.

Ernest Adams and Robert Fagot (1959) derived some empirical consequences of the additivity of utilities:

(1) *Weak ordering* of compound consequences; i.e., the preference or indifference relation ($\gtrsim$)[9] must hold between all pairs of compound consequences, and the relation must be transitive.

(2) If two compounds have a common component, then the direction of preference holding between compounds must remain the same if another common component replaces the first (*Independence Condition*); for example, if $(o_i, o_q) \gtrsim (o_i, o_r)$, then $(o_j, o_q) \gtrsim (o_j, o_r)$.

---

[9] $o_i \gtrsim o_j$ means $o_i > o_j$, or $o_i \sim o_j$.

(3) If $(o_i, o_p) \gtrsim (o_j, o_q)$, and if $(o_j, o_r) \gtrsim (o_k, o_p)$, then $(o_i, o_r) \gtrsim (o_k, o_q)$. (This is *not* the transitivity condition. Why?)

The three consequences must hold in the choices if there exist any utility values for the components such that preference between compounds corresponds to the sums of the component utilities. If the consequences, hold, however, it does not guarantee that the additive utility model holds, since the three consequences do not exhaust the empirical consequences of the model; nonetheless, it would be encouraging.

To test the model, Adams and Fagot had Ss pretend to be personnel managers who had to choose between job applicants who varied in "intelligence" and "ability to handle people" (four possible levels of each). Six of 24 Ss satisfied the model perfectly; for all of the remaining Ss, even the ordinal model [consequence (1)] failed. Analysis of the data suggested that when an S was sufficiently attentive to the task to be transitive, he was also additive.

Adams and Fagot suggested that one could take their consequences as axioms of choice for models weaker than the additive one; for example, consequence (1) would be the axiom for an *ordinal model,* and consequences (1) and (2) would be the axioms for an *independence model.*

Duncan Luce and John Tukey (1964) went further and developed a set of axioms sufficient to imply the additive utility model.[10] Their axioms include consequences (1) and (3); consequence (2) is a theorem in their system. They show that if preferences follow the axioms that they put forth, then numerical assignments can be made to the components such that the compound with the greater sum of component values is the preferred one. The axioms form a basis for utility measurement for both components simultaneously, and therefore Luce and Tukey designated the theory as *simultaneous conjoint measurement.* (It has come to be called *additive conjoint measurement,* to contrast it with nonadditive versions which have been developed.)

As in the case of N–M utility measurement, the numbers assigned by additive conjoint measurement are not unique. The numbers (utilities) assigned to one set of components may be altered by a positive linear transformation, but only if a positive linear transformation with the same slope (*a* coefficient) is applied to the other set of components. If the two component utilities are transformed, the compound utilities, being the sums of the components, naturally must change.

Let us illustrate:

$$u'(o_i) = a\, u(o_i) + b_1$$
$$u'(o_p) = a\, u(o_p) + b_2$$
$$u'(o_i, o_p) = u'(o_i) + u'(o_p)$$
$$= a\,(u(o_i) + u(o_p)) + (b_1 + b_2)$$
$$= a\,(u(o_i, o_p)) + b,$$

---

[10] Debreu (1960) had earlier published some related work.

where $b = b_1 + b_2$. The compound utilities are linearly transformed with the same scale unit transformation a and a constant transformation equal to the sum of the constants for the component transformations.

The requirements for the component transformations can be illuminated this way: Suppose $(o_i, o_p) > (o_j, o_q)$. For additive utility this implies $u(o_i, o_p) > u(o_j, o_q)$. Substituting component utilities for compound utilities yields $u(o_i) + u(o_p) > u(o_j) + u(o_q)$, which rearranges to $u(o_i) - u(o_j) > u(o_q) - u(o_p)$. Thus, the existence of additive utilities implies that the difference between utilities for the first components can be meaningfully compared in magnitude to differences for the second components. If different unit changes (a) were allowed for the first and second components, $u(o_q) - u(o_p)$ could be made larger than $u(o_i) - u(o_j)$, contradicting the above implication.

The Luce–Tukey formalization requires two infinite sets of components, and thus, like N–M theory, cannot be put to a strict test. Weaker axioms, for example, the consequences of Adams and Fagot, permit the transformations of utilities we have discussed, but such transformations are only a subset of the allowable ones.

One interesting aspect of modern additive utility theory, from the viewpoint of utility measurement, is that it provides (in principle) utility measurement at interval scale strength from preferences between sure thing alternatives. Preferences between sure things have, in recent times at least, been conventionally related to ordinal utility. N–M derived cardinal utility on the basis of preference between gambles; gambles, however, are not a necessary feature of a cardinal utility theory.

A further contrast between the N–M and additive utility axioms is that the N–M axioms are often thought of as rational norms. Even though people may not adhere to these axioms in actual decision making, one could argue cogently that it would be the wiser way to so adhere. Such cannot be said for additive utility theory. It may be true for some sets of components that additive utility axioms hold. But, except for weak ordering, it can hardly be argued that the axioms for additive utility constitute general abstract norms for behavior.

Other Multidimensional Utility Theories

There are a variety of possible multidimensional alternatives to additive utility theory. We have already mentioned one in connection with intransitivity. Recall that May offered Ss hypothetical marriage partners varying in intelligence, wealth, and looks. Each possible consequence, then, might be assigned three numbers (utilities), but Ss might choose between two alternatives not by adding the numbers, but by adding the dimensions on which one consequence is superior to the other.

Another possible method for choosing between consequences is by *lexicographic ordering*. This requires that the dimensions be ordered in importance. Preference between consequences is determined by the utility magnitudes for the most important dimension alone, unless there is a tie on that dimension; then, preference would be determined by the magnitudes on the second most important dimension, etc. Hausner (1954) and Thrall (1954) presented axioms leading to such a theory.

Adams (1960) presented an example where lexicographic ordering might hold. Suppose a man is ill and several medicines are available to treat him which vary in cost and effectiveness. Assuming that no medicine is prohibitively expensive, it is reasonable to think that he would choose strictly on the basis of effectiveness, unless two medicines were equally effective; then he would choose on the basis of cost.

It should be clear that "majority vote" and lexicographic ordering, like additive utility, cannot be advanced as norms for rational choice. They are all, instead, possible models for describing the structure of human preferences. It remains for empirical investigation to determine if and when the various models apply.

4.8 TEMPORAL AND CONTEXTUAL EFFECTS ON UTILITY

It is easy, when considering the utility theory literature, to get the impression that the utility of an entity for a person is a kind of universal constant—though its numerical representation may vary subject to transformational constraints. A little thought can convince one, however, that the "utility" of a "consequence" is dependent on temporal and contextual aspects of the choice situation.

Consider the obvious fact that the pleasure which P^A can expect to receive from an entity requires time and relates to starting time and duration of consumption. Jeremy Bentham (1876, p. 29), recognizing this, asserted that the following circumstances determine the value of a pleasure or pain: intensity, duration, certainty, and propinquity. Duration and propinquity are temporal factors. If one enjoys tennis, for example, the opportunity to play for ten minutes would have less attraction than the opportunity to play for one hour. Likewise, if one had to choose between playing tennis and receiving $5, it would make a difference whether the tennis were to be played within the next week or only after a year had passed (i.e., the propinquity would matter).

Economists have generally assumed that marginal utility for successive amounts of a commodity continually decreases. But what does this mean? Assume that I am offered one, two, three, etc., glasses of lemonade. Each successive glass is supposedly less valuable to me; this makes sense in terms of satisfaction of thirst, but only, I should think, if the successive glasses are to be drunk successively. What if I drink one glass a week and keep any excess frozen? Then would not each glass have about the same "marginal" utility. The marginal utility for money is usually thought to decrease as one gains more and more, yet it is not obvious to me that my successive monthly paychecks have less and less subjective value. Apparently, then, it is ambiguous simply to refer to the utility function for various amounts of a commodity. The scheduling for the reception and consumption of the commodity can drastically affect value.

Von Neumann and Morgenstern (1953, p. 19) recognized that temporal factors complicate the exposition of utility: "however, it would be an unnecessary complication as far as our present objectives are concerned, to get entangled with the problems of preference between events in different periods of the future. It seems, however, that such difficulties can be obviated by locating all 'events' in which we are interested in one and the same, standardized moment, preferably in the immediate future." What the implications of the "standardized moment" are for the measurement of utility has never been explained, nor is there any evidence that the concept has affected experimental procedures for utility measurement.

The temporal aspects of preference are extremely important for everyday decisions; thus, would it not be more desirable to attempt to systematize such aspects rather than to avoid the issue? Some theoretical and experimental work along these lines has commenced.

One approach is to have P^A choose between *consumption programs* instead of entities. A consumption program specifies that entity o_i is to be consumed in time interval 1, and entity o_j is to be consumed in time interval 2, etc. The various alternatives might be thought of as commodity bundles with specified consumption schedules. Suppose program 1 is preferred to program 2. Then suppose each program is postponed by one time unit. Then if, as seems likely, the difference in utility between the programs decreases, we say that *time perspective* exists (Koopmans, Diamond, & Williamson, 1964). Suppose $o_i > o_j$. If two programs are the same except for reversal of ordering for o_i and o_j and if the program with o_i first is preferred, we speak of *impatience* (Diamond, 1965).

There is some related psychological research, which was conducted independently of the theoretical work on utility. For example, Mischel and Metzner (1962) were concerned with the effects of age on willingness to postpone consumption. *S*s were given a choice between a 5¢ candy bar today and a 10¢ candy bar tomorrow (or later). A larger percentage of the older children than the younger children preferred to wait for the larger candy bar.

In addition to these temporal effects, the context of the choice can affect preference (and thus utility). For example, if a person were offered a choice between a knife and a sporting pass, his preference (utility) would depend on whether he happened to be under attack at the moment. Obviously, circumstances can drastically alter preferences; measured utilities, at best, can only reflect a person's extant circumstances. Even the value of money to a person is very much dependent on circumstances; does it matter what a laboratory experiment tells us about the relative utilities of a dime and a dollar if our protagonist badly needs a dime for a phone call and cannot get change for his dollar?

Such considerations led Bohnert (1954) to propose that utility theory has us asking the wrong questions. Instead of asking how much "utility" resides in what entity, should we not inquire as to what circumstances pleasure depends on? Answering this would surely require us to consider the context of choice. Is it a reasonable simplification simply to forget about the temporal and contextual aspects of choice and measure utility functions for "conditions at hand"? Perhaps such a procedure can be defended for some purposes; however any conclusions about utility and marginal utility for specific conditions must not be overly generalized.

4.9 SOCIAL WELFARE AND INTERPERSONAL COMPARISONS OF UTILITY

Social philosphers of the utilitarian stripe (see Section 1.2) have commonly asserted that the best social arrangement would be the one which maximizes the total utility across all members of a society. This sounds properly humanitarian; the major problem with it is that nobody seems to have a very convincing notion of what it might mean.

Let us assume that "society" has an aggregation of goods, jobs, money, services, etc. which can be allocated among its members in a variety of possible ways. Suppose we could measure the interval-scale utility to P^A of each possible commodity bundle he might be offered, and likewise measure the utilities for other members. Then could we not look at the utilities for a particular allocation and sum them, and do likewise for other possible allocations? Would not the allocation with the greatest sum be the indicated one?

Let us examine this method for the very simple case of three members and three possible allocations (Table 4.2). The sum is greatest for a_2, so this would appear to provide the greatest total good for the society. P^A would like the result, since of the three allocations, he receives the most utility from a_2. P^B, however, would prefer a_3, and P^C would prefer a_1. Thus there could very well be a problem in implementing the "greatest utility" maxim "democratically," but that is not of immediate concern to us. Let us suppose that a benevolent despot rules over the society who could impose a_2.

Now according to any theory of interval-scale utility measurement, the par-

TABLE 4.2
Utilities for Three Individuals for Three Allocations

		Individual			
		P^A	P^B	P^C	Sum for a_i
	a_1	2	4	9	15
Allocation	a_2	8	5	6	19
	a_3	5	7	4	16

TABLE 4.3
Same as Table 4.2, with New Utilities u' **Obtained from Linear**
Transformations of Original Utilities

$$u_A' = u_A + 0$$
$$u_B' = 10u_B + 2$$
$$u_C' = 2u_C + 8$$

		P^A	P^B	P^C	Sum for a_i
	a_1	2	42	26	70
Allocation	a_2	8	52	20	80
	a_3	5	72	16	93

ticular numbers employed for an individual are somewhat arbitrary, being subject to any positive linear transformation. Suppose, then, we applied the transformations and obtained the new utilities shown in Table 4.3. Our maxim now says that a_3 is best. The utility theory that we have discussed up to now gives us no reason to prefer one set of utilities over the other. Still another transformation could give a_1 the maximum sum.

A maxim that specifies everything specifies nothing. Our interpretation of the maxim has turned out to be meaningless. The result we have come to relates directly to the theory of additive utilities discussed in Section 4.7; let the utilities of the individuals be the "component utilities" of additive utility theory, and let the sum across individuals be the utility of the commodity bundle in additive theory. Recall that additive theory requires that component utilities be transformed with a common multiplier, a. Likewise, by imposing such a condition on our transformations of individual utilities we could have consistency—one allocation would always be maximal.

Cannot we then impose such a restriction? We might, but it would not relieve us of our uncertainty, for we don't know which utilities to start with. Depending on the initial utility assignments any of the allocations could be maximal; the transformational restrictions would only assure that this initial choice would be maintained. The allocation determined by the maxim would still be arbitrarily determined by the initial utility assignments.

Is there not some standard method of initial assignment that would be "fair"? This is where our search has brought us, and here is where we encounter the puzzle of interpersonal comparisons of utility. It is actually the unit for the difference in utilities that concerns us. We can arbitrarily add a constant of 100 or 1,000,000 to one individual's utilities and it will not bias the utility sum in his favor, since this constant would add equally to the sum for all possible allocations. The question, then, can be put in this way: What number shall be assigned to the utility difference for P^A between \$0 and \$1, and what number shall be assigned to P^B? The first thought is, assign the same number. But wait. When are we making such measurements? Before we reallocate the resources, apparently, since the reallocation must depend on our utility measurements. But can we say that the difference in utility is the same for a rich man and a beggar? It is a common belief that a given amount of money means less to a rich man than a poor man. Imagine giving $1 to a rich man, or giving $1 to a beggar; who would care more? Who might be willing to do some unpleasant task to get the $1? Not the rich man. Intuition plus the obvious nonchalance of most rich men over the spending and getting of small amounts of money leads one to feel that a $1 gain does not represent the same amount of utility increment for the rich man and beggar. Likewise, traditional assumptions about decreasing marginal utility of money reflect the same notions.

Also, if one standarized units for $0–$1, there is no necessity that the units be the same for $9–$10; why not standardize on the latter? The particular dollar increment that one standardizes on could arbitrarily affect the final allocation; if people knew what dollar increment were being employed, could they not alter their responses during utility measurement so as to benefit from the final allocation?

It has been suggested that instead of standardizing units on a given commodity, that one use a just-noticeable-difference as a unit. But there is no imperative to accept this idea either (see Luce & Raiffa, 1957, pp. 346–348). In brief, it does not appear that any logically imperative scheme is available for equating utility units across individuals. Therefore, "summation of utilities across individuals" is not a meaningful concept and cannot be used to allocate resources in a society.

There have been attempts to derive a social preference ranking based on individual preference rankings (i.e., ordinal-scale utilities) instead of on interval-scale measurements. This approach is appealing since it skirts the problem of interpersonal comparison of utilities. Unhappily, however, reasonable conditions for deriving a social preference ranking from individual rankings are inconsistent with one another, i.e., in general there may be no social ranking conforming to the desired conditions, a conclusion known as *Arrow's impossibility theorem*. For a detailed discussion, see Arrow (1963); for a summary, see Luce and Raiffa (1957, Chapter 14).

4.10 EVALUATION OF UTILITY THEORY

It might be helpful to point out explicitly some limitations in the intended scope of "utility theory." First, the "utilities" of "consequences" may not reflect the relative satisfaction or pleasure that the consequences would bring to P^A if realized. Generally speaking, utilities represent instead the apparent desirability of the possible consequences to P^A. The point is of no great importance for most experimental studies of decision making, since novel consequences are infrequent. In real life, however, a person must choose between jobs and between marriage partners, for example, without adequate experience with which to evaluate the alternatives. A decision may be rational by whatever decision principle you wish, but if a person's utilities do not correspond well to the potential satisfactions actually inherent in the possible consequences, his rational decision making will be of little avail.

Second, although in general usage "utility" is interpreted to mean "practicability" or "ability to fulfill some necessity," it has a different meaning in the "utility theory" which has concerned us. To a child, for example, the N–M utility for a candy might exceed the N–M utility for spinach, in spite of the greater nutritional value of the latter. In the common language, "utility" might be contrasted with "beauty," yet the N–M utility of a painting could exceed the N–M utility for a "practical" entity such as a tractor. Because of the differences in meaning for "utility," some feel that it is unfortunate that N–M called their magnitude "utility" at all. But "utility" it is, and readers must remember the implications of the term.

Third, to the psychologist, "utility theory" may appear to be a severely limited account of human evaluation, because it has nothing to say about many questions psychologists have great interest in. For example, to what extent are the evaluations of a person inherited, and to what extent learned? What experiences determined or affected the evaluations? Finding numbers to represent desires of some P^A for some limited time period cannot content the psychologist interested in the whys and wherefores of the structure of human preferences. The preceding remark is not intended to deprecate "utility theory," but only to clarify its boundaries.

Now let us attempt to assess impact of utility theory and measurement within decision theory. Beginning with Ramsey and von Neumann and Morgenstern, there has been a large amount of competent and interesting mathematical work in utility theory. The net contribution of theoretical and experimental work in utility to behavioral decision theory, however, has been disappointingly slight. One might have hoped that once the foundations for interval-scale measurement had been laid and once experimental programs to implement the theory had commenced, some agreement concerning the shape of "the utility function" for money and other commodities would be forthcoming. Alas! such has not been the case.

For the most part attempts to measure utility have involved only very small amounts of money. This allows one to offer Ss realistic choices—i.e., they can believe that they will receive their gains and losses. But the results have little to say concerning the conjectures of Bernoulli, Cramer, and others concerning the utility function over vast amounts of money. Nor can one say that, at least up to $1, the function appears to be a logarithmic function, a power function, or whatever. "Up to $1," there appears to be no such thing as "the function." Rather each individual appears to take his own function from a separate mold. Except for monotonic increments, it is very hard to make any general statement about the shapes of the utility functions found—the curvatures are not even the same across individuals, or within for that matter. It would be peculiar, indeed, to see such idiosyncratic and erratic curves extended upwards from about $1 to a few billion dollars. Would there be kinking from cent to cent all the way up? Would there still be large individual differences? Would best fitting simple functions all be from the same family?

Suppose one derived a utility function on the basis of consequences ranging to about $1, and then derived a curve for the same individual on the basis of consequences ranging to about $10. Would the two curves be the same over the common range up to about $1? According to utility theory, yes. But I doubt it. One often finds effects of the stimulus set in psychological scaling, and I fully expect that such effects would occur with the scaling of money. If so, the generality and importance of the particular kinks and twists of an individual's curve found under one set of conditions have to be downplayed.

By having Ss make responses concerning large amounts of money they can imagine receiving, one can measure the utility function for a wide range of dollars. As we have seen, Galanter (1962) used a direct scaling technique and large amounts of imaginary money to derive a utility function. Cent-to-cent kinks naturally do not appear with such methods since successive points are many dollars apart. Although Galanter reported that the best-fitting power function was superior to a best-fitting logarithmic or linear function, this does not prove that no other functions would be worthy of consideration, nor does it prove that all individuals have similar curves. Quite apart from this, since Galanter's technique is controversial, it cannot be said that his experiment has provided a definitive conclusion on the shape of "the utility function" for a large range of dollars.

Is it really important to measure "utilities"? If utilities were really useful in understanding and predicting human behavior, the effort would be worthwhile. So far, such usefulness has not been very convincingly demonstrated. Various authors have compared predictions of choices between gambles based on expected utilities and on actuarial values. The predictions based on the utilities are typically superior, but only slightly so. It is doubtful that the gain is very often worth the effort, at least when relatively small amounts of money are involved. As we shall see in later chapters, empirical studies of decision making typically forgo measurement of utilities; instead, behavior is analyzed in terms of objective quantities such as amount of money. Why is utility measurement neglected, when the theory of decision making emphasizes the importance of the subjective evaluation of consequences? Authors do not tell us, but we may speculate. I suppose utility measurement is neglected because it involves a lot of work, because people are not really sure which measurement technique or techniques are "valid," and because utilities would often make no important difference in the interpretation of the results.

4.11   SUMMARY

Von Neumann and Morgenstern devised a set of axioms for preference between gambles such that numbers (utilities) with these properties could be assigned to entities: (1) the preferred gamble has the higher expected utility; and
(2) the same would be true if a new set of numbers were assigned, related
to the first by a positive linear transformation. Mosteller and Nogee set out to
test the descriptive adequacy of N–M theory by measuring the utility for small
amounts of money for real Ss. The utility functions they found were markedly
idiosyncratic. A possible criticism of their technique is that people do not, as
they assumed, use objective probabilities for decision making. Davidson, Suppes,
and Siegel followed up a method suggested by Ramsey for measuring utility
which was free of this criticism. The utility functions for money which they
found were also idiosyncratic. Furthermore, the method yields utility intervals
rather than point estimates. Both the Mosteller and Nogee and the D–S–S methods required a set of closely spaced and ordered consequences.

Various multidimensional utility theories have been proposed: for example,
additive, lexicographic, and "majority rule." These theories do not have the normative appeal of the expected utility theories, and they have not resulted in
improved techniques for utility measurement on real entities.

Typically Ss do not even exhibit the preference consistency required by N–M
utility theory axioms. This has led to the development of stochastic analogues
of expected utility theories. The values which Ss place on various entities is
clearly a function of consumption schedules and context. Thus, a utility theory
such as the one of N–M can, *at best,* provide a snapshot of a person's values
under specified conditions. Theoretical and experimental work has commenced
on the effects of timing and context on preference.

If, as seems likely, SEU models of choice are not completely adequate, then
measurement techniques assuming this model must be suspect. One can question
whether the predictive benefits received from the measurement of utility justify
the effort entailed.

REFERENCES

Adams, E. W. "Survey of Bernoullian Utility Theory," in H. Solomon (ed.), *Mathematical Thinking in the Measurement of Behavior.* Glencoe, Ill.: The Free Press,
1960, pp. 151–268.
Adams, E., & Fagot, R. F. "A Model of Riskless Choice," *Behavioral Science*
(1959), **4,** 1–10.
Arrow, K. J. *Social Choice and Individual Values,* 2nd ed. New York: Wiley,
1963.
Bentham, J. *An Introduction to the Principles of Morals and Legislation.* Oxford:
The Clarendon Press, 1876 (reprint of 1823 ed.).
Bernoulli, D. "Exposition of a New Theory on the Measurement of Risk," translated
by L. Sommer. *Econometrica* (1954), **22,** 23–26.

Bohnert, H. G. "The Logical Structure of the Utility Concept," in R. M. Thrall, C. H. Coombs, & R. L. Davis (eds.), *Decision Processes*. New York: Wiley, 1954, pp. 221–230.

Coombs, C. H., & Komorita, S. S. "Measuring Utility of Money through Decisions," *American Journal of Psychology* (1958), **71**, 383–389.

Davidson, D., & Marschak, J. "Experimental Tests of a Stochastic Decision Theory," in C. W. Churchman, & P. Ratoosh (eds.), *Measurement: Definition and Theories*. New York: Wiley, 1959, pp. 223–269.

Davidson, D., McKinsey, J. C. C., & Suppes, P. "Outlines of a Formal Theory of Value, I," *Philosophy of Science* (1955), **22**, 140–160.

Davidson, D., & Suppes, P. "A Finitistic Axiomatization of Subjective Probability and Utility," *Econometrica* (1956), **24**, 264–75.

Davidson, D., Suppes, P., & Siegel, S. *Decision Making: An Experimental Approach*. Stanford, Calif.: Stanford University, 1957.

Davis, J. M. "The Transitivity of Preferences," *Behavioral Science* (1958), **3**, 26–33.

Debreu, G. "Topological Methods in Cardinal Utility Theory," in K. J. Arrow, S. Karlin, & P. Suppes (eds.), *Mathematical Methods in the Social Sciences, 1959*. Stanford, Calif.: Stanford University, 1960, pp. 16–26.

Diamond, P. A. "The Evaluation of Infinite Utility Streams," *Econometrica* (1965), **33**, 170–177.

Edwards, W. "The Theory of Decision Making," *Psychological Bulletin* (1954), **51**, 380–417.

Farquharson, R. *Theory of Voting*. New Haven, Conn.: Yale University, 1969.

Fishburn, P. C. "The Irrationality of Transitivity in Social Choice," *Behavioral Science* (1970), **15**, 119–123.

Friedman, M., & Savage, L. J. "The Utility Analysis of Choices Involving Risk," *Journal of Political Economy* (1948), **56**, 279–304.

Galanter, E. "The Direct Measurement of Utility and Subjective Probability," *American Journal of Psychology* (1962), **75**, 208–220.

Gulliksen, H. "Measurement of Subjective Values," *Psychometrika* (1956), **21**, 229–244.

Hausner, M. "Multidimensional Utilities," in R. N. Thrall, C. H. Coombs, & R. L. Davis (eds.), *Decision Processes*. New York: Wiley, 1954, pp. 167–180.

Hurst, P. M., & Siegel, S. "Prediction of Decisions from a Higher Ordered Metric Scale of Utility," *Journal of Experimental Psychology* (1956), **52**, 138–144.

Koopmans, T. C., Diamond, P. A., & Williamson, R. E. "Stationary Utility and Time Perspective," *Econometrica* (1964), **32**, 82–100.

Luce, R. D., & Raiffa, H. *Games and Decisions*. New York: Wiley, 1957.

Luce, R. D., & Suppes, P. "Preference, Utility, and Subjective Probability," in R. D. Luce, R. R. Bush, & E. Galanter (eds.), *Handbook of Mathematical Psychology*, Vol. III. New York: Wiley, 1965, pp. 249–410.

Luce, R. D., & Tukey, J. W. "Simultaneous Conjoint Measurement: A New Type of Fundamental Measurement," *Journal of Mathematical Psychology* (1964), **1**, 1–27.

Markowitz, H. "The Utility of Wealth," in *Mathematical Models of Human Behavior*. Stamford, Conn.: Dunlap, 1955, pp. 54–62.

May, K. O. "Intransitivity, Utility, and the Aggregation of Preference Patterns," *Econometrica* (1954), **22,** 1–13.

Mischel, W. & Metzner, R. "Preference for Delayed Reward as a Function of Age, Intelligence and Length of Delay Interval," *Journal of Abnormal and Social Psychology* (1962), **64,** 425–431.

Mosteller, F., & Nogee, P. "An Experimental Measurement of Utility," *Journal of Political Economy* (1951), **59,** 371–404.

Preston, M. G., & Baratta, P. "An Experimental Study of the Auction-Value of an Uncertain Outcome," *American Journal of Psychology* (1948), 183–193.

Ramsey, F. P. *The Foundations of Mathematics.* New York: Harcourt Brace, 1931.

Shanteau, J. C., & Anderson, N. H. "Test of a Conflict Model for Preference Judgment," *Journal of Mathematical Psychology* (1969), **6,** 312–325.

Siegel, S. "A Method for Obtaining an Ordered Metric Scale," *Psychometrika* (1956), **21,** 207–216.

Stevens, S. S. "Measurement, Psychophysics, and Utility," in C. W. Churchman & P. Ratoosh (eds.), *Measurement: Definitions and Theories.* New York: Wiley, 1959, pp. 18–63.

Stigler, G. J. "The Development of Utility Theory," *Journal of Political Economy* (1950), **58,** 307–327, 373–396.

Suppes, P., & Walsh, K. "A Non-Linear Model for the Experimental Measurement of Utility," *Behavioral Science* (1959), **4,** 204–211.

Thrall, R. M. "Applications of Multidimensional Utility Theory," in R. M. Thrall, C. H. Coombs, & R. L. Davis (eds.), *Decision Processes.* New York: Wiley, 1954, pp. 181–186.

Tversky, A. "Intransitivity of Preferences," *Psychological Review* (1969), **76,** 31–48.

Vickrey, W. "Measuring Marginal Utility by Reactions to Risk," *Econometrica* (1945), **13,** 319–333.

von Neumann, J., & Morgenstern, O. *Theory of Games and Economic Behavior,* 3rd ed. Princeton, N. J.: Princeton University, 1953.

Woodworth, R. S., & Schlosberg, H. *Experimental Psychology,* 2nd ed. New York: Holt, 1954.

CHAPTER 5

Gambling Behavior

In this chapter we review additional empirical studies of choice between gambles by human Ss. In part, the research we review was stimulated by the belief that the SEU model for human choice might be erroneous or too awkward, and that an alternative formulation might be useful. The data do lead one to doubt the general adequacy of the SEU model for human decision making, but a superior alternative is not currently available.

5.1 UTILITY OF GAMBLING

It is a common sense notion that many people enjoy participating in gambling games; they do not always gamble simply out of concern for possible monetary gains. Many participants in gambling games realize that the "house" has the odds set in its favor; nonetheless, these people are apt to make statements such as: "I realize that I will probably lose money, but I enjoy gambling. After all, you spend money on the theater because you enjoy it. Why shouldn't I spend money on an evening's gambling?" Our interest is not in what people enjoy doing in the evening; but the casual gambler's explanation seems on the face of it not to jibe well with formalizations of choice discussed in the previous chapter. There, choice was related to expected gains. Perhaps some revisions in our approach might be necessary for a satisfactory theory of choice.

As we noted (Section 4.1), von Neumann and Morgenstern were well aware of the issue of a "utility of gambling," but they thought the concept to be elusive and difficult to formalize. Of course, the acceptance of gambles with negative expected values need not contradict EU theory—witness the proposed utility curve of Friedman and Savage (Section 4.5). Their curve, however, strikes one as contrived, and it lacks independent experimental support.

The pioneers in the empirical measurement of utility were concerned lest a "utility of gambling" disturb their measures. Mosteller and Nogee (1951, see Section 4.2) had Ss write their strategies out on paper, as instructions to their "agents." The idea was that if the instructions were different from what the writer was actually doing, the difference might be attributed to a utility of gambling. Indeed, differences were found for some Ss, but interpretation of such differences is moot.

Davidson, Suppes, and Siegel (Section 4.3) were likewise concerned about possible effects of utility of gambling. Recall that the first phase of their utility measurement required that a value c be found such that $bE^*c \sim aE^*a$, which means that S had to choose between a gamble and the sure thing a. If S had a positive utility of gambling, would not his choice be biased toward bE^*c? In subsequent steps, a gamble was always paired with a gamble—not a sure thing. An attempt was made to guard against any erroneous determination of c, and therefore of other values, by checking c for consistency in subsequent choices between gambles. Small adjustments in c (at most $2\cent$) were required for one-third of the Ss. The assumption here would seem to be that if there is a utility of gambling, it is approximately constant for different gambles, so one need only worry when a sure thing is involved.

The only attempt at systematic formalization and measurement of the "utility of gambling" as such seems to be Royden, Suppes, and Walsh (1959). These authors assumed that any "utility of gambling" would most likely vary depending on the particular gamble offered. These authors tested the assumption that Ss evaluate a gamble by taking the sum of the expected *monetary* value of a gamble plus a "utility of gambling" for the gamble. Given a choice, S is presumed to prefer the gamble with the greatest sum.

This model was tested on university students and sailors. No simple or uniform utility of gambling functions were found, nor did the model appear to have particular merit for predicting choices. This experiment does not encourage one to believe that a "utility of gambling" concept is going to be very useful.

It is curious that if an S behaves according to the EU model, he could be interpreted as adhering to the model of Royden *et al.* The converse is not necessarily true, however.

There is little or no current research concerning a "utility of gambling" as such. However, this vague entity, "utility of gambling," would seem to relate to the ideas of "variance preference" and "risk," which we discuss next.

5.2 PROBABILITY AND VARIANCE PREFERENCE

A gamble can be thought of as a probability distribution with the various possible payoffs plotted along the abscissa and the probabilities plotted on the ordinate. It is common in mathematical statistics to describe probability distributions in terms of "moments" from which various descriptors derive: namely, expected value, variance, skewness, and kurtosis.[1] Higher moments and related descriptors

---

[1] These descriptors are usually discussed in the elementary statistics course assumed as a background. Roughly speaking, the variance of a gamble describes its dispersion, or degree of spread of possible payoffs. A sure thing has zero variance, whereas a gamble

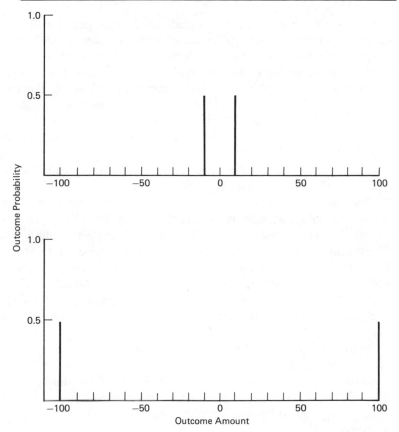

Figure 5.1. Graphs of two two-outcome zero-EV gambles, one with relatively small variance (upper) and one with relatively large variance.

could be calculated, but these four typically exhaust an investigator's interest. The basic assumption for each of the family of expected value theories (Section 2.8) is that preference is determined by only one of the descriptors, namely, expected value; the other descriptors of a gamble have no effect on its desirability.

The possibility that other descriptors might, in fact, affect desirability has been recognized for many years (for example, Fisher, 1906). In particular, it has been thought that the variance of a gamble could affect its desirability. A gamble with a high variance might include the possibility of a large gain or loss. Another gamble with the same expected value might offer an opportunity for only a small gain or loss (see Figure 5.1). It certainly seems reasonable that these could

---

with large possible winnings and losses has a large variance. Skewness relates to the symmetry of the distribution. Kurtosis relates to the relative concentration of possible payoffs in the center and the tails of the distributions.

differ in attractiveness; in fact, one individual might prefer a high-variance gamble, whereas another might prefer a small-variance gamble.

It is important to emphasize, however, that even if variance (and other higher-order descriptors) has no effect for one kind of EV theory, it can have an effect for an alternative kind. For example, suppose EU theory perfectly described the preferences of P^A; then the utility variance of a gamble has no effect on its desirability. But if value were measured in dollars instead of utility, OEV theory might not adequately describe the preferences, and the desirability of a gamble might be related to its variance in dollars, as well as to other descriptors. Individual differences in utility functions might, in the OEV theory context, appear as differences in preferences for variances.

What one would really like to know is whether preferences are affected by variance in utility, as well as by expected utility (or SEU). To study the issue, one would like to construct gambles equal in expected utility (or SEU) but differing in variance of the utilities. But how is one to measure utility? The more prominent measurement techniques assume, in effect, the validity of some expected utility theory of choice. To the extent that variance in utility affects preference, however, these theories for the measurement of utility must be invalid. Hence, one cannot use such measurements to equate "true" expected utilities.

Up to now this difficulty has not been overcome. Instead, investigators have set out to examine what effects monetary variance has on choice behavior when expected monetary values are controlled. Rather than aiming at supplementing utility theory with variance preferences, investigators have aimed to show that utility theory provides an unsatisfactory explanation for observed variance preferences.

The earlier experiments used two-outcome gambles exclusively. For such gambles, the EV, variance (Var), and skewness (Sk) are given by the following formulas, where payoff a occurs with probability p, and payoff b occurs with probability $1 - p$:

$$\text{EV} = pa + (1 - p)b \tag{5.1}$$
$$\text{Var} = p(1 - p)(a - b)^2 \tag{5.2}$$
$$\text{Sk} = \frac{1 - 2p}{\sqrt{p(1 - p)}} \tag{5.3}$$

These formulas include three independent parameters, p, a, and b, so two-outcome gambles can be constructed to vary independently in EV, Var, and Sk. However, once these three quantities are determined, the Kurtosis and any higher-order descriptors are completely determined; i.e., kurtosis cannot be controlled independently.

From these formulas it follows that: for specified payoffs a and b, the variance is greatest when $p = 1/2$ and decreases monotonically as p becomes greater or smaller than $1/2$; for specified p, variance increases directly with the difference between a and b; skewness depends only on p, not on a or b.

Ward Edwards (1953, 1954a,b) used two-outcome gambles to test the hypothesis that Ss' preferences are affected by the specific probabilities involved. Indeed, such preferences were found when OEV was controlled; for example, when offered choices between gambles with OEV = 0, Ss showed a marked tendency to choose the gamble with $p = 1/2$. Edwards called the phenomenon *probability preference*. Though the phenomenon appears to be reliable, its interpretation is problematical. Such preferences need not conflict with the SEU model, since gambles equal in OEV would most likely be unequal in SEU. The problem is to find a utility and/or subjective probability function that would explain the results and that would not look peculiar. Another possibility: although Edwards controlled OEVs, he did not control the variances of his gambles. Thus, one could wonder whether his results reflected variance preferences.

It follows from Equation 5.3 that a preference for a given probability can be interpreted as a skewness preference, since a one-to-one relationship exists between skewness and p. As we have noted, skewness and variance can be independently varied so that the effects of each can be observed. Indeed, Edwards (1954c) himself noted that variances can affect preferences when OEV and probabilities are controlled.

Clyde Coombs and Dean Pruitt (1960) undertook a more systematic and ambitious attack on the problem. They constructed a set of two-outcome gambles differing systematically in variance and skewness, each with OEV = 0. They wished to do more than simply see whether skewness and variance affect preference independently. In addition they tested the hypothesis that ideal variance and skewness levels exist. According to the hypothesis, for a given OEV and skewness level, S prefers gambles having one value of variance—the *ideal variance*—above all others; gambles with progressively higher or lower variance are progressively less desirable. The *ideal skewness* is comparable, except that it pertains to gambles with given OEV and variance levels. The ideal variance and ideal skewness are presumed to vary among individuals.

The hypothesis was borne out quite well for variance, with about equal numbers of Ss preferring low, middle, and high variance bets. The ideal variance for an S was dependent on the skewness level. The hypothesis was somewhat less satisfactory for skewness due to a bias in favor of gambles with $p = 1/2$ (in agreement with Edwards' results); except for this, Ss tended to have ideal skewness values at the two ends of the skewness scale.

Sarah Lichtenstein (1965) employed three-outcome gambles varying independently in OEV, variance, and skewness. Because three outcomes were employed instead of two, probability level was not confounded with skewness. Ss did not choose between pairs of alternatives as in previous studies discussed; instead, they bid on gambles offered singly. If they wished to play a gamble, they stated the largest amount of money they would pay for the opportunity.

If they preferred not to play the gamble, they stated the smallest amount of money that would induce them to play the gamble. *S* was told that his bid would be accepted only if it fell within the top quarter of the bids of another group of *S*s. Actually there was no other group, and the bid was accepted on a random one-third of the trials. Since the play was for real money, *S*s should have been motivated to bid carefully; however, the ruse was necessary to discourage *S* from submitting dishonestly low bids. Apparently *S*s were duped. (In succeeding chapters we shall have other evidence concerning the poor capacity of *S*s for perceiving a random sequence.)

Three levels of OEV were used for the gambles: $-83\cancel{c}$, $0\cancel{c}$, and $+83\cancel{c}$. OEV was a very strong determinant of the amount bid. The mean bids for the three OEV levels were $-91\cancel{c}$, $-11\cancel{c}$, and $67\cancel{c}$, respectively, where the minus sign indicates that *S*s wished to be paid to accept the gambles. The mean bid over the entire experiment was $12\cancel{c}$ below the mean OEV. The variance ranged from 0.25 to 4.00. Generally speaking, *S*s appeared to like a gamble more the lower the variance. This contrasts to the spread of "ideal variances" across *S*s noted by Coombs and Pruitt (1960).

Lichtenstein found no evidence for skewness or probability preferences. A few zero-OEV constant-variance two-outcome gambles were offered to *S*s in addition to the three-outcome gambles. No evidence was found for skewness preferences with these gambles either. The bids showed only small variability across gambles. A search was made for possible effects of kurtosis, but none were detected. In additional research, Van der Meer (1963) found skewness and variance preferences, whereas Slovic and Lichtenstein (1968), using bidding responses, did not. Conditions leading to the appearance or non-appearance of such effects are not currently well-understood. One might aspire to explain the effects of variance and skewness in terms of the SEU or EU model. The problem is, however, to find an elegant interpretation. At the present time it is difficult to foresee whether the concepts "variance and skewness preferences" have a useful future within decision theory.

5.3   RISK

The term "risk" is commonplace in the decision theory literature. Many times, however, the meaning intended is not at all clear. At other times the meaning is clear, but different authors are obviously using the term differently. In this section we consider some of the various research areas and concepts to which the term "risk" has been applied.

Risky Decision Situations

"Risk" has been used in categorizing decision situations. Recall that in Chapter 2 we said that decisions could be made under one of several conditions: certainty, risk, ignorance, and rational competition. The "risky condition" was said to exist if the state of nature was determined by specified probabilities known to the protagonist.

Many authors use "risk taking" to refer to real-life or experimental conditions involving uncertain events, whether or not the probabilities are well-specified for the protagonist. For example, Kogan and Wallach's (1967) review, "Risk Taking as a Function of the Situation, the Person, and the Group," covers individual and group decision making under both conditions of risk and ignorance. It does not cover the condition of rational competition—"risk taking" is less often applied to such situations in the technical literature. In its everyday meaning, "risk" refers to possible loss, bodily harm, etc. "Risk taking" as a technical term, however, need not relate to possible loss.

Riskiness of Gambles

"Risk" is sometimes used in everyday life to characterize an alternative rather than a decision situation as a whole, and the same is true for the technical literature. The implication here is that different gambles (alternatives) differ in degree of riskiness and that gambles can be ordered in "riskiness." The primary motivation for considering the "riskiness" of different gambles is to allow construction of a descriptive model for choice behavior that might be superior to the SEU model. When authors get down to the brass tacks of defining riskiness, they seem to defer to the everyday notion that risk implies some possibility of loss, and thus they only consider gambles with at least one negative consequence.

Let us consider the possible ways in which the riskiness of a gamble might be defined. It might be defined completely *objectively,* i.e., riskiness might be said to depend only on the parameters specifying the gamble; variance, for example, is defined this way. It might be defined completely *subjectively,* i.e., the riskiness might be defined entirely according to the response of the individual *S,* so that the degree of "riskiness" of a gamble for one *S* need have no relation to the degree of "riskiness" of the same gamble for another *S.* Alternatively, "riskiness" might have a *hybrid* definition, i.e., the relative "riskiness" of gambles might have objective constraints but still depend in detail on the responses of the particular individual.

One objective definition of *level of risk* was given by Dean Pruitt (1962), based on the idea that the "riskiness" of a gamble should be greater the greater the probability of loss and the greater the magnitude of any possible loss. He defined *level of risk* to be $\Sigma_i p_i v_i$, where the summation is over only those consequences entailing loss, and where the losses v_i are entered as positive quantities. Level of risk was a component of a model used for predicting choice between gambles, the *pattern and level of risk model.* Although *level of risk* was defined objectively, the model also includes a hybrid *utility of risk,* a function of level of risk, which becomes progressively negative as level of risk increases via increments in the magnitudes of the losses. The model appeared to be promising, but apparently has not been followed up.

David Meyers and Clyde Coombs (1968) presented a hybrid definition of riskiness. They investigated the following "coin-toss game": N coins, each of denomination x, are tossed and P^A receives x for each head and loses x for each tail. Regardless of the values of N or x, the OEV for the gamble is zero. Meyers and Coombs assumed that the gambles defined by varying N and x differed in "riskiness," where "riskiness" was assumed to increase with both N and x. (Note that the probability of losing equals the probability of winning regardless of the sizes of N and x; the size of the maximum and mean possible loss, however, increases with both N and x). These constraints on riskiness did not enforce exact uniformity between Ss in the riskiness levels of different gambles. Meyers and Coombs did not aspire to measure the riskiness of the various gambles for different Ss. Instead, they tested a choice model which assumed that an ideal level of risk existed which could differ among individuals and that the desirability of a gamble for a given S is determined by the difference between the gamble's riskiness and the ideal riskiness for the S. Experimental tests confirmed the predictions of the model quite well.

A game with N coins is equivalent (logically, at least) to N plays with one coin. The work of Meyers and Coombs on the effect of the number of plays of a gamble on its attractiveness is most welcome, as this important variable has been virtually ignored within experimental psychology. Paul Samuelson (1963) has reported some results in this area which, though anecdotal, are entirely convincing. He asked some colleagues whether they would accept a bet on the outcome of a coin flip, where they would receive $200 if they won but would lose $100 otherwise. They could name heads or tails for the win. No one accepted, though the OEV for the gamble is $50. A common counter, however, was: "Offer me 100 repetitions of the same gamble and I'll accept." Why accept 100 of an item one would not want one of? Samuelson noted that with one bet the probability of losing money was $1/2$, but for the positive-EV gamble the probability of losing money over 100 trials reduced to less than 0.01, and thus the offer would be less "risky." (Note, however, that although the probability of ending up "in the red" decreases as N increases, the maximum possible amount one could lose increases proportionally to N.) This line of reasoning implies that the assumption of Meyers and Coombs for zero-EV gambles, that riskiness increases with N, would not apply to positive-EV gambles.

Paul Slovic (1967) interpreted the rating of degree of risk ("virtually no risk" to "extremely great risk") of a gamble by S to be the *perceived risk* of the gamble. Perceived risk could be interpreted as a subjectively defined risk. When the probability of loss ranged from 0.2 to 0.8 and the amount to lose ranged from $1 to $4, probability of losing was a stronger correlate of "perceived risk" than amount to lose. Slovic used a special type of "duplex gamble" which allowed winning probability to vary independently of losing probability. Winning probability correlated strongly (but negatively) with "perceived risk" as well as losing probability, so "perceived risk" apparently depends on more than the negative consequences.

Risk-Taking Tendencies

As we noted, in everyday usage "risk" refers to a situation or a choice that involves possible loss or danger and the loss or danger implied is apt to be substantial. Auto racing, skydiving, and mountain climbing are said to be "risky," as are investments in which one can "lose his shirt." Is risk taking reasonable for a von Neumann-Morgenstern rational man? In the case of investments, at least, the "risky" investments have often turned out to be the most profitable. Risky sports such as race driving, mountain climbing, and bullfighting can lead to great fame and fortune. The quest for status within a male group can lead men to take extraordinary risks. According to one psychiatrist, the short life expectancy of Green Beret commanding officers in Vietnam—three months—resulted from the continual risk taking needed to gain and hold control of the group.[2] Psychoanalytically, one might postulate a "death-wish" to account for activities involving danger to one's life. But such a postulate need not be required.

It has been thought that different individuals are characterized by different levels of *risk-taking tendency* (RTT), and that RTT might be an important determiner of an individual's behavior in many situations. Thus, there have been attempts to devise psychological tests to measure RTT.

Michael Wallach and Nathan Kogan (1959, 1961) developed the *choice-dilemmas questionnaire* to measure RTT. The questionnnaire involves twelve hypothetical situations, in each of which Mr. A. has a choice, for example, of staying with his present job or going to another potentially better job. Each S was asked to check, for each situation, the smallest probability for success on the new job (or whatever) which he felt should exist before Mr. A. should accept the job. Whenever S gave a low response, for example, one in ten, he was rated high in RTT, whereas when he specified a higher probability of success, for example, eight in ten, he was rated low in RTT, i.e., "conservative." Though, literally, Ss were supposed to be advising someone else, it was presumed that such advice reflected the S's own tendencies to take risks. The final score for an S was based on his average response. The highest risk taker, according to this test, is the one who advises going for a specified gain at the lowest probability. The choice-dilemmas questionnaire has been given to many different groups. It was found, for example, that elderly Ss were more "conservative" than young Ss. The difference was due to items comparing a sure-thing financial situation to a risky one involving greater possible gain. It has also been found

---

[2] Dr. Peter Bourne, *New York Times,* May 17, 1968.

that groups responding in consensus to questionnaire items after discussion tend to give lower probabilities, i.e, exhibit greater RTT, than the mean of responses made individually.[3] The phenomenon has been dubbed the *risky shift*. A review of work with the choice-dilemmas questionnaire is given in Kogan and Wallach (1967).

One can ask, why speak of risk-taking tendencies? Cannot the responses be viewed within the framework of SEU or EU theory? For example, could not the age difference be due to the greater value placed on financial security by older people? The choice-dilemma researchers have paid scant heed to such possibilities.

A comparable approach to measurement of RTT was taken by Liverant and Scodel (1960). They offered Ss a choice between 28 two-outcome zero-EV gambles. They took as a measure of "degree of risk taking" the largest amount of money an S could possibly win with the chosen gamble. (Might this be a measure of "greed"?) The largest amount was associated not only with the smallest probability of winning but with the largest possible stake. The authors' aim was to relate RTT to personality variables. Using similar gambles, Pruitt and Teger (1969) showed that group discussion aiming at consensus can result in preference for riskier gambles. (The "risky shift" has not always appeared for choices among gambles; see Pruitt and Teger (1969) for a discussion of some possibly critical conditions.)

Torrance and Ziller (1957) illustrate still another approach to the measurement of RTT. They used a questionnaire that concerned the S's past history and self-perceptions concerning fighting, contact sports, taking dares, etc. The resulting Risk Scale has had some predictive success with military men.

A test to predict RTT in real situations would be of considerable practical interest. For example, Gumpper and Smith (1968) administered the Torrance-Ziller and choice-dilemmas questionnaires to high- and low-accident truck drivers, on the hypothesis that high risk takers would have more accidents. Neither test differentiated the two groups, however.

Psychological testing specialists have been concerned about the effects of risk taking on test scores. S's score can be affected by his willingness to risk a guess and the amount of penalty levied for an incorrect guess. Willingness or reluctance to guess seems to be a general trait of an S over different kinds of tests. When hesitant Ss were forced to guess, their test scores improved (Sherriffs & Boomer, 1954; Slakter, 1969); this result, however, must depend on the size of the penalty.

We might question whether there is any such thing as a risk-taking tendency

---

[3] This effect was noticed by President Kennedy: "The trouble is that, when you get a group of senators together, they are always dominated by the man who takes the boldest and strongest line." From Arthur M. Schlesinger, Jr., *A Thousand Days*, Houghton Mifflin, Boston, 1965, p. 812.

in general. Would the person who invests in long shots also tend to pick fights and drive carelessly? On the contrary, might not careless driving compensate for lack of physical prowess? For further discussion see Slovic (1962, 1964).

In summary, the term "risk taking" has been applied at times so broadly so as to be nearly synonmous with decision making. Although the term "risk," in its everyday meaning, implies the possibility of harm or loss, the term doesn't always have this connotation in the psychological literature. The "perceived riskiness" of gambles depends on the probability of gain as well as the probability of loss. The riskiness of gambles has entered into models for decision making; according to one, for zero-EV gambles S is supposed to choose the gamble nearest his ideal risk level. Various tests to measure "risk-taking tendencies" have been developed, but one can question the generality of any such concept.

5.4   THE ROLE OF AMBIGUITY IN CHOICE

Suppose P^A is shown two urns, each containing a total of 10 balls, some red and the rest black. He is assured that the first urn, $U(5-5)$ has 5 red balls and 5 black balls, whereas the second urn, $U(?)$, has an unspecified division between red and black balls. P^A is then told he may choose one urn and pick "red" or "black." One ball will be randomly selected from the chosen urn, and P^A will receive \$1 if he named the selected color. Let us suppose first of all that P^A has no preference for red over black for either urn. For $U(5-5)$ this is reasonable since P^A realizes that red and black have equal chances of occurring (P^A is free from color biases). For $U(?)$ he doubts strongly that the red and black balls are equal in number; if he knew which color predominated he would choose it, but he hasn't the "foggiest." Thus he couldn't care less which color he chooses for $U(?)$.

Our interest is not in P^A's choice of color—it is in his choice of the urn from which the ball is to be drawn. As we shall see, there is a reasonable amount of evidence that Ss prefer $U(5-5)$. A logical analysis from the standpoint of SEU theory, however, implies that there is no reason for Ss to prefer one urn to the other. These facts have led to severe doubts about the descriptive adequacy of SEU theory and, as well, have given rise to doubts about the "rationality" of SEU axioms.

Daniel Ellsberg (1961) has characterized the feature of $U(?)$ that leads to its rejection as *ambiguity*, by which he refers to the uncertainty that P^A has in regard to $p(\text{red})$ and $p(\text{black})$. According to SEU theory, since $p(\text{red}) = p(\text{black})$, $p(\text{red})$ and $p(\text{black})$ must both equal 0.5, the same as for $U(5-5)$. Yet for $U(5-5)$ P^A knows $p(\text{red})$ is 0.5; for $U(?)$, however, there might be 3 red balls in the urn, or 2, or 7, or 10, in which cases, $p(\text{red})$ would be 0.3, 0.2, 0.7, or 1.0. In other words, for $U(5-5)$ $p(\text{red}) = 0.5$ because there is a very good reason it should; for $U(?)$ $p(\text{red}) = 0.5$ only because there is no evidence that it should be higher or lower.

In Chapter 2 we mentioned various conditions under which decisions could be made: certainty, risk, ignorance, and rational competition. The situation with $U(5\text{--}5)$, which involves well-specified probabilities, exemplifies the condition of risk. The situation of $U(?)$ could be said to exemplify the condition of ignorance, since the probability of red could vary anywhere from 0 to 1. "Ambiguity" includes the condition of ignorance, but it also includes cases intermediate between risk and ignorance, for example, the case of an urn that could contain anywhere from 2 to 8 red balls.

The notion of ambiguity can be thought of in terms of a probability distribution of probabilities. In the case of $U(?)$, for example, S is told that there could be any number of red balls from 0 to 10. We can imagine P^A thinking to himself: "There might be 4 red balls, in which case the probability of red would equal 0.4, or there might be 7 red balls, in which case the probability would be 0.7, etc., for each number from 0 to 10. But I don't know which situation exists." There are 11 possible exclusive conditions for the urn (0 to 10 red balls), and we might ask, what is the probability for each possible condition? Although there are no conventional or objective probabilities to assign to the condition, SEU theory accepts subjective probabilities. It might be possible to measure the probabilities for a given individual for the 11 possible states. In which case, one could plot a probability distribution of a probability, as in Figure 5.2a.

It is possible to consider such a distribution for $U(5\text{--}5)$, except that, ideally, there would be a point distribution at 0.5, as in Figure 5.2b. Actually, P^A might have some doubts that the probability for red really is 0.5—experimenters sometimes use ruses and sometimes make mistakes—but even then the distribution of probabilities might be as in Figure 5.2c, concentrated at $p(\text{red}) = 0.5$ but with small values elsewhere. (Of course, if P^A doubts the experimenter, he might doubt that the urn has 10 balls, or that all balls must be red and black.)

Savage (1954, p. 58) mentioned this "second-order" distribution of probabilities in his book, *The Foundations of Statistics,* but reasoned that people average over the distribution to come out with an expected probability to use in decision making. This resultant probability is the expected value of the second-order probability distribution. The final conclusion that the probability of red for a ball drawn from the urn is 0.5 is equivalent to saying that the mean of the second-order probability distribution is 0.5.[4] According to SEU theory, the dispersion, i.e., the variance of the second-order distribution, should have no bearing on preference. The evidence, however, is to the contrary.

It is tempting to identify ambiguity with the variance of the second-order probability distribution, but no one has offered a precise definition of ambiguity so far, so no exact relationship between ambiguity and variance should be as-

---

[4] It is possible to conceive third and higher-order distributions as well. These could be averaged out also.

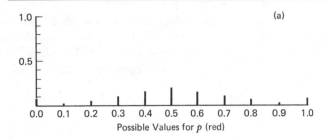

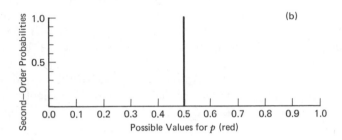

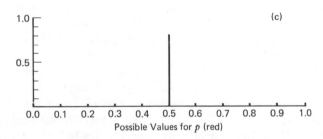

Figure 5.2. "Second-order" probabilities of the various possible values of $p(\text{red})$. (a) Hypothetical second-order probabilities for $U(?)$. (b) The situation for $U(5-5)$, when P^A "knows" there are 5 red balls. (c) A situation in which P^A believes $p(\text{red}) = 0.5$ is highly likely, but does not exclude other possibilities altogether.

sumed. There are at least two experimental methods for varying degree of ambiguity, however, and both can be interpreted as inducing changes in the variance of the second-order distribution.

John Chipman (1960) drew a "random" sample of 10 balls from an urn. Through a ruse, the proportion was predetermined. Apparently the total number of balls was unspecified, but the larger the sample portion, the better the probability estimate should be and the smaller the ambiguity should be. Chipman did not vary sample size in his experiment, so no validation of this method of ambiguity variation was possible. In fact, Chipman's work pre-dated the publications on ambiguity, and his work was conducted for other purposes. Nonetheless, his results contain peculiarities which suggest the presence of an ambiguity effect.

Selwyn Becker and Fred Brownson (1964) set limits to the maximum and minimum number of red balls an urn could contain. Greatest ambiguity, presumably, existed when the limits were 0 and 100, less when the limits were 15 and 85, less still for 25 and 75, etc. They found that most Ss were willing to pay money to avoid the more ambiguous choice, and that the amount they were willing to pay varied directly with the difference in ambiguity (range) between gambles. When the ambiguity difference was greatest, Ss were willing to pay an average of 36¢ to avoid the ambiguous gamble, even though the OEV for each choice was 50¢.

We should clearly distinguish between the variance of the second-order distribution, which apparently relates to "ambiguity," and the variance of a gamble. The gamble "bet on red for $U(5–5)$" has, in the usual view of things, exactly the same variance as the gamble "bet on red for $U(?)$." In spite of logical differences between the two types of variance, there may be a behavioral connection. Becker and Brownson presented evidence that ambiguity aversion and preference for small variance may reflect the same attitude in Ss. In a supplementary test, they found that all Ss with an aversion to ambiguity preferred $50 certain to 50–50 gamble for $0 or $100; i.e., they preferred the small-variance gamble. The S who preferred the ambiguous gamble also preferred the high-variance gamble.

The evidence relating to the effect of ambiguity on choice behavior might lead us to conclude that man is irrational, since he does not follow SEU principles. As usual, however, there are possible "outs." Fellner (1961) has questioned whether it is reasonable to insist that subjective probabilities add to 1, as they must for SEU theory. Could the probabilities be "nonadditive" (see Section 3.5)? If they add to 1, then when two exclusive and exhaustive events such as red and black have equal probabilities, these probabilities must each equal $\frac{1}{2}$; however, if the probabilities could add to less than 1, the probabilities need not equal $\frac{1}{2}$. Even though red and black have equal probabilities for the ambiguous urn, these probabilities might, say, be 0.4. Then preference for the unambiguous situation would relate to differences in SEU between "red for $U(5–5)$" and "red for $U(?)$."

Toda and Shuford (1965) were able to rationalize the ambiguity effect in terms of a utility for being right or wrote quite apart from the money gained. For example, if an S guessed black and it turned out that there were 10 red balls, it is as if the experimenter made a fool of S. If S guessed wrong with $U(5–5)$, however, it would simply be bad luck.

In summary, Ss generally appear to prefer situations with well-specified probabilities to situations with ambiguous probabilities, even though by additive SEU theory they should be indifferent. Several concepts have been put forward to rationalize this behavior, or at least to assist in describing it. It is not clear at the present time, however, which of these explanations will turn out to be most useful.

5.5 THE INTERACTION OF UTILITY AND SUBJECTIVE PROBABILITY

> "I still feel just as convinced as ever that as soon as I start playing on my own account I can't fail to win."
> "But what makes you so sure?"
> "Well, since you ask me—I don't know. All I can tell you is that I *must* win, that it is the only way out for me. Well, maybe that's why I feel so sure."
>
> (from *The Gambler* by Dostoevsky[5])

The *objective probability* of a die landing ace is 1/6 regardless of whether this result will yield $1, $1,000, or a loss of $10,000. There is a widespread suspicion, however, that *subjective probability* varies depending on the value of the associated consequence. In the Dostoevsky quote above, the protagonist is in desperate straits and therefore believes he will win. He apparently feels that the roulette wheel is sympathetic to his needs.

We might say that an *optimist* is one who believes that outcomes will be biased according to his desires. Thus the gambler would be an optimist. However, it is possible for the interaction to work the other way; i.e., a person could think: "If it's good, it won't happen to me; if it's bad, it will happen to me." The gambler might then respond: "I must win, so I'll surely lose." Such a person might be called a *pessimist*. What then do we call the person not characterized by interaction? A *realist?* Perhaps. But the "realist" need not have an "accurate" or "objective" appraisal of probabilities.

If, as evidence suggests, subjective probability and utility interact, it would be a serious blow to SEU theory. According to the theory, there is supposed to be a specific utility for a consequence regardless of the gamble into which it enters. Likewise, an event is supposed to have a specific probability regardless of the consequence with which it is associated. Otherwise, it would be pointless to try to measure utilities of consequences and subjective probabilities of events and to predict choices from them. There would be no such thing as the "utility of 10¢" per se, since, quite apart from the allowable transformations, the quantity would differ depending on the event associated with it. Likewise, one could

---

[5] F. Dostoevsky, *The Gambler,* translated by A. R. MacAndrew, Bantam Books, New York, 1964, p. 47.

not speak of an event E^* as having a "subjective probability of $1/2$," for, in association with other payoffs, the event's probability would differ. Of course, one could claim that the SEU theory still holds for each choice, but one must know how to determine each utility and subjective probability separately for each gamble. As we have seen, however, SEU measurement procedures are already complicated. Any additional burden would have to be a light one. Edwards (1962), for example, hoped that the interaction might depend only on the sign of the utility (i.e., gain or loss), but not the amount. Experimental results suggest, however, that his hope, itself, was subject to optimistic interaction.

Now for the evidence: Rose Marks (1951) and Francis Irwin (1953) conducted similar experiments to determine whether the value of a consequence could affect subjective probability. Decks of ten cards were used containing marked and unmarked cards. (The marks were obvious—not the surreptitious kind used by gambling cheats.) S was told how many of each kind of card were in the deck, and then had to state whether he thought a random card picked from the deck (by himself) would be marked. Decks with various numbers of marked cards were employed. In the Desirable condition, S gained a point if he actually drew a marked card (regardless of his prediction), whereas in the Undesirable condition he lost a point if he drew a marked card (regardless of his prediction).

For all decks, Ss predicted more marked cards in the Desirable than in the Undesirable condition (see Figure 5.3). Objectively, of course, Ss could expect to get a marked card equally often, whether it was desirable or not. Furthermore, the number of points they received depended only on the presence or absence of marked cards and thus in no way depended on Ss' predictions. Why, then, should Ss predict marked cards more often when they are desirable? It appeared that subjective probability for marked cards was higher when the cards were more valuable than when they were less valuable. The effect was considerably stronger for Marks' children (fifth and sixth grades) than for Irwin's college students. The effect in children did not depend on sex, IQ, or socioeconomic level.

The interpretation of this *Marks-Irwin effect* is open to question. Viewed in terms of decision theory, the two choices (predictions) available to S at any given time offered the same expected number of points regardless of S's choice. Therefore, one choice was as good as the other, and nothing S could do would scandalize any canon of decision theory.

It has been suggested that Ss' responses reflected "wishes" or "hopes" rather than "expectations" (Rotter, 1954). There have been several attempts to meet this objection. Irwin (1953) required confidence ratings along with predictions on the hypothesis that if wishes were governing responses rather than "true expectations," the confidence ratings would be lower for predictions of desirable outcomes than for predictions of undesirable outcomes. Confidence ratings were

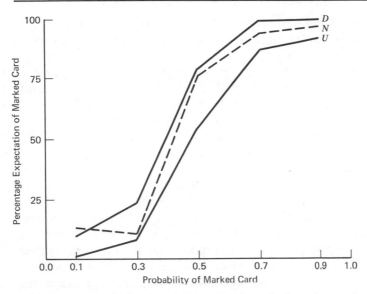

Figure 5.3. Percentage expectation of the marked card as a function of probability of marked card and value of marked card. The marked card was desirable for graph *D*, undesirable for graph *U*, and neither desirable nor undesirable for graph *N*. (From Irwin, 1953.)

the same for both, however. Crandall, Solomon, and Kellaway (1955) instructed *S*s on the importance of accurate predictions in order to reduce wishful predictions, but there is no assurance that such instructions are effective. The Marks-Irwin effect appeared in their results. Pruitt and Hoge (1965) found the effect with a variety of alternative measures of subjective probability; they found that incentives for accurate probability estimations decreased the magnitude of the effect, but did not eliminate it. Irwin and Graae (1968) likewise found the effect when *S*s were financially motivated to make accurate predictions. In brief, it appears safe to say that subjective probability is influenced by the value of the associated consequence.

It remains to consider whether the effect is a function of the sign of the consequence alone (discontinuity hypothesis) or depends on the magnitude of the consequence in some regular way. Crandall, Solomon, and Kellaway (1955) offered five levels of payoff for the marked cards: $-25\cancel{c}$, $-5\cancel{c}$, $-0\cancel{c}$, $+5\cancel{c}$, and $+25\cancel{c}$. The average percentage of predictions of the marked card were 41, 49, 53, 55, and 58, respectively. This tentatively suggests that the magnitude of the effect depends on more than the sign. Pruitt and Hoge (1965) also used five payoff levels; but the subjective probability functions did not appear to have consistent shapes across conditions. Irwin and Graae (1968), who offered incentives for accurate predictions, found strong evidence against the dicontinuity hypothesis; *S*s showed a clear preference for the more desirable event even when both events had positive or both had negative payoffs associated with them. The preference for the more desirable card, however, varied only weakly with the magnitude of the difference in payoff.

Slovic (1966) likewise found interaction effects which could not be accounted for by the discontinuity hypothesis. He also noted large individual differences; both "pessimistic" and "optimistic" response patterns appeared. Slovic suggested that optimists might generally take greater risks than pessimists.

We have discussed the effect of value on subjective probability. It is also possible to consider the effect of subjective probability on value. Such an effect is hypothesized in the adage, "The grass always looks greener on the other side of the fence." The adage, appropriately translated, became part of Lewinian theory: a barrier tends to enhance a positive valence. The theory was tested by Feather (1959), who indeed found that candies requiring a high performance level to win appeared more desirable to primary school boys than candies requiring a lower performance level. The effect was more pronounced for skill and achievement-oriented conditions than for chance and relaxed conditions. One wonders, however, whether the Ss' preference responses for the candies were not confounded unnecessarily with the desire of the Ss to succeed at the more challenging task.

In summary, contrary to the requirements of SEU theory, subjective probabilities appear to interact with values of the associated consequences. Optimistic interaction between subjective probability and value is generally observed, but pessimistic interaction can occur as well. The pattern of the interaction cannot be easily described, but subjective probability certainly depends on more than the sign of the associated consequence.

5.6   REGRET AND PREFERENCE STRENGTH

The concept of "regret" was introduced in Section 2.10. The "regret" for a consequence was defined to be the difference between the payoff and the maximum possible payoff for the same state of nature. A regret matrix can always be found for each payoff matrix. If probabilities are specified for each state of nature, and expected regret can be calculated for each choice. The difference in expected regret for two choices equals the difference in expected payoff for the same two choices, though the signs differ. Thus, postulating that Ss prefer the choice with the smallest expected regret is no different from postulating that Ss prefer the choice with the largest expected payoff. In spite of this redundancy between expected regret and expected payoff, evidence exists that "regret" may prove to be a useful concept for understanding choice behavior.

Max Schoeffler (1962) had Ss "bid" on 100 successive trials by stating a number on each trial between 0 and 30. Then a random number N was presented from a rectangular probability distribution. If the bid was less than or equal to N, S received the amount of his bid in "make-believe dollars." If his bid exceeded N, in different conditions he either won nothing or lost the amount of his bid. Schoeffler found that the mean bid reflected a *regret equalization hypothesis*, which states that the mean bid is placed so that the expected regret due to overbidding equals the expected regret due to underbidding. If the range for N is 8–15, the hypothesis predicts a mean bid of 9.7, close to the actual result, whereas maximization of OEV (or, equivalently, expected regret minimization) requires that S bid 8. It is not clear how to generalize the hypothesis to any type of payoff matrix, since, in general, the consequences available to S cannot be unambiguously attributed to "overbids" or "underbids."

Jerome Myers and his colleagues discovered another behavioral phenomenon which suggests that regret can affect choice (Myers & Sadler, 1960; Myers & Katz, 1962; Suydam & Myers, 1962). Ss had to make a sequence of choices between two decks of cards. One deck had cards worth either $+1$ or -1. At the beginning of each trial the top card from this deck was turned up, so S knew its value. The other deck consisted of cards with a wider range of values with plus and minus signs balanced so that the EV was zero. In different conditions the range of values for this deck varied from narrow to wide. S could choose either the known value of $+1$ or -1 from the first deck or the unknown top card from the second deck. It is hardly a surprise that Ss chose the unknown card more often when the known alternative was -1 than when it was $+1$. Of greater interest is a peculiar interaction which appeared between the range of the unknown deck and the sign of the known card. The effect is schematized in Figure 5.4. The effect, which we might dub the *Myers effect*, has appeared with monetary payoffs as well as with symbolic payoffs, and with a rating-scale response as well as with simple choice.

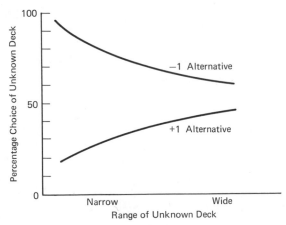

Figure 5.4. Graph illustrating the type of interaction found between range of "unknown" deck and sign of sure-thing alternative. A bias toward choosing the unknown deck is found in experimental data and is included in the figure.

That Ss do not choose consistently is, of course, contrary to a deterministic SEU theory. More to the point of our present discussion, however, is the fact that the effect is inconsistent with any workable stochastic version of SEU theory, as well. Suppose the two known alternatives each have a utility (which is also an SEU). The prospect of drawing a card from the unknown deck, of, say, narrow range, likewise has an SEU associated with it, which depends on the utilities and subjective probabilities for the various possible consequences. Now the SEU for the wide range cards may be higher or lower, but if it is higher, the percentage choice for the unknown deck should increase against both sure-thing alternatives, whereas if SEU is lower for the higher range, percentage choice should go down against both sure-thing alternatives. The interaction shown in Figure 5.4 belies either possibility. Of course, if SEU remains the same, choice probabilities should not change at all. There are no other possibilities within SEU theory, so SEU theory fails (unless one allows SEU to vary according to the set of alternatives available).

Ward Edwards developed an index on two-alternative payoff matrices—the *relative expected loss*—which appeared to be remarkably successful in predicting the probability that one alternative would be chosen over another (Edwards, 1956; Taub & Myers, 1961). As Suydam (1965) has shown, this index relates linearly to another index which we will call the *expected regret ratio* (R).[6] In addition, she pointed out that the index predicts the Myers effect.

The expected regret ratio is defined for two-alternative decision situations with specified probabilities. Let ER_1 and ER_2 be the expected regrets for alternatives a_1 and a_2. By definition, the expected regret ratio,

$$R_{12} = \frac{ER_2}{ER_1 + ER_2} \tag{5.4}$$

Also,

$$R_{21} = \frac{ER_1}{ER_1 + ER_2} = 1 - R_{12} \tag{5.5}$$

The hypothesis advanced by Edwards, in terms of R, is that the greater R_{12}, the greater the probability that a_1 will be chosen over a_2. Suydam has extended the hypothesis to include mean strength of preference ratings. Generally speaking, one might say that the hypothesis concerns the strength of preference for one alternative over another. Let $p(a_1, a_2)$ be the probability that a_1 is chosen when paired with a_2. Let the prime indicate another decision situation with different alternatives a_1' and a_2'. Then the hypothesis says that if $R_{12}' > R_{12}$, $p(a_1', a_2') > p(a_1, a_2)$.

---

[6] Suydam (1965) calls it the "expected loss ratio." Though "loss" has some precedence, "loss" can mean negative payoff as well as regret, so we use the latter term.

TABLE 5.1
Expected Regret Ratios Predicting the Myers Effect

		Payoff Matrix				Regret Matrix				ER	R_{12}
(a)	a_1	-4	-2	$+2$	$+4$	3	1	0	0	1	
	a_2	-1	-1	-1	-1	0	0	3	5	2	0.67
(b)	a_1	-8	-4	$+4$	$+8$	7	3	0	0	2.5	
	a_2	-1	-1	-1	-1	0	0	5	9	3.5	0.58
(c)	a_1	-8	-4	$+4$	$+8$	9	5	0	0	3.5	
	a_2	$+1$	$+1$	$+1$	$+1$	0	0	3	7	2.5	0.42
(d)	a_1	-4	-2	$+2$	$+4$	5	3	0	0	2	
	a_2	$+1$	$+1$	$+1$	$+1$	0	0	1	3	1	0.33

$\left.\begin{array}{l}\text{(a)}\\\text{(d)}\end{array}\right\}$ Narrow Range a_1

$\left.\begin{array}{l}\text{(b)}\\\text{(c)}\end{array}\right\}$ Wide Range a_1

Table 5.1 shows four payoff matrices, with sure-thing alternatives of $+1$ or -1 paired with narrow and wide range alternatives. (These do not match any actual experiments, but they do illustrate the nature of the situation.) The ordering of the R_{12}'s, where a_1 is always the gamble and a_2 the sure thing, matches the ordering for choice probabilities shown in Figure 5.4; thus, the expected regret ratio hypothesis can predict the Myers effect (though it cannot predict the exact choice probabilities for the various situations).

Edwards (1956), Taub and Myers (1961), and Suydam (1965) reported correlations in the 0.90's between preference strength and R, when R was calculated from monetary payoffs. Thus it would appear that regret, in the form of R, is extremely relevant to choice behavior.

My own analysis and research on this index, however, has shown that the situation is not as clear-cut as previous reports would indicate (Lee, 1971a). Mosteller and Nogee (1951) suggested that choice probability increases monotonically with difference in expected utility between the two alternatives. Their data supported this idea, though not very precisely. Myers, Reilly, and Taub

(1961) likewise reported a relation between objectively expected value difference—which presumably relates closely to expected utility difference—and
choice probability. Indeed, it would be surprising if the two were not related.
Suppose $p(a_1, a_2) = 0.6$, when expected value difference $D_{12} = \$0.50$; if EV_1
were increased by \$1.00 so that D_{12} became \$1.50, would it not be remarkable
if S were not tempted to choose a_1 more frequently, i.e., if $p(a_1, a_2)$ did not
increase? Immersed as we are in expected value theory and its ramifications,
we could hardly imagine that no such relationship exists.

Nonetheless, the correlations found between R_{12} and $p(a_1, a_2)$ are so high
that it is doubtful that any other variable could be very influential unless it were
strongly confounded with R_{12} in past experiments. Indeed, previous experiments
investigating the relationship between R_{12} and $p(a_1, a_2)$ have used sets of gamble
pairs with strongly confounded R_{12} and D_{12}.

The same pair of gambles constituting a payoff matrix can be indexed and
scored as either R_{12}, D_{12}, and $p(a_1, a_2)$, or R_{21}, D_{21}, and $p(a_2, a_1)$. *A priori*
it would appear to make no particular difference, so past experimenters have
been rather arbitrary in their scoring. However, $R_{12} > 1/2$ if and only if
$D_{12} > 0$, and $R_{12} < 1/2$ if and only if $D_{12} < 0$. Thus, if one payoff matrix is
scored so that D_{12} is positive and another scored so that D_{12} is negative, there
must be confounding of R and D. Furthermore, such arbitrary scoring results
in arbitrarily inflated correlations between R and p, as well as arbitrary verifica-
tions of Edwards' hypothesis. If, for example, R_{12} is 0.8 and $p(a_1, a_2)$ is 0.75,
R_{21} must be 0.2 (Equation 5.5) and $p(a_2, a_1)$ must be 0.25. Suppose, in addition, that R_{12}' for another pair of gambles is 0.85, and $p(a_1', a_2')$ is 0.70. Then
by scoring R_{12} and R_{12}' the prediction proposed by Edwards would fail, since
the larger R does not associate with the larger p. But if we score R_{21}' and
$p(a_2', a_1')$, the prediction holds.

It is possible to construct sets of gamble pairs unconfounded in D and R.
Using such sets, I have determined that D and R both affect preference strength,
but they can interact strongly (Lee, 1971b). Furthermore, there are strong
but poorly understood influences other than D and R which affect preference strength. OEV is an excellent predictor of stochastic preference; i.e., the
alternative with the higher OEV was chosen more than 50 percent of the time
for the large majority of gamble pairs that have been used in research. Actually,
since $D_{12} > 0$ if and only if $R_{12} > 0.5$, Edwards' (1956) rule for predicting
stochastic preference in terms of his expected loss index amounts to nothing
more and nothing less than prediction that the higher-EV gamble will be
stochastically preferred.

In summary, the concept of regret appears to hold some promise for dealing
with certain choice data. The regret equalization hypothesis appears promising
for situations in which each of the possible regrets can be attributed to underbidding or overbidding. The expected regret ratio (R) succeeds in predicting
the Myers effect and, in addition, appears to have a role in predicting strength

of preference in choice between gambles. Its role in this regard, however, is by no means so overpowering as the initial research reports imply. Expected value difference and other factors are important determiners of preference strength, as well. The gamble with the higher expected value is generally preferred stochastically to the other alternative.

5.7 EFFECTS OF SEQUENCE AND BANKROLL

Sequence

If S's responses in the "same" decision situation differ systematically depending on choices, outcomes, and consequences on preceding trials, we speak of the *effect of sequence.* Jerome Myers and Jane Fort (1963) offered Ss, on each of a series of trials, the opportunity to accept or reject a gamble which could result in winning or losing. Ss were more apt to accept a gamble on a trial if, on the previous trial, they had accepted a gamble and won than if they had accepted a gamble and lost. If Ss did not accept a gamble, they were still allowed to see what the consequence would have been. Ss were more apt to accept the gamble if they had accepted the previous gamble and lost than if they had not gambled but had seen that they would have lost.

Robert Munson (1962) studied choice between gambles in an actual carnival gambling situation. He found that when one of the participants won a large payoff on a low probability gamble, there was increased play for that particular gamble by other customers. William McGlothlin (1956) likewise studied gambling in a real-life situation—the race track. He found a negative correlation between the proportion of persons with winning tickets for a given race and the amount bet per person on the next race. This does not appear to agree with the finding of Myers and Fort (1963) that winning increases the tendency to gamble, since it implies a greater tendency to gamble after losing than after winning. McGlothlin's findings, however, can be interpreted to say that when a longshot wins a race, people bet more on the next race. This may reflect the same tendency found by Munson for people to get unduly optimistic when they note a longshot paying off.

The notion of a "gambler's fallacy" has existed for a long time. This relates to an alleged tendency for gamblers to believe that mechanical randomizers such as roulette wheels exhibit sequential tendencies; in particular, according to the "gambler's fallacy," as a series of "red" events occur on a roulette wheel, the probability of "black" increases, as if "black" had to "catch up" with "red." As we shall see in Chapter 6, there is experimental evidence confirming the existence of such beliefs for people in general. In brief, there can be no doubt of the existence of sequential effects on choice between gambles. We have only mentioned a very small portion of the evidence. Such effects do not accord with the standard SEU theory.

Bankroll

In the course of a night of gambling, a person may find his bankroll increasing, i.e., he may find himself winning, or he may find his bankroll diminishing. The folklore is that the gambling behavior of a person depends on the current size of his "wad." A bankroll effect may be thought of as a special type of sequence effect which relates to cumulative effects of winning or losing over many trials; the typical analysis of "sequence effects" concerns only a few previous trials.

Authorities on poker strategy (and amateurs as well) consider bankroll to be an important determinant of betting, but they are not entirely clear and consistent on what the effects are. Moss stated that in his opinion, the man who is losing is less likely to bluff than the man who is even or a little ahead, particularly if the man losing cannot afford his loss very well.[7] However, he states that the man who is well ahead is not likely to bluff, either, unless he is a "bluffer by nature." Scarne mentioned that a big winner frequently seems to go on a betting spree, but that a heavy loser may tend to bluff in order to "steal the pot" or to "change his streak of bad luck."[8] I believe that a fair summary of this expert advice might read: "If a poker player is either ahead or behind, his tendency to gamble on weak hands may either increase or decrease (not respectively)."

Perhaps objective research could provide more insight than informal observations. There has been very little research devoted to effect of bankroll, per se. Some authors have, however, attempted to determine, in experiments aimed primarily in other directions, whether choices were affected by prior winnings and losses.

First let us ask, is there any good reason why the bankroll should affect choice? Yes, indeed. Suppose, first, that gains and losses can move S up and down a utility curve. Then depending on past gains, the prospect of an additional gain of, say, $10, could imply a variety of possible utility increments, and a like assertion holds for each possible consequence. If utilities of the consequences can change with bankroll, choices can certainly change as well. Even with the utility curve proposed by Markowitz (Section 4.5) on which S can make no systemic movements, temporary movements up or down the curve are postulated until S can absorb his gains or losses into his customary position. Mosteller and Nogee (1951) suggested that any effects of bankroll on choice could be avoided in an experimental session by postponing observations of the random events until all choices had been indicated.

Another possible way for bankroll to affect choice: S might vary his choice behavior with his bankroll in order to decrease the chances of gambler's ruin,

[7] J. Moss, *How to Win at Poker*, Garden City Books, Garden City, N.Y., 1950, p. 27.
[8] J. Scarne, *Scarne on Cards*, Crown, New York, 1949, p. 308.

i.e., complete loss of his bankroll and thus inability to accept any further offerings. The probability of ruin has been shown to be a function of the amount of P^A's starting capital, the stake to be wagered at each trial, the capital of the opponent (or, equivalently, the amount P^A must win before he will quit), the probability that P^A will win his wager on a trial, and the amount he can win with his stake.[9]

Ruin considerations constituted more than an academic exercise for Edward Thorp (1962), a mathematician who devised a method to play "twenty-one" (a card game) in a casino with odds favorable to him, i.e., with the OEV to him positive. With two wealthy backers, he went to Nevada to try his system. To maximize OEV he should have bet the house limit whenever a favorable situation occurred, i.e., one with positive EV (the EV for a particular situation might not be positive). But this method would have made the probability of ruin too high, and thus might have required a premature and inconclusive termination of the test. Instead, Thorp employed a scheme which kept the probability of ruin low by varying the stakes according to the favorability of the odds and the amount of past winnings.[10]

Now for some experimental findings. Mosteller and Nogee (1951) collected some information on bankroll effects for some pilot Ss. They found a clear tendency for a number of Ss to be more willing to accept a given gamble for those periods of time when they had a large number of winnings in front of them than when they had only a meager supply. Lichtenstein (1965) found no effect of total amount won or lost in a given session on the amounts Ss were willing to bid for a gamble.

Greenberg and Weiner (1966) devoted an experiment primarily to effect of amount won or lost. They controlled amount won or lost through nine phony "random" draws, so that different groups of Ss "won" $1.20, nothing, or lost $1.20, and did so with one , four, or eight winning instances. All Ss were then offered the opportunity to choose one of 20 zero-EV gambles and then one of 100 gambles. Choices appeared to be independent of amount won, but were affected by number of winning trials. Individuals with either very high or very low number of winning trials preferred the high-risk gambles (low probability of high payoff), whereas individuals with the intermediate number tended to prefer more conservative gambles.

In summary, choice behavior in the same decision situation differs systemati-

---

[9] An introduction to the probability of "ruin" is given by Feller (1950, Chapter 14).

[10] Thorp "cleaned up" with his system. In order to dampen the fires of greed in the heart of the reader, however, let me venture to judge that Thorp's system is not a simple get-rich-quick scheme. The system itself is complicated. If the casino recognizes you as a "trouble-maker" (i.e., a winner) they can invite you to leave, bring out a "mechanic" (crooked dealer), or shuffle frequently, which cuts your advantage. Rough-arm tactics are apparently not out of the question either. Furthermore, the house rules have been changed to decrease the effectiveness of the system.

cally depending on choices, outcomes, and consequences on previous trials. It need not be unreasonable for a person to alter his behavior as his bankroll waxes and wanes, but psychological research here is scanty and inconclusive.

5.8   EFFECTS OF IMAGINARY MONEY

Many experiments in decision theory have used payoffs in "imaginary money," poker chips, or points. Sometimes chips, for example, might be used simply as a convenient coin for the experimental sessions, to be redeemed in real money at the end. At other times, however, S is instructed to try to gain as many chips as possible, though he realizes that no pecuniary interest is served from his accumulations. When imaginary money is employed, S is typically instructed to respond as he would if the payoffs were dollars, cents, or whatever, though he realizes that he will actually neither gain nor lose money as the result of his choices. Experimenters typically hope that their results are general, and, in particular, they hope their results would be virtually the same if real money had been employed.

In spite of such hopes, skepticism is rampant. Even if Ss prefer more chips to fewer and more imaginary money to less, the shape of the utility functions need not be the same for symbolic and monetary payoffs. Furthermore, though the intentions of the Ss may be pure, they simply may not know how they would "really" react if the consequences were amounts of real money. In addition, if such attitudinal factors as interest in the task and time spent deciding affect choice, one can well imagine that choices might differ for real and imaginary payoffs.

Needless to say, there are obstacles to the widespread use of real-money payoffs. As we noted in regard to utility measurement, large sums of money cannot be offered in laboratory experiments. Funds are not available for large winnings, and if they were, eyebrows—not to say the tops of heads—would be raised if it were discovered that college students were receiving tens, hundreds, or thousands of dollars of public money for an hour's worth of "gambling" in a university's psychological laboratory. Likewise, large losses by Ss would have repercussions, even if most Ss in an experiment won. For that matter, small losses by Ss would be awkward as well; for could one ask the student employment service to send over Ss, and then have some leave the experiment poorer than when they entered, or could one require students in a class to serve as Ss, and then require them to pay the experimenter? Yet realistic experiments on choice must include the possibility of loss.

The foregoing considerations mean that experiments with real money have offered Ss the prospects of only relatively small gains or losses. Several techniques have been used to assure that Ss don't end up as losers. One technique is to offer them an initial bankroll large enough to absorb losses resulting from their choices. Another technique is to offer any S who is behind near the end of the session some terminal choices with particularly favorable consequences or with rigged outcomes so that S will not leave a loser, though hopefully, he is unaware of the ruse and believes that he could have lost during the experimental session.[11] Some techniques for allowing the entries of payoff matrices to be reasonably large without having total payoff over many choices mount extravagantly are to mix favorable and unfavorable decision situations together so that gains and losses tend to cancel, or to notify S that only one of the decision situations will be played "for real," but that this one will be determined randomly at the end of the session.

In addition to worrying about the effects of chips or imaginary money on choice, one can conduct experiments to determine if such effects exist. For best control, an experiment should compare exactly the same task using real and symbolic money. Such experiments are hard to come by.

Edwards (1953) compared worthless chip, imaginary money, and real money sessions in a "probability preference" experiment. The pattern of preferences were highly similar across conditions. One graph does suggest some modest differences for the imaginary money condition, but since imaginary money sessions took place first and real money sessions took place last, one cannot be sure that any effects were not due to order of treatment.

Slovic, Lichtenstein, and Edwards (1965) hypothesized that highly motivated Ss produce more inconsistent and disorderly response patterns than bored, unmotivated Ss, who would rather exert themselves as little as possible by adopting simple strategies. They assumed that high motivation results from individual sessions, a small number of choices, real payoffs, and ample time for decisions, whereas low motivation results from group sessions, a large number of choices, imaginary payoffs and short choice-times. They pointed out that the relatively orderly data found by Coombs and Pruitt (1960; see Section 5.2), for example, existence of an ideal variance, may have resulted from the "low-motivation" conditions that prevailed. Slovic *et al.* made an experimental comparison between "low-" and "high-motivation" conditions. Indeed, they found the effects they hypothesized, but where effects appeared, reality of payoff was confounded with so much else that there is no reason to assume that payoff reality had any effect. Indeed, the data from three groups which differed only in payoff reality appeared to be very similar.

Slovic (1969) conducted to well-controlled study of the effect of payoff reality on choices between gambles. Ss under the hypothetical payoff condition were particularly attracted to gambles with the larger possible winning amount, whereas Ss under the real payoff conditions took a more cautious and balanced view of the alternatives. There have been a number of "probability prediction" experiments (Chapter 6) showing that Ss make optimal predictions more frequently if they receive monetary reward for a correct prediction rather than simply knowledge of results (see Section 6.4). As far as I know, however, such

[11] Argyris (1968), among others, notes that so many psychologists have been using so many ruses that Ss are becoming skeptical concerning any instructions given them.

studies have not compared imaginary money, points, or poker chip rewards with real money payoffs.

Although a number of other studies could be cited, it is clear that the comparative effects of real versus symbolic rewards in decision making have not been thoroughly investigated, and any general conclusions would be premature. Further experimentation on this topic would be definitely worthwhile.

5.9 GAMBLING IN EVERDAY LIFE

> And now that I have told of gluttony,
> I'll take up gambling, showing you thereby
> The curse of chance, and all its evils treat;
> From it proceeds false swearing and deceit,
> Blaspheming, murder and—what's more—the waste
> Of time and money;
>
> (from *Canterbury Tales* by Chaucer[12])

The term "gambling" in everyday life typically refers to gambling games such as roulette, poker, and blackjack, or to betting on sporting events. The term "gambling" is also used figuratively at times to refer to particularly risky decisions in less frivolous areas such as business, war, etc.

The assumption within decision theory—not typically made explicit—would seem to be that the same or very similar principles of behavior lie behind decision making under uncertainty whether the decision takes place in a gambling game or not. The metaphor of general decision making as gambling is by no means recent (though the appeal of the metaphor is limited by the undesirable connotations of the word "gambling" to many people). In the seventeenth century Pascal argued that acceptance of the Christian faith was a favorable wager, regardless of how small the probability of its truth, since the payoff in eternity for acceptance would be infinite.[13] This type of argument has continued—I heard it used by a high school classmate who became a minister—but since gambling has generally been considered to be a disreputable activity in religious circles, the argument has not been fully utilized.

The insurance business was at one time outlawed and operated clandestinely because it was perceived to be a form of gambling. The relationship between risk taking in business and in gambling was likewise recognized by a tract from eighteenth century England which complained that a card-player who lost his

---

[12] G. Chaucer, *Canterbury Tales,* Rendered into Modern English by J. U. Nicolson, Garden City Publishing Company, Garden City, New York, 1934, pp. 300–301 (quoted from Marx, 1952, p. 180).

[13] B. Pascal, *Pensées: Thoughts on Religion and Other Subjects,* Washington Square Press, New York, 1965, p. 72.

estate was a "cull," whereas the merchant who lost his goods in a shipwreck was only a "bankrupt," though "one cannot command the winds and the waves, any more than the other can the aces and honors"; furthermore, "their designs are the same, equally tending to advance their family, and to serve their country."[14] The analogy between gambling and business is not uncommon today, but I suspect that the analogy is not popular with bankers and financiers, at least when they deal with the public.

Considering the presumed close relationship between behavior in gambling games and decision making under uncertainty in general, some naturalistic observations on gambling and gamblers would seem appropriate to this chapter. Such observations provide a useful supplement to information gained from laboratory experiments. Gambling games have been universal across human cultures and across history. The characters in the prehistorical mythology of Egypt, Greece, and India made fateful decisions via gambling devices. Zeus, Poseidon, and Hades divided the world by casting lots. The Vedas tell of gambling large stakes on chariot races and of dice games with loaded dice, with the wife as the stake after all possessions, including slaves and brothers, had been gambled away (Wykes, Chapter 2).

Mechanical devices for gambling seem to have existed early in all cultures. Manufactured dice with six sides appeared in antiquity, but much of the dice-playing in ancient times and the Middle Ages was with an astragalus—an ankle bone with four sides from a sheep or similar animal. Playing cards first appeared in Europe around the fourteenth century, but did not spread rapidly because of their expense. Roulette wheels can be traced to eighteenth century French casinos, but spinning devices for gambling, of which they are a variant, occurred widely throughout history and cultures.

Gambling equipment has been, throughout history, closely associated with religion and superstition; in fact, it cannot be said whether the devices were first used as mechanisms for divination or for gambling. Nonetheless, religions have generally opposed gambling. The ancient Jews prohibited gamblers from testifying in court, on the grounds that they were unreliable and avaricious. The Koran forbids gambling. In the Middle Ages the Christian Church opposed the use of gambling devices for divination, which was associated with sorcery. Legal prohibitions of gambling have, likewise, been widespread. The Romans promulgated many laws against gambling, but these probably had little success. Laws in Middle Age England and France limited gambling for money to noblemen.

It is not entirely clear why there has been so much opposition by state and church to gambling, but reasons can be surmised. Leaders may have been disturbed that people should be so avid in attending to non-productive games when the prosperity and security of the state demanded greater economic achievement and military preparedness. Gambling contributes to neither. In addition, it must

---

[14] Marx (1952, pp. 184–185).

have been a great nuisance to have to deal with the miseries, deprivations, and passions that resulted when the head of a family gambled away all his possessions. Cheating in gambling has always been rather easy, though difficult to police, so gambling has often been associated with gangsters. Laws against gambling could protect the innocent from the wolves.

State and religion have not opposed all forms of gambling at all times. Both government and churches have found lotteries to be useful for fund raising. Public lotteries first appeared in sixteenth century Italy and spread rapidly throughout Europe. England raised money this way to finance public utilities, ransom prisoners, and colonize America. Lotteries were reputable in the early years of the United States. They were used to support the Continental Army and to provide for such venerable academic institutions as Harvard, Yale, and Princeton. (Financially beleaguered college presidents take note!)

In spite of many legal restrictions on gambling in the U.S. today, staggering sums are bet each year. For example, in 1962 attendance at horse tracks in the U.S. was over 50 million, twice that of major league baseball. Pari-mutuel betting was $3.6 billion, with $288 million going to the states.[15] John Scarne (1961, p. 32) estimated that illegal betting on horseracing was much more extensive, amounting to perhaps $50 billion. Considering all forms of betting, Scarne estimated that Americans wagered $500 billion in 1960, 98% of it illegally (Scarne, 1961, p. 1).[16]

A survey showed that 74% of adult women and 67% of adult men participate in some form of gambling. The large majority, 70%, claimed that they gamble to win money, whereas 25% said they gamble for pleasure, of which one-fifth said they found nothing more exciting. Of those who did not gamble, most said they could not afford it or they knew they couldn't win. The alleged sinfulness of gambling only influenced 2 percent of the non-gamblers (Scarne, 1961, Chapter 1).

According to the U.S. Public Health Service, there are six million compulsive gamblers in the U.S. These people literally beg, borrow, and steal to get money to gamble. In spite of long histories of loss, they feel that good luck is just around the corner. Psychologists have postulated various devious motives behind such behavior. Gambling has been said, for example, to be a substitute for sexuality—hetero-, homo-, or solitary. According to Bergler (1957), the compulsive gambler has an unconscious desire to lose, i.e., he is masochistic. Gamblers

---

[15] *Time*, April 5, 1963, p. 29.

[16] $500 billion was more than half the gross national product in 1960, so the figure may be hard to believe. Note, however, that a man can go to the race track with $50, put up several hundred dollars in bets during the course of the evening, and still go home with some money—probably less than $50. Most of the wagering would not represent any net transfer of funds. Scarne estimated net transfer from gambling in 1960 as $50 billion, still a substantial fraction of the gross national product.

Anonymous is an organization of compulsive gamblers who try to help each other; it is modeled after Alcoholics Anonymous.[17]

5.10 SUMMARY

In this chapter we have summarized a variety of experimental results concerning human choice between gambles. When OEV is controlled, preferences are affected by (1) the "utility of gambling," (2) the variance and skewness of a gamble, and (3) the "riskiness" of a gamble. Factors (1), (2), and (3) have been studied separately, and the relationships between them have not been clearly articulated. They are apparently highly similar. The SEU model might account for at least some of the results attributed to factors (1), (2), and (3), but the problem is to find acceptable utility (and subjective probability) functions.

The notion of "risk" is widespread, but the term is used with various meanings. The fact that people take "risks," i.e., subject themselves to possible "loss," need not, of itself, be evidence against the SEU theory. There are often dearly prized social rewards for risk taking (if one survives). There is some evidence that preference is affected by the "ambiguity" of a gamble, i.e., by the extent to which S lacks confidence in the probabilities he assigns to events. People generally prefer to avoid ambiguous situations, a fact not easily reconciled with usual interpretations of SEU theory. The not uncommon presumption that subjective probabilities are affected by the associated payoffs has been confirmed by laboratory studies. In general, people are "optimistic," i.e., believe chance to "secretly favor" themselves. An index based on "regret," the expected regret ratio, is an important determinant of strength of preference for one gamble over another, and it can predict the interaction found between the range of a gamble and the sign of a sure-thing alternative. The effects of bankroll and sequence on choice are not consistent with the "simple" form of SEU theory, but could be consistent with versions allowing S to move up and down on his utility function. In some situations the player may change his behavior as a function of his bankroll in order to avoid "ruin." A survey of participation in gambling games shows that the appeal of gambling transcends culture and era. Presumably, behavior in gambling games reflects principles common to choice in all risky situations, though one can hardly assume that choice behavior depends only on the abstract specification of the alternatives.

Many of the results presented in this chapter are incompatible with an SEU model for human decision making, or at least with the standard version. If SEU theory is descriptively inadequate, methods for measuring utility based on it, in particular, the D–S–S procedure (Section 4.3), are of doubtful validity. There is at present, however, no demonstrably superior alternative model.

---

[17] *Gamblers Anonymous* (1964).

REFERENCES

Argyris, C. "Some Unintended Consequences of Rigorous Research," *Psychological Bulletin* (1968), **70**, 185–197.

Becker, S. W., & Brownson, F. O. "What Price Ambiguity? Or the Role of Ambiguity in Decision-Making," *Journal of Political Economy* (1964), **72**, 62–73.

Bergler, E. *The Psychology of Gambling.* New York: Hill and Wang, 1957.

Chipman, J. S. "Stochastic Choice and Subjective Probability," in D. Willner (ed.), *Decisions, Values and Groups.* New York: Pergamon, 1960, pp. 70–95.

Coombs, C. H., & Pruitt, D. G. "Components of Risk in Decision Making: Probability and Variance Preferences," *Journal of Experimental Psychology* (1960), **60**, 265–277.

Coombs, C. H., & Meyer, D. E. "Risk-Preference in Coin-Toss Games," *Journal of Mathematical Psychology* (1969), **6**, 514–527.

Crandall, V. J., Solomon, D., & Kellaway, R. "Expectancy Statements and Decision Times as Functions of Objective Probabilities and Reinforcement Values," *Journal of Personality* (1955), **24**, 192–203.

Edwards, W. "Probability-Preferences in Gambling," *American Journal of Psychology* (1953), **66**, 349–364.

Edwards, W. "Probability-Preferences among Bets with Differing Expected Values," *American Journal of Psychology* (1954a), **67**, 56–67.

Edwards, W. "The Reliability of Probability-Preferences," *American Journal of Psychology* (1954b), **67**, 68–95.

Edwards, W. "Variance Preferences in Gambling," *American Journal of Psychology* (1954c), **67**, 441–452.

Edwards, W. "Reward Probability, Amount, and Information as Determiners of Sequential Two-Alternative Decisions," *Journal of Experimental Psychology* (1956), **52**, 177–188.

Ellsberg, D. "Risk, Ambiguity, and the Savage Axioms," *Quarterly Journal of Economics* (1961), **75**, 643–669.

Feather, N. T. "Success Probability and Choice Behavior," *Journal of Experimental Psychology* (1959), **58**, 257–266.

Feller, W. *An Introduction to Probability Theory and Its Applications,* Vol. 1. New York: Wiley, 1950.

Fellner, W. "Distortion of Subjective Probabilities as a Reaction to Uncertainty," *Quarterly Journal of Economics* (1961), **75**, 670–689.

Fisher, I. *The Nature of Capital and Income.* New York: Macmillan, 1906.

Gamblers Anonymous. Los Angles, Calif.: The G. A. Publishing Co., 1964.

Greenberg, M. G., & Weiner, B. "Effects of Reinforcement History upon Risk-Taking Behavior," *Journal of Experimental Psychology* (1966), **71**, 587–592.

Gumpper, D. C., & Smith, K. R. "The Prediction of Individual Accident Liability with an Inventory Measuring Risk-Taking Tendency," *Traffic Safety Research Review* (1968), **12**, 50–55.

Irwin, F. W. "Stated Expectations as Functions of Probability and Desirability of Outcomes," *Journal of Personality* (1953), **21**, 329–335.

Irwin, F. W., & Graae, C. N. "Tests of the Discontinuity Hypothesis of the Effects of Independent Outcome Values upon Bets," *Journal of Experimental Psychology* (1968), **76,** 444–449.

Kogan, N., & Wallach, M. A. "Risk Taking as a Function of the Situation, the Person, and the Group," in *New Directions in Psychology III.* New York: Holt, 1967, pp. 111–278.

Lee, W. "Preference Strength, Expected Value Difference, and Expected Regret Ratio," *Psychological Bulletin* (1971a), **75,** 186–191.

Lee, W. "The Effects of Expected Value Difference and Expected Regret Ratio on Preference Strength." *American Journal of Psychology* (1971b), **84,** in press.

Lichtenstein, S. "Bases for Preferences among Three-Outcome Bets," *Journal of Experimental Psychology* (1965), **69,** 162–169.

Liverant, S., & Scodel, A. "Internal and External Control as Determinants of Decision Making under Conditions of Risk," *Psychological Reports* (1960), **7,** 59–67.

Marks, R. W. "The Effect of Probability, Desirability, and 'Privilege' on the Stated Expectations of Children," *Journal of Personality* (1951), **19,** 332–351.

Marx, H. L. (ed.) *Gambling in America.* New York: H. W. Wilson, 1952.

McGlothlin, W. H. "Stability of Choices among Uncertain Alternatives," *American Journal of Psychology* (1956), **69,** 604–615.

Meyer, D. E., & Coombs, C. H. "Risk Preference in Coin-Toss Games," *Proceedings of the 76th Annual Convention of the American Psychological Association* (1968), **3,** 55–56.

Mosteller, F., & Nogee, P. "An Experimental Measurement of Utility," *Journal of Political Economy* (1951), **59,** 371–404.

Munson, R. F. "Decision-Making in an Actual Gambling Situation," *American Journal of Psychology* (1962), **75,** 640–643.

Myers, J. L., & Fort, J. G. "A Sequential Analysis of Gambling Behavior," *Journal of General Psychology* (1963), **69,** 299–309.

Myers, J. L., & Katz, L. "Range of Payoffs and Feedback in Risk Taking," *Psychological Reports* (1962), **10,** 483–486.

Myers, J. L., Reilly, R. E., & Taub, H. A. "Differential Cost, Gain, and Relative Frequency of Reward in a Sequential Choice Situation," *Journal of Experimental Psychology* (1961), **62,** 357–360.

Myers, J. L., & Sadler, E. "Effects of Range of Payoffs as a Variable in Risk Taking," *Journal of Experimental Psychology* (1960), **60,** 306–309.

Pruitt, D. G. "Pattern and Level of Risk in Gambling Decisions," *Psychological Review* (1962), **69,** 187–201.

Pruitt, D. G., & Hoge, R. D. "Strength of the Relationship between the Value of an Event and Its Subjective Probability as a Function of Method of Measurement," *Journal of Experimental Psychology* (1965), **69,** 483–489.

Pruitt, D. G., & Teger, A. I. "The Risky Shift in Group Betting," *Journal of Experimental Social Psychology* (1969), **5,** 115–126.

Rotter, J. B. *Social Learning and Clinical Psychology.* New York: Prentice-Hall, 1954.

Royden, H. L., Suppes, P., & Walsh, K. "A Model for the Experimental Measurement of the Utility of Gambling," *Behavioral Science* (1959), **4,** 11–18.

Samuelson, P. A. "Risk and Uncertainty: A Fallacy of Large Numbers," *Scientia* (1963), **57,** 1–6.

Savage, L. J. *The Foundations of Statistics.* New York: Wiley, 1954.

Scarne, J. *Scarne's Complete Guide to Gambling.* New York: Simon and Schuster, 1961.

Schoeffler, M. S. "Prediction of Some Stochastic Events: A Regret Equalization Model," *Journal of Experimental Psychology* (1962), **64,** 615–622.

Sherriffs, A. C., & Boomer, D. S. "Who is Penalized by the Penalty for Guessing?" *Journal of Educational Psychology* (1954), **45,** 81–90.

Slakter, M. J. "Generality of Risk Taking on Objective Examinations," *Educational and Psychological Measurement* (1969), **29,** 115–128.

Slovic, P. "Convergent Validation of Risk Taking Measures," *Journal of Abnormal and Social Psychology* (1962), **65,** 68–71.

Slovic, P. "Assessment of Risk Taking Behavior," *Psychological Bulletin* (1964), **61,** 220–233.

Slovic, P. "Value as a Determiner of Subjective Probability," *IEEE Transactions on Human Factors in Electronics* (1966), **7,** 22–28.

Slovic, P. "The Relative Influence of Probabilities and Payoffs upon Perceived Risk of a Gamble," *Psychonomic Science* (1967), **9,** 223–224.

Slovic, P. "Differential Effects of Real versus Hypothetical Payoffs on Choices among Gambles," *Journal of Experimental Psychology* (1969), **80,** 434–437.

Slovic, P., & Lichtenstein, S. "Importance of Variance Preferences in Gambling Decisions," *Journal of Experimental Psychology* (1968), **78,** 646–654.

Slovic, P., Lichtenstein, S., & Edwards, W. "Boredom-Induced Changes in Preferences among Bets," *American Journal of Psychology* (1965), **78,** 208–217.

Suydam, M. M. "Effects of Cost and Gain Ratios, and Probability of Outcome on Ratings of Alternative Choices," *Journal of Mathematical Psychology* (1965), **2,** 171–179.

Suydam, M. M., & Myers, J. L. "Some Parameters of Risk-Taking Behavior," *Psychological Reports* (1962), **10,** 559–562.

Taub, H. A., & Myers, J. L. "Differential Monetary Gains in a Two-Choice Situation," *Journal of Experimental Psychology* (1961), **61,** 157–162.

Thorp, E. O. *Beat the Dealer: A Winning Strategy for the Game of Twenty-One.* New York: Random House, 1962.

Toda, M., & Shuford, E. H., Jr. "Utility, Induced Utilities, and Small Worlds," *Behavioral Science* (1965), **10,** 238–254.

Torrance, E. P., & Ziller, R. C. "Risk and Life Experience: Development of a Scale for Measuring Risk-Taking Tendencies," USAF Personnel and Training Research Center, Research Report No. 57–23, V, 1957.

Van der Meer, H. C. "Decision-Making: The Influence of Probability Preference, Variance Preference and Expected Value on Strategy in Gambling," *Acta Psychologica* (1963), **21,** 231–259.

Wallach, M. A., & Kogan, N. "Sex Differences and Judgment Processes," *Journal of Personality* (1959), **27,** 555–564.

Wallach, M. A. & Kogan, N. "Aspects of Judgment and Decision Making: Interrelationships and Changes with Age," *Behavioral Science* (1961), **6,** 23–36.

Wykes, A. *The Complete Illustrated Guide to Gambling.* Garden City, N. Y.: Doubleday, 1964.

CHAPTER 6

Probability Learning

6.1 HISTORICAL INTRODUCTION

In this chapter we consider the large body of experimental and theoretical work concerned with the predictions people make about which random event of a set will occur on each of a series of trials. If P^A must predict which event will occur when the outcome is random, one might think he would predict the event that seems most probable to him. Thus, the topic would seem to be a sub-area of subjective probability in which P^A indicates the most probable event without indicating his judgments as to the probabilities of the various events. This was called qualitative probability in Chapter 3.

We might inquire, however, concerning why P^A should predict the most probable event; if he has no motive to do this, one could doubt that he would. One might postulate an intrinsic type of payoff to P^A if he predicts correctly, and some other lesser intrinsic payoff (punishment) for an incorrect prediction. With such an interpretation, we could set up a payoff matrix, with the possible choices P^A can make being the possible predictions. Seen in this light, a prediction is a kind of decision. We now can understand why P^A should predict the most probable event: this will maximize his expected payoff (Section 6.2 elaborates this idea).

When the predictions are viewed as decisions, then experimental results pose serious difficulties for decision theory, and the method of attacking these difficulties sheds considerable light on the nature of decision theory in the conceptualization of man. Here, also, we have a direct confrontation of decision theory and mathematical learning theory, and the working out of this confrontation illuminates the nature of mathematical methodology in psychology.

The term *probability learning,* which is often used to refer to the type of studies considered in this chapter, was apparently originated by Egon Brunswik (for example, Brunswik & Herma, 1951).[1] The situations to which the term

---

[1] "Probability learning" experiments were conducted in the 1930's, but the term did not come into use until the 1950's.

applies are viewed as generalizations of the usual learning situations in which a reward is coupled to a response in a regular and deterministic manner. In probability learning experiments, the reward is coupled to a response only probabilistically. This is a more realistic approximation to many learning situations encountered by man and animals (Tolman & Brunswik, 1935; Brunswik, 1939, 1943).

Although the term "probability learning" applies to both animal and human experimentation, the basic paradigm with humans requires P^A to "predict" which of a set of random events will occur on each of a series of trials, so the term *probability prediction* is often used in place of "probability learning." Since the area of probability learning is not primarily concerned with the learning of probabilities, as the term suggests, the alternate terminology may be less misleading.

The early history of experimentation in probability learning was traced by Jenkins and Stanley (1950) in their review of the area of "partial reinforcement." The ideas of partial reinforcement and probability learning are highly similar: both relax the experimental arrangement in which a reward is deterministically coupled to a particular response. Partial reinforcement, however, need not imply that the reward to a response be randomly determined. In classical conditioning experiments, for example, the reinforcement might be introduced on every other trial, or every third trial in a regular sequence (fixed-ratio reinforcement). There is nothing probable about what will happen on a trial. A rat in a Skinner box may only be rewarded once every five minutes at the most, regardless of how many responses he makes before that time interval is up (fixed-interval reinforcement). Here again, the relation between the response and reward is not deterministic, since a response may not evoke a reward, but neither is it probabilistic.

Partial reinforcement was employed in early conditioning experiments. Pavlov noted in a classical conditioning experiment[2] that he could omit the reinforcement (noxious stimulation) on some of the trials during learning without slowing the course of learning. During the 1930's Skinner and his colleagues made extensive use of partial reinforcement techniques. The germinal experimental papers in probability learning, however, were not published until 1939. Lloyd Humphreys (1939a) studied the effect of giving reinforcement (air-puff) in a classical eyelid conditioning experiment on only a random 50% of the trials, versus all trials for another group. Acquisition of the eyeblink response proceeded at the same rate for the two groups. During extinction, however, when the reinforcement was never given, the eyeblink response decreased faster for

---

[2] Classical conditioning is a procedure whereby a response normally evoked by an *unconditioned stimulus* (*reinforcement*) comes to be evoked by another stimulus which was initially ineffective. For example, salivation is normally evoked by food; but if a bell is rung before presenting food over a series of trials, the bell becomes a *conditioned stimulus* which can evoke salivation by itself.

the group with 100% reinforcement than for the group with 50% reinforcement. Humphreys interpreted these results to be inconsistent with a conditioning theory positing specific increments and decrements of excitatory strength with reinforcements and non-reinforcements, respectively. Instead, he followed the conceptualization of Tolman and Brunswik (1935) and postulated that the acquisition and extinction were related to the expectancy of the noxious stimulation (air-puff). According to Humphreys, the conditioned stimulus (light) is reacted to provided that the expectancy of the air-puff is high enough. During extinction, those Ss having 100% reinforcement quickly lose expectancy of air-puff because the change of conditions is so obvious. The other Ss, with 50% reinforcement originally, are slower to note the change, so the expectancy of air-puff decreases more slowly for them.

Humphreys' result and theory led him to perform the first study of human prediction of a Bernoulli binary series.[3] He set out to study the acquisition and extinction of expectancy directly using a situation analogous to classical conditioning (Humphreys, 1939b). His aim was to investigate the course of verbal expectancies in a situation similar to his classical conditioning experiment. At the beginning of a trial, a ready light came on. This was the analogue of the conditioned stimulus. The "conditioned response" was S's prediction that a second light would come on. The "reinforcement" (unconditioned stimulus) consisted of the actual appearance of the second light. Humphreys' experiment came to be called the "verbal conditioning" experiment (a term he didn't use). Comparison of the classical conditioning and verbal conditioning experiments can be summarized as follows:

	Classical Conditioning	Verbal Conditioning
Conditioned Stimulus	light comes on	ready light comes on
Unconditioned Stimulus (Reinforcement)	air-puff to eye	second light comes on
Conditioned Response	eyelid response	prediction of second light

During acquisition one group had 100% reinforcement (the second light always came on) and the other group had random 50% reinforcement. Each time the

---

[3] A Bernoulli binary series is a series of two discrete events with constant probabilities over trials. The event occurring on any trial is independent of events occurring on other trials in the series. An example is the series of heads and tails obtained by flipping a coin over successive trials.

The series used by Humphreys was not exactly Bernoulli, since the series was controlled for relative frequency of events within successive blocks of trials. This has been a common practice.

ready light came on commencing a trial, S wrote on a sheet of paper whether he expected the second light to come on or not for that trial. Then the light would or would not come on.

The verbal prediction responses had different properties from the eyelid responses. Whereas acquisition in the classical conditioning experiment was the same for the 50% and the 100% reinforcement groups, in the verbal conditioning experiment acquisition was markedly different: the 100% reinforcement group came rather quickly to expect the second light to come on for every trial, whereas Ss in the 50% group predicted the light would come on only about 50% of the time. Initial response levels for both groups in the verbal case were about 50% whereas they were lower for the classical case.

During "extinction" in the verbal case, the second light never came on. Although the 100% reinforcement group started extinction at a higher initial level of responding than the 50% group, it "extinguished" faster. This appears to be the main similarity between the results in the two experiments.

Note that in the 100% reinforcement group, Ss came to expect (predict) the reinforcement on 100% of the trials, and in the 50% reinforcement group, Ss came to expect reinforcement on 50% of the trials. For $X\%$ of reinforcement, would Ss come to expect reinforcement on $X\%$ of the trials? Humphreys published no conjectures about what would happen with other reinforcement percentages.

Grant, Hake, and Hornseth (1951) did extend the Humphreys "verbal conditioning" experiment (as they called it) to other reinforcement percentages. Different groups of Ss received 100%, 75%, 50%, 25%, and 0% reinforcement. There were 60 acquisition trials and 30 extinction trials. Figure 6.1 shows the results for acquisition and extinction. The authors noted that in the final block of acquisition trials, the mean probability (relative frequency) of "light to come on" predictions matched the reinforcement probability. They suggested that this is a general result which would be true of other reinforcement probabilities as well. The paper of Grant, Hake, and Hornseth is the source of the *probability matching generalization*, which states that for a series of Bernoulli trials, the prediction probabilities come to equal the reinforcement probabilities. Further research has shown that this generalization has definite limitations. This research, and accompanying theory, is the subject of Sections 6.4 and 6.5.

Note on terminology: In the early literature on probability learning, reinforcement was said to occur only when one of two possible events occurred, for example, "light on." This usage derived by analogy from the classical conditioning paradigm, as explained. During the 1950's, however, it became common to say that reinforcement occurred whichever event occurred, though the kind of reinforcement (for example, "light on" or "light not on") differed. We follow this newer usage, though it is not universal even today. In the early literature *nonreinforcement* was said to occur if the event identified with reinforcement did not occur. In some more recent research, however, S is sometimes not in-

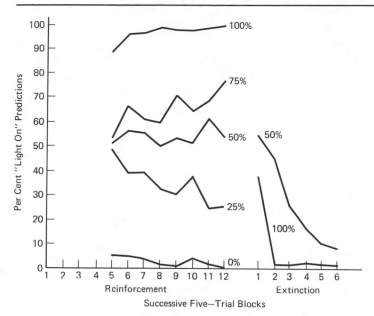

Figure 6.1. Percent "light on" predictions for reinforcement and extinction trials. The percentage of reinforcement of "light on" during the reinforcement trials is given next to each curve. The earlier reinforcement trials are omitted, since the curves become jumbled together. During extinction all groups received 0% reinforcement. The group trained on 100% reinforcement extinguished faster than the group trained on 50% reinforcement. Extinction curves for the 75% and 25% groups are omitted, but, except for the first block of trials, these curves were very close to the 50% curve. (From Grant, Hake, & Hornseth, 1951.)

formed at all regarding which event occurred, and the term *nonreinforcement* is used with respect to such trials. We follow this more recent usage. By our usage, to say that "reinforcement" occurred is synonomous with saying that *feedback* was given regarding the correct response. To say that "nonreinforcement" occurred is synonomous with saying that feedback was withheld.

6.2 DECISION THEORY AND PROBABILITY MATCHING

The probability matching generalization generated a good deal of interest, in large part because two areas of mathematical psychology had something to say about the result. Since probability matching is not the optimal strategy for maximizing the expected number of correct predictions, the results appeared to contradict a "decision theory" view of man. On the other hand, the probability matching result was in perfect accord with some mathematical learning theory models.

Let H be the higher probability event in a Bernoulli binary series, and let L be the lower probability event. $\pi = p(H)$. Let h be a prediction by P^A that H will occur, and l be a prediction that L will occur. For each choice h, the probability of being correct is π, whereas for each choice l, the probability is $1 - \pi$. By definition π is greater than 0.5, since it is the probability of the more probable event: it follows that $1 - \pi$ is less than 0.5.[4] Then the probability of being correct for any trial in the series is greater for response h than for response l. *The strategy for maximizing the expected number of correct predictions is to choose h on every trial.* This strategy is often called the *optimal* or

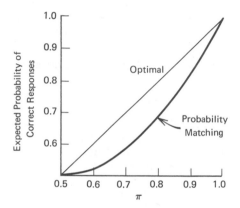

Figure 6.2. The expected probability of correct responses for the optimal strategy and probability matching as a function of π.

rational strategy, though, as we shall see, the notion that choosing so as to maximize the expected number of correct choices is "optimal" or "rational" is open to question. In any case, unless otherwise qualified, by *optimal strategy* we shall mean the one giving the maximum expected number of correct choices. It should be noted that the optimal strategy need not always give a higher number of correct predictions than an alternative strategy. By chance, P^A could get more correct predictions with another strategy. But the optimal strategy maximizes the expected value of the random variable, "number of correct predictions."

The expected probability of success on a trial with a probability matching strategy is $\pi^2 + (1 - \pi)^2$. This is less than the probability of success with the optimal strategy, π, for every $\pi > 0.5$. Figure 6.2 shows the expected probability of success for the optimal strategy and probability matching as a function of π.

Note on terminology: The term *correct* is used in two senses in the probability

---

[4] When we consider series with more than two events, H is still the most probable event, but $p(H) = \pi$ need not be greater than 0.5.

prediction literature. Sometimes, "correct prediction" means the prediction corresponding to the event actually occurring on a trial; in this sense, h is a correct prediction on a trial if and only if H happens to occur on the trial, and l is a correct prediction if and only if L happens to occur on the trial. "Correct" was used in this sense in the preceding paragraphs. Some authors, however, refer to h as the "correct" response and l as the incorrect response, regardless of whether H or L happens to occur on a trial, because h is the choice P^A "should" make (i.e., the optimal choice). To distinguish the two senses, we use *empirically correct* for the former sense, and *strategically correct* for the latter. Unless qualified, we use "correct" for "empirically correct." An S's performance is usually scored according to his percentage of strategically correct choices.

The preceding discussion of optimal strategy related only to the probability of a correct choice. There was no analysis of a payoff matrix with some decision principle. It is possible to justify the same optimal strategy, however, with a payoff matrix analysis. Suppose the value to P^A of a correct prediction is 1, and the value for an incorrect prediction is some lesser amount, say, 0. Then we have the following payoff matrix for P^A's decision situation on a trial:

	H	L
h	1	0
l	0	1

$$EV_h = \pi \cdot 1 + (1 - \pi) \cdot 0 = \pi \qquad (6.1a)$$
$$EV_l = \pi \cdot 0 + (1 - \pi) \cdot 1 = 1 - \pi \qquad (6.1b)$$

$EV_h > EV_l$ if and only if $\pi > 1 - \pi$, but the latter condition is true by assumption. By the EV principle, which would seem to be appropriate here, h is the optimal choice on a trial. Since the payoff matrix remains the same over successive trials, h is the optimal choice for every trial, and the optimal strategy is to choose h on every trial.

When the values are given as 1 and 0 for correct and incorrect predictions, the EV for either choice is equal to the probability of being correct for that choice. But the particular numbers chosen to represent the values of "correct" and "incorrect" have no bearing on the conclusion about optimal strategy. Any other numbers would yield the same conclusion (as long as the value for "correct" is greater than the value for "incorrect"). For present purposes there is no need to be concerned with problems of utility measurement, since with only two different consequences, utilities can be assigned arbitrarily (preserving relative preference).

In view of the preceding analysis, the probability matching result appears to indicate a deviation from "rational" behavior. Even if an S had a subjective probability different from the objective one used for the analysis, he should still make the same choice on each trial, assuming that the subjective probability remains constant over trials, as the objective probability does. Deviation of subjective probability from objective probability could require that P^A choose l, but then l would have to be chosen on every trial. Likewise, even if the utility of a "correct" or an "incorrect" consequence differed, depending on whether the choice were h or l, consistency would be required in choices across trials.

Are we to conclude, then, that man is irrational? Not unless we wish to—for one can always find some way to rationalize observed behavior, if one wishes. Flood (1954) asserted that Ss do not recognize the Bernoulli sequence as random, but if they did, they would choose optimally (some relevant evidence is presented in Section 6.4). In other words, man chooses optimally within the constraints of his information-processing capabilities. Simon (1956) extended the idea and combined it with the minimax regret decision principle to show how probability matching could be seen as optimal, but his explanation seems contrived. Siegel (1959) rationalized choice variation by assuming that P^A has a utility for varying his choices in addition to a payoff utility (see Section 6.5).

Rather than concerning themselves with the issue of man's "rationality," mathematical learning theorists attempted to explain probability matching as the natural result of a learning process. We consider this approach next.

6.3 MATHEMATICAL LEARNING THEORY FOR PROBABILITY PREDICTION

At about the same time as the probability matching generalization was formulated—the early 1950's—mathematical learning theory was entering a period of vigorous expansion. Mathematical learning theory readily accounted for probability matching, and the conjunction of the experimental findings with the mathematical approach generated considerable interest. Since that time, "decision theory" has often been pitted against "mathematical learning theory" for various kinds of experiments. Because mathematical learning theory has been so important as a contender to decision theory, we present a brief introduction to it. Detailed accounts are given by Bush and Mosteller (1955), Estes (1959), Suppes and Atkinson (1960), Sternberg (1963), Atkinson and Estes (1963), Atkinson, Bower, and Crothers (1965), and Neimark and Estes (1967).

We consider two general approaches, *mathematical operator* and *stimulus sampling*. The *mathematical operator* approach works like this: Some mathematical function is hypothesized which transforms the probability of a particular response when a particular reinforcement occurs. Best known is the *linear operator model*. If the probability of a particular response, say h, on trial n is p_n and reinforcement k occurs, then the probability of h on trial $n + 1$ is

$$p_{n+1} = \alpha_k p_n + (1 - \alpha_k)\lambda_k, \tag{6.2}$$

where α_k and λ_k are constants independent of p_n.[5] For the two-alternative experiment we have been discussing, k has two different values. When one reinforcement occurs (say, H), p_n is transformed to p_{n+1} according to Equation 6.2, with constants α_1 and λ_1; when L occurs, constants α_2 and λ_2 apply. When H occurs on trial n, the constants are such that $p_{n+1} > p_n$, and when L occurs, the different constants are such than $p_{n+1} < p_n$. If $\pi = 0.75$, then on the average there will be three increments of p to one decrement. But the decrement is larger than an increment, so at asymptote, the mean value of p equals 0.75. Likewise, $p = \pi$ for any π. The linear operator approach is particularly associated with Bush and Mosteller (1955).

In the *stimulus sampling* approach, the "stimulus" (or, more generally, the total stimulating situation) is represented by a number N of discrete *elements*. On a trial, certain of the elements are *sampled;* only the sampled elements bear on the response probabilities for S for that trial. Various assumptions have been made about the sampling process, leading to different classes of models. Sometimes it is assumed that the *probability* that an element is sampled is fixed, and sometimes it is assumed that the *number* of elements sampled on a trial is fixed.

Each element exists in (is *conditioned* to) one of a number of states corresponding to the possible reinforcements.[6] The response probability on a trial for h, say, equals the proportion of sampled elements in state H. For example, suppose the stimulating situation in a probability learning experiment could be represented by five elements, and suppose three elements were sampled on a trial. If two of the elements sampled were conditioned to H and one to L, then $p(h)$ *for that trial* would be 2/3. Had different elements been sampled, a different probability might exist.

Learning takes place because reinforcement can change the states of the *sampled* elements. For example, if the reinforcement were H, the sampled element in state L would be changed to state H (or, in some models, change of state occurs only with some probability). The larger the probability of reinforcement H, the higher the average proportion of elements conditioned to H, and the higher the mean $p(h)$ across trials. For some of the simpler stimulus sampling models, the mean $p(h)$ across trials equals π, the probability of reinforcement H; i.e., the models account for probability matching.

The stimulus sampling approach traces to papers by Estes (1950) and Estes and Burke (1953). The language of the theory suggests that the "stimulus elements" might be identified with specific aspects of S's environment or his sensory mechanisms. In practice, however, such identification is seldom attempted. The number of elements representing a situation, the number sampled, and other

---

[5] α is Greek alpha; λ is Greek lambda.
[6] In some models elements may exist in a "neutral" state, even if "nonreinforcement" never terminates a trial. "Neutral states" are sometimes assumed to characterize elements at the beginning of the learning session.

assumptions are typically chosen with regard to mathematical simplicity and accuracy of the model in accounting for observed behavior, rather than by any apparent correspondence of the elements to impinging sensation.

"Mathematical learning theory" models have by now been applied to such a wide variety of tasks that it is, perhaps, just as well to refer to this body of work as "stochastic theory" or "stochastic modeling." For example, stochastic models have been constructed for signal detection (see Section 7.7) and for interpersonal interaction (Section 9.1). Originally, mathematical learning theory seemed to enjoy the upper hand over decision theory for dealing with probability learning. As we noted, however, decision theory can be altered to be compatible with probability matching. In addition, subsequent empirical research, which we consider next, demonstrated that probability learning is not an invariable result, so any theory requiring it is severely limited. As we shall see in Section 6.5, both decision theory and mathematical learning theory have attempted to accommodate the new findings. "Mathematical learning theory," like "decision theory," makes no flat predictions on the basis of which it stands or falls. Specific models make flat predictions, but if the predictions turn out to be false, it is the model which is rejected (or accepted merely because a preferable model is lacking): mathematical learning theory per se is not subject to rejection on empirical grounds.

6.4 EXPERIMENTAL VARIABLES AFFECTING $p(h)$

The probability matching generalization has been confirmed, or approximately so, in many experiments. Nonetheless, it is clear by now that $p(h)$ is subject to experimental conditions: $p(h)$ does not invariably equal π. We now consider experimental variables affecting $p(h)$.

Before proceeding, we should note that most discussions of $p(h)$ have concerned the mean value across all Ss in a particular experimental condition. Even if mean $p(h)$ equals π, it does not imply that all the individual Ss probability match—indeed, it could be that none do. It is quite clear that individual differences in $p(h)$ exist. Models predicting probability matching ostensibly apply to individual Ss, however, so the common tendency to judge models by mean $p(h)$ is somewhat misleading. In accordance with common practice, the forthcoming discussion primarily deals with mean $p(h)$, though individual levels are occasionally considered.

Number of Trials

Typically, $p(h)$ changes from the beginning of an experiment to the end. Discussions of $p(h)$ and comparisons of $p(h)$ usually concern the level occurring at "asymptote," i.e., after a stable value for $p(h)$ obtains. However, in many, if not all, of the experiments apparently supporting the probability matching generalization, it is doubtful that asymptote was reached. For instance, it surely was not reached in the experiment of Grant, Hake, and Hornseth (1951) giving rise to the generalization (see Figure 6.1, in particular for the 75% and 25% reinforcement groups).

Present evidence strongly suggests that when probability matching appears to hold for experiments using only about up to 250 trials, with additional trials $p(h)$ would exceed π. Estes (1962a) analyzed six experiments which used from 300 to 450 trials; the mean response probability was 0.02 higher than the mean π of 0.72. Edwards (1961a) used 1000 trials; in the last 80 trials, 64 of 80 Ss had $p(h)$ greater than π (but only 7 Ss chose h *exclusively* in the final block of 80 trials). If the experiment had been run for only 200 trials, probability matching would have been confirmed.

So how many trials are necessary to reach asymptote? The only general answer is that one can never be sure that asymptote has been reached. For a while, the reputed number of trials necessary in probability learning experiments escalated from 75, to 150, to 250, to 400 or more. No limit can be given, however. Although Edwards (1961a) apparently felt his Ss had reached asymptote somewhere over 500 trials, my own impression from his graphs is that $p(h)$ was still increasing at the end of the experiment for some groups. Derks (1962) found that $p(h)$ increased steadily over 1000 trials, and asymptote had apparently not yet been reached. Beach and Shoenberger (1965) found that $p(h)$ increased throughout 1500 trials, and had not, apparently, stabilized by the end.[7]

Although $p(h)$ has seemed to be stable from about 200 trials upwards (for several hundred more) in some experiments, a reported $p(h)$ value should not be thought of as an asymptotic level, but as the value relating to the trial numbers over which the estimate was made.

Number of Events

A Bernoulli series may have more than two possible outcomes, and in some experiments S has been required to predict from among more than two possibilities. Let H be the highest probability event and $\pi = p(H)$, as before; but with more than two events, π need not exceed 0.5.

It has been reported for a number of experiments that for a given π, the larger the number of alternative events, the higher is $p(h)$. For example, Gardner (1958) found that for $\pi = 0.7$, and with 1, 2, 4, or 7 equally probable alternatives to H, $p(h)$ was 0.73, 0.75, 0.81, and 0.83 respectively. A similar increment in $p(h)$ occurred for $\pi = 0.6$. (The values of $p(h)$ were for trials 281–420; it appeared that $p(h)$ values were still increasing at the end of the experiment.) Similar findings were reported by Gardner (1957) and by Cotton and Rechtschaffen (1958). The following papers reported $p(h)$ exceeding π in series with more than two events, but they had no control groups with only two events for comparison: McCormack (1959), Swensson (1965), Jones (1961), and

---

[7] We should note that this was in a ten-event prediction task, with $\pi = 0.25$.

Beach and Shoenberger (1965). Such overshooting of π has not always occurred, particularly for three-event series (Neimark, 1956; Gardner, 1958; Jones, 1961; Little, Brackbill, & Kassel, 1962). This may be due to an insufficient number of trials, to population differences, or to procedural differences.

In the preceding experiments, increase in the number of possible outcomes was accompanied by an increase in the number of possible predictions. It is possible, however, to increase either quantity singly. One can increase the number of events while keeping the number of possible responses at two by requiring S to predict only "H" or "not H." Using this technique, Gardner and Forsythe (1961) found no effect on $p(h)$ of the number of events. (Also, see Jones (1961).)

Increase in the number of response categories can be effected while keeping the number of events constant by giving S response alternatives with corresponding events that actually never occur. Using this technique, Gardner (1961) found a small increase in $p(h)$ with an increase in the number of response alternatives, but it appears that neither increase in the number of response categories nor events taken singly can account for their joint effects on $p(h)$.

Payoff

The payoffs in a probability prediction task might be only *intrinsic,* for example, the satisfaction of being correct. Or, we could include *extrinsic* rewards, such as money, in the payoff matrix. How do extrinsic rewards affect $p(h)$? A large number of relevant experiments have been performed.

Siegel and Goldstein (1959) had Ss predict which of two lights would come on, with $\pi = 0.75$. Three groups of Ss were used. Group I had usual probability prediction instructions with no payoffs. Group II received 5¢ for each correct prediction, but had no gain or loss for incorrect predictions. Group III had a 5¢ gain for each correct prediction, and, in addition, a 5¢ loss for each incorrect prediction. During the final 20 of 300 trials, the $p(h)$ values for the three groups were 0.75, 0.86, and 0.95, respectively.

Derks (1962) found the same ordering as Siegel and Goldstein for the conditions no-payoff, reward, and reward-loss, but the differences were not statistically significant. Myers, Fort, Katz, and Suydam (1963) found an increase in $p(h)$ for reward-loss groups over no-payoff groups for π series of 0.6, 0.7, and 0.8. Nagamachi (1960) found that adding punishment (buzzer-shock) for an incorrect response increased $p(h)$ over that for a control group, showing that loss alone can affect $p(h)$, as well as reward alone. Swensson (1965), in a three-event task with $\pi = 0.6$, found that 5¢ reward and loss gave a $p(h)$ of 0.77, versus 0.67 for a control group (trials 121–160).

Increase in $p(h)$ going from no payoff to some payoff is a more reliable effect than in going from a low payoff to a higher payoff, for example, by multiplying a symmetrical payoff matrix by a constant. Myers *et al.* (1963) found that the increase in reward and loss from 1¢ to 10¢ (different groups) increased $p(h)$

for the $\pi = 0.6$ Ss, only slightly for the 0.8 Ss, and not at all for the 0.7 Ss. Brackbill, Kappy, and Starr (1962) found with children (2nd grade) that $p(h)$ for reward groups was about 0.8, compared to 0.7 for a no-payoff group. The amount of reward, however, had relatively little effect. Suppes and Atkinson (1960, Chapter 10) found some increase in going from 5¢ reward and loss to 10¢ $(p(h)$ of 0.64 and 0.69 when $\pi = 0.6)$.

It is not necessary that the extrinsic rewards for "correct" be the same for different choices, and likewise for the incorrect consequences. In a two-event probability learning task, there are four possible consequences, so the payoff matrix can have four independent monetary amounts. Actually, some such experiments were discussed in Section 5.6. In our present symbolism, $p(h)$ is strength of preference for one gamble (prediction) over the other. Recall from Section 5.6 that expected regret ratio appeared to be a more powerful determinant of $p(h)$ than expected value difference. Multiplicative increments in the payoff matrix, such as those discussed in the preceding paragraph, increase expected value difference, but leave expected regret ratio unchanged. The weak and inconsistent effects noted for such multiplicative increments confirms the conclusions of Section 5.6.

Although multiplicative differences in the payoff matrices have little effect on $p(h)$ when the matrices apply to different Ss, a notable effect can be found if the payoff matrix is changed for a group of Ss partway through the experiment. A multiplicative decrement in payoffs lowers $p(h)$. This is known as a *negative contrast effect,* since it is the contrast between the two payoff matrices that is the determinant of the lowered $p(h)$. A multiplicative increase in the payoff matrix does not induce a positive contrast effect—Ss remain at the same level (Swensson, 1965; Schnorr & Myers, 1967; Castellan, 1969).

In an attempt to induce optimal responding, Das (1961) told Ss that only correct predictions of H would count for imaginary points—correct predictions of L would not count for any points. Even this payoff scheme didn't induce complete optimality.

Instructions

The payoff matrix itself can be considered to be instructions to S (Edwards, 1961b). The present subsection concerns the effects on $p(h)$ of other kinds of instructions (verbal explanations).

A number of authors have discussed probability matching in relation to the perception of randomness by S. Flood (1954) suggested that Ss do not understand the random nature of the outcome series (typically, they are not told it is random), and that the performance might very well be different (optimal, perhaps) if they did understand the series. Goodnow (1955) indicated a similar view. She felt that Ss take a "problem-solving" approach to the probability prediction task, whereas a "gambling" approach would yield more correct predictions. If S sees the task as "problem solving," then: (a) he believes there is some strategy that will enable him to predict correctly on 100% of the trials, which, in turn, implies that both responses will have to be used, and (b) he believes he should keep searching for a solution, since once the solution is found, the number of previous failures becomes unimportant. On the other hand, if S sees the task as "gambling," then: (a) he believes that no strategy will enable him to predict correctly on 100% of the trials, so there is no need to use both responses, and (b) he perceives his total success to depend on gains and losses all throughout his performance, not just at the end. In short, Goodnow believed that the "gambling" outlook would lead S to perform more optimally than the "problem-solving" outlook; she did not, however, expect that the "gambling" outlook would lead to 100% optimal responding, since this method of responding is boring and since some Ss may believe they can devise gambling schemes to beat the odds.

To test her ideas, Goodnow had two groups perform ostensibly different tasks, though the series of outcomes had the same pattern of H and L. The "problem-solving" group was told that they were participating in a learning experiment, and were led to believe that a solution would yield 100% correct responses. The "gambling" group used a kind of slot machine; on each trial an S placed a chip in the machine, and pressed one of two buttons. He then found out whether he "won" (was correct) or did not win (was incorrect). Ss were told they were participating in an experiment on gambling, and that they would be paid according to the numbers of wins and losses. For the last 20 of 120 trials, when π was 0.7, $p(h)$ was 0.66 for the problem-solving group and 0.82 for the gambling group; when π was 0.9, $p(h)$ was 0.96 for both groups.

Considering that there is not too much room for improvement when $\pi = 0.9$, Goodnow's ideas would seem to have some validity. But there were so many differences between the groups that the source of the effect is unclear. For one thing, we have already seen that the inclusion of extrinsic payoffs can increase $p(h)$, even if the task and instructions are otherwise the same. For example, the tasks were very different, quite apart from payoffs and instructions, and this might have caused some differences (task effects are discussed in the succeeding subsection). Then again, verbal instructions inducing a problem-solving or gambling outlook might have caused differences in $p(h)$. To verify this, verbal instructions alone should be varied, while task and payoffs are kept constant. Some such experiments have been conducted.

McCracken, Osterhout, and Voss (1962) used a variety of instructions. Their instructions (2) and (3) were similar to the "problem-solving" and "gambling" instructions. Instruction (2) told Ss to try to predict each outcome correctly. Instruction (3) told Ss that there was no pattern to discover, that they should get as many correct as possible, and that they might not be able to get every prediction correct. There was no difference for the two groups; both reached about the probability matching level of 0.7 in 140 trials. The experiments later tried a more emphatic version of instruction (3): instruction (4) told Ss to ignore a trial-by-trial approach, since there was no pattern or system to the events, and that Ss could not get all predictions correct. This instruction increased $p(h)$ to about 0.9.

Instructions similar to "problem-solving" versus "gambling" have been employed in a variety of probabilistic tasks, and have not succeeded in producing different levels of optimal responding (Anderson & Grant, 1957; Lee & Janke, 1965; Edwards, 1962, mentioned unpublished results; Van der Meer, 1960). Nor is there unanimity concerning what the relative effects of these instructions should be. Van der Meer (1960), in contrast to Goodnow, hypothesized that Ss should perform more optimally with the problem-solving instructions.

Some experimenters, thinking that Ss misperceive the trial-by-trial stability of π, have emphasized this stability with instructions. Tversky and Edwards (1966) told Ss either that the event probability was stationary or that the probability would vary over trials in an unspecified way. Actually, the probability was stationary and equal for both groups. $p(h)$ was higher for the group with "stationary" instructions, but this group by no means performed optimally.

McCracken et al. (1962) used one of the more extreme instructions possible in an attempt to induce optimal responding. One group of Ss was told that they should always predict the more frequent event, since there was no pattern or sequence and this would yield the maximum number of correct predictions. By the end of 140 trials, the Ss had a $p(h)$ of about 0.96, versus a π of 0.7. With these instructions, Ss have only to perceive which event occurs more frequently. Indeed, Neimark and Shuford (1959) required Ss to estimate the overall proportion of H events, and found they could do this quite accurately. They also found that $p(h)$ was enhanced when Ss had to make overall proportion estimates as well as making predictions.

Galanter and Smith (1958) told Ss that the prediction on a specific trial would also have to apply for a given number of subsequent trials. This enhanced $p(h)$ somewhat (also see McCracken et al., 1962).

Task

Under "task" we consider the physical features of probability prediction experiments. Ss have been asked to predict a wide variety of events, for example, lights, colors, words, binary symbols (1,0), playing cards, pictures, and others. Experimenters typically use only one type of event, so it is not known whether type of event affects $p(h)$. For about the same instructions, payoffs, number of trials, π, and number of events, results seem similar, however, so type of event is presumably not very critical.

Wykoff and Sidowski (1955) had Ss perform a task that, on the face of it, did not appear to be a prediction experiment, but rather a motor skills task. A target would sweep clockwise or counter-clockwise, with specified probabilities. The task for S was to stay on target for a given period of time. If the time required for S to be on target was high enough, successful completion required that S anticipate from which direction the target would come. For the last 120 (of 320) trials, probability of anticipation of the high probability side was 0.93 (versus $\pi = 0.75$) or 0.78 (versus $\pi = 0.6$). Perhaps the skill set was critical here.

A number of experimenters have presented the same sequence in two different ways: one way suggested that the outcomes were random and that S could not learn to be correct on each trial, and the other way allowed S to infer that he could so learn. Here "gambling" and "problem-solving" outlooks were induced by the nature of the task, however, and not by verbalized instructions.

The basic idea of the "gambling" task is to allow S to see the random mechanism that generates the outcomes, and let him observe the generation of random outcomes. In contrast, for the problem-solving task, a sequence of outcomes is prepared ahead of time, and S is not told how they were generated. (An intermediate case would be to tell S the events were generated randomly, but not let him see the generation.) For example, Rubinstein (1959) had Ss predict whether the Jack or King would come up from a deck consisting of two Kings and one Jack. The deck was shuffled before each trial in front of the Ss. This group had a $p(h)$ higher than the control groups with prearranged sequences of colors ($p(h) = 0.78$ versus $\pi = 0.67$, 126 trials).

Morse and Runquist (1960) had Ss predict whether a rod dropped from a vertical position onto the floor would end in a position crossing the floorboard lines or not. Then the same Ss had to predict which of two lights would come on. The same sequence for the lights was used that had happened to occur with the rod. Ss performed more optimally with the rod task. Empirical probability of H in the rod task was about 0.65, whereas $p(h)$ was about 0.8. In the light prediction task, probability matching occurred.

Nies (1962) showed S a box containing marbles of two colors. He had to guess which color would come out when the marbles were shaken in the box, and one was allowed to fall out into a trough. The marble was replaced for the next trial. Actually, an experimental confederate stated an "observed" color according to a predetermined random sequence so that a control group could be employed using the same sequence, but without an apparent random device present. Whereas the control group came to about a probability matching $p(h)$ of 0.7 after 200 trials, $p(h)$ for the Ss who saw the marbles drawn from the box was 0.77. Nies also examined effects of different instructions on the experimental group. Ss who were told the ratio of colors had a $p(h)$ of about 0.77 from the start, whereas Ss who were simply asked to predict, or were told that marbles rolled out in a definite pattern, approached this level gradually.

Peterson and Ulehla (1965) used a technique which was free from certain possible flaws in the preceding work. A single S threw a die with four black and two white sides ($\pi = 0.67$). He predicted each outcome. A paired S later saw the same outcome sequence of black and white on cards in an obviously prearranged sequence, and had to predict this sequence. Many such pairs of Ss were used, with, of course, different sequences. During the third 100 trials, Ss who threw the die had a $p(h)$ of about 0.88, whereas the control group had a $p(h)$ of 0.78. (Even this was above the π of 0.67, possibly because of the monetary payoffs employed for correct predictions.)

In summary, it seems clear that Ss who can see for themselves that the outcomes are being generated by a random mechanism perform more nearly optimally than Ss who have sequences generated in an unknown manner. However, this increment in optimal performance only moves Ss about one-fourth to one-half the distance to complete optimal performance.

6.5   THEORY RELATING TO *p(h)* VARIATIONS

When it became clear that (mean) $p(h)$ was subject to systematic variations, mathematical theories predicting only probability matching were seen to be inadequate. Both "stochastic" and decision theory models were developed that allowed for systematic variations in $p(h)$.

Richard Atkinson (1962) developed a "weak-strong" stimulus sampling model, which allows $p(h)$ to vary over a wide range. The original twist in this model is that the conditioning of an element can be in either a "weak" or "strong" state. On each trial exactly one element of N is sampled. If the sampled element is conditioned weakly to response l, reinforcement of l either leaves the conditioning unchanged, or, with some probability, changes it to the strong state. Reinforcement of h would either leave the conditioning in the weak l state, or, with some probability, change it to the weak state of h. And so forth. The probabilities for state changes are called "conditioning parameters," and depending on their values, the model predicts different levels for $p(h)$. The model has been applied with apparent good success to the data of several experiments (Myers & Atkinson, 1964).

Frank Restle (1961, Chapter 6) developed what he called "schema theory," or what has been referred to as "runs" theory. The theory encompasses two central ideas. One is that S pays attention to runs of the same event, and that he stores the runs as such in memory. The second idea is that S searches in his memory and finds a run at least as long as that current run. S's present response is based on what that remembered run did.[8] Suppose, for example, that the events S has seen most recently have been   . . . *LHHH*. A run of three H's is current. S searches his memory. If he comes up with a run of three H's, he would predict l, since a change of event occurred after the three similar

---

[8] Overall's (1960) "cognitive probability" model is rather similar. This model also assumes that behavior depends on memory for the outcome in a previous similar situation.

events. If a longer run is remembered, he would predict h. Longer runs are more salient than shorter ones in the memory. Using these ideas, Restle derived a formula for the prediction probability for any given current length of run. His theory implies that Ss will do slightly better than probability matching with two choices, and better still with more than two choices. It has been successful with some other experimental findings as well. It does not, however, predict varying levels of $p(h)$ depending on motivational conditions or instructions. It has had certain other difficulties as well (Restle, 1966; Rose and Vitz, 1966).

Sidney Siegel (1959) developed a decision theory model which incorporates the following hypotheses: (1) it is boring for P^A to make the same response on trial after trial; (2) P^A nonetheless does value being correct in his predictions, the more so when monetary reward depends on it; (3) the preceding two motivations are balanced with one another so as to produce a maximum of overall satisfaction. Siegel's model can be seen as an attempt to save decision theory, in spite of data showing approximate probability matching, as well as an attempt to explain how certain variations in the prediction task can affect $p(h)$.

He actually developed several models. We discuss his so-called Model I.

> *Symbolism:*
> $p = p(h)$
> $a =$ marginal utility of a correct prediction
> $b =$ marginal utility of varying one's responses

Siegel assumed there are two components to P^A's total expected utility: expected utility of a correct prediction, u_r, and utility for varying one's responses, u_v. P^A has all possible p values from 0 to 1 for his choice set, and is assumed to choose the p value maximizing the total expected utility,

$$u(p) = u_r + u_v \tag{6.3}$$

u_r is proportional to the probability of making a correct prediction, $\pi p + (1 - \pi) \cdot (1 - p)$. u_v is proportional to the following formula: $p(1 - p)$. This formula was chosen because it is maximum when $p = 1/2$ (when responses vary the most), is zero when p is equal to 0 or 1 (when there is no response variability), and is symmetric around $p = 1/2$. The symmetry feature seems desirable since it seems reasonable that the value of response variability be the same when $p = 0.7$ as when $p = 0.3$; the same division of responses into two types holds for either case.

The marginal utilities, a and b, are the relative weights which P^A places on being correct and varying his responses, respectively. Then the total expected utility

$$
\begin{aligned}
u(p) &= u_r + u_v \\
&= a[\pi p + (1 - \pi)(1 - p)] + bp(1 - p)
\end{aligned} \tag{6.4}
$$

The maximum total expected utility is obtained when

$$p = \frac{a(2\pi - 1)}{2b} + \frac{1}{2},$$

or, letting $\alpha = a/b$, when

$$p = \alpha \left(\pi - \frac{1}{2} \right) + \frac{1}{2} \tag{6.5}$$

The particular value of p that P^A should choose, given π, is a function of α. This value of p can range anywhere from 0.5 (when $\alpha = 0$, i.e., when only the utility of variability has any importance to P^A) to 1 when $\alpha \geq 1/(2\pi - 1)$. Probability matching would occur for $\alpha = 1$. Figure 6.3 illustrates how u_r and u_v vary as a function of p. The optimal strategy is that p maximizing the sum of u_r and u_v.

Does the model work? As a qualitative test of the notion of utility of variability, Siegel, Siegel, and Andrews (1964, Chapter 4) performed an experiment in which, by the use of a mirror on some trials, S could make the optimal prediction with the left or right hand on different trials, versus the usual condition where the optimal prediction would be made with only one hand for every trial. The mirror condition, which allowed S to cater to his yearning to vary his responding (right and left hand) while continuing to choose h, did indeed increase $p(h)$ to about 0.82, versus 0.75 for the control group.

Siegel aspired, however, that the model make precise quantitative predictions

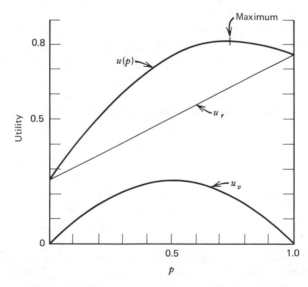

Figure 6.3. Utility of variability (u_v), utility for being correct (u_r), and total utility $(u(p))$ as a function of p for Siegel's Model I. For the graphs shown, $\pi = 0.75$, $a = 1$, and $b = 1$; the total utility is a maximum when $p = 0.75$. (From Restle, 1964.)

about p. If one takes the p from a single experiment, one can estimate α from Equation 6.5:

$$\alpha = \frac{p - 1/2}{\pi - 1/2} \tag{6.6}$$

Such calculations can always be performed regardless of p, and prove nothing about the quantitative validity of the model. If one assumes further, however, that α is a quantity independent of π, then one can run a new group of Ss, with a new π but the same payoff conditions and instructions, and predict the p value for the new group, using α and Equation 6.5.

Siegel *et al.* (1964) reported experiments of this type. The quantitative predictions were confirmed to a highly satisfactory degree. Extensions of Model I allowed for more than two alternatives and for unequal rewards depending on which response was correctly made. The same general technique of verification was employed, using parameter estimates from one π condition to estimate p for another π condition. The results were again highly satisfactory.

Not all results have accorded so well with the model, however. Little, Brackbill, and Kassel (1962) found that different π levels resulted in different estimated α's. Messick (1965) gave Ss in one group only one possible response for predicting each of two possible events, and gave another group five equivalent ways of predicting each event. According to Siegel's way of reasoning, one might suppose that S could satisfy his need for response variability by using the five equivalent responses associated with H. This would imply that more optimal responses would occur when five equivalent responses were allowed, but such was not observed. Restle (1964) expressed concern that Ss generally perseverate their responses, in comparison to a random sequence, and that if there were a utility for response variation, this would not be expected. One could also add that in studies of probabilistic discrimination learning (Section 6.11) a good deal of response variation can occur consistent with an optimal strategy, yet optimal responding does not typically occur. In addition, stochastic modelers might note that Siegel's model does not deal with sequential aspects of choice. In brief, although Siegel's attempt to rationalize observed behavior in probability prediction tasks was clever and instructive, one cannot conclude that he succeeded.

It cannot be said that either mathematical learning theory or decision theory has proved to be highly successful in accounting for the rich and often bewildering complexity of the experimental data. Neither "theory" has invalidated the other, nor is this likely to happen. It is entirely credible that in the future the two "theories" may be perceived to be more similar and less irreconcilable than they have been. Both theories will have to accept the same well-established empirical findings, and in many cases the different interpretations of the results may turn out to be merely terminological. For example, Siegel's utility of variability model is a special case of Luce's stochastic "beta model." Data confirming

Siegel's model could be equally well interpreted as supporting the beta model (Luce & Suppes, 1965, pp. 374–375). Siegel (1961) and Radlow (1964, p. 273) broached the possibility of modeling subjective probability revisions in terms of stimulus sampling theory, and Myers and Atkinson (1962) described some parameters of a stochastic model in terms of the decision theory concept of regret.

6.6 THE STRUCTURE OF RESPONSE SEQUENCES

> "Of course, after the red has come up ten times in a row, hardly anyone will persist in betting on it."
>
> (from *The Gambler* by Dostoevsky[9])

> "I have seen men, ardently desirous of having a son, who could learn only with anxiety of the births of boys in the month when they expected to become fathers. Imagining that the ratio of these births to those of girls ought to be the same at the end of each month, they judged that the boys already born would render more probable the births next of girls."
>
> (from *A Philosophical Essay on Probabilities* by Laplace (1951, p. 162))

The first quotation refers to the gambling game of roulette. It refers to the belief that people expect the black to come up after a long run of red. Actually, assuming that the roulette wheel operates as it is designed to, the probability of red or black remains the same regardless of any combinations of previous outcomes. The second quotation illustrates a similar fallacy in thinking. The sex of a child is actually independent of the sex of previous children. The outcomes, red and black, and the outcomes, male or female, are Bernoulli series. We might wonder whether the fallacies attributed to people in the above sources would exist in predictions of Bernoulli series in the laboratory.

Murray Jarvik (1951) examined the predictions made by Ss in a two-event probability prediction experiment, and he found that the runs of past events do indeed affect future prediction. The exact technique by which runs are analyzed varies somewhat from experimenter to experimenter. The technique we explain is not precisely what Jarvik did, but it is very close. On each trial, as S is about to predict, there has just been a run of zero, one, two, three or more H events in a row. To say that there has been a run of zero H events means that the immediately preceding event was L. To say that there has been a run of two H events means that the preceding three events were LHH. Each trial, then, can be classified according to the run length of the preceding H events.

---

[9] F. Dostoevsky, *The Gambler*, translated by A. R. MacAndrew, Bantam Books, New York, 1964, p. 146 (a novel written in 1866).

Then $p(h)$ can be calculated separately for each class of trials. Jarvik found that the $p(h)$ values for different classes differed. $p(h)$ was higher after a run of one H event than after a run of zero H events (after an L). However, $p(h)$ became lower again after a run of two H events, and for longer runs yet, became lower yet.

Similar effects have by now been found by many experimenters. Most work has been done with college students, but the effect was also found in grade school children (Atkinson, Sommer, & Sterman, 1960; Craig & Myers, 1960), though not in preschool children (Craig & Myers, 1960; Bogartz, 1965). Figure 6.4 illustrates the effect of run length on $p(h)$, as found by a number of experi-

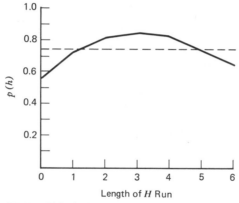

Figure 6.4. $p(h)$ as a function of the number of immediately preceding H outcomes in a row. The data are fictitious, but represent the features such plots often reveal. The horizontal dashed line represents the result to be expected if response probability were independent of run length. The initial, increasing segment of the runs curve illustrates a "positive recency effect," whereas the successive, declining segment illustrates a "negative recency effect," or "gambler's fallacy." We assume that $\pi = 0.75$ and appropriate probability matching holds. Probability matching may, as for the curve above, represent an average of "overmatching" for runs of moderate length and "undermatching" for very short and long runs.

menters. The highest $p(h)$ is placed in the region of run length two to four, which is more typically found than the peak after a run of one found by Jarvik. The initial rising part of the graph illustrates the *positive recency effect,* i.e., the increment of $p(h)$ following recent occurrences of H. The subsequent, declining part of the curve illustrates the *negative recency effect,* i.e., a decline in $p(h)$ as run length of H increases. The negative recency effect is also known as the *gambler's fallacy.* The presence of a negative recency effect in Jarvik's data confirms, in a laboratory setting, the existence of thought processes noted in the above quotations.

Subsequent experimenters have noted a flaw in Jarvik's technique, namely, that his experimental sequences were not truly random. The sequences were constrained so that the event proportions in successive blocks of trials exactly equalled the nominal probability π. Such a constraint takes the form, for example, of requiring that 15 out of every 20 successive trials be H if $\pi = 0.75$. In a truly random sequence the number of H events in each block of 20 trials is a random variable. Furthermore, when such constraints are introduced, there are fewer long homogeneous runs of H events than one would expect in a truly Bernoulli series. To illustrate, suppose that three out of every successive four events had to be H. Then the longest possible run of H events would be six (in two successive blocks of four trials), whereas in a truly random series, longer runs would show up.

Jarvik was not alone in so constraining his sequences. Actually, such constraints have been typical in probability prediction studies beginning with Humphreys. There seems to be no evidence that such constraints affect overall $p(h)$, but it does appear that such constraints affect the appearance of recency effects.

A number of experimenters have obtained the positive-negative recency curve using series that were less restricted in the longer run lengths (Nicks, 1959; Anderson & Whalen, 1960; Edwards, 1961a; Derks, 1962). These recency curves were less bowed (i.e., flatter) than Jarvik's, and generally peaked after run lengths of two and three, rather than a run length of one. One study found only positive recency effects (Feldman, 1959), and another found no recency effects in early trials (Friedman et al., 1964).

Evidence exists that the nature of the bow-shaped recency curve changes over the course of many trials. The nature of this change has not always been the same in different experiments, however. Edwards (1961a) reported that the negative recency part of the curve dropped out over the course of 1000 trials. Lindman and Edwards (1961) reported that the disappearance had started during the second hundred trials. In other studies there did not appear to be a diminution over the first several hundred trials (Anderson & Whalen, 1960; Atkinson, Sommer, & Sterman, 1960). Derks (1962, 1963) found that over the course of 1000 trials, the negative recency effects disappeared first, then the positive recency effects dropped out, leaving no recency effects at all. Friedman et al. (1964), however, found that in the beginning Ss had no recency effects, but that over the course of many trials they developed a positive recency effect. Witte (1964) found that negative recency could last over several days' sessions including 900 trials, but it finally appeared to diminish.

Different experimenters give different interpretations to the disappearance of the negative recency effect over trials. Estes (1964) considers the negative recency effect to be a habit carried over from life into the laboratory, which is gradually extinguished. Edwards (1961a) suggests that the gambler's fallacy is a "highly intellectual response" which would not occur in later trials when Ss become bored.

If the gambler's fallacy is a pre-experimental response tendency learned in everyday life, it is not clear where it is learned. According to folklore, it applies in everyday life to situations where it is not valid and could not have been learned, for example in expectancies of the sex of unborn children. The effect might be learned in situations of probability sampling without replacement and inappropriately generalized to replacement situations such as Bernoulli series.[10] Goodnow, Rubinstein, and Lubin (1960) and Witte (1964) have shown how previous experience with events sequences of short or long runs will affect behavior when Ss are transferred to Bernoulli series. With short-run sequences, the negative recency effect has a certain validity. Such short-run sequences in life might disincline people to expect long runs generally.

The appearance of the negative recency effect in experimental data was a source of annoyance to stochastic modelers. The typical stochastic model predicts that the longer the run of any event, the more likely is S to predict that event. In other words, only the positive recency effect should occur. The finding that the negative recency effect declined over trials provided considerable satisfaction. Restle's (1961, Chapter 6) schema model, on the other hand, was able to account for the presence of the gambler's fallacy.

Run length need not be the only pattern affecting $p(h)$. Consider the alternating pattern $HLHLHL$. Anderson (1960) and Anderson and Whalen (1960) found that as such an alternation sequence continues, the effect of an L becomes less effective in decreasing $p(h)$. In other words, Ss come to expect the alternation to continue.

$p(h)$ is dependent not only on past events, but on past responses as well. Nicks (1959) found that the previous response affected the $p(h)$ for the forthcoming response, but observation of runs of more than one previous response produced no further differentiation. The response tended to be the same as the previous one.

Next consider the effect of past responses and events taken in conjunction. For example does $p(h/hH) = p(h/lH)$? That is, given that the previous event was H, does it make any difference what the previous response was? The answer generally found is that the previous response does make a difference. For example, a number of studies were analyzed by Myers and Atkinson (1964) which showed that for the same previous event, h is more likely if the preceding re-

---

[10] Suppose we have an urn with five red balls and five black balls. The probability of "red" is 0.5. Suppose the first ball drawn randomly is red. Before drawing a second ball we could "replace" the red ball just drawn back in the urn, in which case the probabilities for the second draw would be the same as for the first draw. If, however, we proceed "without replacement," the first ball drawn would be set aside, so the probabilities for the second draw would be 4/9 for red and 5/9 for black. When there is no replacement, the accumulation of samples of one color increases the probability for the other color. A Bernoulli series, with constant probabilities over trials, can be thought of as generated by replacement sampling.

sponse was h; i.e., there is a degree of response perseveration. It has been found, however, that when the previous event is L, children tend toward response alternation (Brackbill, Kappy, & Starr, 1962; Brackbill & Bravos, 1962).

Feldman and Hanna (1966) pointed out that apparent effects of previous responses on future responses could be largely attributed (in their data, anyway) to the effects on the previous responses of events preceding them. That is, given enough preceding events, only slight further predictability of the forthcoming response can be obtained by considering previous responses.

6.7   WHAT Ss THINK THEY ARE DOING

We have seen how different theorists view probability learning, and how behavior is affected by different experimental variables. But what do Ss consciously think about the task? Most experiments have not been concerned with this. Nonetheless, some experimenters have questioned Ss on this topic, and some indications are available, though not in a systematic way.

It appears that most Ss think that there is some patterning to the sequence they see. They believe that the next event depends somehow on what the recent events have been. Many are willing to offer hypotheses about these dependencies, even though there have been a sufficient number of events to refute such hypotheses (Jarvik, 1951; Morse & Runquist, 1960; Hake & Hyman, 1953). Sometimes Ss think that a particular event was put in to "throw them off," and that what they guessed was actually what should have come up. If the experimenter reads the answers, then the possibility occurs to S that the event may be dependent on his response. His task, perhaps, is to outguess the experimenter (Feldman, 1961). Sometimes the experiment is seen as one in extra-sensory perception, although the task was not so presented (Rubinstein, 1959).

Even when a task was used in which the events were apparently generated by a random device, Ss looked for patterns (Nies, 1962). The majority of these Ss also said they knew the wisest procedure would be to bet consistently on the more likely alternative, but for some reason they did not follow their own counsel (see also Tversky & Edwards, 1966). Perhaps it is boring to always make the same choice; perhaps it would be embarrassing; would the experimenter approve of such a procedure?

S may choose the less frequent event in order to test a hypothesis concerning its appearance on a given trial. Actually, the hypothesis could be checked while the more frequent event is chosen, but Ss seem resistant to this idea (Bruner, Goodnow, & Austin, 1956, p. 194). Though they apparently do not express the idea directly, it is as if they believe that the outcomes may be dependent on their responses. This is doubtless often true in life; also, as we shall see, this is true in some experiments.

Ss sometimes seem quite interested in the less frequent event. If they can learn when to predict it, they will have the situation mastered. This leads to testing of this less frequent event by choosing it (Bruner *et al.,* 1956, p. 194). Some experimenters consider that *S* has a higher utility for predicting *L* than for predicting *H*. *L* occurs less often, and correct prediction of it is more difficult; hence, the greater satisfaction with success. From a strict expected utility point of view, however, such utilities cannot justify inconsistent choosing over trials. They can at most require that *L* be predicted on every trial, instead of *H*.

6.8 PREDICTION WITHOUT FEEDBACK

In some probability learning experiments, "reinforcement," i.e., *feedback* concerning the correct prediction, is omitted on some trials. Feedback may be given on all of the first *N* trials to acquaint *S* with the series, and then eliminated henceforth. Or, "nonreinforced" trials may be interspersed throughout the entire sequence.

A third method is to tell or suggest to *S* what the probabilities for the possible events are, and then have him guess without any feedback at all. A task which seems closely related is to have *S* attempt to produce a list of random numbers, such as would be found in a random number table. Here the experimenter does not imply that each number given by *S* can be scored right or wrong, but quite possibly the same response tendencies would be operating.

The first use of "nonreinforced" trials in probability learning apparently occurred by accident. Estes (1964, p. 105) related how, through an error in communication, *S*s who were supposed to be shifted to a different π were continued with no reinforcement at all. *S*s continued with the same $p(h)$ as before, a result confirmed by Neimark (1956). It has also been found that when nonreinforced trials are interspersed with reinforced trials, they have little effect on $p(h)$, or in some cases, perhaps some slight decremental effect (Atkinson, 1956; Anderson & Grant, 1957; Greeno, 1962).

Continuance at the same $p(h)$ is rather curious. It is not obvious that this would occur. On the one hand, one might think that nonreinforcement would result in a decrement toward equal probability for the various predictions, since there is no reinforcement favoring one over the other. On the other hand, one might believe that *S*s would perform more optimally without feedback, since it would be impossible to try to figure out sequential patterns when no outcomes are known. There are indeed, some data for related probabilistic tasks indicating that *S*s sometimes perform somewhat more optimally without feedback than with feedback (Bruner *et al.,* 1956, pp. 208–216; Lee & Zentall, 1966).

Approximate "probability matching" without feedback does not require that *S* have previous experience with feedback. Senders and Sowards (1952) had *S*s guess whether a light and tone came on at different times, or at the same time, for a series of trials without feedback. Actually, all pairs were simultaneous. If the experimenter suggested that, for example, 75% of the pairs were simultaneous, then Ss guessed "simultaneous" on 75% of the trials.

Given the probability $p(h)$ for guessing, we might ask further whether the sequences of guesses without feedback is Bernoulli. Bendig (1951) had Ss guess whether a head or tail would appear when a coin was flipped, for three successive trials. With feedback there were considerably more repetitions than one would expect by chance. (The response perseveration under feedback has been previously mentioned.) Without feedback, however, there appeared to be about the expected number of response repetitions, except that there were too many Ss with one repetition (guess sequences like "head, tail, tail,") and not enough with two repetitions ("head, head, head") or with zero repetitions.

Guessing experiments without feedback have sometimes been presented to Ss as studies in extra-sensory perception; sometimes the experimenters so intended the experiment, and sometimes ESP was simply used as a rationale to justify having Ss guess numbers with no knowledge of results. Goodfellow (1938) analyzed data collected from a radio audience in a test of ESP. One of two symbols, such as circle or cross, was to be chosen randomly, and then five persons in the radio studio concentrated on the symbol chosen. People listening to the broadcast tried to guess which symbol had occurred by using ESP. Five trials were employed. The results appeared to be a strong confirmation of ESP. Goodfellow showed, however, that the statistical reasoning confirming ESP was faulty, in part because Ss do not guess symbol sequences in a random fashion. The pattern of guesses 11212 (and its counterpart 22121) was used most often, whereas the patterns 22222 and 21212 and their counterparts were used much less than one would expect by chance. The probability of repeating the first guess on the second trial was about 0.5, indicating no strong tendency to repeat or alternate (Skinner, 1942).

Such guessing experiments without feedback have also been performed with more than two alternatives, and it appears that the sequences are not random (Sheffield, 1949). Failure to recognize that Ss do not produce a random sequence of guesses of digits resulted in an erroneous conclusion in academic psychology, paralleling the ESP case. Consider a paired associates experiment in which the responses are digits. Thorndike postulated a "spread of effect" such that if a response were rewarded (correct) it would strengthen the "bonds" between adjacent stimulus-response pairs, even when the adjacent responses were incorrect. Such appeared to be the case, until a series of experiments showed that the results came about because of a tendency by Ss to guess digits in certain nonrandom patterns (Sheffield, 1949; Fagan & North, 1951; Jenkins & Cunningham, 1949; Hilgard & Bower, 1966).

A number of experiments have required Ss to attempt to produce "random" series, i.e., Bernoulli series with equiprobable events. Although such experiments are usually not discussed in relation to the probability learning literature, they seem related to some of the preceding experiments. Chapanis (1953) investigated the attempted random sequences of digits produced by naive Ss and by Ss sophisticated in statistical theory. The sophisticated Ss produced more nearly random sequences than the naive Ss, but both groups produced nonrandom response patterns. Most Ss preferred certain digits to others, although the preferred digit varied among the Ss. Repetitive pairs and triplets were avoided, for example, 000, 111, 110, 131. Decreasing sequences, for example, 987, were highly preferred, but increasing sequences were not.

Hansel (1966, pp. 138–139) requested Ss to produce random series from the symbols A, B, C, D, and E. Repetitions of the same letter seldom appeared. Hansel noted how failure of humans to generate random sequences allowed an erroneous "confirmation" of ESP. An experiment had been performed in which one person chose one of five lights, and the other was supposed to guess which light was chosen. Better than "chance" performance (20% success) occurred. However, if S realized, consciously or not, that the experimenter changed his choice on successive trials, then by changing also, S's chance of success would increase to 25%.

6.9 PREDICTION OF BINARY SERIES WITH STRUCTURE

In the present context, a series of discrete events is said to have structure if, unlike a Bernoulli series, the event probabilities on trial n are conditional on the events which happened to occur previous to trial n. Since many real-life series have structure in this sense, it is of interest to investigate event predictions for these series as well as for Bernoulli series.

One important class of structured sequences are the *Markov chains*. In a *Markov chain of order 1*, the conditional probabilities applicable on trial n differ depending on the outcome that happened to occur on trial $n - 1$, but given that outcome, the dependency goes no further back. The *order* of a Markov chain gives the number of preceding trials affecting a trial's probabilities.

A Markov chain of order 1 can be specified by a *conditional probability matrix* giving the probabilities for the events on trial n as a function of the outcome on trial $n - 1$. For a two-event series, the matrix might be

		Trial $n - 1$	
		E_1	E_2
Trial n	E_1	0.8	0.4
	E_2	0.2	0.6

If the previous outcome were E_1, $p(E_1)$ would be 0.8, but if the previous outcome were E_2, $p(E_1)$ would be 0.4.

When Ss are presented such sequences with instructions to predict the forthcoming event, they come to *roughly* match the conditional probabilities of the events. That is, given that the preceding event was E_1, they tend to predict E_1

about 0.8 of the time, but given that the preceding event was E_2, they tend to predict E_1 about 0.4 of the time. Thus they have some awareness, consciously or not, of the effect of the previous outcome on the forthcoming event (Hake & Hyman, 1953; Engler, 1958; Anderson, 1960; Chapman, 1961).

Conditional probability matching does not optimize the expected percentage of correct predictions. The optimal strategy is to predict whichever event has the higher probability conditional on the previous outcome. For the preceding example, the optimal strategy would be to always predict E_1 after an E_1 outcome, and always predict E_2 after and E_2 outcome. With other conditional probability matrices, the optimal strategy might be to predict the same event on *every* trial, or to predict the event *opposite* to the preceding outcome.

Prediction of the opposite event would be required, for example, with the following order 1 series:

Trial $n - 1$

		E_1	E_2
Trial n	E_1	0.3	0.7
	E_2	0.7	0.3

In this type of series, the forthcoming outcome tends to differ from the preceding one, and Ss tend to predict the event differing from the preceding one. The better-known stochastic models, however, assume that occurrence of E_1 on trial $n - 1$ increases the probability of predicting the same event, an implication inconsistent with the experimental results. Some modified models were constructed which assume a different set of stimulus elements for each type of previous event. Such models had some, but not perfect success (Engler, 1958; Anderson, 1960).

Ss have been asked to predict sequences of greater complexity than the Markov chain of order 1. They have some success in such situations, but the further back the dependencies go (i.e., the greater the number of previous outcomes affecting current probabilities), the more trouble Ss have in making effective use of such dependencies (Wolin, Weichel, Terebinski, & Hansford, 1965; Feldman & Hanna, 1966).

Experiments concerned with the learning of nonprobabilistic (i.e., deterministic) series are enlightening in this regard. Goodnow and Pettigrew (1956) found that 25% of the Ss did not learn the sequence *LLRLLR* etc. perfectly in 100 trials. Galanter and Smith (1958) found a median of 49 trials to criterion in learning repetitions of the sequence 01001. (See also Restle, 1966.) If such difficulties occur in learning such simple deterministic sequences, it is not surprising to find even greater difficulties when the probabilistic element enters.

Goodnow and Pettigrew stated that Ss report hypotheses far more complicated than the patterns that are presented. It is sometimes asserted that Ss do poorly in the Bernoulli series task because they expect a more complex sequence, such as is typically found in life. They do worse, if anything, however, when they get what they expect—complexity. There are, of course, many possible complex sequences, and just because S expects complexity does not mean he expects the particular structure that occurs.

6.10 CONTINGENT PROBABILITY LEARNING

Consider the following paradigm. There are two light bulbs, left and right, and S has two choices, left and right. He is correct if he chooses left and the left bulb lights up, or if he chooses right and the right-hand bulb lights up. There is a probability π_1 that the left bulb will light up if he chooses left, and a probability π_2 that the right-hand bulb will light up if he chooses right. The left bulb never lights up if S chooses right, nor does the right-hand bulb ever light up if he chooses left.

This experimental paradigm is called *contingent probability learning* because the information received by S on a trial is contingent on which choice he makes (Detambel, 1955). In contrast, the procedure we have concentrated on previously is called *noncontingent probability learning*. In the usual form of the noncontingent task, one or the other of the bulbs is scheduled to light up on a trial and does so regardless of what S chooses. Because in the contingent task the observed outcome depends in part on what S does, the task has been described as one in which S "attempts to control an uncertain event" (Estes, 1954). But S has some control over the expected percentage of correct responses in each paradigm; in the contingent task, the optimal strategy is to choose the bulb with the higher π (which may be less than 0.5).

The two tasks can be usefully compared in terms of sample spaces. First consider diagram (a) below, which concerns the noncontingent task.

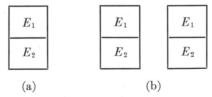

(a)   (b)

On each trial event E_1 or E_2 will occur (say left or right-hand bulb lights up). S must predict which will happen, and is correct if he predicts accurately. He can choose either E_1 or E_2 for his prediction. Now consider (b), which refers to the contingent task. Let E_1 mean that the light comes on. The two sample spaces refer to two light bulbs. If the left sample space is chosen, event E_1 will occur with probability π_1, and if the right-hand sample space is chosen, then event E_1 will occur with probability π_2. Here S does not have a choice of predicting E_1 or E_2. Instead his job is to choose the sample space such that E_1 has the highest probability of occurring. In order to maximize the number of successful trials, S should always choose the left space if $\pi_1 > \pi_2$, and always the right-hand space if $\pi_2 > \pi_1$.

We have identified task (a) with the noncontingent task, and (b) with the contingent. This correspondence is dependent on the occurrence of the usual feedback conditions. If the feedback conditions are changed, (a) can be "contingent" and (b) "noncontingent." Thus, in general, we might refer to (a) as *event prediction* and (b) as *space prediction*. The essence of the event prediction task is that exactly one thing of a given set will happen, and S is to make one choice attempting to predict it. Suppose S is not told the outcome unless he predicts correctly. This would make no difference (at least logically) if there were only two possible events. If there were more than two events, however, it would make a difference, since S would not know which event occurred on those trials when he guessed incorrectly. Cole (1965) has utilized such a task, which he called the "search task," since when Ss were wrong, they had to make successive guesses until they were correct. Since the information given to S depends on his choice, the task might be called "contingent."

In addition, a space prediction task can be "noncontingent." Suppose after choosing a space, S could see the outcomes for all spaces; i.e., with N spaces (light bulbs), any from 0 to N bulbs would light up, based on independent (or possibly dependent) sampling according to the probabilities π_1, π_2, etc. Since the feedback would be the same regardless of the choice, the task could be called noncontingent. This task, too, has been used (Anderson & Grant, 1957).

Henceforth in this section, "contingent" will refer to the contingent space prediction task, as is customary. In most of the experiments on contingent probability learning, the Ss have been misled concerning the nature of the feedback. The instructions have led Ss to believe that the task was contingent event prediction. They were told, for example, that exactly one light could come on during a trial, and that if S pressed the correct button, the corresponding light would come on. Otherwise, S was to assume that some other light would have come on had it been chosen. In many of the contingent experiments such instructions were given because a stochastic model for the contingent task was being tested which assumed that Ss so believed (Detambel, 1955; Brand, Sakoda, & Woods, 1957b). In a two-alternative task, for example, the models assume that if the left light is chosen and turns out to be not correct, then the increase in probability of predicting the right-hand light for the next trial is the same as it would be for the noncontingent event prediction task. The formula for the probability of making choice a_1 based on this idea is $p(a_1) = (1 - \pi_2)/(2 - \pi_1 - \pi_2)$ (Estes, 1954; Bush & Mosteller, 1955, p. 288). If it so happens that $\pi_2 = 1 - \pi_1$, as in the noncontingent case, then the formula reduces to $p(a_1) = \pi_1$, probability matching.

This formula has had good, although not perfect, success; if anything, Ss seem to behave somewhat more optimally than the formula implies (Brand, Sakoda, and Woods, 1957a,b; Neimark, 1956; Woods, 1959). Do Ss accept the instruction that exactly one bulb could light on each trial? There is some evidence both ways. Woods (1959) had one group of Ss press the other button if they were unsuccessful in their first choice, whereupon the second light would come on (it actually might not have had they pressed this button first). Ss in this group performed no differently from Ss run in the usual way, suggesting that this latter group accepted the idea that the other button would have produced success. Detambel (1955) used three choices, two of which had zero probabilities of success. After the experiment, many Ss noted that only one button ever produced success, so they apparently rejected the implication that if the one "effective" button failed on a trial, one of the others would have been correct. These Ss also performed more optimally than Detambel's model implies. But this was an extreme case. Typically, all buttons have some probability of success. Nonetheless, in principle, Ss should be able to realize that the instructions are false; in principle, the feedback should allow them to tell that they are correct randomly with different probabilities for different choices, and that if these probabilities do not add to one, something must be phony. It appears by now, however, that most Ss are not that astute in dealing with probabilistic sequences.

Some Ss have been told that the light which would come on was determined randomly, and others were told that it was determined by some plan. Variation of this type seemed to have little or no effect on choice behavior (Brand *et al.,* 1957b). Motivation provided by the cessation of a noxious stimulus (noise) for a correct choice had no noteworthy effect on performance (Woods, 1959).

A three-alternative contingent task in which one alternative is successful with a non-zero probability π and the other two with probability zero has been extensively used in the study of probability learning with children. The higher the π, the more Ss choose the button which could be rewarded. For optimal success they should choose that button on every trial, regardless of π, but that did not happen. When π was 1.0 they came close to this, however. Younger children (ages 3 and 5) performed more optimally than the older ones (Stevenson and Weir, 1959). Feebleminded children did as well or better than normals (Stevenson and Zigler, 1958).

6.11 PROBABILISTIC DISCRIMINATION LEARNING

In a discrimination learning situation, S must learn to respond differently depending on which stimulus is present. In the ordinary discrimination learning paradigm, the stimulus present on a trial provides S with enough information to make the correct response with certainty. In *probabilistic discrimination learning,* however, the correct response is only probabilistically related to the stimulus, so perfect responding is not possible. For example, suppose that either of two stimuli, denoted T_1 and T_2, can occur on a trial. On a T_1 trial, the experimenter commences the trial by saying the nonsense syllable MEF. On a T_2 trial the experimenter commences the trial by saying ZIL. After presentation of the stimulus, S must guess either a_1 or a_2 (Popper & Atkinson, 1958). After the guess, the experimenter states the correct response for that trial. In ordinary discrimination learning, it might be that a_1 is the correct answer for T_1 trials, and a_2 is the correct answer for T_2 trials. In probabilistic discrimination learning, however, there is only some probability π_1 that a_1 is the correct response on a T_1 trial, and some probability π_2 that a_1 is the correct response on a T_2 trial.[11]

The optimal strategy for maximizing the expected percentage of correct responses is, on T_1 trials, to always respond a_1 if $\pi_1 > 0.5$, and a_2 if $\pi_1 < 0.5$, and on T_2 trials to always respond a_1 if $\pi_2 > 0.5$, and a_2 if $\pi_2 < 0.5$. Optimal performance may require giving the same response on every trial regardless of the stimulus present, for example, if $\pi_1 > 0.5$, and $\pi_2 > 0.5$.

There need not be the same number of stimuli as responses. For example, there may be six stimuli, $T_1, T_2, \ldots, T_6$, two responses, and a probability for each stimulus that a_1 is correct, $\pi_1, \pi_2, \ldots, \pi_6$. The stimuli may be points on a continuum x, in which case there would be a $\pi(x)$ function (Lee, 1966). The reinforcements for a given stimulus have been Bernoulli series, but there are many other possibilities.

The prediction of a Markov series resembles probabilistic discrimination learning in that a "stimulus" is present on each trial which identifies the reinforcement probabilities operating. In a Markov series of order 1, the "stimulus" is the outcome on the preceding trial. For order 2 series, the "stimulus" is the preceding two outcomes, etc. In spite of the similarity, however, the term "probabilistic discrimination learning" is customarily used only when there is a series of stimuli separate from the series of events to be predicted.

How do Ss respond in probabilistic discrimination learning? Suppose that only stimulus T_1 were presented. Then the situation would simply be noncontingent probability learning. Likewise for T_2, except that π would differ. Based on results from noncontingent probability learning, one might expect that if the stimuli are clearly discriminable, Ss might probability match to each one separately, i.e., for T_1 trials $p(a_1) = \pi_1$, and for T_2 trials $p(a_1) = \pi_2$. Such *conditional probability matching* describes the mean response probabilities (across Ss) quite

---

[11] The original conceptualization of probabilistic discrimination learning appeared in Burke and Estes (1957) and Estes, Burke, Atkinson, and Frankmann (1957). The definitions in these two sources may not appear to jibe with my definition (indeed, they appear not to jibe perfectly with each other). Burke and Estes (1957) distinguished between "classical" and "probabilistic" discrimination learning; their classical case would appear to be the same as my "probabilistic" case. Their probabilistic case seems on the surface to be rather different, but a deeper analysis reveals that it differs from the former paradigm (in Estes *et al.,* at least) only in the number of stimuli that can commence a trial. Instead of only two, there are a large number, and for each there are reinforcing probabilities for a_1 and a_2. I do not consider the distinction to be important enough to require the two terms. "Probabilistic discrimination learning" is the better term for the paradigm discussed in the present section.

well for a number of experiments (Estes *et al.,* 1957; Popper & Atkinson, 1958; Atkinson, Bogartz, & Turner, 1959; Lee & Zentall, 1966). Of course, since response probabilities in the noncontingent task depend on many experimental variables, one would expect the same to be the case for probabilistic discrimination learning. In some experiments Ss performed more optimally than conditional probability matching (Howell & Funaro, 1965; Bourne, 1963; Lee & Janke, 1964), but the specific conditions resulting in such improved performance are not well researched. Lee and Zentall (1966) found that a small monetary incentive did not yield increased optimal responding.

Performance of S when T_1 is present is clearly a function of π_1, but such performance is somewhat dependent on π_2 as well (Popper & Atkinson, 1958; Atkinson, Bogartz, & Turner, 1959). Such dependence might be attributed to *generalization.* In fact, a paradigm invented to study spatial generalization, the so-called "horse-race technique," is a form of probabilistic discrimination learning. In the "horse-race" paradigm, S sees a row of perhaps seven light bulbs. Each bulb represents a horse. At the start of each trial, one bulb lights up. This means that horse has been entered in a race (but not with the other horses, i.e., the other bulbs). S is to predict whether the horse wins. The experimenter says whether he won, based on a Bernoulli reinforcement series with a π value conditional on that horse. Each horse (bulb) has a different probability π_i of winning (Brown, Clark, & Stein, 1958). When the horse in the middle position won 0.8 of his races and the others each won 0.2 of theirs, approximate conditional probability matching held for the middle and end horses, but there was a generalization gradient of response probability in between (see Figure 6.5). In other words, the response probability for a stimulus (horse) depends on the π_i's for adjacent stimuli. (Also see Simon (1964) and Evans (1961); but no gradient was found by Dixon and Wickens (1961).) Such generalization was also noted in direct subjective probability estimates (Brown *et al.,* 1958; Simon, 1964).

Instead of discrete light bulbs in a row, we might have a continuum x of possible stimuli, one of which is selected at random on each trial from a probability distribution. The probability of reinforcement for a_1 could then be described by a function, $\pi(x)$, and response probability conditional on a stimulus by a function $g(x)$. According to one stochastic model (Lee, 1966), if a new reinforcement function $\pi'(x)$ is related to the original one by a linear function $\left(\pi'(x) = a\pi(x) + b\right)$, then the new response function $g'(x)$ should equal $ag(x) + b$. Unpublished experiments did not accord perfectly with this implication.

In many discrimination learning experiments the stimuli vary on some attribute that has no bearing on the correct response. These attributes are then called *irrelevant variables.* A discrimination learning experiment with irrelevant variables is usually called a *concept learning* task. In most concept learning tasks, a stimulus has one correct response on each trial so that S may learn to respond correctly on each trial. However, in some "concept learning" experiments probabilistic reinforcement has been used, so perfect responding is not possible. In the literature under discussion the reinforcement of the non-optimal response is called *misinformative feedback;* the probability of misinformative feedback is the same for all stimuli.

Since irrelevant variables usually mislead S and impair his performance in concept learning tasks, we might expect similar impairment with probabilistic reinforcement. Such is the case. The greater the number of irrelevant variables, the poorer the performance (Pishkin, 1960; Johannsen, 1962). With only one irrelevant dimension and about 200 trials, however, performance was close to

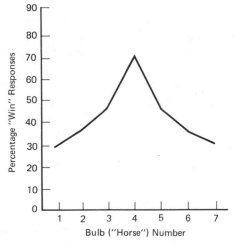

Figure 6.5. Percentage of "win" responses as a function of number (position) of the "horse." Reinforcement percentage of win was 80 for horse 4 (middle) and 20 for all others. The graph illustrates generalization between adjacent stimuli (horses). (From Brown, Clark, & Stein, 1958.)

probability matching; but a misinformative feedback probability of 0.4 or higher prevented learning from taking place at all (Morin, 1955; Johannsen, 1962). Bourne's (1963) Ss improved over several days of extended training, and with misinformative feedback of 0.15, came to respond optimally.

Typically, summing over all stimuli, the number of reinforcements of a_1 and a_2 are equal. It is possible to alter this, for example by presenting stimulus T_1 more often than stimulus T_2. Suppose this is done, and in addition, assume that S is unable to pick out a relevant stimulus variable. Then he perceives a series of reinforcements of, say 70% a_1 and 30% a_2. To S the situation is similar to noncontingent probability learning. Mandler, Cowan, and Gold (1964) noted that early in a concept learning task, before the relevant stimulus variable was learned, Ss simply matched response probabilities to the overall reinforcement probabilities. Lee and Janke (1965) noted a similar finding: certain Ss never did come to learn the relevance of the stimulus variable, and simply probability matched to the overall reinforcement probabilities.

Probabilistic Paired Associates Learning

In the usual paired associate learning task, there is one proper response to each of a set of stimuli. This task has been modified so that the correct response for a stimulus is determined randomly from a set of possibilities. The resulting task is similar to probabilistic discrimination learning with these differences: First, the stimuli are usually presented in a systematic rather than a random order. Second, instead of having a common choice set for all stimuli, the set of possible correct responses differs from stimulus to stimulus. Third, the Ss may be unable to make any response at all on a trial, especially in the earlier trials, since they can't always remember which words are used as reinforcements to a stimulus.

In spite of the differences, results with probabilistic paired associates learning are generally in accord with what we have learned about probabilistic discrimination learning, i.e., approximate conditional probability matching obtains. With a given probability for the most likely reinforcement, the more alternative reinforcements there are, the greater the percentage of optimal responses (Voss, Thompson, & Keegan, 1959; Erdelyi, Watts, & Voss, 1964).

6.12 CONTINUOUS RESPONSE DIMENSION

In the experiments discussed so far in this chapter, S has been required to make a choice on each trial from a discrete set of possibilities. In other experiments, however, S has had to choose from a continuum of possibilities. Suppes and Frankmann (1961) had Ss predict where along the rim of a circular disc a "target" would appear in a pseudo "radar fire-control task." After each prediction, S received feedback (reinforcement) based on a random sample from a continuous probability distribution located along the rim of the disc. The task is a variation of noncontingent probability learning in which the possible events and responses form a continuum. Viewing the task in this light, one would expect that the distribution of responses would approximately match the distribution of reinforcements. But the continuous task has special features making the preceding analysis dubious. For one thing, the continuous task has an infinite number of possible responses, and, as we saw (Section 6.4), the number of alternatives can affect optimal responding. Of course, due to Ss' limited discriminative capacities, the possible number of psychologically relevant responses must be relatively small. Likewise, a reinforcement cannot be effective at only the exact point of occurrence; its effect must generalize to adjacent regions as well.

Before considering the results, let us consider the optimal strategy. It is not as easy to speak of a "correct" prediction in the continuous case as in the discrete case, since the probability of predicting *exactly* which reinforcement will occur is zero, regardless of where one predicts. If, however, we can assume that S considers himself to be correct if his prediction error is very small, then, in general, the strategy for maximizing the correct number of predictions is to predict the mode of the reinforcement distribution on each trial.[12]

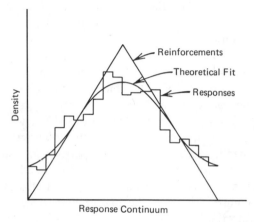

Figure 6.6. The response histogram (step function) for a continuous response probability prediction experiment. The response (and reinforcement) continuum was located around the rim of a circle. The reinforcement distribution was triangular, but because of a "smearing" of the effect of reinforcement in the stochastic model used, the fitted theoretical response distribution had a different shape. (From Suppes & Frankman, 1961.)

The results of the Suppes and Frankmann experiment are given in Figure 6.6. The variance of the response distribution was larger than the variance of the reinforcement distribution, and the shape was different. The authors developed a stochastic model for their data. The model is basically a one-element stimulus sampling model (which predicts probability matching in the discrete case), to which a "smearing distribution" was added to account for generalization of a reinforcement to nearby regions. The model could account for the differences between the reinforcement and response distributions.

Rosenberg (1963) performed a similar experiment in which he used two different normal distributions for reinforcements, one with smaller variance and the other with larger variance. For each case the response variance roughly equalled the reinforcement variance. The shape of the response distributions

---

[12] The mode of a distribution is the value with the greatest density, i.e., the value occurring with greatest relative frequency. Strictly speaking, the optimal strategy is to always predict that value which has the highest probability of success, given the region of tolerance for error. In special circumstances this may not be the mode.

was leptokurtic, rather than normal; that is, relative to a normal distribution, there were too many predictions at the center of the distribution (optimal predictions) and too many far away from the center.

The distinction between the discrete and continuous cases is not as clear-cut as we have suggested. For example, in the Suppes and Frankmann experiment, the reinforcements were not actually from a continuous distribution—reinforcements were only given at discrete locations, but these were so numerous that Ss could not realize it. Also, in some experiments discussed below, Ss responded with numbers to the nearest unit.

An experiment may have both discrete responses and reinforcements, and still be very similar to the continuous case. For example, in one discrete noncontingent task, Ss were required to predict which of ten bulbs mounted in a row would light. The same sort of reinforcement generalization appeared here as in the continuous task: a bulb was chosen more often if it was near a bulb with high reinforcement probability instead of a bulb with low reinforcement probability. On the other hand, McCormack (1959) performed a similar experiment using five bulbs, but did not discover any generalization. Intuitively, generalization would seem more likely to occur with many bulbs than with few, because the greater the number of bulbs, the harder it is to keep track of the separate reinforcement histories.

Because no neat and psychologically valid distinction can be made between "continuous" tasks and tasks with a substantial number of ordered events, this section includes discussion of both types of experiments. For simplicity, both types will be called "continuous."

Effect of Payoff

We noted that the optimal strategy for maximizing the number of correct predictions is to predict the mode of the reinforcement distribution on each trial. However, as in the discrete case, it is possible to alter the optimal strategy by changing the payoff scheme. Suppose, for example, that the payoff is inversely proportional to the difference between the prediction and the reinforcement. Then prediction of the median of the reinforcement distribution maximizes the expected payoff. If the payoff is inversely proportional to the squared difference between the prediction and the reinforcement, then prediction of the mean of the reinforcement distribution is optimal. If the reinforcement distribution is symmetrical and has a central mode (for example, the normal distribution), then all three payoff schemes require the same optimal strategy, since the mode, median, and mean are the same. For other shapes, the optimal strategies can differ.

Messick and Rapoport (1965a) had Ss predict a number from 0 to 9 which was drawn from a J-shaped distribution. One group of Ss got paid only if they predicted the reinforcement exactly (mode strategy optimal), and another group was paid according to the difference between the prediction and the reinforcement (median optimal). Although neither group used a strictly optimal strategy, the former group was closer to a mode strategy, and the latter group was closer to a median strategy.

Peterson and Miller (1964) had Ss predict the supposed speed of cars passing a stop sign. The reinforcement distribution was J-shaped, and the reinforcements were chosen by random sampling. Payoffs for different groups made the mode, the median, or the mean optimal. Ss were quite good in coming to make appropriate predictions under mode and median schedules, but had difficulty with the mean schedule, which required them to minimize the square of error.

Schoeffler (1962) used an altogether different type of payoff scheme. The concept of expected regret equalization proved to be useful in predicting asymptotic responses (see Section 5.6 for further discussion of Schoeffler's research).

Reinforcement Distribution with Constraints

We saw that the continuous response task bears a close resemblance to non-contingent probability learning with discrete events. There are also continuous response analogies to the prediction of a structured series of discrete events. The continuous response analogy to a discrete Markov series of order 1 occurs when the reinforcement distribution is conditional on the previous reinforcement.

Lee and Garner (1966) studied the prediction of such a sequence. The reinforcement on trial n, x_n, was determined by adding to x_{n-1} a random sample from a normal distribution with a mean of zero.[13] If the payoff scheme requires predicting the mode, median, or mean, the optimal strategy is to predict that x_n will equal x_{n-1}. In contrast to the previous experiments in this section, the optimal strategy for this task requires different responses on succeeding trials.

Series were derived for a large and a small normal distribution standard deviation. The average standard deviations for Ss" predictions relative to the previous outcome, x_{n-1}, approximately matched the standard deviations used to construct the series. This result is analogous to the approximate conditional probability matching seen in the prediction of Markov series of discrete events (Section 6.9).

Discrimination Learning

In the continuous task version of probabilistic discrimination learning, the reinforcement distribution depends on which stimulus initiates a trial. Suppes and Rouanet (1964) ran a discrimination learning variation of the experiment of Suppes and Frankmann (1961). One of four bulbs lit up to begin each trial, indicating which of four reinforcement distributions would be used. Ss responded more nearly optimally than in the non-discrimination task.

---

[13] The sequence of daily prices of a share of stock is well modeled by this type of series (Godfrey, Granger, & Morgenstern, 1964).

In the previous experiment the stimuli were discrete. There has also been considerable research on continuous stimulus experiments with continuous responses. Many of these experiments have not involved probabilistic reinforcement, but others have. We begin by describing a non-probabilistic experiment.

Summers (1962) had Ss learn to predict the length of a line based on a three-variable stimulus. The variables (which are often called *cues*) were angle (X_1), area (X_2), and color (X_3) of a triangle. Each variable could assume any of eight values, which were quantified as 1, 2, . . . , 8. The length of the line Y was entirely determined by the stimulus:

$$Y = 2X_1 + 1.5X_2 + X_3 \qquad (6.7)$$

Of course, Ss cannot attain perfect responding, even if the reinforcements are deterministic. They actually attained a correlation between response and reinforcement of about 0.41, although the correlation still appeared to be increasing over trials.

Yntema and Torgerson (1961) used a similar task, except that the cues were not combined in the simple additive manner of Equation 6.7. Ss apparently took note of the interactions between cues in making their judgments.

Hammond and Summers (1965) combined two cues in an additive manner; however, one cue was linear and the other nonlinear: $Y = X_1 + \sin X_2$. The instructions for different groups differed in detail concerning the nonlinear cue. Mean correlations between predictions and Y for the various instructional groups ranged from 0.49 to 0.85. The poorest group had the least information about the nonlinear cue, and those Ss relied more heavily on the linear cue. The size of the correlation related directly to the level of detail in the instructions.

The validity of a cue is related to the size of its coefficient (see Equation 6.7). If S utilized only one cue and ignored the rest, he could do best by utilizing the cue with the highest validity (coefficient). Uhl (1963) compared the performance of Ss when the cues were equally valid with that when the cues had unequal validities. Ss performed better with unequal cue validities. Note that the most extreme case of unequal validities is for only one cue to be relevant.

The paradigm becomes probabilistic discrimination learning when the reinforcement Y' is determined by adding a random value from a probability distribution to Y. Then Y' cannot be perfectly predicted from the stimulus, even in principle. In Peterson, Hammond, and Summers (1965) the reinforcement depended on a random value drawn from a rectangular probability distribution centered on Y. The probabilistic reinforcement reduced the correlation between the cues and the reinforcements (between Y and Y') from 1 to 0.83. A correlation analysis of responses indicated that Ss did somewhat better than conditional probability matching. (Of course, as we have seen, for non-probabilistic reinforcements, Ss do worse than "conditional probability matching," which implies a correlation of 1 between responses and reinforcements.)

Todd and Hammond (1965), also using probabilistic reinforcement, compared performance under "outcome feedback" (the usual kind) with "lens model feedback." Lens model feedback includes the correlation between S's responses and the reinforcements, the correlation between cues and the reinforcements, and correlation between the cues and S's predictions. The lens model feedback was given every 25 trials. Performance under lens model feedback was superior to performance under outcome feedback, presumably because it easily allowed the Ss to compare the relative importance they were giving to the different cues with the actual relative validities. Addition of outcome feedback to lens model feedback effected no improvement.

Some mention should be made of the heavy reliance on correlational analysis in the literature on continuous stimulus, continuous response probability learning. Correlations between predictions and reinforcements may often be useful in comparing different experimental conditions, but from the viewpoint of decision theory, correlations are not entirely satisfactory. Suppose that S is to receive payoff according to the accuracy of his prediction—an entirely reasonable arrangement. Correlations are not very good indicators of accuracy; of two Ss, the one with the lower correlation could be the more accurate, i.e., the one with the lower correlation might deserve higher payoffs.

6.13 SUMMARY

In probability learning experiments, a reward is not coupled to a response in a regular and deterministic manner. The experiments involve, instead, a kind of partial reinforcement. It is the probability learning experiments with humans that has concerned us. Since humans are required to "predict" which event will occur, the area is often called "probability prediction." The simplest experimental paradigm—and the one which has received the most attention—requires S to predict the forthcoming outcome of a two-event Bernoulli series. The early experiments of this type led to the *probability matching generalization,* according to which event predictions appear in the same proportions as the outcomes. The generalization was troublesome from the viewpoint of decision theory, since the optimal strategy for maximizing the expected number of correct predictions or for maximizing expected payoff for the more reasonable looking payoff matrices is to predict the more probable event H on *every trial.* Probability matching accorded perfectly, however, with some stochastic learning models. Actually, probability matching at best described mean results across Ss, not individual results, and even the mean response probability $p(h)$ proved to be susceptible to experimental conditions such as number of trials, number of alternative events, payoffs, and instructions. If Ss can see for themselves that outcomes are generated by a random mechanism rather than being pre-arranged, or if they are convinced of the fact by instructions, they predict H more than they otherwise would.

To account for these experimental findings, revised stochastic models were developed which allowed $p(h)$ to deviate from π. From the decision theory side, Siegel attempted to rationalize observed results by postulating that Ss like to vary their responses, and that $p(h)$ represents a balance maximizing the sum of utility of variability and the utility of the consequence. Siegel's approach was not completely successful, but it was an interesting attempt to rationalize behavior which, on the surface, appears irrational. It cannot be said that either mathematical learning theory or decision theory has proved to be highly successful in accounting for the rich and often bewildering complexity of the experimental data. Neither approach has been able to invalidate the other, nor is this likely to happen.

Even when the sequence of reinforcements is Bernoulli, the sequence of responses typically is not. For one thing, the "gambler's fallacy" has often been found in experimental results: after several outcomes of one kind in a row, Ss become more likely to predict the alternate event. In some experiments, at least, the "fallacy" has disappeared over the course of several hundred trials. Ss seem unable to recognize the simplicity of a Bernoulli series; they therefore attempt to figure out the patterning involved.

The Bernoulli series is the simplest probability prediction task S can be asked to do, but other tasks have been studied as well. In a Markov series, in contrast to a Bernoulli series, the event probabilities vary from trial to trial, depending on the previous outcome or outcomes. In the Markov series or order 1, Ss predictions, conditional on the previous outcome, roughly match the event probabilities conditional on the previous outcome. This behavior is not optimal, but it represents a degree of adaptive responding. As the order (complexity) of a Markov series becomes greater and greater, Ss become less and less able to recognize the dependencies involved.

In *contingent probability learning,* in contrast to the noncontingent case, the feedback (reinforcement) provided on each trial is dependent on the S's response. Feedback is given only for "correct" responses; S is not allowed to observe the occurrence of an event he didn't predict. In the usual form of the contingent task ("space prediction"), S is led to believe that exactly one prediction can be correct on a trial, as in the noncontingent case, but actually, zero, one, or more predictions might be "correct."

In probabilistic discrimination learning, the event probabilities are dependent on the stimulus presented on a trial. The stimuli may form a discrete set or a "continuum." Approximate conditional probability matching rather than optimality characterizes Ss' responses. The feedback to one stimulus may generalize and affect the responses to a similar stimulus. The use of "misinformative feedback" turns the concept learning task into probabilistic discrimination learning. Finally, we allowed the responses (and reinforcements) to exist on a continuum. An important factor in these experiments is the generalization between adjacent regions of the continuum. Here we considered experiments with multiple-cue continuous stimuli and unidimensional continuous responses.

A truly wide variety of probability learning situations have been studied. Optimal responding, as we have used the term, characterizes none of these situations. Ss have considerable difficulty in adequately comprehending even quite simple probabilistic data. Any conception of man as a rational being will have to depend on fairly weak standards for information-processing ability.

REFERENCES

Anderson, N. H. "Effect of First-Order Conditional Probability in a Two-Choice Learning Situation," *Journal of Experimental Psychology* (1960), **59,** 73–93.

Anderson, N. H. "An Evaluation of Stimulus Sampling Theory: Comments on Professor Estes' Paper," in A. W. Melton (ed.), *Categories of Human Learning.* New York: Academic Press, 1964, pp. 129–144.

Anderson, N. H., & Grant, D. A. "A Test of a Statistical Learning Theory Model for Two Choice Behavior with Double Stimulus Events," *Journal of Experimental Psychology* (1957), **54,** 305–317.

Anderson, N. H., & Whalen, R. E. "Likelihood Judgements and Sequential Effects in a Two-Choice Probability Learning Situation," *Journal of Experimental Psychology* (1960), **60,** 111–120.

Atkinson, R. C. "An Analysis of the Effect of Nonreinforced Trials in Terms of Statistical Learning Theory," *Journal of Experimental Psychology* (1956), **52,** 28–32.

Atkinson, R. C. "Choice Behavior and Monetary Payoff: Strong and Weak Conditioning," in J. H. Criswell, H. Solomon, & P. Suppes (eds.), *Mathematical Methods in Small Group Processes.* Stanford, Calif.: Stanford University, 1962, pp. 23–34.

Atkinson, R. C., Bogartz, W. H., & Turner, R. N. "Discrimination Learning with Probabilistic Reinforcement Schedules," *Journal of Experimental Psychology* (1959), **57,** 349–350.

Atkinson, R. C., Bower, G. H., & Crothers, E. J. *An Introduction to Mathematical Learning Theory.* New York: Wiley, 1965.

Atkinson, R. C., & Estes, W. K. "Stimulus Sampling Theory," in R. D. Luce, R. R. Bush, & E. Galanter (eds.), *Handbook of Mathematical Psychology,* Vol. 2. New York: Wiley, 1963, pp. 121–268.

Atkinson, R. C., Sommer, G. R., & Sterman, M. B. "Decision Making by Children as a Function of Amount of Reinforcement," *Psychological Reports* (1960), **6,** 299–306.

Beach, L. R., & Shoenberger, R. W. "Event Salience and Response Frequency in a Ten-Alternative Probability-Learning Situation," *Journal of Experimental Psychology* (1965), **69,** 312–316.

Bendig, A. W. "The Effect of Reinforcement on the Alternation of Guesses," *Journal of Experimental Psychology* (1951), **41,** 105–107.

Bogartz, R. S. "Sequential Dependencies in Children's Probability Learning," *Journal of Experimental Psychology* (1965), **70,** 365–370.

Bourne, L. E., Jr. "Long-Term Effects of Misinformative Feedback upon Concept Identification," *Journal of Experimental Psychology* (1963), **65,** 139–147.

Brackbill, Y., & Bravos, A. "The Utility of Correctly Predicting Infrequent Events," *Journal of Experimental Psychology* (1962), 648–649.

Brackbill, Y., Kappy, M. S., & Starr, R. H. "Magnitude of Reward and Probability Learning," *Journal of Experimental Psychology* (1962), **63,** 32–35.

Brand, H., Sakoda, J. M., & Woods, P. J. "Contingent Partial Reinforcement and the Anticipation of Correct Alternatives," *Journal of Experimental Psychology* (1957a), **53,** 417–424.

Brand, H., Sakoda, J. M., & Woods, P. J. "Effect of a Random versus Pattern Instructional Set in a Contingent Partial Reinforcement Situation," *Psychological Reports* (1957b), **3,** 473–479.

Brody, A. L. "Independence in the Learning of Two Consecutive Responses per Trial," *Journal of Experimental Psychology* (1958), **56,** 16–20.

Brown, J. S., Clark, F. R., & Stein, L. "A New Technique for Studying Spatial Generalization with Voluntary Responses," *Journal of Experimental Psychology* (1958), **55,** 359–362.

Bruner, J. S., Goodnow, J. J., & Austin, G. A. *A Study of Thinking.* New York: Wiley, 1956.

Brunswik, E. "Probability as a Determiner of Rat Behavior," *Journal of Experimental Psychology* (1939), **25,** 175–197.

Brunswik, E. "Organistic Achievement and Environmental Probability," *Psychological Review* (1943), **50,** 255–272.

Brunswik, E., & Herma, H. "Probability Learning of Perceptual Cues in the Establishment of a Weight Illusion," *Journal of Experimental Psychology* (1951), **41,** 281–290.

Burke, C. J., & Estes, W. K. "A Component Model for Stimulus Variables in Discrimination Learning," *Psychometrika* (1957), **22,** 133–145.

Bush, R. R., & Mosteller, F. *Stochastic Models for Learning.* New York: Wiley, 1955.

Castellan, N. J. "Effect of Change of Payoff in Probability Learning," *Journal of Experimental Psychology* (1969), **79,** 178–182.

Chapanis, A. "Random-Number Guessing Behavior," *American Psychologist* (1953), **8,** 332.

Chapman, J. P. "The Spacing of Sequentially Dependent Trials in Probability Learning," *Journal of Experimental Psychology* (1961), **62,** 545–551.

Cole, M. "Search Behavior: A Correction Procedure for Three-Choice Probability Learning," *Journal of Mathematical Psychology* (1965), **2,** 145–170.

Cotton, J. W., & Rechtschaffen, A. "Replication Report: Two- and Three-Choice Verbal-Conditioning Phenomena," *Journal of Experimental Psychology* (1958), **56,** 96.

Craig, G. J., & Myers, J. L. "A Developmental Study of Sequential Two-Choice Decision Making," *Child Development* (1963), **34,** 483–493.

Das, J. P. "Mathematical Solution in the Acquisition of a Verbal CR," *Journal of Experimental Psychology* (1961), **61,** 376–378.

Derks, P. L. "The Generality of the "Conditioning Axiom" in Human Binary Prediction," *Journal of Experimental Psychology* (1962), **63,** 538–545.

Derks, P. L. "Effect of Run Length on the 'Gambler's Fallacy'," *Journal of Experimental Psychology* (1963), **65,** 213–214.

Detambel, M. H. "A Test of a Model for Multiple-Choice Behavior," *Journal of Experimental Psychology* (1955), **49,** 97–104.

Dixon, B. D., & Wickens, D. D. "Spatial Generalization of Voluntary Responses under Two Techniques of Study and Two Levels of Anxiety," *Journal of Experimental Psychology* (1961), **61**, 508–509.

Edwards, W. "Reward Probability, Amount, and Information as Determiners of Sequential Two-Alternative Decisions," *Journal of Experimental Psychology* (1956), **52**, 177–188.

Edwards, W. "Probability Learning in 1000 Trials," *Journal of Experimental Psychology* (1961a), **62**, 385–394.

Edwards, W. "Costs and Payoffs are Instructions," *Psychological Review* (1961b), **68**, 275–284.

Edwards, W. "Dynamic Decision Theory and Probabilistic Information Processing," *Human Factors* (1962), **4**, 59–73.

Engler, J. "Marginal and Conditional Stimulus and Response Probabilities in Verbal Conditioning," *Journal of Experimental Psychology* (1958), **55**, 303–317.

Erdelyi, M., Watts, B., & Voss, J. F. "Effect of Probability of Competing Responses in Probabilistic Verbal Acquisition," *Journal of Experimental Psychology* (1964), **68**, 323–329.

Estes, W. K. "Toward a Statistical Theory of Learning," *Psychological Review* (1950), **57**, 94–107.

Estes, W. K. "Individual Behavior in Uncertain Situations: An Interpretation in Terms of Statistical Association Theory," in R. M. Thrall, C. H. Coombs, & R. L. Davis (eds.), *Decision Processes*. New York: Wiley, 1954, pp. 127–137.

Estes, W. K. "The Statistical Approach to Learning Theory," in S. Koch (ed.), *Psychology: A Study of a Science*, Vol. 2. *General Systematic Formulations, Learning, and Special Processes*. New York: McGraw-Hill, 1959, pp. 380–491.

Estes, W. K. "Learning Theory," in P. R. Farnsworth, O. McNemar, & Q. McNemar (eds.), *Annual Review of Psychology*, Vol. 13. Palo Alto, Calif.: Annual Reviews, Inc., 1962a, pp. 107–144.

Estes, W. K. "Theoretical Treatments of Differential Reward in Multiple-Choice Learning and Two-Person Interactions," in J. H. Criswell, H. Solomon, & P. Suppes (eds.), *Mathematical Methods in Small Group Processes*. Stanford, Calif.: Stanford University, 1962b, pp. 133–149.

Estes, W. K. "Probability Learning," in A. W. Melton (ed.), *Categories of Human Learning*. New York: Academic Press, 1964, pp. 89–128.

Estes, W. K., & Burke, C. J. "A Theory of Stimulus Variability in Learning," *Psychological Review* (1953), **60**, 276–286.

Estes, W. K., Burke, C. J., Atkinson, R. C., & Frankmann, J. P. "Probabilistic Discrimination Learning," *Journal of Experimental Psychology* (1957), **54**, 233–239.

Estes, W. K., & Straughan, J. H. "Analysis of a Verbal Conditioning Situation in Terms of Statistical Learning Theory," *Journal of Experimental Psychology* (1954), **47**, 225–234.

Evans, W. O. "Two Factors Affecting Stimulus Generalization on a Spatial Dimension," *Journal of Experimental Psychology* (1961), **61**, 142–149.

Fagan, C. A., & North, A. J. "A Verification of the Guessing Sequence Hypothesis about Spread of Effect," *Journal of Experimental Psychology* (1951), **41**, 349–351.

Feldman, J. "On the Negative Recency Hypothesis in the Prediction of a Series of Binary Symbols," *American Journal of Psychology* (1959), **72**, 597–599.

Feldman, J. "Simulation of Behavior in the Binary Choice Experiment," *Proceedings of the Western Joint Computer Conference* (1961), **19**, 133–144. Reprinted in E. A. Feigenbaum & J. Feldman (eds.), *Computers and Thought*. New York: McGraw-Hill, 1963, pp. 329–346.

Feldman, J., & Hanna, J. F. "The Structure of Responses to a Sequence of Binary Events," *Journal of Mathematical Psychology* (1966), **3**, 371–387.

Flood, M. M. "Environmental Non-Stationarity in a Sequential Decision-Making Experiment," in R. M. Thrall, C. H. Coombs, & R. L. Davis (eds.), *Decision Processes*. New York: Wiley, 1954, pp. 287–299.

Friedman, M. P., Burke, C. J., Cole, M., Keller, L., Millward, R. B., & Estes, W. K. "Two-Choice Behavior under Extended Training with Shifting Probabilities of Reinforcement," in R. C. Atkinson (ed.), *Studies in Mathematical Psychology*. Stanford, Calif.: Stanford University, 1964, pp. 250–316.

Galanter, E. H., & Smith, W. A. S. "Some Experiments on a Simple Thought Problem," *American Journal of Psychology* (1958), **71**, 359–366.

Gardner, R. A. "Probability-Learning with Two and Three Choices," *American Journal of Psychology* (1957), **70**, 174–185.

Gardner, R. A. "Multiple-Choice Decision-Behavior," *American Journal of Psychology* (1958), **71**, 710–717.

Gardner, R. A. "Multiple-Choice Decision-Behavior with Dummy Choices," *American Journal of Psychology* (1961), **74**, 205–214.

Gardner, R. A., & Forsythe, J. B. "Two-Choice Decision Behavior with Many Alternative Events," *Journal of Experimental Psychology* (1961), **62**, 631.

Godfrey, M. D., Granger, C. W. J., & Morgenstern, O. "The Random Walk Hypothesis of Stock Market Behavior," *Kyklos* (1964), **17**, 1–30.

Goodfellow, L. D. "A Psychological Interpretation of the Results of the Zenith Radio Experiments in Telepathy," *Journal of Experimental Psychology* (1938), **23**, 601–632.

Goodnow, J. J. "Determinants of Choice-Distribution in Two-Choice Situations," *American Journal of Psychology* (1955), **68**, 106–116.

Goodnow, J. J., & Pettigrew, T. F. "Some Sources of Difficulty in Solving Simple Problems," *Journal of Experimental Psychology* (1956), **51**, 385–392.

Goodnow, J. J., Rubinstein, I., & Lubin, A. "Response to Changing Patterns of Events," *American Journal of Psychology* (1960), **73**, 56–67.

Grant, D. A., Hake, H. W., & Hornseth, J. P. "Acquisition and Extinction of a Verbal Conditioned Response with Differing Percentages of Reinforcement," *Journal of Experimental Psychology* (1951), **42**, 1–5.

Greeno, J. G. "Effects of Nonreinforced Trials in Two-Choice Learning with Noncontingent Reinforcement," *Journal of Experimental Psychology* (1962), **64**, 373–379.

Hake, H. W., & Hyman, R. "Perception of the Statistical Structure of a Random Series of Binary Symbols," *Journal of Experimental Psychology* (1953), **45**, 64–74.

Hammond, K. R., & Summers, D. A. "Cognitive Dependence on Linear and Nonlinear Cues," *Psychological Review* (1965), **72**, 215–224.

Hansel, C. E. M. *ESP: A Scientific Evaluation*. New York: Scribner's, 1966.

Hilgard, E. R., & Bower, G. H. *Theories of Learning,* 3rd ed. New York: Appleton-Century-Crofts, 1966.

Howell, W. C., & Funaro, J. F. "Prediction on the Basis of Conditional Probabilities," *Journal of Experimental Psychology* (1965), **69,** 92–99.

Humphreys, L. G. "The Effect of Random Alternation of Reinforcement on the Acquisition and Extinction of Conditioned Eyelid Reactions," *Journal of Experimental Psychology* (1939a), **25,** 141–158.

Humphreys, L. G. "Acquisition and Extinction of Verbal Expectations in a Situation Analogous to Conditioning," *Journal of Experimental Psychology* (1939b), **25,** 294–301.

Jarvik, M. E. "Probability Learning and a Negative Recency Effect in the Serial Anticipation of Alternative Symbols," *Journal of Experimental Psychology* (1951), **41,** 291–297.

Jenkins, W. O., & Cunningham, L. M. "The Guessing-Sequence Hypothesis, the 'Spread of Effect,' and Number-Guessing Habits," *Journal of Experimental Psychology* (1949), **39,** 158-168.

Jenkins, W. O., & Stanley, J. C., Jr. "Partial Reinforcement: A Review and Critique," *Psychological Bulletin* (1950), **47,** 193–234.

Johannsen, W. J. "Concept Identification under Misinformative and Subsequent Informative Feedback Conditions," *Journal of Experimental Psychology* (1962), **64,** 631–635.

Jones, J. E. "Deviations from Matching Behavior in Probability Learning," *Journal of Psychology* (1961), **52,** 335–345.

Kroll, N. E. A. "Learning of Several Simultaneous Probability Learning Problems as a Function of Overall Event Probability and Prior Knowledge," *Journal of Experimental Psychology* (1970), **83,** 209–215.

Laplace, P. S. *A Philosophical Essay on Probabilities.* Translated by F. W. Truscott and F. L. Emory. New York: Dover, 1951.

Lee, W. "Conditioning Parameter Model for Reinforcement Generalization in Probabilistic Discrimination Learning," *Journal of Mathematical Psychology* (1966), **3,** 184–196.

Lee, W., & Garner, W. R. "Prediction and Estimation of a Random Fluctuation," *Journal of Experimental Psychology* (1966), **71,** 516–520.

Lee, W., & Janke, M. "Categorizing Externally Distributed Stimulus Samples for Three Continua," *Journal of Experimental Psychology* (1964), **68,** 376–382.

Lee, W., & Janke, M. "Categorizing Externally Distributed Stimulus Samples for Unequal Molar Probabilities," *Psychological Reports* (1965), **17,** 79–90.

Lee, W., & Zentall, T. "Factorial Effects in the Categorization of Externally Distributed Stimulus Samples," *Perception and Psychophysics* (1966), **1,** 120–124.

Lindman, H., & Edwards W. "Unlearning the Gambler's Fallacy," *Journal of Experimental Psychology* (1961), **62,** 630.

Little, K. B., Brackbill, Y., & Kassel, S. H. "A Test of a General Utility Theory Model for Probability Learning," *Journal of Experimental Psychology* (1962), **63,** 404–408.

Luce, R. D., & Suppes, P. "Preference, Utility, and Subjective Probability," in Luce, R. D., Bush, R. R., & Galanter, E. (eds.), *Handbook of Mathematical Psychology,* Vol. 3. New York: Wiley, 1965, pp. 249–410.

Mandler, G., Cowan, P. A., & Gold, C. "Concept Learning and Probability Matching," *Journal of Experimental Psychology* (1964), **67,** 514–522.

McCormack, P. D. "Spatial Generalization and Probability-Learning in a Five-Choice Situation," *American Journal of Psychology* (1959), **72,** 125–138.

McCracken, J., Osterhout, C., & Voss, J. F. "Effects of Instruction in Probability Learning," *Journal of Experimental Psychology* (1962), **64,** 267–271.

Messick, D. M. "The Utility of Variability in Probability Learning," *Psychonomic Science* (1965), **3,** 355–356.

Messick, D. M., & Rapoport, A. "A Comparison of Two Payoff Functions on Multiple-Choice Decision Behavior," *Journal of Experimental Psychology* (1965a), **69,** 75–83.

Messick, D. M., & Rapoport, A. "Expected Value and Response Uncertainty in Multiple-Choice Decision Behavior," *Journal of Experimental Psychology* (1965b), **70,** 224–230.

Morin, R. E. "Factors Influencing Rate and Extent of Learning in the Presence of Misinformative Feedback," *Journal of Experimental Psychology* (1955), **49,** 343–351.

Morse, E. B., & Runquist, W. N. "Probability-Matching with an Unscheduled Random Sequence," *American Journal of Psychology* (1960), **73,** 603–607.

Myers, J. L., & Atkinson, R. C. "Choice Behavior and Reward Structure," *Journal of Mathematical Psychology* (1964), **1,** 170–203.

Myers, J. L., Fort, J. G., Katz, L., & Suydam, M. M. "Differential Monetary Gains and Losses and Event Probability in a Two-Choice Situation," *Journal of Experimental Psychology* (1963), **66,** 521–522.

Nagamachi, M. "The Effect of Buzzer-Shock upon the Predictive Behavior in a Two-Choice Situation," *Psychologia* (1961), **3,** 159–164.

Neimark, E. D. "Effects of Type of Nonreinforcement and Number of Alternative Responses in Two Verbal Conditioning Situations," *Journal of Experimental Psychology* (1956), **52,** 209–220.

Neimark, E. D., & Estes, W. K. (eds.) *Stimulus Sampling Theory.* San Francisco: Holden-Day, 1967.

Neimark, E. D., & Shuford, E. H. "Comparison of Predictions and Estimates in a Probability Learning Situation," *Journal of Experimental Psychology* (1959), **57,** 294–298.

Nicks, D. C. "Prediction of Sequential Two-Choice Decisions From Event Runs," *Journal of Experimental Psychology* (1959), **57,** 105–114.

Nies, R. C. "Effects of Probable Outcome Information on Two-Choice Learning," *Journal of Experimental Psychology* (1962), **64,** 430–433.

Overall, J. E. "A Cognitive Probability Model for Learning," *Psychometrika* (1960), **25,** 159–172.

Peterson, C. R., Hammond, K. R., & Summers, D. A. "Optimal Responding in Multiple-Cue Probability Learning," *Journal of Experimental Psychology* (1965), **70,** 270–276.

Peterson, C., & Miller, A. "Mode, Median, and Mean as Optimal Strategies." *Journal of Experimental Psychology* (1964), **68,** 363–367.

Peterson, C. R., & Ulehla, Z. J. "Sequential Patterns and Maximizing," *Journal of Experimental Psychology* (1965), **69,** 1–4.

Pishkin, V. "Effects of Probability of Misinformation and Number of Irrelevant Dimensions upon Concept Identification," *Journal of Experimental Psychology* (1960), **59,** 371–378.

Popper, J., & Atkinson, R. C. "Discrimation Learning in a Verbal Conditioning Situation," *Journal of Experimental Psychology* (1958), **56,** 21–25.

Radlow, R. "Decision Making and the Theory of Learning," in S. Messick & A. H. Brayfield (eds.), *Decision and Choice.* New York: McGraw-Hill, 1964, pp. 267–275.

Restle, F. *Psychology of Judgment and Choice.* New York: Wiley, 1961.

Restle, F. "Siegel's Contributions to Learning Theory," in S. Messick & A. H. Brayfield (eds.), *Decision and Choice.* New York: McGraw-Hill, 1964, pp. 276–283.

Restle, F. "Run Structure and Probability Learning: Disproof of Restle's Model," *Journal of Experimental Psychology* (1966), **72,** 382–389.

Rose, R. M., & Vitz, P. C. "Role of Runs in Probability Learning," *Journal of Experimental Psychology* (1966), **72,** 751–760.

Rosenberg, S. "Behavior in a Continuous-Response Task with Noncontingent Reinforcement," *Journal of Experimental Psychology* (1963), **66,** 168–176.

Rubinstein, I. "Some Factors in Probability Matching," *Journal of Experimental Psychology* (1959), **57,** 413–416.

Schnorr, J. A., & Myers, J. L. "Negative Contrast in Human Probability Learning as a Function of Incentive Magnitudes," *Journal of Experimental Psychology* (1967), **75,** 492–499.

Schoeffler, M. S. "Prediction of Some Stochastic Events: A Regret Equalization Model," *Journal of Experimental Psychology* (1962), **64,** 615–622.

Senders, V. L., & Sowards, A. "Analysis of Response Sequences in the Setting of a Psychophysical Experiment," *American Journal of Psychology* (1952), **65,** 358–374.

Sheffield, F. D. " 'Spread of Effect' without Reward or Learning," *Journal of Experimental Psychology* (1949), **39,** 575–579.

Siegel, S. "Decision Making and Learning under Varying Conditions of Reinforcement," *Annals of the New York Academy of Sciences* (1961), **89,** 766–783.

Siegel, S. "Theoretical Models of Choice and Strategy Behavior: Stable State Behavior in the Two-Choice Uncertain Outcome Situation," *Psychometrika* (1959), **24,** 303–316.

Siegel, S., & Goldstein, D. A. "Decision-Making Behavior in a Two-Choice Uncertain Outcome Situation," *Journal of Experimental Psychology* (1959), **57,** 37–42.

Siegel, S., Siegel, A. E., & Andrews, J. M. *Choice, Strategy, and Utility.* New York: McGraw-Hill, 1964.

Simon, H. A. "A Comparison of Game Theory and Learning Theory," *Psychometrika* (1956), **21,** 267–272. Reprinted in H. A. Simon, *Models of Man.* New York: Wiley, 1957, pp. 274–279.

Simon, S. H. "Differential Prediction and Postdiction of Win-Lose Events in a Spatial-Generalization Problem," *Journal of Experimental Psychology* (1964), **67,** 342–351.

Skinner, B. F. "The Processes Involved in the Repeated Guessing of Alternatives," *Journal of Experimental Psychology* (1942), **30,** 495–503.

Sternberg, S. "Stochastic Learning Theory," in R. D. Luce, R. R. Bush, & E. Galanter (eds.), *Handbook of Mathematical Psychology,* Vol. 2. New York: Wiley, 1963, pp. 1–120.

Stevenson, H. W., & Weir, M. W. "Variables Affecting Children's Performance in a Probability Learning Task," *Journal of Experimental Psychology* (1959), **57,** 403–412.

Stevenson, H. W., & Zigler, E. F. "Probability Learning in Children," *Journal of Experimental Psychology* (1958), **56,** 185–192.

Summers, S. A. "The Learning of Responses to Multiple Weighted Cues," *Journal of Experimental Psychology* (1962), **64,** 29–34.

Suppes, P., & Atkinson, R. C. *Markov Learning Models for Multiperson Interactions.* Stanford, Calif.: Stanford University, 1960.

Suppes, P., & Frankmann, R. W. "Test of Stimulus Sampling Theory for a Continuum of Responses with Unimodal Noncontingent Determinate Reinforcement," *Journal of Experimental Psychology* (1961), **61,** 122–132.

Suppes, P., & Rouanet, H. "A Simple Discrimination Experiment with a Continuum of Responses," in R. C. Atkinson (ed.), *Studies in Mathematical Psychology.* Stanford, Calif.: Stanford University, 1964, pp. 317–357.

Swensson, R. G. "Incentive Shifts in a Three-Choice Decision Situation," *Psychonomic Science* (1965), **2,** 101–102.

Todd, F. J., & Hammond, K. R. "Differential Feedback in Two Multiple-Cue Probability Learning Tasks," *Behavioral Science* (1965), **10,** 429–435.

Tolman, E. C., & Brunswik, E. "The Organism and the Causal Texture of the Environment," *Psychological Review* (1935), **42,** 43–77.

Tversky, A., & Edwards, W. "Information versus Reward in Binary Choices," *Journal of Experimental Psychology* (1966), **71,** 680–683.

Uhl, C. N. "Learning of Interval Concepts: I. Effects of Differences in Stimulus Weights," *Journal of Experimental Psychology* (1963), **66,** 264–273.

Van der Meer, H. C. "The Influence of Instruction in a Two-Choice Probabilistic Learning Task under Partial Reinforcement," *Acta Psychologica* (1960), **17,** 357–376.

Voss, J. F., Thompson, C. P., & Keegan, J. H. "Acquisition of Probabilistic Paired Associates as a Function of $S\text{-}R_1$, $S\text{-}R_2$ Probability," *Journal of Experimental Psychology* (1959), **58,** 390–399.

Witte, R. S. "Long-Term Effects of Patterned Reward Schedules," *Journal of Experimental Psychology* (1964), **68,** 588–594.

Wolin, B. R., Weichel, R., Terebinski, S. J., & Hansford, E. A. "Performance on Complexly Patterned Binary Event Sequences," *Psychological Monographs* (1965), **79,** No. 7 (Whole No. 600).

Woods, P. J. "The Effects of Motivation and Probability of Reward on Two-Choice Learning," *Journal of Experimental Psychology* (1959), **57,** 380–385.

Wykoff, L. B., & Sidowski, J. B. "Probability Discrimination in a Motor Task," *Journal of Experimental Psychology* (1955), **50,** 225–231.

Yellott, J. I., Jr. "Probability Learning with Noncontingent Success," *Journal of Mathematical Psychology* (1969), **6,** 541–575.

Yntema, D. B., & Torgerson, W. S. "Man-Computer Cooperation in Decisions Requiring Common Sense," *IRE Transactions on Human Factors in Electronics* (1961), **HFE-2,** 20–26.

CHAPTER 7

Probabilistic Categorization and ROC Curve Analysis

7.1 INTRODUCTION

A common task is: given an object, place it correctly in one of a discrete number of *categories*. The "object" need not be a "thing" of the sort that can be picked up and moved around. It can simply be a perceivable property or set of properties used as a basis for categorization.[1] Often objects can be assigned to categories without error; we do not consider this case in the present chapter. We might say we are concerned with *probabilistic categorization*.[2] To illustrate: (1) A doctor categorizes a patient as having a particular disease, rather than another, on the basis of symptoms; however, the doctor may be wrong even if he is perfectly competent since two different diseases can produce the same symptoms. (2) A zoologist categorizes an insect specimen into one of several related species; because of variability within each species, members of different species may be very similar in appearance, so the categorization could be wrong.

To a large extent, we will discuss the utilization of "signals" to make one or another of a discrete set of inferences about the state of nature. For example, radar blips are often ambiguous. Just before the Pearl Harbor attack, radar blips were interpreted to mean that American planes were in the air; actually, the blips represented Japanese planes. We shall largely be concerned with a more

---

[1] The term "classification" might be used instead; likewise, for "category" we might substitute "class" or "concept." Sometimes distinctions are made between these terms, but definitions in this area are loose and variable.

[2] "Concepts" are typically treated in non-probabilistic terms; however, Bruner, Goodnow, and Austin (1956), in *A Study of Thinking,* a book largely devoted to the learning of "deterministic" concepts, include a chapter, "On categorizing with probabilistic cues."

mundane case. A laboratory subject (S) listens through earphones and on the basis of a property of a time interval "categorizes" that interval as one in which a very low-intensity signal was present or one in which no signal was present; in such a situation S can be correct only with some probability, regardless of his strategy for responding.

The theory of greatest concern to us for dealing with the preceding experimental situation is called *signal detection theory*. This chapter might well have been so titled, for this theory and the experimental work inspired by it constitute well-nigh the entire chapter. Logically, however, signal detection theory is a special case of the decision theory of categorization. In my opinion, it is more enlightening to approach the topics considered in this chapter from the broader viewpoint.

Typically categorization involves multidimensional stimuli and many categories, but for simplicity our analysis will concentrate on two categories whose combined set of members differ only along a single dimension. The multidimensional extension of the theory, however, is closely related to *discriminant analysis* (Rozeboom, 1966; Wilks, 1962), a statistical technique for classifying, say, persons into categories (for example, "normal," "neurotic," or "psychotic") on the basis of a set of test scores for each person (Eysenck, 1961).

7.2 DECISION THEORY OF CATEGORIZATION

As stated, our analysis will concentrate on two categories whose combined set of members differ only by their various values along a single dimension x. The different values of members of a category compose a probability distribution. Generally, we take this distribution to be continuous and to have a specified probability density at each value of x. Often we assume that the distribution is normal (Gaussian). Except for minor modifications like substituting discrete probabilities for probability densities, the exposition applies for discrete distributions as well as for continuous ones. For the sake of brevity, we usually leave the reader to make the necessary adjustments.

We assume that one category is chosen randomly, and that a sample value x is then chosen randomly from the category (distribution) and presented to S (who takes the part of the protagonist, P^A, in our decision analysis). S must then state from which category the sample point x derived. We call the x presented to S the *observation*. To be specific, suppose that x is "height," and that there are two categories consisting of adult men (category b_2) and adult women (category b_1). Suppose the heights for each category compose a normal probability distribution. (See Figure 7.1. Of course, a finite set of objects cannot compose a continuous probability distribution. The reader is assumed to be capable of surmounting this sort of license.) The height of a particular person, x_i, is presented to S, and he must state whether the object (person) characterized by observation x_i is male or female; i.e., is the object a member of category

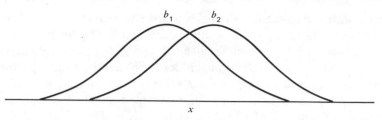

Figure 7.1. Hypothetical distributions of measurements on attribute *x* (height) for categories (sets) b_1 and b_2, women and men, respectively.

b_1 or of category b_2? But how can you tell a person's sex from his height? A person 65 inches tall could be male or female. True. Nonetheless, if a response is required, one choice may be better than the other.

If some assumptions are met, decision theory can specify what response *S* should give. As we know from Chapter 2, different decision principles exist which give different decision specifications. We will consider two: the expected value (EV) principle, and the maximin principle.

Expected Value Principle

A decision theory solution must specify a choice for each possible observation *x* which might appear.[3] Once we know the conditional probabilities $p(b_1|x)$ and $p(b_2|x)$, the EV solution is very simple. We assume that a payoff matrix exists, as follows:

State of Nature

		b_1	b_2
	a_1	a	b
Choice			
	a_2	c	d

a_1 is the response, "the category represented is b_1," and a_2 corresponds to b_2 similarly. *a, b, c, d* are the payoffs. It is assumed that the payoff to *S* depends only on the state of nature and on the choice, and, with these specified, the payoff is independent of the observation sampled from the state of nature. For a given x_i, if we know $p(b_1|x_i)$ and $p(b_2|x_i)$, we can calculate the expected value for a_1 and a_2, and by the EV principle we choose the alternative with the higher EV. In other words, for a given x_i and the corresponding conditional

---

[3] In the abstract, we should keep open the possibility of a mixed strategy specification; for the decision principles we shall discuss, however, mixed strategies for a given observation are not required.

probabilities, the situation simplifies to the situation of Chapter 2; one can forget about other possible x values and the distributions of x for b_1 and b_2.

The conditional probabilities $p(b_1|x)$ and $p(b_2|x)$ are called *posterior* probabilities since these are the probabilities for b_1 and b_2 which apply *after* observation x is presented. There are also *prior* probabilities, $p(b_1)$ and $p(b_2)$, which apply *before* the observation is presented and might represent the relative frequencies of sampling of distributions b_1 and b_2. The prior probabilities and the distributions for b_1 and b_2 are important because with them we can use Bayes' formula to calculate the posterior probabilities we need. The details are given later in this chapter.

Let $p = p(b_2|x)$. There exists a *critical value of p*, p_c, such that the EV principle implies the following: whenever $p > p_c$, one choice is specified, and whenever $p < p_c$, the alternate choice is specified. This critical value, p_c, is a function of the payoffs alone.

By definition of expected value, the EV's for the two choices are

$$EV_1 = (1 - p)a + pb$$
$$EV_2 = (1 - p)c + pd$$

Define D to be

$$
\begin{aligned}
D &= EV_2 - EV_1 \\
&= (1 - p)(c - a) + p(d - b) \\
&= [(a - c) + (d - b)]p - (a - c) \quad\quad (7.1)
\end{aligned}
$$

Since the payoffs a, b, c, and d are constants, D is a linear function of p. Generally, the slope of this function $((a - c) + (d - b))$ will be positive (for example, if $a > c$, and $d > b$, which merely states that S is better off when he is "right" than when he is "wrong"). We exemplify such a function in Figure 7.2. The value of p for which $D = 0$ is p_c; it can be determined from Equation 7.1 by setting $D = 0$ and solving for p:

$$p_c = \frac{(a - c)}{(a - c) + (d - b)} \quad\quad (7.2)[4]$$

Note on Figure 7.2 that p_c is the value of p where the D function crosses the abscissa. Also note that for any value of $p > p_c$, $D > 0$ and the EV principle specifies a_2. For any $p < p_c$, $D < 0$ and the EV principle specifies a_1.

It is possible for the graph of Figure 7.2 to have a negative slope, for example, under the unusual circumstances that S is paid better for being "wrong" than "right." Nonetheless, D would still be a linear function of p; therefore, to one

---

[4] $0 < p_c < 1$ if we can avoid $a = c$ and $b = d$, and if we avoid dominance. By assumption, we do so avoid. Diagrammatically, these assumptions forbid that the slope of D versus p (Fig. 7.2) be zero; therefore, the function must cross the abscissa.

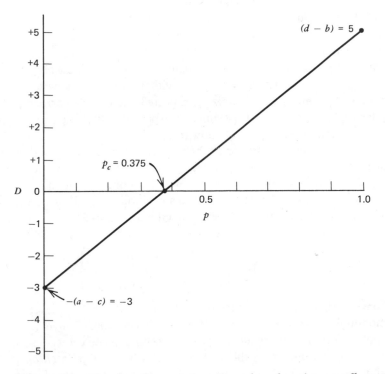

Figure 7.2. The function relating D and p for the payoff matrix shown.

side of p_c D would always have the same sign and the same choice would be specified, and to the other side of p_c, the other choice would always be specified.

Henceforth, assume that the slope of D is positive, i.e., $(a - c) + (b - d) > 0$, i.e., $(a - c) > -(d - b)$. Then the EV principle specifies the following decision rule:

$$\text{If } p \begin{Bmatrix} > p_c \\ = p_c \\ < p_c \end{Bmatrix}, \text{ choose } \begin{Bmatrix} a_2 \\ a_1 \text{ or } a_2 \\ a_1 \end{Bmatrix}.$$

If $p_c = 0.5$, this rule is equivalent to maximizing the expected number of correct categorizations, since one then chooses a_2 if $p(b_2|x) > 0.5$, i.e., if, given

x, b_2 is more probable than b_1. In Chapter 6 we discussed this reasoning, and there it implied that S should always predict the more probable event in a two-choice noncontingent probability learning task. The reasoning here is precisely the same, except that with different observations, different "events" (b_1 or b_2) may be more probable. The reader should be able to see at this point that our "probabilistic categorization" task is a "probabilistic discrimination" task (Section 6.11) with a continuum of observations (these were called stimuli in Chapter 6). This chapter, then, might be said to elaborate the material on probabilistic discrimination, particularly with regard to "signal detection."

From Equation 7.2 one can deduce the necessary and sufficient conditions for $p_c = 0.5$, namely, that $(a - c) = (d - b)$. A special case of this is the symmetric payoff matrix for which being "right" for either choice is equally valuable ($a = d$), and being "wrong" for either choice is, likewise, equally valuable ($b = c$). A strategy of maximizing expected number of correct choices is, then, equivalent to a strategy of maximizing expected value when payoff depends only on being right or wrong, not on how one is right or wrong.

Figure 7.3 relates posterior probability to x for the two equal-variance normal distributions of Figure 7.1, assuming equal prior probabilities. Here p and x are related by a one-to-one monotonic function, which, indeed, is always the case for two equal-variance normal distributions regardless of the values of the prior probabilities. For this type of functional relationship, the decision rule can be translated to:

$$\text{If } x \begin{Bmatrix} > x_c \\ = x_c \\ < x_c \end{Bmatrix}, \text{ choose } \begin{Bmatrix} a_2 \\ a_1 \text{ or } a_2 \\ a_1 \end{Bmatrix}.$$

where x_c is the *critical value* of x. Decision theory divides the observational continuum into two response regions; observations above x_c should receive response a_2, and observations below x_c should receive response a_1. Because x_c divides the continuum in this fashion, it has been called a *cutoff point,* a *cutoff,* and a *cut-point.* The same terms might apply to the critical probability, p_c.

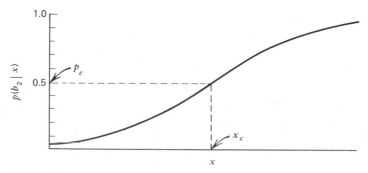

Figure 7.3. Posterior probability $p(b_2|x)$ as a function of x, for the distributions of Figure 7.1.

In general, however, decision theory does not specify such a single cutoff point[5] on the x continuum. When, for example, two normal distributions have unequal variances, the function relating p and x is nonmonotonic. In this case, the cutoff on p does not imply a single cutoff on x. Instead, there may be two critical x_c values, implying two response regions for one response (a_1) at the extremes of x and a central response region for the alternate response (see Figure 7.4). Or, if p_c is large enough, there may be no x_c value; all observations would then require the a_1 response. In Figure 7.4, $\sigma_2 < \sigma_1$. Were the reverse true, the central response region would be for a_1 instead of a_2.

More generally, one could consider any possible function relating p and x, for example, the function of Figure 7.5. Based on the cutoff rule for p, there would be several response regions for both a_1 and a_2.

Calculation of Posterior Probabilities. We have described the expected value solution, given the posterior probabilities and the payoff matrix. We now discuss the calculation of posterior probabilities.

Posterior probabilities are calculated by utilizing Bayes' formula, which was described in Section 3.2. Recall that Bayes' formula concerns the calculation of the posterior probability that any of an exclusive, exhaustive set of hypotheses is true, given the following three inputs:

(1) data bearing on the probability (i.e., data having different probabilities of occurring under different hypotheses);
(2) the probabilities of the hypotheses *prior* to receiving the data; and
(3) the likelihoods for the data conditional on the various hypotheses.

The hypotheses (the H_j's of Chapter 3) are the states of nature, b_1 and b_2. The datum is the observation x which is exhibited to S. The prior probabilities, $p(b_1)$ and $p(b_2)$, have been mentioned previously. The likelihoods are the densities of the unit probability distributions for b_1 and b_2, $f(x|b_1)$ and $f(x|b_2)$. Densities are used in place of the probabilities $(p(E|H_j))$ of Chapter 3 because the distribution of the data given a hypothesis is continuous under the present assumptions.

Bayes' formula states that

$$p = p(b_2|x) = \frac{f(x|b_2)p(b_2)}{\displaystyle\sum_{i=1}^{2} f(x|b_i)p(b_i)} \tag{7.3}$$

---

[5] The term "single cutoff point" is probably a redundancy. If there is more than one x_c value, are they all cutoff points? Although I have found no authoritative answer to this question, I believe that the implication of the cutoff terminology is uniqueness and shall reserve the terminology "cutoff point" and its variations for the case of a single critical value. The terminology, then, would always apply to the p continuum, but only sometimes to the x continuum.

If S knows the terms of the right-hand side, he can, in principle, calculate the posterior probability, and he can compare this with the p_c value determined from the payoff matrix. Strictly speaking, in order to follow the dictates of decision theory (EV principle), S need not be able to calculate p exactly—he need only be able to determine whether p is larger or smaller than p_c. It is not clear how S would make this comparison, however, without calculating p.

The prior probabilities do not affect p_c, but they do affect p, and this can affect which choice is specified. Let us consider how and why this happens. Relative prior probability can be illustrated by relative area of probability distribu-

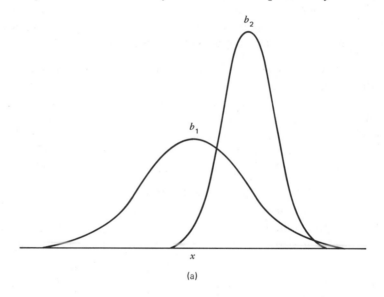

(a)

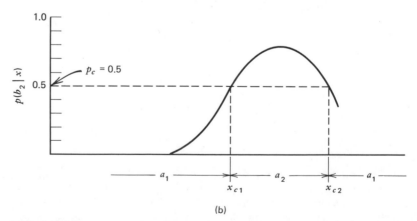

(b)

Figure 7.4. Two unequal-variance normal distributions and the function for them relating posterior probability and x.

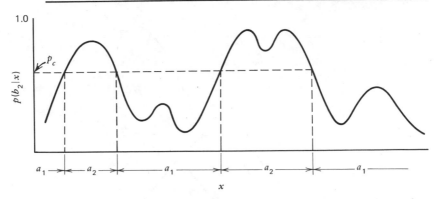

Figure 7.5. An irregular function relating posterior probability and x. The appropriate responses for stimuli from various regions of x are shown.

tions. The solid lines of Figure 7.6(a) represent two distributions with equal areas, i.e., $p(b_1) = p(b_2)$. The dotted line represents a doubling of the area of b_2, i.e., $p'(b_1) = 0.5p'(b_2)$, or $p'(b_1) = 0.33$, and $p'(b_2) = 0.67$. With the larger prior probability for b_2, an observation is more likely to have derived from b_2 than before. This is reflected in the posterior probability functions, p' and p, of Figure 7.6(b). The observation x_i would require decision a_1 for $p(b_2) = 0.50$, but would require decision a_2 for $p(b_2) = 0.67$.

Likelihood Ratio. The likelihood ratio of x for hypothesis b_2 over hypothesis b_1 is defined to be

$$L(x) = L_{21}(x) = \frac{f(x|b_2)}{f(x|b_1)} = \frac{1}{L_{12}(x)} \tag{7.4}$$

Probability densities must be non-negative, but otherwise may have any values; therefore, generally, $0 \le L(x) \le \infty$. For normal distributions $f(x)$ must be positive for any x; therefore, $0 < L(x) < \infty$. The posterior probability $p(b_2|x)$ can be written in terms of the likelihood ratio by substituting $L(x)$ into Equation 7.3 and rearranging.

$$p = p(b_2|x) = \frac{1}{\dfrac{1}{L(x)}\dfrac{p(b_1)}{p(b_2)} + 1} \tag{7.5}$$

Likewise, by rearranging Equation 7.5 we obtain

$$L(x) = \frac{p(b_1)}{p(b_2)}\left(\frac{p}{1-p}\right) \tag{7.6}$$

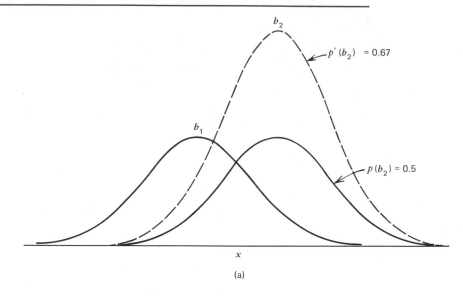

(a)

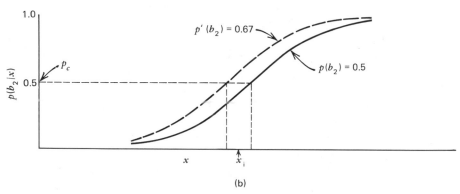

(b)

Figure 7.6. Illustration of how increasing the prior probability of b_2 alters choice specified by the EV principle for stimulus x_i.

From Equations 7.5 and 7.6 we can see that as $L(x)$ goes from 0 to ∞, $p(b_2|x)$ goes from 0 to 1, and that the two quantities are monotonically related (for constant prior probabilities). Therefore, the decision rule can be stated in terms of the likelihood ratio instead of p:

$$\text{If } L(x) \begin{cases} > L_c(x) \\ = L_c(x) \\ < L_c(x) \end{cases}, \text{ choose } \begin{cases} a_2 \\ a_1 \text{ or } a_2 \\ a_1 \end{cases}.$$

$L_c(x)$, the *critical likelihood ratio,* can be calculated from Equation 7.6 by substituting p_c for p. Or, one can substitute Equation 7.2 into Equation 7.6, obtaining

$$L_c(x) = \frac{p(b_1)}{p(b_2)} \frac{(a - c)}{(d - b)},$$ (7.7)

which allows one to calculate L_c from the payoffs and prior probabilities directly.

Note that if $p_c = 0.5$, then by Equation 7.2, $(d - b) = (a - c)$, so from Equation 7.7

$$L_c(x) = \frac{p(b_2)}{p(b_1)}$$ (7.8)

If, furthermore, the prior probabilities are equal, $L_c(x) = 1$.

Likelihood ratio, by its definition in Equation 7.4, is strictly determined by x, and thus is invariant to changes in payoffs and prior probabilities. The critical likelihood ratio, however, is a function of both payoffs and prior probabilities. Likelihood ratio need not be monotonic with x. Because $L(x)$ is monotonic with p, whenever p is monotonic with x, so is $L(x)$, but when p is non-monotonic with x, so is $L(x)$; likewise, if $L(x)$ is non-monotonic with x, so is p.

The critical likelihood ratio, $L_c(x)$, in the literature of interest to us, is often denoted β and is called the *criterion*.[6] Since a decision principle is often called a criterion also, we must take care to distinguish between the two meanings. Henceforth in this chapter, "criterion" will only mean the critical likelihood ratio, β. Sometimes it is assumed that S used a critical likelihood ratio in making his choices, but it is not necessarily assumed that the value employed was one specified by decision theory. One still speaks of S's "criterion."

Effect of Subjective Probability and Utility. We have seen that for each value of x, the EV principle states that the same choice must be made for each occurrence of x (unless $x = x_c$). If S responds on the basis of utilities instead of objective payoffs, there will still be some p_c based on these utilities. Likewise, if the posterior probabilities for each x are subjective and do not correspond with the objective ones, the SEV or SEU principle specifies a choice for each x, and it will be the same each time the same x occurs. Thus, the x continuum must still be divided into response regions, and only one response may be given for repeated trials with the same observation. If posterior subjective probability is monotonic with x, there must be a cutoff point on x, although it might be displaced from the cutoff point calculated from objective parameters.

As in Chapter 6, simple subjectivization of value and probability cannot account for choice inconsistency within a given situation (for a given x, in the present case). By allowing subjective quantities to vary from trial to trial, how-

---

[6] β is small Greek beta.

ever, doubtless any manner of responding might be accommodated within a framework of maximization of expected utility.

Maximin Principle

It is possible to apply other decision principles to the categorization task, though, up to now, no other principles have been shown to be very helpful for either normative or descriptive purposes. The *maximin principle* is worth discussing, however, because it is prominent in the technical literature, and because it can clarify the EV principle by contrast. As mentioned in Chapter 2, statisticians typically enter losses instead of gains in their payoff matrices and speak of the *minimax principle*. Regardless of these variations, the decisions specified are the same, and thus the maximin and minimax principles are equivalent.

It is assumed that S is ignorant of the prior probabilities, but that he knows the likelihoods for each state (i.e., he knows $f(x|b_1)$ and $f(x|b_2)$). Recall from Chapter 2 that the gist of the maximin principle is this: For each option (or mixed strategy) there is a minimum payoff (or expected payoff) across the possible consequences for that option. The maximin principle specifies that P^A should choose the option (or strategy) which makes the minimum payoff as large as possible (i.e., maximal).

For the situation at hand, the two states of nature possible are b_1 and b_2. The situation here differs from the case presented in Chapter 2 in that an observation x is presented which bears on the decision. The set of possible strategies is thereby enlarged, since a choice or strategy must be specified for each possible observation. Nonetheless, an important basic principle of Chapter 2 still applies. There exists an admissible (undominated) set of strategies, and this set is equivalent to the set of possible EV principle strategies for the various possible values of $p(b_1)$. A maximin strategy is admissible, and therefore the maximin solution must be one of the possible EV solutions for different $p(b_1)$. The set of *possible* EV solutions is the set of all possible posterior probability cutoffs, or equivalently, the set of all possible likelihood ratio cutoffs. In other words, the maximin solution must be of the form,

$$\text{if } L(x) \begin{Bmatrix} > \beta \\ = \beta \\ < \beta \end{Bmatrix}, \text{ choose } \begin{Bmatrix} a_2 \\ a_1 \text{ or } a_2 \\ a_1 \end{Bmatrix}.$$

The problem is reduced, then, to finding a criterion (β) for which the minimum (expected) gain is maximal. In general, the β specified by the EV principle does not equal the β specified by the maximin principle.

The expected payoffs for a strategy given b_1 and b_2 are designated g_1 and g_2.

$$g_1 = ap(a_1|b_1) + cp(a_2|b_1)$$
$$g_2 = bp(a_1|b_2) + dp(a_2|b_2)$$

With integral calculus, the conditional response probabilities can be calculated

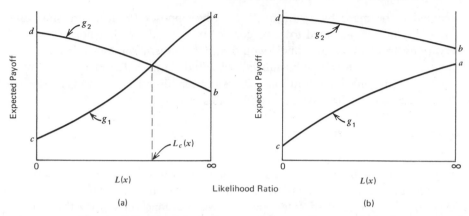

Figure 7.7. Hypothetical expected payoffs g_1 and g_2 for states of nature b_1 and b_2, as a function of likelihood ratio used as a cutoff point. Panels (a) and (b) represent different types of payoff matrices.

for each possible $L(x)$. $p(a_1|b_1)$ and $p(a_1|b_2)$ increase monotonically with $L(x)$ whereas $p(a_2|b_1)$ and $p(a_2|b_2)$ decrease monotonically with $L(x)$. $(p(a_1|b_1) + p(a_2|b_1) = 1.)$ If $a > c$, as we assume, g_1 would have a maximum of a for $p(a_1|b_1) = 1$ $(L(x) = \infty)$ and a minimum of c for $p(a_2|b_1) = 1$ $(L(x) = 0)$. As $L(x)$ goes from zero to infinity, g_1 increases. Likewise, as $L(x)$ increases, g_2, which has a maximum of d, decreases to a minimum of b $(d > b$, by assumption).

Figure 7.7 illustrates the situation. In panel (a), the two graphs, g_1 and g_2, cross. The value of $L(x)$ where they cross is the β specified by the maximin principle, since here the minimum of (g_1, g_2) is as large as possible. The two graphs might not cross, as in panel (b). Here the minimum of (g_1, g_2) is as large as possible when $L(x) = \infty$; thus, the maximin solution is to choose a_1 regardless of x. This guarantees a payoff of at least a.

Even though in principle one must examine an infinity of possible $L(x)$ values to find the maximin solution, in fact the monotonicity of g_1 and g_2 with $L(x)$ means that the solution can be found relatively easily, particularly with a computer. Note that g_1, g_2, and $L(x)$ are unaffected by changes in the prior probabilities, and therefore so is the maximin solution. This might be considered a strong point of the maximin principle, for if reliable information about the prior probabilities were lacking the maximin principle could still be used (use of expected value principle requires that the prior probabilities be specified). On the other hand, if information about prior probabilities were available, one feels that this information should affect the choice to be made; with the maximin principle, it would not. As noted in Section 2.4, some authorities feel that subjective prior probabilities may be used, in which case one would never *have* to resort to the maximin principle for lack of prior probabilities.

The maximin principle could best be justified if the choice of b_1 or b_2 were assumed to be made by a "rational" P^B who opposes P^A in a zero-sum game. This P^B would be assumed to have control over b_1 and b_2 but not over the observations from b_1 or b_2, which would still be drawn randomly from the distributions. Under these circumstances, P^A could do no better than to follow the dictates of the maximin solution. The situation described, however, does not characterize any of the tasks discussed in this chapter.

Extensions of the Theory

The basic ideas of the decision theory of categorization can be extended to encompass more than two options, more than two states of nature, and more than one observational dimension. The mathematics becomes more complicated, however. For the kind of categorization we are concerned with, there are, by definition, the same number of possible choices as states of nature. For three categories, say, three normal distributions along a single dimension, there would, in general, be three types of response regions. With the EV principle, the boundaries of the regions would depend on the payoffs and the prior probabilities.

A two-dimensional category might be represented by a bivariate normal distribution in x and y. Instead of response regions along a line, one would have response areas on the (x, y) plane. For three-dimensional stimuli one would have response volumes. The lines (surfaces for three dimensions) of separation between response regions for multivariate normal distributions with equal covariance matrices would be straight lines (planes for three dimensions) (Anderson, 1958).

Two multidimensional categories may be considered to vary along the single dimension of likelihood ratio. Each possible observation of each category has a single-valued likelihood ratio $L_{21}(x, y)$; instead of plotting density as a function of x, as in Figure 7.1, one could plot density as a function of the single dimension L_{21}. Then even though the categories are multidimensional, the decision rule is to use a cutoff point on a unidimensional continuum (likelihood ratio). With more than two categories each observation has more than one likelihood ratio associated with it, so such simplification is not possible.

7.3 SIGNAL DETECTION THEORY

We have now laid the groundwork for *signal detection theory* (also known as *detection theory* or the *theory of signal detectability*). The theory arose in the early 1950's as an outgrowth of the theory of signal detection in physical communication systems (Peterson, Birdsall, & Fox, 1954; Van Meter & Middleton, 1954). The prime mover of the theory within psychophysics was Wilson Tanner, Jr. (Tanner & Swets, 1954).

Introductory presentations of detection theory are: Egan and Clarke (1966), Clarke and Bilger (1963), Swets, Tanner, and Birdsall (1961), Green (1960),

Swets (1961), and Levitt (in press). The important papers of the first ten years have been collected into a book by Swets (1964). In addition, there is a textbook on *Signal Detection Theory and Psychophysics* by David Green and John Swets (1966). This is the basic reference source for detection theory, and we shall refer to it frequently.

Detection theory applies the principles of decision theory to psychophysical tasks such as the *yes-no detection task*. This task requires S to indicate on each trial whether "signal" or "noise" (no signal) was present. For signal, he responds "yes," and for noise, "no." The terminology "noise" derives from the theory of communication, where "noise" is random, unwanted interference with the signal, for example, the "static" of radio communications. "Noise," however, need not be aural—it can occur for any sensory modality.

Noise in detection theory can be *internal* or *external*. Internal noise is due to processes within S, perhaps random neural activity. Internal noise is assumed to be present at all times, even during signal presentation, though its level varies randomly. Typically, however, detection experiments include experimenter-controlled "noise," or "background" stimulation, which is present during both "signal" and "noise" trials. For the aural modality, this might be "white noise," a "hissing" sound produced by a random combination of a wide range of frequencies. Although we speak of "signal" trials, it would be more accurate to refer to these as "signal plus noise" trials, since "noise" is present on both types of trials.

We refer to the detection task in which only internal noise is presumed to be present as the *absolute detection task*. The presentation of external noise does not eliminate internal noise, but internal noise is usually presumed to be small compared to the external noise, so that the level of external noise can be taken to approximate total noise level.

Detection theory can be divided into a *distributional theory* and a *decision theory*. The distributional theory concerns the variable effects presumed to be evoked along some subjective continuum by signal or noise on successive trials. It is assumed that these variations can be described by a continuous probability distribution. Different distributions are ascribed to signal and noise, but both distributions exist on the same subjective continuum. When signal is presented on a trial, the subjective effect is presumed to be a random sample point (value) from the signal distribution; when noise is presented, the subjective effect is presumed to be a random value from the noise distribution. Because the signal and noise distributions may overlap, the relationship between the continuum value perceived by S and the stimulus presented by the experimenter is ambiguous.

The task for S, according to these assumptions, is to observe a value drawn randomly from one of two distributions and to state which distribution (signal or noise) the sample derived from. This is precisely the task to which the decision theory we have discussed applies. The two "categories" are "signal" and "noise." The "members" of each category are the varying subjective effects produced by each category over successive presentations.

The experimenter cannot know the particular observation made by S on a trial, i.e., the value of x. He can only know that the category presented was signal or noise. Indeed, the continuous subjective distribution for signal or noise is only a hypothesis. In a detection experiment it is natural to refer to signal and, perhaps, noise as the stimuli. Therefore, it could be awkward to call x the stimulus, although, in principle, it is analogous to what we called the stimulus in discussing probabilistic discrimination learning (Section 6.11).

The shapes of the distributions for signal and noise are sometimes assumed a priori and sometimes derived on a theoretical basis. When the a priori approach is taken, the distributions are typically assumed to be normal.[7] One then examines the data to see whether they conform reasonably well to the assumption. Alternatively, the distributions for noise and signal might be derived theoretically. Such derivations concern the performance of a hypothetical physical device called the *ideal detector* or *ideal observer,* which is designed to categorize stimulation impinging on it as signal or noise according to an optimal (decision-theoretic) procedure. These derivations require exact mathematical specification of the nature of signal and noise, for example, in terms of frequency components, relative amplitude of the components, time of onset, etc. There are actually different ideal observers, depending on the mathematical nature of the stimuli. The distributions for signal and noise for these detectors may or may not be normal.

The ideal observer is the detection theory form of normative decision theory. The analysis of ideal observers is an extremely important part of detection theory, but it involves specialized mathematics, and we refer the interested reader to Green and Swets (1966).[8]

So much for distributional theory. The decision theory of detection theory is precisely the decision theory for categorization which we have discussed. The states of nature are "signal presented" (b_2) and "noise presented" (b_1). The possible choices are "yes" (a_2) and "no" (a_1). An *extrinsic* payoff matrix might be employed, giving S money or points depending on his choice and the state of nature, or an *intrinsic* payoff matrix might be assumed, with subjective values determined by S's attitude and the instructions.

To maximize expected payoff, a posterior probability cutoff must be determined. If the posterior probability that the observation is "signal" is monotonic

---

[7] The normal distribution assumption for the variable internal effects of a "signal" have long been part of Thurstone's (1927) scaling theory, and similar assumptions antedated Thurstone.

[8] The theory of ideal detectors has been for the most part developed by persons interested in physical communications systems, not by psychologists. The theory was then applied to psychophysics. For a communications engineering treatment of ideal detectors, see Van Trees (1968, Ch. 4).

with the observational continuum then a cutoff point should be formed on the continuum, and the decision should be based on the relation of the observation to the cutoff point. If the payoff matrix or prior probability is varied, then location of the theoretical cutoff point can be varied.

Detection theory can readily account for differences in the percentages of correct signal identifications between experiments even when the signal intensity is the same for both. Differences in instructions can, in effect, vary an intrinsic payoff matrix and thus vary the cutoff point. For example, if the experimenter somehow encourages S to respond "yes" if there is "any chance" he will be correct, this in effect specifies a low cutoff point and a relatively high percentage of correct identifications of the signal (*hits*). It will likewise, however, result in a high percentage of incorrect decisions, "signal" (*false alarms*). Instructions for S to be more conservative, i.e., not to respond "yes" unless he is "sure," will result in higher cutoff point, a lower percentage of hits, and a lower percentage of false alarms. This is illustrated in Figure 7.8.

If signal and noise have normal distributions with means M_2 and M_1 respectively, and a common standard deviation σ, then, by definition,

$$d' = \frac{M_2 - M_1}{\sigma} \tag{7.9}$$

d' is taken in detection theory to measure the inherent discriminability between the signal and noise, i.e., the *detectability* of the signal, given the prevailing noise. According to detection theory, "attitude," "motivation," "response

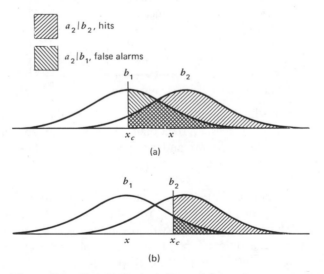

Figure 7.8. The theoretical hit and false alarm probabilities are given by the proportions of the b_2 and b_1 distributions above the cutoff point x_c. These probabilities both decrease if x_c increases.

biases," and "payoffs" affect the criterion employed by S, and thus affect the hit rate, but they do not affect d'.

The two categories we have been concerned with are "signal" and "noise." Actually, as we have noted, the relevant decision theory can deal with categories in general, so "detection theory" can be extended to other psychophysical tasks besides "detection." For example, the two categories might be "signal$_1$" and "signal$_2$" instead of "signal" and "noise," in which case the experiment would concern discriminability between signals rather than detection per se. Such extensions of "detection theory" are commonplace. Nonetheless, for concreteness and uniformity, our exposition will proceed in terms of "signal" and "noise."

7.4 THE ROC CURVE

The results of a detection experiment for an S can be summarized by a table of response probabilities conditional on the presentation of noise or signal. Such a table is shown below, together with the conventional designation for each probability. (This is not a payoff matrix.)

		Stimulus	
		b_1 (noise)	b_2 (signal)
Response	a_1 (no)	$p(a_1\|b_1)$ correct rejection	$p(a_1\|b_2)$ miss
	a_2 (yes)	$p(a_2\|b_1)$ false alarm	$p(a_2\|b_2)$ hit
Column Sum		1	1

Since each column in this table must sum to one, the table contains two independent numbers (two degrees of freedom). Two such independent numbers are $p(a_2|b_2)$ and $p(a_2|b_1)$, the *hit* and *false alarm* probabilities. As we have seen, if the cutoff point is somehow changed, these two numbers will change also.

The two numbers can be plotted as a single point on a two-dimensional graph with $p(a_2|b_2)$ on the ordinate and $p(a_2|b_1)$ on the abscissa. If a new cutoff point is utilized, new response probabilities will result and a different point can be plotted. There will be a different point on the graph for each possible cutoff point. The curve that results from plotting all possible such points (corresponding to all possible cutoff points) is called an "ROC (*receiver-operating-characteristic*) curve." Figure 7.9(b) illustrates an ROC curve for the two normal distributions (categories) of Figure 7.9(a).

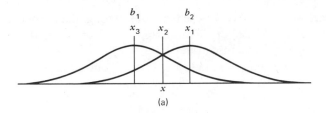

(a)

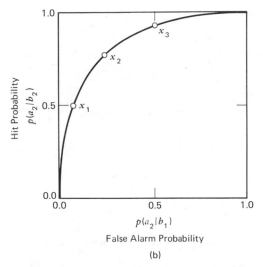

(b)

Figure 7.9. (a) Two categories, b_1 and b_2, with three possible cutoff points, x_1, x_2, and x_3. (b) The ROC curve for the two distributions, showing the points resulting from cutoffs at x_1, x_2, and x_3.

All points on the same ROC curve are assumed to refer to the same two distributions, and therefore to the same d'. Thus, provided that the assumptions behind the d' measure are valid, an ROC curve can be identified with its d' value. Because any point on an ROC curve refers to the same d', and thus the same detectability of the signal, the curve has received the alternative designation, *isosensitivity curve* (Luce, 1963b, p. 131).

Figure 7.10 illustrates four values of d' and the associated ROC curves. Note that all the curves are symmetrical about the negative diagonal. Also note that the higher the d', the higher the ROC curve, which means that for any false alarm probability, the higher the d', the higher the hit probability.

As d' approaches 0, the ROC curve merges with the positive diagonal of the graph. ROC curve points would occur below this diagonal only if the decision rule were reversed, i.e., if stimuli higher than x_c received an a_1 ("no") response and the stimuli below x_c received the a_1 ("yes") response. This might happen if S decided to do as *badly* as possible or if the payoff matrix were structured so that S received more payoff when he was wrong than when he was right. These conditions would seldom if ever appear in practice, thus ROC curves nearly always appear above the diagonal.

If $\sigma_1 \neq \sigma_2$, then d' cannot be employed. Instead, one could report a

$$d_a' = \frac{M_2 - M_1}{\sigma_1} \tag{7.10}$$

The ROC curve in this case would be asymmetrical (thus the subscript a) about

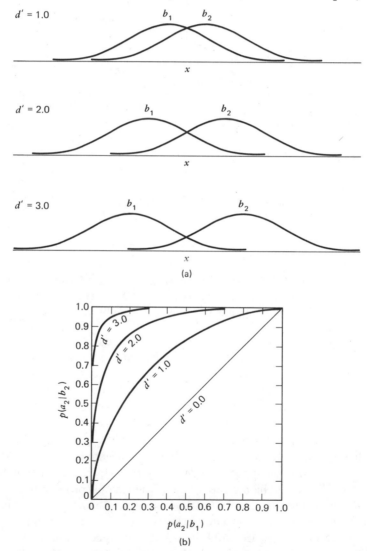

(a)

(b)

Figure 7.10. Three levels of d' are shown in (a). In (b) the corresponding ROC curves are shown.

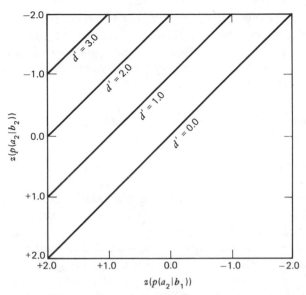

Figure 7.11. z-ROC curves for four d' values. The positive and negative ends of the axes are oriented opposite to the usual convention. This is necessary if the points at the lower and upper ends of a curve are to correspond for the regular and the z-ROC curves. Sometimes the sign labels of the axes are reversed to give the graph a more conventional appearance, but even then the curves are plotted as if the axes were oriented as shown.

the negative diagonal through $(1/2, 1/2)$. In addition to d_a' one needs to know σ_1/σ_2 in order to specify the ROC curve.

Instead of plotting the response probabilities directly, one often plots the deviate of the unit normal distribution associated with that probability. For example, when $p(a_2|b_2)$ is 0.7, one observes from a table of the unit normal distribution the abscissal value (z) above which 0.7 of the area falls. This z, -0.52, is plotted instead of $p(a_2|b_2)$. If we have equal-variance normal distributions, the ROC curve in such a plot is a straight line with 45° slope (see Fig. 7.11). We will call such a plot a *z-ROC curve* when we want to differentiate it from the ROC curve with probability coordinates. Otherwise we simply call it an ROC curve.

Like the untransformed ROC curve, when $\sigma_1 \neq \sigma_2$, the z-ROC curve is not symmetrical about the negative diagonal (through $(0, 0)$); standard sources state that the z-ROC curve is still a straight line, but with a slope of σ_1/σ_2 (Green & Swets, 1966, p. 64). The z-ROC curve referred to is generated by a letting a single cutoff x_c take different values; but, as we noted, if the normal distributions have unequal variances, a likelihood ratio decision principle would, in general, specify two critical x_c's. Thus, the straight line z-ROC curve for

$\sigma_1 \neq \sigma_2$ is not strictly generated by different decision theory criteria. In most cases, however, I expect that the difference between the straight lines and the strictly decision-theoretic ROC curves would be slight because the third response region resulting from the second x_c typically involves only a small percentage of the total number of trials.[9]

7.5 METHODS FOR OBTAINING EMPIRICAL ROC CURVES

The *theoretical* ROC curves we have been discussing were derived mathematically on the basis of distributional and decision-theoretic assumptions. *Empirical* ROC curves are plotted from data collected from real *S*s in the laboratory. There is no a priori necessity that theoretical and empirical curves should coincide, since the distributional and decision-theoretic assumptions may be singly or jointly faulty. Failure of the curves to coincide indicates that at least one assumption is incorrect. Coincidence between curves does not prove that the assumptions are correct, however, since very similar curves can be derived from different assumptions. Still, the coincidence encourages the theoretician. But because of the limitations in the precision of the data, it is often difficult to assert with total confidence that coincidence did or did not occur.

Several methods are available for obtaining empirical ROC curves. We describe the three most prevalent: (1) varying the payoff matrix, (2) varying the prior probabilities, and (3) the rating method.

Varying the Payoff Matrix. A detection experiment is run like this: On each trial the experimenter chooses to present signal (b_2) or "noise" (b_1). The choice on a particular trial is determined randomly, with $p(b_2)$ (the prior probability) equal to some set value, typically 0.5. Suppose that an extrinsic payoff matrix is employed; say that *S* is to receive 1ϕ for a correct response and -1ϕ for an incorrect response.

From the responses the experimenter can estimate $p(a_2|b_2)$ and $p(a_2|b_1)$. These data provide one point of an empirical ROC curve. As we have seen, different points of an ROC curve can be generated by utilizing different criteria. As Equation 7.7 shows, if a different payoff matrix is employed, a different criterion can result—though, assuredly, the new payoff matrix *could* be designed to keep the criterion constant. The method consists, then, of collecting new sets of data with different payoff matrices, ones which require new criteria. One obtains an ROC curve point for each set of data so collected, and attempts to match these points to the best-fitting theoretical curve.

---

[9] Levitt (in press) presents a figure comparing untransformed ROC curves generated by strictly decision-theoretic (likelihood ratio) variation, and by variation of a single cutoff on *x*. For his parameters ($d' = 0.2$, $\sigma_1/\sigma_2 = 0.67$), the two curves differ notably. The standard deviation difference, however, seems extreme for such a small d'.

Varying the Prior Probabilities. The rationale here is very similar, except that the criterion changes for different data sets are brought about by variation of $p(b_2)$. It is clear from Equation 7.7 that such changes should produce different criteria. The experiment is run in essentially the same way as before. Previous to the collection of each new set of data the experimenter informs S of the prior probability, by saying, for example, "for this block of trials, signals will occur 75 percent of the time." Alternatively, the experimenter could give feedback after each trial and allow S to infer the prior probabilities. The data collected for each prior probability provide one point on an empirical ROC curve.

The Rating Method. In the rating method, for each trial S makes an estimate of the posterior probability of the signal, $p(b_2|x)$. Typically, an exact estimate is not given. Instead, S categorizes a trial into one of several posterior probability categories. These categories might be defined numerically; for example, there might be five categories: 0.0–0.20, 0.21–0.40, 0.41–0.60, 0.61–0.80, and 0.81–1.0. Alternatively, verbally designated confidence categories might be employed, for example, "sure the signal was not present," "think the signal was not present," "even chance that the signal was present," "think the signal was present," and "sure that the signal was present." S is instructed that these categories are to cover the posterior probabilities in an exclusive and exhaustive manner, just as the numerically defined categories do. The response might have the appearance of a "yes" or "no" response plus an auxiliary confidence rating, for example, "signal-certain," or "no signal-fairly certain." Such a set of response categories forms an ordering of posterior probabilities, however, from "no signal-certain," which corresponds to the lowest values of $p(b_2|x)$, to "signal-certain," which corresponds to the highest. With four degrees of confidence and two detection responses ("signal" or "no signal") there would be eight categories of posterior probability.

One obtains a point on an empirical ROC curve for each boundary between confidence categories. With N categories there would be $N-1$ category boundaries and thus $N-1$ points on an ROC curve. The succeeding exposition gives the method of calculating an empirical ROC curve from rating data. An explanation of the method is given in terms of detection theory.

Figure 7.12(a) shows the b_1 and b_2 distributions, which we assume to be equal-variance normal distributions. The three vertical lines are three posterior probability category boundaries: t_1, t_2, and t_3. (As we have noted, for two equal-variance normal distributions, posterior probability and x are monotonically related; therefore, the category boundaries can be located on the x continuum in order.) The four posterior probability categories are designated w_1, w_2, w_3, and w_4, where w_1 is the category with the highest probabilities of signal. S's response on each trial is usually assumed to be strictly determined by the location of the sample value in relation to the boundaries; for x_i S would re-

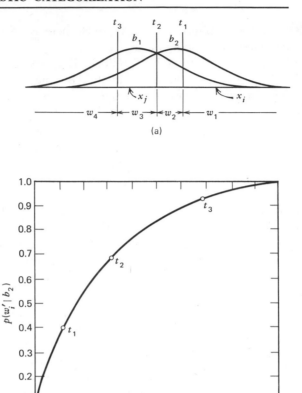

Figure 7.12. Two categories (a) and the associated ROC curve (b). w_i's are rating categories t_j's are boundaries between rating categories.

spond w_1; for x_j S would respond w_3. From the data it is possible to calculate $p(w_1|b_2)$, the probability of response w_1 conditional on the presentation of b_2. This should be the same as the hit probability $p(a_2|b_2)$ had the usual type of yes-no experiment been conducted and had S used a cutoff at t_1. Likewise, one can calculate $p(w_1|b_1)$, which should be the same as the false alarm probability $p(a_2|b_1)$ had S used a cutoff at t_1 in the usual yes-no experiment. Thus $p(w_1|b_2)$ and $p(w_1|b_1)$ give the coordinates of an ROC curve point corresponding to a cutoff at t_1.

Next accumulate the reponses w_1 and w_2, i.e., form a single category from w_1 and w_2. One can observe from the data the probability that this combined category w_2' is used given presentation of b_2, $p(w_2'|b_2)$; this would also be the hit probability $p(a_2|b_2)$ had S used a cutoff t_2 in a yes-no task. $p(w_2'|b_1)$ would be the false alarm probability $p(a_2|b_1)$ under the same conditions. Thus $p(w_2'|b_2)$ and $p(w_2'|b_1)$ are the coordinates of the ROC curve for a cutoff at t_2. Likewise, the combination of w_1, w_2, and w_3 (w_3') would provide the coordinates for the ROC curve for a t_3 cutoff.

Table 7.1 illustrates the steps in calculating an ROC curve from rating data. The data are fictitious and designed to be consistent with Figure 7.12. $N(w_i b_j)$ is the number of trials on which the experimenter presented b_j and S responded w_i. $N(b_j)$ is the total number of trials on which b_j was presented.

The ROC curve coordinates are given in Table 7.1(c). $p(w_i'|b_2)$ and $p(w_i'|b_1)$ are the coordinates for boundary t_i. The terms "hit probabilities" and "false alarm probabilities" are put in quotation marks because, strictly, in the rating experiment there are no hits or false alarms. A hit means that S cor-

TABLE 7.1
Calculation of ROC Curve: Rating Method

Response

	w_1	w_2	w_3	w_4	Total
Noise, b_1	11	20	38	31	100
Signal, b_2	40	29	24	7	100

(a) Response Frequencies $N(w_i b_j)$

	w_1'	w_2'	w_3'	w_4'
Noise, b_1	11	31	69	100
Signal, b_2	40	69	93	100

(b) Cumulative Response Frequencies $N(w_i'b_j) = \sum_{k=1}^{i} N(w_k b_j)$

	w_1'	w_2'	w_3'	
Noise, b_1	0.11	0.31	0.69	"False Alarm Probabilities"
Signal, b_2	0.40	0.69	0.93	"Hit Probabilities"

(c) Conditional Response Probabilities

$$p(w_i'|b_j) = \frac{N(w_i'b_j)}{N(b_j)}$$

rectly gave a "yes" response, but in the rating experiment S is not giving a "yes" response; he is at most giving the probability that the "yes" response is correct. Figure 7.12(b) gives the three points of the ROC curve derived via the rating method. Typically, more than four rating categories are used and more than three points are obtained. For verbally (or even numerically) defined confidence categories, different Ss might locate the boundaries at different locations, i.e., Ss may utilize different criterial boundaries; nonetheless, each category boundary should give a point on the proper ROC curve.

In contrast to the payoff and prior probability techniques, only one series of trials is required to obtain an ROC curve from the rating technique; essentially, this is because the relevant probabilities for different cutoffs are being obtained throughout the one series. The rating technique is, therefore, more efficient than the other two techniques mentioned; an equally reliable ROC curve can be obtained with fewer total trials (Egan, Schulman, & Greenberg, 1959). There is more information, in the technical sense of information theory, in the confidence categorization responses than in the yes and no responses alone.

Other Methods.   The three major methods used to derive empirical ROC curves and their rationales have been presented. Other methods exist as well. One can use different instructions for different trial blocks, encouraging various degrees of laxness in the criterion (Egan, Schulman, & Greenberg, 1959). One can use response latencies instead of confidence ratings (Carterette, Friedman, & Cosmides, 1965); this works, I suppose, because of the relationship between response latency and confidence (Section 3.5). ROC curves are drawn as part of Thurstone category scaling, although they have not been recognized as such (Lee, 1969); see Torgerson (1958, pp. 244–5) for examples. Finally, if the experimenter gives misinformative feedback about the signal with different probabilities for different trial blocks, an ROC curve can be calculated. This method results in a different shape for the ROC curve because S is misled about the distributions (Kinchla & Atkinson, 1964; Lee, 1966).

7.6   FORCED-CHOICE PROCEDURE

The forced-choice procedure is a major procedural alternative to the yes-no task. Instead of having S respond "yes" or "no" after each trial, there are two presentation intervals for each trial, with signal in one and noise in the other; S must state in which interval the signal appeared, the first or second.[10] More

---

[10] For a single trial the forced choice procedure is the same as the well-known *method of constant stimuli* and the *method of paired comparisons*. In the forced-choice procedure, however, both (or all m) categories reappear in successive trials. In the method of constant stimuli, one stimulus is presented on every trial, and the other stimulus generally differs from trial to trial. In the method of paired comparisions, both generally differ from trial to trial.

generally, the signal can appear in any one of m presentation intervals, and S is instructed to identify the interval. (As in the yes-no procedure, the two stimuli need not be "signal" and "noise.") The procedure is known as forced choice since S must identify one of the presentation intervals with the signal (or whatever). The name for the procedure cannot be taken literally to differentiate it from the yes-no procedure, however, which requires ("forces") S to respond "yes" or "no." The forced-choice procedure for auditory stimuli involves successive temporal intervals. For visual presentation of stimuli, instead of the two temporal intervals one might have two spatial positions; during a single time span a signal appears in one of the positions.

The forced-choice procedure has been favored because biases are less apt to affect the data than in the yes-no task. For example, a bias to be cautious in stating that a signal had occurred would affect response probabilities in the yes-no task, but such a bias becomes irrelevant if S must state that the signal was in one interval or the other. There might be, however, a bias to say that signal was in the first interval rather than the second. Such interval biases have been less of a problem than yes-no biases. To see if interval biases exist simply observe the proportion of responses of each kind. If the signal appears equally often in each interval, so will the responses unless there is a bias.

We now analyze the forced-choice technique in terms of decision theory. Let us follow the usual detection theory assumption that for each stimulus, signal (s) and noise (n), there exists an associated probability distribution internal to S. For now, assume that these are normal distributions with $\sigma_s > \sigma_n$ (see Figure 7.13). Suppose there are two temporal intervals; then S notes two values on the same internal continuum and associates one with the first interval and one with the second (Figure 7.13).

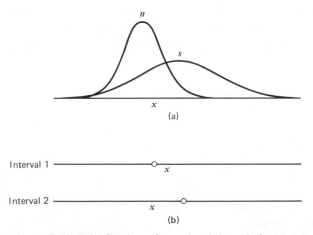

Figure 7.13. Distributions for noise (n) and signal (s). In the forced-choice procedure, interval 1 contains a sample point from s or n, and interval 2 contains a sample point from the alternate distribution.

At this point, S has two possible decisions available, and he must choose between them. There are two possible states of nature: sn (signal first, then noise) and ns (noise first, then signal). Thus a 2×2 payoff matrix can be constructed:

		b_1	b_2
		(sn)	(ns)
a_1:	"signal first"	1	0
a_2:	"signal second"	0	1

We have made the payoff matrix symmetric, since typically both S and the experimenter care only if S is right or wrong—not for which interval he is right or wrong.

Now, what is the optimal strategy? Initially, assume that S's "observation" is $x_2 - x_1$, the difference between the stimulus samples for the second and first intervals. For a given state of nature, this difference has a probability distribution, since each component has a distribution. If we assume that the sample points in the two intervals are uncorrelated (independent), then it is well-known from statistical theory that the distribution of $x_2 - x_1$ given ns is a normal distribution with mean $M_s - M_n$ and standard deviation $\sigma_{ns} = \sqrt{\sigma_s^2 + \sigma_n^2}$.

The distribution of $x_2 - x_1$ given sn is the reflection of the distribution given ns about $x_2 - x_1 = 0$, so the standard deviation is the same, but the mean is $M_n - M_s$. The distributions of $x_2 - x_1$ under the two hypotheses are shown in Figure 7.14. By now the analogy with the yes-no decision analysis should be apparent. Given the observation $x_2 - x_1$, which category did it derive from, sn or ns? By our earlier reasoning for this type of problem, a cutoff strategy is required. Note that even though the two distributions s and n had unequal variances, the two difference distributions in the forced-choice situation have equal variances.

From here on out one can proceed as in the yes-no case, since formally the situation is the same. We can, for example, consider a d' which measures the discriminability between ns and sn. Since $\sigma_{sn} = \sigma_{ns}$, there is no problem (in theory) about a d' not being valid because of unequal variances.

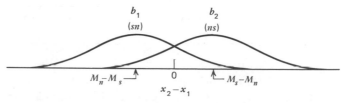

Figure 7.14. The distribution of $x_2 - x_1$ for signal first (sn) and signal second (ns) for the forced-choice procedure.

Let us for the moment assume that $\sigma_n = \sigma_s = \sigma$ for our original distributions. Then d_{yn}' (yes-no d') is:

$$d_{yn}' = \frac{M_s - M_n}{\sigma}$$

The forced-choice d_{fc}' is:

$$d_{fc}' = \frac{M_{ns} - M_{sn}}{\sigma_{fc}} = \frac{(M_s - M_n) - (M_n - M_s)}{\sqrt{\sigma_n^2 + \sigma_s^2}}$$

$$= \frac{2(M_s - M_n)}{\sqrt{2\sigma^2}} = \frac{\sqrt{2}\,(M_s - M_n)}{\sigma}$$

$$= \sqrt{2}\,d_{yn}'$$

In other words, the forced-choice d' is larger than the yes-no d' for the same s and n distributions. S can be expected to get more correct responses with the forced-choice procedure than with the yes-no procedure for the same stimuli. This is understandable because in the forced-choice procedure S has two presentations on which to base his response rather than one.

It is possible to find ROC curves for the forced-choice situation as well as for the yes-no situation. The same techniques can be used. One could, for example, vary the payoff matrix or vary the prior probabilities that the signal appears in interval 1. Likewise, one could use the rating technique in the same way it is used in the yes-no situation. These techniques have received little use, however. One need not, in theory, worry about measuring the relative variances, since they should be the same. Since interval biases typically are negligible, one can simply observe the percentage of correct responses in a forced-choice task. This value can be easily translated into a d_{fc}' value, if one wishes, by reference to a table of the normal distribution.

The preceding development is based on the assumption that the "observation" utilized by S is simply the *difference* between sample locations. Suppose S considers the absolute locations of the two samples, however. If $\sigma_s = \sigma_n$, the solution is not affected, since likelihood ratio for the two hypotheses is monotonic with the difference and is independent of the absolute values (Green & Swets, 1966, p. 67). Detection theory is not explicit on the case $\sigma_s \neq \sigma_n$, but it is clear to me that the likelihood ratio must be dependent on absolute locations. Thus, the analysis based on the "sample difference" observation is not strictly justified by decision theory. Nonetheless, it is the standard detection theory analysis for $\sigma_s \neq \sigma_n$.

7.7 THRESHOLD THEORY AND THE ROC CURVE

The idea of a threshold appears in many fields of psychology. In psychophysics, it refers to a signal level which is just great enough to be noticed. In ethology, it refers to a stimulus which is just great enough to release an instinctual behavior pattern. In verbal learning, it refers to a strength of memory just great enough to evoke a response. Although the word "threshold" has been used widely in psychology over many years, its interpretation is not self-evident. (See Corso (1963) for a historical study of the threshold concept.)

If there is a critical value of stimulation for a signal to be "detected," then when signal strength is below this level, the signal ought never to be "detected," and when signal strength is above this level, the signal ought always to be "detected." It has been known from the earliest days of psychophysics, however, that—if by a "detection" one means a "yes" response—no such critical value of signal strength exists. Instead, as the signal strength is increased from very low levels, the probability that an S will report a detection increases in an apparently gradual manner. It was clear from the start, then, that by "threshold" one could not mean such a critical value of signal strength. Nonetheless, the idea of a threshold has adapted to this empirical fact and survived. In many applications the threshold concept is used tautologically; i.e., if a response is observed, then "threshold" must have been exceeded. Within psychophysics, however, the threshold hypothesis has received careful mathematical analysis. Instead of a threshold notion, various threshold models exist which are empirically testable (in principle, at least).

Detection theory denies the existence of a threshold (except possibly one so low that even internal noise regularly exceeds it). Instead, as we have seen, it postulates a subjective continuum on which S can perceive all degrees of intensity (or whatever), however low. If a threshold existed on this continuum, the implication would be that below a particular point S would "sense" nothing. Detection theory postulates only lesser and lesser "sensation" for lower x values. A cutoff point is not a threshold, since it is a boundary for response, set wherever S wills, not a boundary for "sensation."

Opposition to the threshold concept by no means originated with detection theory (Corso, 1963), but such opposition has been one of the central features of detection theory. We now present a mathematical treatment of a simple form of threshold theory against which detection theory first pitted itself. We shall also discuss some revised forms of threshold theory and compare them with detection theory. Later, we shall consider experimental findings bearing on these theories.

Blackwell's High-Threshold Theory.   Blackwell's (1953) high-threshold theory assumes that a variable internal noise level exists, but that noise seldom (virtually never) exceeds the *high threshold*. The effect of the signal likewise varies from trial to trial, exceeding the threshold with some probability $p(s_t|b_2)$ which depends on signal strength (b_2 is signal, b_1 is noise). S responds "signal" (a_2) on a trial which exceeds threshold (s_t) and is correct, since only signal trials exceed threshold. The proper response when threshold is not exceeded (s_0 trials) is ambiguous, since either signal or noise may produce an s_0 trial.

On s_0 trials S guesses "signal" with probability $p(a_2|s_0)$. $p(s_t|b_2)$ is assumed to be fixed for a given signal strength, but S can vary $p(a_2|s_0)$ at will. Variation in $p(a_2|s_0)$ affects correct hit rate and false alarm rate since both signal and noise trials can produce s_0; thus, different points on an ROC curve can be generated by variation in $p(a_2|s_0)$. Such variations might be induced by payoff or instructional variations for different trial blocks. We derive the curve.

$$p(a_2|b_2) = p(s_t|b_2)p(a_2|s_t) + p(s_0|b_2)p(a_2|s_0) \tag{7.11}$$

$p(s_t|b_2) = k$ (k is constant with motivational changes, by assumption)
$p(a_2|s_t) = 1$ (by assumption)
$p(s_0|b_2) = 1 - p(s_t|b_2)$ (by probability theory)
$p(a_2|s_0) = p(a_2|b_1)$ (since S cannot distinguish between s_0 trials, and virtually
   all b_1 trials are s_0 trials)

Substitution for these four terms in Equation 7.11 yields

$$p(a_2|b_2) = (1 - k)p(a_2|b_1) + k \tag{7.12}$$

Equation 7.12 gives the hit rate as a function of the false alarm rate and thus describes an ROC curve. Unlike the ROC curve of detection theory, this one is a straight-line function. Figure 7.15 gives five ROC curves under

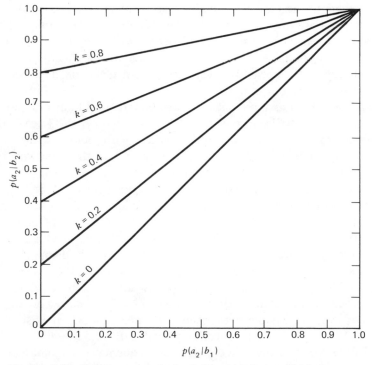

Figure 7.15. ROC curves derived from high-threshold theory.

high-threshold theory. Each ROC curve has a Y-intercept equal to k and an upper bound at $(1, 1)$. As for detection theory, the greater the value of signal strength, the higher the ROC curve.

It is possible to solve Equation 7.12 for $k = p(s_t|b_2)$:

$$k = p(s_t|b_2) = \frac{p(a_2|b_2) - p(a_2|b_1)}{1 - p(a_2|b_1)} \qquad (7.13)$$

k is a hypothetical quantity, but Equation 7.13 allows us to estimate it from the observable quantities $p(a_2|b_2)$ and $p(a_2|b_1)$. High threshold theory considers $p(s_t|b_2)$ to be a true measure of the signal detectability, comparable to d' of detection theory; i.e., it is, in theory, free from the effects of guessing that would affect $p(a_2|b_2)$.

The shape of the ROC curve under high-threshold theory is independent of the assumptions about the shapes of internal distributions associated with b_1 and b_2 trials. Actually, the theory does not require that continuous distributions be postulated at all.

Other Threshold Theories.   High-threshold theory has born the brunt of the attack which signal detection theorists have waged against the threshold concept, partly because the theories were contemporaneous and partly because they implied a clear-cut difference in detection data. Generally, as we shall see, signal detection theory has accorded better with data. This has not brought the demise of threshold theory, however. Instead, various modified forms of threshold theory have appeared which accord with detection data better than high-threshold theory does.

It is possible to assume that noise exceeds threshold on some noteworthy percentage of noise trials. In one such *low-threshold theory* (Luce, 1963a), Ss are presumed to guess "no" on some s_t trials, since some of the s_t trials result from presentation of b_1. (This contrasts with high-threshold theory.) Also, as in high-threshold theory, Ss sometimes guess "yes" on s_0 trials. This theory implies an ROC curve with two straight-line segments, as in Figure 7.16. Although one might think that such an ROC curve could be clearly distinguished from the detection theory ROC curve, real data can often be fit about as well with either type of curve.

Another low-threshold theory assumes that Ss can distinguish between the likelihood ratios of s_t trials, but that s_0 trials are indistinguishable (Green & Swets, 1966, p. 139). This theory implies an ROC curve with two segments: one curved as in detection theory, and one a straight-line segment.

Quantal theory postulates that subjective magnitudes can exist at only discrete values. In this the quantal theories resemble Blackwell's high-threshold theory and Luce's low-threshold theory. However, quantal theory may postulate many discrete steps instead of two. A quantal theory with even as few as five or six

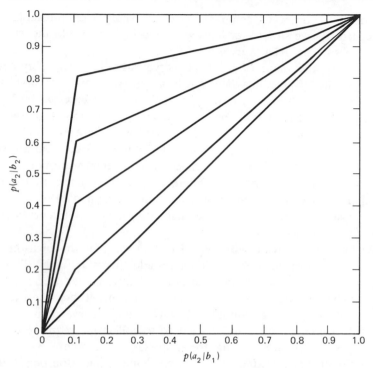

Figure 7.16. ROC curves derived from the low-threshold theory of Luce. The false alarm rate at the kink gives the probability that noise exceeds threshold, a parameter of the theory.

levels could predict essentially the same results as detection theory (see Green & Swets, 1966, pp. 136–138).

7.8 EMPIRICAL ROC CURVES

We consider the shape of empirical ROC curves, i.e., those derived from experimental data, in particular to see what such curves have to say about the relative merits of detection theory and threshold theory.

First, do the various theoretical methods for deriving ROC curves actually work? Are the hit and false alarm rates appropriately altered by variations in the payoff matrix and prior probabilities? Yes. Present S with a different payoff matrix and he will typically change his hit rate and false alarm rate in the direction specified by detection theory. Likewise, change the prior signal probability and S will change his response rates in the appropriate direction. In the rating method, S's posterior probability responses correlate with the state of nature. In brief, the fundamental ideas of detection theory have been well-confirmed in a qualitative sense. ROC curves can therefore be obtained with the methods described. In order to compare detection theory with threshold theory, more is needed. As we saw, detection theory and high-threshold theory predict different shapes for the ROC curve.

Typically, the shape of the ROC curve has been reasonably consistent with detection theory postulates and not in accord with high-threshold theory. Most of these curves, however, have been obtained with external background noise. Hohle (1965) found that for absolute visual detection data, the two theories fit the data about equally well. Hohle used a mixture of prior probability and payoff matrix variation to obtain his ROC curves. Green and Swets (1966, pp. 147, 434) feel that Hohle's experimental parameters were not adequate to produce a situation in which the differences between detection theory and high-threshold theory could appear. Nachmias and Steinman (1963) also studied absolute visual detection and found that rating-scale ROC curves accorded well with detection theory.

Whereas it is obvious for most ROC curves that the high-threshold theory is faulty, it is not obvious that low-threshold theory is faulty. The two straight-line segments of low-threshold theory typically appear to account for results about as well as detection theory. To distinguish between the two formulations we would need a large number of reliable ROC curve points, and it appears that it would be an arduous task indeed to collect the requisite data with methods requiring a separate session for each ROC curve point.

To circumvent this difficulty, Watson, Rilling, and Bourbon (1964) utilized the rating method with a continuous pointer response instead of discrete rating categories. The data were interpreted as coming from 36 discrete rating categories, and the ROC curve appeared to confirm detection theory but not low-threshold theory. The use of the rating technique to compare two-state and detection theory has been controversial, however, since the two-state theory did not originally specify behavior for the rating experiment, so the ROC curve it would predict was not clear (Larkin, 1965; Broadbent, 1966). Krantz (1969) reviewed this controversy and concluded that although evidential arguments against two-state low-threshold theory had been invalid, other evidence against the theory does exist.

More complicated threshold theories can succeed where two-state low-threshold theory fails. Likewise, detection theory can modify its hypotheses when necessary. In brief, it appears hopeless to try to eliminate either all forms of threshold theory or all forms of continuity theory by empirical analysis. The two approaches appear destined to live side by side. The psychologist may choose between them according to his fancy.

Relative Dispersion of Signal and Noise. Many times, in order to fit an empirical ROC curve with normal distribution detection theory, it is necessary to assume that the standard deviation of signal exceeds the standard deviation of noise. This is typically true with visual detection and frequently true with auditory detection. Where a discrepancy exists, increments in signal strength increase the discrepancy.

Invariance of d' Across Methods. Detection theory specifies that the ROC curves should be the same for different methods, if b_1 and b_2 are the same; thus, the d' measures should be the same. The detection theorists consider that one of their major contributions is the unification of different psychophysical methods around the d' measure.

Now, what are the facts? Green and Swets (1966, pp. 110–114) present a comparison of various methods (yes-no, rating, forced-choice) and conclude that d' is independent of the method used to measure it. Nonetheless, discrepant data exist (Swets, Tanner, & Birdsall, 1961; Watson, Rilling, & Bourbon, 1964). It would perhaps be fair to say that if systematic differences in d' are obtained with the different standard methods, it remains to be proved. It is clear, however, that d' does not remain constant in Thurstone category scaling (Lee, 1969).

7.9 OBSERVATIONAL CONTINUUM ALTERNATIVES TO DETECTION THEORY

We said that detection theory consists of a distributional theory and a decision theory. The two need not be wed, to stand or fall in unison. Alternatives to detection theory are possible, which, in contrast to threshold theory, maintain the hypothesis of an observational continuum.

Recall that we began this chapter by discussing the problem of categorization, in particular when the sample derived from one of two possible normal distributions of samples. If S were to guess which distribution the sample derived from and if feedback were provided, he would receive probabilistic reinforcement dependent on the sample location. According to Bayesian terminology, the reinforcement probability function is given by the posterior probability function $p(b_2|x)$.

Formally, the situation is identical to the probabilistic discrimination learning paradigm discussed in Section 6.11 for the case of a stimulus continuum. If the experimental results in probabilistic discrimination are any guide, we would not expect a cutoff point to be used since cutoff behavior implies "all-or-none" responding to a particular observation. According to the results of Chapter 6, Ss respond probabilistically to a given observation.

Even if the cutoff principle for detection were incorrect, it would still be possible for the continuity hypothesis to be correct. Then one might, for example, postulate that S responds to each observation in the same proportions as the reinforcements (feedback) for that observation. This would amount to *conditional probability matching,* or *micromatching* (Lee, 1963; Lee & Janke, 1964, 1965). In this case, there would be a response probability function of x equal to the reinforcement function. Like simple probability matching, micromatching

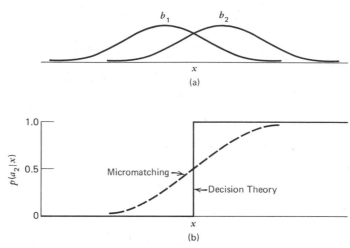

Figure 7.17. (a) Two category distributions. (b) Response probability function for decision theory (assuming $p_c = 0.5$) and for micromatching.

can be derived from simple learning theory axioms (Lee, 1966). Figure 7.17 contrasts the response probability function under decision theory and micromatching.

We need not employ a psychophysical detection task in order to investigate S's behavior in the two-distribution task. In the detection task, the observational continuum is *internal* to S and cannot be observed by the experimenter. Thus, the experimenter cannot directly observe the response probabilities at each observation x. However, it is possible to have S perform the categorization task with the "observation" on an *external* continuum. For example, consider the continuum along the long, horizontal dimension of a plain, white file card. We can locate two normal distributions along such a dimension, randomly choose one of the distributions, and then randomly choose a point from one of the distributions for presentation to S. (See Figure 7.18.) Such distributions are

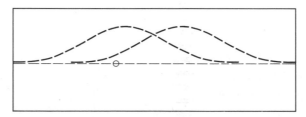

Figure 7.18. A trial observation in an externally distributed stimulus experiment. A dot is shown at some position on a file card. The continuum and the distributions, shown dashed, do not appear on an actual stimulus card.

called *externally distributed* to contrast them with the *internally distributed* ones postulated by Thurstone and decision theories.[11]

How would S go about making such a categorization? With no knowledge of the reinforcement function or of the overall (*molar, marginal,* or *prior*) probabilities (for b_1 and b_2), S could only guess unmethodically, and there would be little point in observing such guessing. If, however, information about the distributions were made available to S, then S's behavior would be of interest. One way of presenting this information is by providing feedback about the source distribution on each of a long series of trials.[12]

It is possible to analyze the data from an *externally distributed stimulus task* in every way detection data is analyzed (although the converse is not true because sample position is unknown in detection trials). Thus, for example, one can plot ROC curves by use of the rating method (Lee, 1963). Figure 7.19 shows curves for two individuals. $S1$ performed close to decision theory and $S2$ performed close to micromatching. The actual d' (a known quantity for externally distributed stimuli) was 1.5. The empirical d', measured from the ROC curve, was close to 1.5 for $S1$, but was about 1.1 for $S2$. Still, the shape of the ROC curve for $S2$ was in accordance with decision theory. Conclusion: if S does not use an optimal strategy, the shape of the ROC curve may appear to confirm detection theory, but the observed d' will be too low.

S need not, of course, perform in the same manner for detection and externally distributed stimulus tasks. Nonetheless, results from externally distributed stimulus experiments prove that Ss do not, as a matter of course, categorize samples from distributions according to strict decision theory principles. In view of these results and in view of the probabilistic responding appearing in a large number of experimental studies (Chapters 5 & 6), one can perhaps be allowed to be skeptical that consistency would hold sway in the detection task.

---

[11] Even in the absolute detection task there must be *some* variation in the external signal from trial to trial, since no signal generator can have perfect precision. Likewise, each externally distributed stimulus sample point must have some internal variation associated with it because of human imprecision. Thus, "both" types of experiments contain both internal and external variation, differing only in the relative amounts. The amount of external variability can be increased by the experimenter at will above some basic minimum. As far as we know, however, the internal variability is not subject to such alterations.

[12] Feedback or some other means of providing information about the distributions is necessary for the application of decision-theoretic principles for the usual detection experiment as well. It is true that one can take a naive S and start him right off in a detection experiment without any feedback or other information about the distributions; his responses can be sensible because he can group the larger observations (x's) together as "yes" responses, and the smaller observations as "no" responses. But the EV principle cannot state *where* a cutoff should occur unless payoffs, prior probabilities, and the likelihood function is known. The typical detection experiment contains many training trials with feedback, which, together with instructions, can, in theory, provide the required information.

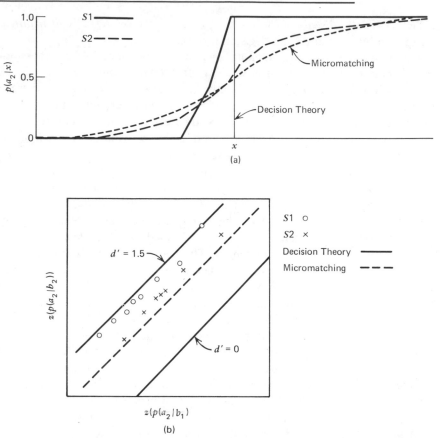

Figure 7.19. (a) Probability of response a_2 as a function of x for two Ss. (b) The z-ROC curve points for the same Ss. (From Lee, 1963.)

Actually, Tanner and Swets affirmed in 1954 that a stable cutoff point in detection is unrealistic, but that instability in the cutoff point is equivalent to a stable cutoff point for a lower d' value. Since then, detection theorists have shown little interest in the possible implication of cutoff point variations for detection data. It is not at all clear what pitfalls exist in accepting d' measures degraded by criterion variance as accurate estimates.

The micromatching theory might, at first, be thought of as an alternate form of the cutoff-variance idea; i.e., with cutoff variance one would expect a continuous response probability function rather than a discrete one (see Figure 7.17), and, depending on the cutoff distribution, the function could equal the one for micromatching. Things are not quite that simple, however. For one thing, the cutoff variance would have to be larger than we could account for from sensory limitations in order to explain results from externally distributed stimuli. Second, the cutoff variance would have to be an inverse function in d' in order to explain the flattening of the choice probability function as d' decreases in the externally distributed stimulus task (Lee & Zentall, 1966). Such flattening would be expected from micromatching, but would have to be handled *ad hoc* with variable-cutoff theory.

Needless to say, if one is willing to allow the cutoff to hop, skip, and cavort around from trial to trial without constraints, then one can hold to the idea that S is utilizing a cutoff point regardless of the choice he makes on any trial. If S says a_2, then one can say the cutoff was to the left of the observation on that trial, and if he says a_1, then one can say that the cutoff was to the right of the observation. If the cutoff is defined in such a way that it is unobservable by the experimenter, then such a theory *can* be tautologically true; by applying suitable constraints, however, a variable-cutoff theory can be made nontautological.

Experimental results with externally distributed stimuli show that the response probability does not exactly accord with micromatching. As in the case of the simple two-choice noncontingent task, experimental variables and individual differences are important determiners of the response probabilities. Nonetheless, micromatching describes average categorization behavior much more accurately than the cutoff theory does.

Schoeffler (1965) has formulated another model for detection that combines the continuity assumption of detection theory with a stochastic learning process. Here, also, there is a smooth function relating choice probability to x. If the trial outcome is b_2 for observation x_i, the probability of a_2 increases for $x \geq x_i$. If the outcome is b_1, the probability of a_1 increases for $x \leq x_i$. The choice probability function at asymptote increases monotonically with x, and as for micromatching, the function becomes steeper for higher d' values.

7.10 EXTENSIONS OF DETECTION THEORY

As we have noted, the basic concepts of detection theory relate to the categorization of an object from one of two or more overlapping sets of objects. Thus, it is to be expected that detection theory ideas would have considerably wider applicability than just to the signal detection situation as we have described it. Indeed, this is the case. As in the detection situation, a prime motivation for the use of detection theory techniques is to separate criterion effects from discriminability effects. We shall consider only some of the areas of application.

Vigilance

In everyday usage, vigilance refers to a careful watchfulness, especially as regards possible danger. In experimental psychology, it has come to mean a special type of signal detection task—one which typically has no real danger associated with it. To be "vigilant" is to be on the lookout for something which could happen at any time, and this meaning is maintained in psychology. In the typical vigilance task a signal is presented at random times without warning, and the subject must respond whenever he detects the signal. By way of contrast, in the typical detection task there is a discrete sequence of trials, and those moments when a signal might occur are clearly specified to S. Although in the vigilance task the signal comes at "random" times, the meaning of "random" varies for different experimental procedures so that some "vigilance" experiments resemble the detection task more closely than other "vigilance" tasks (for example, Mackworth & Taylor, 1963).

Real-life "vigilance" tasks are exemplified by radar-observing and sentry-keeping, tasks in which the signal—appearance of the enemy—occurs only infrequently. Intuition and folklore tell us that under such circumstances the observer becomes less "alert" over time, i.e., he is less apt to "detect" a signal. Although signals occur much more frequently in laboratory studies than in the real-life tasks mentioned, a decrement in the percentage of detections over time has been regularly noted. Needless to say, the experiments concern signals of low magnitude so that there can be some uncertainty about the occurrence. If the signal came from a foghorn placed next to S, we would not expect a decrement in the number of detections over time, regardless of boredom, lapses of attention, or even sleep.

Because of the similarity between "vigilance" and "detection" tasks, Egan, Greenberg, and Schulman (1961) were led to ask whether the decrement in the vigilance task might reflect a change in the criterion rather than a lowering in the discriminability of the signal, presumably because of "boredom," "lapses of attention," or whatnot. If, over time, Ss adopted stricter criteria, the percentage of signals reported would decrease, even if "discriminability" remained the same. Or possibly both the discriminability and the criterion change over time.

In principle, discriminability is said to remain the same if the ROC curve on which S operates remains the same. The criterion is said to change if the point of the curve at which S operates changes. In theory, then, if one could see the ROC curves for early and late in the session, one could see if the curves are the same, and, in addition, if one could determine the point on the curves at which S operated, one could state whether the criterion changed.

The application of ROC curve techniques to the vigilance task is not, however, straightforward. In the detection task the false alarm rate is easy to measure; it is the proportion of noise trials with a_2 responses. Since there are no discrete trials in a vigilance task, it is not at all clear what a "false alarm rate" might refer to. One solution is to arbitrarily divide the total time into intervals of, say, 10 seconds, and to take the false alarm rate to be the proportion of b_1 intervals with a_2 responses. The false alarm rate, then, is clearly dependent on the time interval arbitrarily chosen, although one hopes that one's final conclusions are not so dependent.

Determination of the hit rate is less devious, since the total number of signals presented gives a definite denominator for the calculation. The question arises, however, when should a response be considered a response to the previous signal? If the response is too soon it must be ruled to be a false alarm, because reaction time limitations would prevent responses to a signal from appearing too soon. On the other hand, how long should one wait after the signal presentation before the response is considered to be a false alarm? The issue did not occur for the discrete trial detection task since there was a definite interval for the a_1 or a_2 response.

Egan, Greenberg, and Schulman (1961) had Ss try to detect auditory signals in noise in a vigilance task (which they called the *method of free response*). Ss worked at different times under four instructions (from strict to lax). Under the strict instructions they were to have high probability that a signal was present before responding, and under lax instructions the probability could be lower. Egan *et al.* then calculated the average response rate as a function of time after onset of the signal. The results for one S are presented in Figure 7.20. As we mentioned, it is not possible to state exactly which responses were to the signals; however, the responses associated with the sharp peak can be interpreted as hits, whereas the responses occurring after the peak can be considered as false alarms. Egan *et al.* developed a model which allowed them to analyze the data accordingly and arrive at a measure of discriminability. Note in Figure 7.20 that as the S becomes lax, both the hit and the false alarm probabilities increase. This confirms the suspicion that the hit rate alone does not tell the whole story and that detection theory concepts might be useful.

Egan *et al.* did not analyze the vigilance decrement, but other workers have attempted to determine whether the decrement is criterial. A certain amount of positive thinking is required of the reader of this vigilance literature. For example, though the model of Egan *et al.* avoids the assumption of equal-variance normal distributions as unrealistic, succeeding experimenters make this assumption but give no empirical confirmation. Such an assumption allows d' and β to be inferred from one ROC curve point, but the values are invalid if the assumption is false. Furthermore, these experimenters typically assume an arbitrary temporal decision interval as a unit for the calculation of false alarm rates. Intervals ranging at least from one second to one minute have been employed. It is not clear that the conclusions are entirely independent of this arbitrary choice.

Disregarding these uncertainties, what has been concluded from the experiments? There has been no concensus. Some experimenters report criterion shifts, and others report d' decrements with time. Perhaps different types of vigilance tasks gives different results (Poulton, 1966).

But in spite of the theoretical and experimental difficulties of applying detection theory concepts to the vigilance situation, similar principles undoubtedly apply across tasks. As we have seen, S can adjust a confidence criterion in the vigilance task so that as he becomes more lax, he has both more hits and false

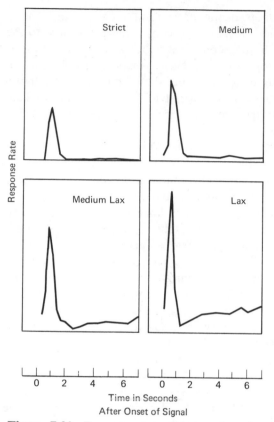

Figure 7.20. Response rate for one S under four instructions in a vigilance task. (After Egan *et al.*, 1961.)

alarms. Likewise, it appears that the criterion is responsive to changes in the payoff matrix. (See Egan *et al.*, 1961; Broadbent & Gregory, 1963b; Levine, 1966.)

Memory

Consider the following recognition memory task:

Stage (1): A set of stimuli (the "old" set) is presented to S for inspection. Stage (2): A larger set of stimuli is now presented to S, which consists of the "old" set and a "new" set intermixed. S examines each stimulus and states that it is "old" (he "recognizes" it as a member of the "old" set), or that it is "new" (he does not "recognize" it). The stimuli are typically presented one at a time.

Compare Stage 2 with the detection task. An "old" stimulus compares with the signal, and the "new" stimulus compares with noise. On each trial S must make a categorization on the basis of an observation. One can observe conditional probabilities that S says "old" when the stimulus is old and when it is new, and plot these "hit" and "false alarm" probabilities on ROC curve coordinates. Several such points can form an ROC curve for memory (which has also been designated the MOC curve—M for memory). A d' measure taken from such a curve would indicate how well S can discriminate between the "old" and "new" stimulus sets.

In contrast to the detection and vigilance situations, the members of a single category are obviously distinct entities (different words, numbers, or whatever) quite apart from any hypothetical internal probability distributions. Nonetheless, each member is assumed to give rise to some value on a hypothetical subjective continuum of *familiarity,* and if the category members are presented in random order they give rise to random values from a probability distribution of familiarity. Decision theory would then require a critical likelihood ratio, and if the likelihood ratio is monotonic with "familiarity," a cutoff point on the familiarity continuum would be required. The location of the cutoff point should depend on prior probabilities of "old" and "new," and on payoffs.

Determination of the empirical MOC curve is free of some of the special difficulties in finding the ROC curve for vigilance. There are discrete trials so the hit and false alarm proportions can be calculated directly. On the other hand, as for vigilance studies, one must be wary of plotting an MOC curve with points based on data collected in successive time intervals. If feedback to the responses is given after each response, or if S is allowed to view the "old" set again before new data are collected, S will learn and improve his d' for the second set of data. If no feedback or review is given, forgetting may take place, which implies a decrease in d'.

The rating method, however, allows the MOC curve for an individual to be plotted from the data of a single session. Furthermore, it is an efficient method. This is important because the number of "old" and "new" stimuli is likely to be relatively small. Because of these factors, the rating method has been widely employed for obtaining MOC curves. Even with the rating method the data for a given S is apt to be so meager that data are pooled across Ss to get an "average" MOC curve. This averaging has been a source of considerable concern, since theory typically deals with individual curves, and the average curve may have a different appearance from the individual curves.

Given that an MOC curve can be obtained, we might ask—why bother? The motivations are similar to the reasons in psychophysics; d' can (hopefully) supply a measure of learning uncontaminated by criterion bias. In addition, both threshold and continuum theories exist for memory as well as for detection; empirical MOC curves can (hopefully) eliminate inadequate theory.

Threshold Theory. One possible measure of performance quality for recognition memory would be the proportion of old stimuli recognized as such. An S could obtain a perfect score with this measure, however, without really having learned anything, by always responding "old." Short of this extreme strategy, S's score would be materially affected by response bias. As a protection against the effects of such bias, it has been standard practice to employ the following scoring formula (Woodworth & Schlosberg, 1954, p. 700):

true score = percentage of old stimuli recognized
— percentage of new stimuli falsely recognized

Symbolism:
O, an "old" response
o, an "old" stimulus
N, a "new" response
n, a "new" stimulus

Conversion of the formula to probabilities yields

$$p_t = p(O|o) - p(O|n) \qquad (7.14)$$

James Egan (1958) showed that this standard scoring formula is equivalent to a threshold theory of memory, and he derived the MOC curve implied by the theory. We present the theory.

Let us assume that some old stimuli presented to S exceed a threshold, and that they are recognized by S with probability $p'(O/o)$. Likewise assume that some new stimuli exceed a threshold and are "recognized" as new by S with probability $p'(N/n)$. These probabilities are not under S's control. For stimuli not exceeding threshold S guesses that they are old with probability p_g, which is under S's control. The ordinate of the MOC curve is $p(O/o)$, which consists of $p'(O/o)$ plus correct guesses of "old."

$$p(O|o) = p'(O|o) + p_g(1 - p'(O|o)) \qquad (7.15)$$

The abscissa is

$$p(O|n) = p_g(1 - p'(N|n)) \qquad (7.16)$$

If we solve for p_g in Equation 7.16 and substitute for p_g in Equation 7.15, we obtain

$$p(O|o) = \frac{1 - p'(O|o)}{1 - p'(N|n)} \, p(O|n) + p'(O|o) \qquad (7.17)$$

This is the equation for the MOC curve. Since the p' quantities are constants, the equation specifies a straight line relating $p(O/o)$ and $p(O/n)$. The line has a Y-intercept equal to $p'(O/o)$, the threshold probability for recognition of old, and a slope of $(1 - p'(O/o))/(1 - p'(N/n))$. Depending on the assumptions about $p'(N/n)$, different special cases may be derived. If we assume that $p'(N/n) = 0$ (i.e., that S never *knows* that a stimulus is new), we have the analogue of the "high-threshold" model for detection, which, recall, also predicts the straight line ROC curve (see Equation 7.12). On the other hand, we might assume that $p'(N/n) = p'(O/o)$, i.e., that new stimuli are definitely "recognized" as new at the same rate that old stimuli are recognized as old. Then Equation 7.17 becomes

$$p(O|o) = p(O|n) + p'(O|o)$$

or, by rearranging,

$$p'(O|o) = p(O|o) - p(O|n)$$

Compare this with Equation 7.14 and note that $p_t = p'(O/o)$. Thus the standard correction is equivalent to estimating the common probability with which old and new stimuli exceed their thresholds in a two-threshold model. Other assumptions about $p'(N/n)$ can be made, but as long as it is assumed to be a constant, the MOC curve will be a straight line.

Empirical MOC Curves.   The classical paper in this area is by Egan (1958); this paper has only been published as a technical report and is not widely available, but a summary can be found in Green and Swets (1966, Chapter 12). Egan first presented 100 monosyllabic words, then presented a list which contained these old words and 100 new words interspersed. S had to decide "old" or "new" and give a confidence rating. The data were adequate for plotting individual MOC curves, and these curves clearly accorded with the normal-normal distribution theory but not with the threshold theory discussed. The curves indicated that σ_o exceeded σ_n. A second learning trial dramatically increased the observed d_a'. Pooling of data across Ss appeared to be acceptable.

Successive research with a variety of stimulus materials has generally accorded with these findings. As in the case of detection, however, this does not mean that more complicated threshold theories or, indeed, that other continuum theories could not account for the experimental findings (Murdock, 1965; Norman & Wickelgren, 1965; Bernbach, 1967; Kintsch, 1967).

Murdock (1966) has raised the issue of changes in β versus d' in memory. He attributed differences in recall probability across serial positions to changes in β rather than to changes in d'. This issue is very similar to the analysis of vigilance decrement in detection theory terms.

One could presumably eliminate the contaminating effects of criterion biases by utilizing a forced choice technique, i.e., on each trial S would be presented with both an "old" and "new" stimulus, and be required to identify the "old" (Green & Moses, 1966).

Miscellaneous Applications

We have by no means exhausted the possibilities for applying detection theory techniques. Indeed, whenever there are two stimuli (or stimulus sets) which can be discriminated, but not perfectly, the methods of detection theory can probably be applied.

ROC curves have been drawn for discrimination between tachistoscopically presented visual patterns (Lee, 1965), for discrimination between water and sucrose solutions (Linker, Moore, & Galanter, 1964), for discrimination between short samples of English prose (Ulehla, Canges, & Wackwitz, 1967), for discrimination between lines of slightly different lengths (Creelman, 1965), and for discrimination between constant and flickering light sources (Clark, 1966).

Division of attention has also been analyzed with detection theory. If different messages are presented to S via different sensory channels, S can divide his attention between the channels or attend to one channel and attempt to ignore the second. This attention to one channel will typically improve the reception for that channel, but degrade the reception for the other channel. This deterioration has been interpreted as degradation of d' with constant β in the second channel (Broadbent & Gregory, 1963a; Treisman & Geffin, 1967; Moray & O'Brien, 1967).

Our presentation of signal detection theory and its extensions has largely concerned two categories and one dimension. As we have noted however, human categorizations are usually more complicated than this. There have been some attempts to extend detection theory to these more complicated categorizations, for example to recognition of individual letters, vowels, or words presented visually or aurally (Rodwan & Hake, 1962; Marill & Green, 1960).

Engineers have been very interested in the theory of pattern recognition, in part because they would like to build pattern recognition machines. These would lead to more direct forms of man-computer interaction, because, for example, the computer system would recognize spoken words and numbers, and handwriting. Pattern recognition machines could also possibly perform such practical tasks as specifying the owner of a set of fingerprints. Computer engineers have relied heavily on multidimensional decision theory in their work (Sebestyen, 1962; Rosen, 1967), but their work has generally been independent of the psychophysical literature of detection theory.

7.11 LIMITATIONS AND ALTERATIONS OF DETECTION THEORY

Detection theorists realized from the start that the theory was an idealization and that deviations from it were to be expected. "We probably all agree that, in the strict sense of the word, the human observer cannot be considered as an ideal observer. Few of us would expect perfect computations of likelihood ratios and perfect matching into criterion spaces. However, we might feel that the human observer's sensory system is, in a broad sense, similar to that of an ideal observer in some respects." (Tanner, 1961)

Human Ss do not behave strictly in accordance with the "simple" form of detection theory. The discrepancy is perhaps less apparent and, I would guess, less widely accepted than the discrepancy between "optimal" behavior and "probability matching" that we noted in Chapter 6. The discrepancy of Chapter 6 is apparent for all to see from the data of the simplest experiments, but discrepancy between detection theory and behavior is not apparent from the typical detection data or from an empirical ROC curve.

We have pointed out that the ideal of a perfectly sharp cutoff could hardly hold with the human observer. Quite apart from such a *prima facie* criticism, empirical data exist which, at the least, are bothersome for detection theory. For example, percentage correct responses does not equal that for the ideal observer, measured shifts in criteria induced by experimental variations are less extreme than theory predicts, and sequential dependencies exist which are not predicted by detection theory (Swets, 1961; Green, 1960; Shipley, 1961; Speeth & Mathews, 1961; Ulehla, 1966). Swets (1961) offers the following possibilities for the discrepancy between behavior and the ideal observer: (1) "noisy decision process" (for example, an unstable criterion); (2) discontinuous decision axis; (3) noise inherent in human sensory systems (i.e., the internal noise of the absolute detection task, which is not present for the ideal observer); or (4) faulty memory.

Swets favors the last possibility—faulty memory. The ideal observer is assumed to know exactly which signal it is looking for. If it has uncertainty about the signal, its performance must deteriorate. The human observer might very well have uncertainty about the signal, for example, its frequency, amplitude, duration, time of onset, etc., because of limitations of memory. Experimental techniques have been devised to eliminate various possible sources of uncertainty; for example, need for memory for frequency can be eliminated by making the signal an amplitude increment of a continuous "carrier" tone of the same frequency. Successive elimination of these sources of uncertainty has notably reduced, but not eliminated, the discrepancy between behavior and the ideal observer (Green, 1960; Sorkin, 1965).

An alternative approach for reducing the discrepancy is to alter the assumptions about the ideal observer, for example, by assuming that it can, over time, "forget" the signal specifications. Its performance, then, would be degraded— hopefully to correspond to human performance.[13]

Presumably, if one could align human performance and the ideal observer, one could state that the human detector performs optimally given his inherent information processing limitations. This alteration of the ideal observer corresponds to the model reformulation mentioned in Chapter 1, and is by no means a unique approach by detection theorists. Indeed, we have already seen parallel

---

[13] Luce (1963b, p. 156) has summarized the program of the detection theorists as follows: "As well as I can make out, Tanner proposes to search for assumptions about the information that is available to the ideal observer until he finds a set for which the optimum behavior predicted is that of the human being . . . it seems that two lines are being developed: modifications of the experiments to fit the model and modifications of the model to fit the experiments."

though somewhat different attempts to "rationalize" human choice behavior in previous chapters. Little or nothing has been done within detection theory with the ideas of subjective probabilities, utility functions, or "utility of variability." Instead, detection theorists have concentrated on trying to show that discrepant behavior results from lack of information which the theory assumed to be available to S. The idea is that if S is provided with such information, he will then perform optimally, or if the lack of information is accounted for, the behavior can be interpreted as optimal under the conditions.

7.12 SUMMARY

This chapter has largely concerned signal detection theory and its ramifications. Signal detection theory consists of a distributional theory and a decision theory. The distributional theory concerns the variable effects on the "detector" that "signal" or "noise" (no signal) has on successive trials. Detection theory assumes that the variable effects of signal or noise over trials form a continuous probability distribution. The distribution is often assumed to be normal (Gaussian), but may have other shapes as well. The decision theory used is simply the EV principle applied to probabilistic categorization tasks. For two categories (for example, the signal and noise of a "yes-no" task), the optimal strategy is to respond a_2 or a_1 according to whether a sample point (observation) x has a posterior probability $(p(b_2/x))$ greater or less than a critical probability p_c. The critical probability depends only on the payoff matrix entries. The strategy is more often described instead in terms of a critical likelihood ratio (criterion), which depends on prior probabilities as well as on payoffs. Although optimal strategy can be defined in terms of a cutoff point for posterior probability or likelihood ratio, there may be more than two response regions on the observational continuum. The maximin principle also requires use of a critical likelihood ratio for categorization, but whereas for the EV principle the critical likelihood ratio is dependent on the prior probabilities, for the maximin principle prior probabilities are irrelevant. If the standard deviation σ is the same for both distributions, the discriminability between the categories can be given by $d' = (M_2 - M_1)/\sigma$. In theory, at least, d' is a constant unsusceptible to variations of motivation, payoffs, and prior probabilities, which are supposed to only affect the criterion. Changes in the criterion affect both the "hit probability" and the "false alarm probability." A plot of these probabilities on the ordinate and abscissa, respectively, as the criterion goes from one extreme to the other is called an ROC curve.

In the forced-choice procedure—a major alternative to the yes-no procedure—there are two intervals: one containing signal and one containing noise. S must identify the signal interval. By considering the "observation" to be the difference between the sample points in the two intervals, forced-choice data are amenable to the same type of theory and data analysis as yes-no data. However, because the forced-choice procedure allows S two observations (intervals) rather than one, d_{fc}' is larger than d_{yn}' for the same signal and noise.

Based on a comparison between empirical and theoretical ROC curves, signal detection theory seems to be superior to high-threshold detection theory. The superiority to other threshold theories, for example, low-threshold theory, has not been established. Neither can it be said that detection theory is clearly superior to continuous-observation alternatives not specifying a likelihood ratio cutoff point. The techniques and postulates associated with signal detection theory have been extended to many areas of psychology other than detection, for example, signal discrimination and recognition, vigilance, and short-term memory. Signal detection theory should by no means be thought to give a perfect description of human behavior. But, detection theory is capable of being altered to reflect human limitations. In particular, detection theorists have been concerned with how limitations in human memory may explain discrepancies between the human and the ideal detector.

REFERENCES

Anderson, T. W. *An Introduction to Multivariate Statistical Analysis.* New York: Wiley, 1958.

Banks, W. D. "Signal Detection Theory and Human Memory," *Psychological Bulletin* (1970), **74,** 81–99.

Bernbach, H. A. "Decision Processes in Memory," *Psychological Review* (1967), **74,** 472–480.

Blackwell, H. R. "Psychophysical Thresholds: Experimental Studies of Methods of Measurement," Ann Arbor, Mich.: Bulletin of the Engineering Research Institute (No. 36), University of Michigan, 1953.

Broadbent, D. E. "Two-State Threshold Model and Rating-Scale Experiments," *Journal of the Acoustical Society of America* (1966), **40,** 244–245.

Broadbent, D. E., & Gregory, M. "Division of Attention and Decision Theory of Signal Detection," *Proceedings of the Royal Society of London, Series B* (1963a), **158,** 222–231.

Broadbent, D. E., & Gregory, M. "Vigilance Considered as a Statistical Decision," *British Journal of Psychology* (1963b), **54,** 309–323.

Bruner, J. S., Goodnow, J. J., & Austin, G. A. *A Study of Thinking.* New York: Wiley, 1956.

Carterette, E. C., Friedman, M. P., & Cosmides, R. "Reaction-Time Distributions in the Detection of Weak Signals in Noise," *Journal of the Acoustical Society of America* (1965), **38,** 531–542.

Clark, W. C. "The *Psyche* in Psychophysics: A Sensory-Decision Theory Analysis of the Effect of Instructions on Flicker Sensitivity and Response Bias," *Psychological Bulletin* (1966), **65,** 358–366.

Clarke, F. R., & Bilger, R. C. "The Theory of Signal Detectability and the Measurement of Hearing," in J. Jerger (ed.), *Modern Developments in Audiology.* New York: Academic Press, 1963, pp. 371–408.

Corso, J. F. "A Theoretico-Historical Review of the Threshold Concept," *Psychological Bulletin* (1963), **60**, 356–370.

Creelman, C. D. "Discriminability and Scaling of Linear Extent," *Journal of Experimental Psychology* (1965), **70**, 192–200.

Egan, J. P. "Recognition Memory and the Operating Characteristic," Bloomington, Ind.: Hearing and Communication Laboratory (Technical Note AFCRC-TN-58-51), University of Indiana, 1958.

Egan, J. P., & Clarke, F. R. "Psychophysics and Signal Detection," in J. B. Sidowski (ed.), *Experimental Methods and Instrumentation in Psychology*. New York: McGraw-Hill, 1966, pp. 211–246.

Egan, J. P., Greenberg, G. Z., & Schulman, A. I. "Operating Characteristics, Signal Detectability, and the Method of Free Response," *Journal of the Acoustical Society of America* (1961), **33**, 993–1007.

Egan, J. P., Schulman, A. I., & Greenberg, G. Z. "Operating Characteristics Determined by Binary Decisions and by Ratings," *Journal of the Acoustical Society of America* (1959), **31**, 768–773.

Eysenck, H. J. "Classification and the Problem of Diagnosis," in H. J. Eysenck (ed.), *Handbook of Abnormal Psychology*. New York: Basic Books, 1961, pp. 1–31.

Green, D. M. "Psychoacoustics and Detection Theory," *Journal of the Acoustical Society of America* (1960), **32**, 1189–1203.

Green, D. M., & Moses, F. L. "On the Equivalence of Two Recognition Measures of Short-Term Memory," *Psychological Bulletin* (1966), **66**, 228–234.

Green, D. M., & Swets, J. A. *Signal Detection Theory and Psychophysics*. New York: Wiley, 1966.

Hohle, R. H. "Detection of a Visual Signal with Low Background Noise: An Experimental Comparison of Two Theories," *Journal of Experimental Psychology* (1965), **70**, 459–463.

Kinchla, R. A., & Atkinson, R. C. "The Effect of False-Information Feedback upon Psychophysical Judgments," *Psychonomic Science* (1964), **1**, 317–318.

Kintsch, W. "Memory and Decision Aspects of Recognition Learning," *Psychological Review* (1967), **74**, 496–504.

Krantz, D. H. "Threshold Theories of Signal Detection," *Psychological Review* (1969), **76**, 308–324.

Larkin, W. D. "Rating Scales in Detection Experiments," *Journal of the Acoustical Society of America* (1965), **37**, 748–749.

Lee, W. "Choosing among Confusably Distributed Stimuli with Specified Likelihood Ratios," *Perceptual and Motor Skills* (1963), **16**, 445–467.

Lee, W. "ROC Curves for Recognition of Visual Patterns," *Psychonomic Science* (1965), **2**, 51–52.

Lee, W. "Conditioning Parameter Model for Reinforcement Generalization in Probabilistic Discrimination Learning," *Journal of Mathematical Psychology* (1966), **3**, 184–196.

Lee, W. "Relationships between Thurstone Category Scaling and Signal Detection Theory," *Psychological Bulletin* (1969), **71**, 101–107.

Lee, W., & Janke, M. "Categorizing Externally Distributed Stimulus Samples for Three Continua," *Journal of Experimental Psychology* (1964), **68**, 376–382.

Lee, W., & Janke, M. "Categorizing Externally Distributed Stimulus Samples for Unequal Molar Probabilities," *Psychological Reports* (1965), **17**, 79–90.

Lee, W., & Zentall, T. R. "Factorial Effects in the Categorization of Externally Distributed Stimulus Samples," *Perception and Psychophysics* (1966), **1**, 120–124.

Levine, J. M. "The Effects of Values and Costs on the Detection and Identification of Signals in Auditory Vigilance," *Human Factors* (1966), **8**, 525–537.

Levitt, H. "Decision Theory, Signal Detection Theory and Psychophysics," in E. E. David, Jr. & P. B. Denes (eds.), *Human Communication: A Unified View*. New York: McGraw-Hill, in press.

Linker, E., Moore, M. E., & Galanter, E. "Taste Thresholds, Detection Models, and Disparate Results," *Journal of Experimental Psychology* (1964), **67**, 59–66.

Lockhart, R. S., & Murdock, B. B., Jr. "Memory and the Theory of Signal Detection *Psychological Bulletin* (1970), **74**, 100–109.

Luce, R. D. "A Threshold Theory for Simple Detection Experiments," *Psychological Review* (1963a), **70**, 61–79.

Luce, R. D. "Detection and Recognition," in R. D. Luce, R. R. Bush, & E. Galanter (eds.), *Handbook of Mathematical Psychology*, Vol. 1. New York: Wiley, 1963b, pp. 103–189.

Mackworth, J. F., & Taylor, M. M. "The d' Measure of Signal Detectability in Vigilance-Like Situations," *Canadian Journal of Psychology* (1963), **17**, 302–325.

Marill, T. M., & Green, D. M. "Statistical Recognition Functions and the Design of Pattern Recognizers," *IRE Transactions on Electronic Computers* (1960), **9**, 472–477.

Moray, N., & O'Brien, T. "Signal-Detection Theory Applied to Selective Listening," *Journal of the Acoustical Society of America* (1967), **42**, 765–772.

Murdock, B. B., Jr. "Signal-Detection Theory and Short-Term Memory," *Journal of Experimental Psychology* (1965), **70**, 443–447.

Murdock, B. B., Jr. "The Criterion Problem in Short-Term Memory," *Jourrnal of Experimental Psychology* (1966), **72**, 317–324.

Nachmias, J., & Steinman, R. M. "Study of Absolute Visual Detection by the Rating-Scale Method," *Journal of the Optical Society of America* (1963), **53**, 1206–1213.

Norman, D. A., & Wickelgren, W. A. "Short-Term Recognition Memory for Single Digits and Pairs of Digits," *Journal of Experimental Psychology* (1965), **70**, 479–489.

Peterson, W. W., Birdsall, T. G., & Fox, W. C. "The Theory of Signal Detectability," *Transactions of the IRE Professional Group of Information Theory* (1954), **PGIT-4**, 171–212.

Poulton, E. C. "Engineering Psychology," in P. R. Farnsworth, O. McNemar, & Q. McNemar (eds.), *Annual Review of Psychology*, Vol. 17. Palo Alto, Calif.: Annual Reviews, Inc., 1966, pp. 177–200.

Rodwan, A. S., & Hake, H. W. "The Discriminant-Function as a Model for Perception," *American Journal of Psychology* (1964), **77**, 380–392.

Rosen, C. A. "Pattern Classification by Adaptive Machines," *Science* (1967), **156**, 38–44.

Rozeboom, W. W. *Foundations of the Theory of Prediction*. Homewood, Ill.: Dorsey Press, 1966.

Schoeffler, M. S. "Theory for Psychophysical Learning," *Journal of the Accoustical Society of America* (1965), **37**, 1124–1133.

Sebestyen, G. S. *Decision-Making Processes in Pattern Recognition.* New York: Macmillan, 1962.

Shipley, E. F. "Dependence of Successive Judgments in Detection Tasks: Correctness of the Response," *Journal of the Acoustical Society of America* (1961), **33**, 1142–1143.

Sorkin, R. D. "Uncertain Signal Detection with Simultaneous Contralateral Cues," *Journal of the Acoustical Society of America* (1965), **38**, 207–212.

Speeth, S. D., & Mathews, M. V. "Sequential Effects in the Signal Detection Situation," *Journal of the Acoustical Society of America* (1961), **33**, 1046–1054.

Swets, J. A. "Is There a Sensory Threshold?" *Science* (1961), **134**, 168–177.

Swets, J. A. (ed.) *Signal Detection and Recognition by Human Observers.* New York: Wiley, 1964.

Swets, J. A., Tanner, W. P., Jr., & Birdsall, T. G. "Decision Processes in Perception," *Psychological Review* (1961), **68**, 301–340.

Tanner, W. P., Jr. "Physiological Implications of Psychophysical Data," *Annals of the New York Academy of Sciences* (1961), **89**, 752–765.

Tanner, W. P. Jr., & Swets, J. A. "A Decision-Making Theory of Visual Detection," *Psychological Review* (1954), **61**, 401–409.

Thurstone, L. L. "Psychophysical Analysis," *American Journal of Psychology* (1927), **38**, 368–389.

Torgerson, W. S. *Theory and Methods of Scaling.* New York: Wiley, 1958.

Treisman, A., & Geffin, G. "Selective Attention: Perception or Response?" *Quarterly Journal of Experimental Psychology* (1967), **19**, 1–17.

Ulehla, Z. J. "Optimality of Perceptual Decision Criteria," *Journal of Experimental Psychology* (1966), **71**, 564–569.

Ulehla, Z. J., Canges, L., & Wackwitz, F. "Signal Detectability Theory Applied to Conceptual Discrimination," *Psychonomic Science* (1967), **8**, 221–222.

Van Meter, D., & Middleton, D. "Modern Statistical Approaches to Reception in Communication Theory," *Transactions of the IRE Professional Group on Information Theory* (1954), **PGIT-4**, 119–141.

Van Trees, H. L. *Detection, Estimation, and Modulation Theory,* Part I. New York: Wiley, 1968.

Watson, C. S., Rilling, M. E., & Bourbon, W. T. "Receiver-Operating Characteristics Determined by a Mechanical Analog to the Rating Scale," *Journal of the Acoustical Society of America* (1964), **36**, 283–288.

Wilks, S. S. *Mathematical Statistics.* New York: Wiley, 1962.

Woodworth, R. S., & Schlosberg, H. *Experimental Psychology,* Revised ed. New York: Holt, 1954.

CHAPTER **8**

Information, Dynamic Decision Theory, and Bayesian Statistics

This chapter is concerned with the relationship between information and decision making. In real life, before making a decision, one often gathers information relevant to the decision. How much information should be gathered, why is such information worth having, and how much should one pay to get it?

Information need not come from an auxiliary information-gathering process. When a sequence of related decisions is made, past outcomes can be informative concerning the probabilities of the states of nature and thus can bear on forthcoming decisions. The topic of information gathering in decision making relates closely to current discussions concerning the "classical" and "Bayesian" approaches to statistical theory and method; we shall examine this controversy in the latter part of the chapter.

8.1 WHY INFORMATION AFFECTS DECISION MAKING

By "information" we typically refer to "data," "observations," or "communications" which change P^A's subjective probabilities for the states of nature in a decision situation. The EVs for the various choices depend, of course, on these probabilities, so if the probabilities change, the EVs for the possible choices change. Therefore, an alternative that has the highest EV before receipt of information might not afterwards. Information not only can change the EVs for the various choices; it can also alter the choice specified as optimal by the EV principle.

Though "information" is usually conceived to affect decisions via probabilities of states of nature, we can also imagine P^A receiving "information" bearing on his evaluation of consequences, i.e., on his utility function. Changes in the utility matrix, of course, can affect the optimality of an alternative.

8.2 AMBIGUOUS PROBABILITIES AND RELEVANT INFORMATION

Is it always possible to acquire information relevant to a decision? I refer here not to the practical matter of locating an accessible information source, but the theoretical issue of whether information could possibly be made available. Information relevant to the probabilities cannot always be made available. The probabilities must be ambiguous if they are to change. Recall from Section 5.4 that a subjective probability is said to be ambiguous if P^A has room for doubt about his estimate. In particular, we used the term in relation to an urn with an unknown proportion of red balls.

Suppose, for example, that a red or black ball is to be drawn randomly from an urn. If the contents of the urn are unknown to P^A, then he must use ambiguous probabilities in making his decisions (we assume he wants to use a decision criterion affected by the probabilities). Information, in principle, could be made available to P^A. For example, random samples could be drawn and displayed to P^A; these samples would be replaced in the urn and would not affect the objective probabilities for the states of nature, but they could very well affect the subjective probabilities on which the decision must be based.[1] In the extreme case the entire contents of the urn might be exhibited to P^A. He would then realize that the urn contains, say, eight red balls and two black balls. At this point no more information about the probabilities could be made available. (We assume an honest random draw and the impossibility of P^A's receiving any information about the outcome of the draw that "counts" until he has committed himself to a decision.)

This section, I admit, may appear tautological. When I stated, "The probabilities must be ambiguous if they are to change," does this not simply mean that, by definition, ambiguous probabilities are those susceptible to change due to evidence? Perhaps, but rather than become involved in this question, I would prefer simply to point out that there are situations in which one could not aspire to gather relevant information, as well as situations in which one could so aspire;

---

[1] Since there is reference to both "objective" and "subjective" probabilities, do I assume a disparity conception of probability (Section 3.3)? I don't think so, necessarily. If the urn contains eight red and two black balls, I say the objective probability for red is 0.8, and I assume that if P^A knew the contents his subjective probability would be 0.8. Of course, the measured subjective probability for a real person could deviate from this value.

these situations can be illustrated by the unambiguous and ambiguous urns, respectively.

8.3 SOME TERMINOLOGICAL PITFALLS

This chapter concerns a variety of types of decision situations, and it would be helpful to have a standard terminology for differentiating them. Unfortunately, the terminology in the area is most confusing. Not only do different authors use the same term differently, but it appears to me that a single author is sometimes inconsistent in his various papers, or even within a single paper. Nonetheless, it hardly seems possible to proceed without reference to such terminology. In this section I will only attempt an introduction to the terminology and the various uses of some important terms. I hope that this will assist the reader who consults source materials by leading him to be wary of terminology and to search for the meaning intended within each specific context.

First, a distinction is made between *static* and *dynamic* decision theory (or situations). Apparently all decision making falls under one rubric or the other, though for a given situation it may be difficult to say which. If forced to define these terms, I would say that a decision situation is *dynamic* if (1) information to P^A from past decision outcomes or from information-gathering processes is available and can lead to better decision making for forthcoming decisions than would otherwise be possible, or if (2) decisions made by P^A affect which subsequent decision situations he will face; if neither (1) nor (2) holds, the situation is *static*.

Ward Edwards (1961, 1962) is primarily responsible for the use of these terms in psychology. But his explanations of the terms seem confusing to me, so the above definitions do not correspond exactly to his own. In Edwards (1962) he appears to give *static* theory little or no domain, since it can apparently involve only a single choice. He doesn't say exactly that, but everything involving a sequence of decisions appears to be a type of dynamic situation. He includes as a *dynamic* subclass a *static sequential decision task* and says that research on preferences between bets has been characteristically of this type. In an earlier review, however, Edwards (1961) asserts that most research on preferences between gambles (up to 1960 at least) has concerned *static* decision theory (not *static sequential,* which is a subclass of dynamic).

The term *sequential* has been used with variety of meanings. In every case P^A is conceived to have a series of steps, actions, or decisions to make, or at least he has the option of making such a series. As we have seen, Edwards (1962) essentially makes "sequential" equivalent to "dynamic." According to Amnon Rapoport (1968) a *sequential decision problem* consists of static decision problems repeated. (In "static decision problems" P^A never makes another decision based on what he learned; yet learning in the sequential case is supposed to be possible.)

Sequential analysis or *sequential testing* is a method for experimentation developed within the field of statistics; it has also been used as a model for human behavior (see Section 8.6). A decision-theoretic outgrowth of sequential analysis which accounts for payoffs is sometimes called *sequential decision making* (Section 8.7). Both fields are concerned with step-by-step collection of observations (information); the number of steps to be taken is not set ahead of time; instead, the accumulated observations are tested after each step to determine whether information-gathering should cease or continue. Sequential analysis and sequential decision making would typically be considered examples of dynamic decision making.

We have yet to consider another common designation—the *multistage decision process*. According to Rapoport (1967), this is one with many stages involving sequential decisions; at the beginning of stage k, P^A obtains information about the "state" of the system, then makes a decision; the system then assumes a new state dependent on the previous state, the previous decision, and a stochastic variable. *Dynamic programming* is a technique for finding the optimal decisions for such situations, and in fact, Rapoport (1968) uses "dynamic programming model" synonomously with "multistage decision problem." Multistage decision processes are discussed in greater detail in Section 8.11. The terms *multistage experimentation* and *multistage procedure* have been used as synonyms for *sequential analysis*, as defined in preceding paragraph (Wald, 1950, pp. 28–29; Wilks, 1962, p. 474). Thus, they do not mean the same thing as *multistage decision process* as defined in the present paragraph.

Rapoport (1966) identifies multistage decision making with a subclass of Edwards' (1962) dynamic decision making, in particular with case 6. In this case, according to Edwards, both environment and information about it are affected by decisions. For all the other "dynamic" cases, the environment is not affected by decisions. Finally, note that in Fishburn's (1964) classification, the *multistage decision process* is considered to be a type of *sequential decision process* (which differs from the sequential decision making mentioned above).

8.4   WHERE THE INFORMATION COMES FROM

It is helpful to delineate several sources of information that P^A might use to adjust his probabilities:

(1) On the one hand, P^A can observe the states of nature which occur subsequent to his decisions. If P^A begins with ambiguous probability estimates and makes a sequence of decisions involving the same or related event probabilities, he can, in principle, arrive at better estimates of these probabilities. P^A, then, receives his information along with his payoffs, i.e., he "learns while he earns." In probability prediction experiments, for example, P^A may start out with ambiguous and inaccurate probability estimates, but over many trials his estimates become less ambiguous and more accurate. If the event probabilities change

over time his task is more difficult, but he can still use past events to estimate probabilities for the forthcoming decision if the changes are "lawful."

(2) The information may come from an auxiliary information-gathering process preceding the decision. This case can be further subdivided:

(2a) The number of observations may be controlled by the experimenter or some other power. For example, in probabilistic discrimination and signal detection experiments (Chapters 6 and 7), a single observation is typically made available on each trial prior to the decision. The observation alters P^A's prior probabilities into posterior probabilities which allow more effective decision making. Though only one observation is typically allowed, the experimenter could allow exactly two observations (for example, two presentations of the "signal" in a detection task) before each decision, or some other set number. In psychophysics this method has been dubbed the *fixed-observation procedure*.[2]

(2b) The number of observations before deciding may be left entirely to the discretion of P^A; he can go on making observations as long as he wishes. If he is not required to state ahead of time or at any time how many observations he wishes to make until he decides to stop, the task is *sequential analysis* (Section 8.6) or *sequential decision making* (Section 8.7). The terms *optional stopping, sequential-observation,* and *deferred-decision* procedure are also used. If P^A must state how many observations he wants ahead of time, the terms *predetermined-observation* and *fixed stopping* procedure are used.[3]

(2c) P^A may be allowed to make as many observations as he wishes, as long as the number doesn't exceed some value N set by the experimenter or some other power in advance. This is known as a *truncated sequential procedure*.[4]

There are other possibilities as well. For example, there might be some probability, known to P^A, that a current observation will be the last one allowed. Or P^A may simply understand that the experimenter may require him to cease making observations at any time.

Note that the same breakdown could apply to a sequence of decisions. There could be a set number known to P^A, P^A could be allowed to continue as long as he wished, or as long as he wished up to a limit, etc. Generally speaking, the more information P^A receives, the better his decisions will be. However, in real life, information comes at a price—in money, other resources, discomfort, and time. To simulate this in laboratory experiments, P^A may be required to pay for his information, and the more he requests, the more he must pay. Thus he must balance the value of the information received against the cost. Even in the absence of monetary costs, however, P^A won't take the time to make endless observations.

---

[2] Birdsall and Roberts (1965).
[3] *Ibid.* Also, Fried and Peterson (1969).
[4] Blackwell and Girshick (1954, p. 91).

8.5   BAYESIAN PROBABILITY REVISION

As we have said, information can affect decisions by affecting the probabilities of the states of nature. A quantitative explanation of these probability changes is centered around Bayes' formula (Chapters 3, 7). Does Bayes' formula, however, describe the impact of information on the probabilities of real people? A body of experimental work has been devoted to investigation of this question. We shall consider the basic theory, method, and results.

Recall that Bayes' formula describes the impact of observable events (data) on prior probabilities. In particular, according to Equation 3.7, if H_j's form a set of n exclusive, exhaustive events (hypotheses) and if an event E is observed, the posterior (new) probability for an event H_j is

$$p(H_j|E) = \frac{p(E|H_j)p(H_j)}{\displaystyle\sum_{j=1}^{n} p(E|H_j)p(H_j)} \tag{8.1}$$

The relevant experiments typically employ only two hypotheses, H_1 and H_2. Thus, we have

$$p(H_1|E) = \frac{p(E|H_1)p(H_1)}{\displaystyle\sum_{j=1}^{2} p(E|H_j)p(H_j)} \tag{8.2}$$

and

$$p(H_2|E) = \frac{p(E|H_2)p(H_2)}{\displaystyle\sum_{j=1}^{2} p(E|H_j)p(H_j)} \tag{8.3}$$

Since the denominators in Equations 8.2 and 8.3 are identical, if we divide Equation 8.3 by Equation 8.2 we obtain

$$\frac{p(H_2|E)}{p(H_1|E)} = \frac{p(E|H_2)p(H_2)}{p(E|H_1)p(H_1)} \tag{8.4}$$

$p(H_2)/p(H_1)$ is the prior odds for H_2 over H_1, and is often denoted Ω_0.[5] $p(E|H_2)/p(E|H_1)$, a ratio of two likelihoods, was called a likelihood ratio in Chapter 7 (see Equation 7.4), though it was defined there in terms of continuous instead of discrete sample spaces. As before, let us denote the likelihood ratio $L(E)$, or $L_{21}(E)$ if we wish to emphasize that the likelihood for H_2 is in the numerator. The left term of Equation 8.4 is the posterior odds in favor of

---

[5] Ω is capital Greek omega.

H_2, and is often denoted Ω_1. Then Equation (8.4) can be written

$$\Omega_1 = L(E)\Omega_0, \qquad (8.5)$$

or the posterior odds equals the prior odds multiplied by the likelihood ratio for the observed event.

Let us consider the details of a "typical" experiment on Bayesian probability revision. Ss are informed that there are two urns (or bags, or whatever) containing balls (or chips) of two colors, say red and black. In one urn black balls predominate, $p(\text{black}) = p$, whereas in the other urn red balls predominate, $p(\text{red}) = p$. One of the urns is chosen randomly, with probability of choice for each equal to $1/2$. H_2 is the hypothesis that the black-predominant urn was chosen; H_1 is the hypothesis that the red-predominant urn was chosen. Exactly one of these hypotheses is true. Next a ball is drawn randomly from the chosen urn and exhibited to S. The prior odds Ω_0 should be, and presumably is, 1. Equation 8.4 or 8.5 can be used to calculate the posterior odds. Instead of seeing only one ball, S might see a sequence of such samples, each drawn independently with replacement of the previous sample before the new drawing (replacement keeps the probabilities constant for each draw). For the situation under consideration,

$$L(E) = \left(\frac{p}{1-p}\right)^{b-r}, \qquad (8.6)$$

where b and r are the number of black and red balls drawn when a total of $b + r$ samples was taken (singly and independently). Note that $p/(1-p) > 1$, and if H_2 is true, we would expect $(b-r)$ to be positive (though it wouldn't always be), so $L(E) > 1$, and the posterior odds in favor of black would increase relative to the prior odds. If $r > b$ in a series of samples, however, $L(E)$ would be less than 1, and the posterior odds in favor of H_2 would be less than the prior odds. Note that the adjustment in odds for the conditions at hand depends only on the difference between the number of red and black balls sampled, and, given this difference, is entirely independent of the total number of balls sampled, $b + r$. Thus observation of 4 black balls and 0 red balls would have exactly the same impact (likelihood ratio) on Ω_0 as 1004 black balls and 1000 red balls.

Ss are provided with varying numbers of samples and then are asked to estimate the posterior probabilities for H_1 and H_2. Direct probability estimates are required (Section 3.4), and the method used typically assures that the probabilities do sum to 1 (for example, Ss, perhaps, have to adjust a pointer to divide a line of length 1 into two lengths representing the probabilities for H_1 and H_2).

The first question is, considering the prior odds and the $L(E)$ from the samples, do the Ss' estimates for Ω_1 match the value required by Bayes' formula, as stated in Equation (8.5). The answer is clearly no. Experiments have consistently shown that Ss seldom give probability (or odds) estimates according with Bayes' formula. Typically, observations have much less impact on the odds than Bayes' formula requires; this has been called the *conservatism effect* (Edwards & Phillips, 1964). It is as if Ss are reluctant to change their estimates to the extent justified by the available data. Under some circumstances, however, revisions are greater than Bayes' formula requires.

If we rearrange Equation 8.5 and take logarithms we obtain

$$\log_{10} L(E) = \log_{10} \Omega_1 - \log_{10} \Omega_0 \qquad (8.7)$$

This log of the likelihood ratio (LLR) can be calculated from the theoretical value of $L(E)$. A subjective LLR can also be found by using the S's value for Ω_1 in Equation 8.7 (S's value for Ω_0 is typically adjusted to its correct value at the beginning of the trial). The ratio of the S's LLR to the Bayes' formula LLR will be called the *impact ratio,* and this value is often plotted to describe Ss' revisions under different conditions. The impact ratio would be less than 1 for "conservative" revisions and 1 if the revisions accorded with Bayes' formula. Impact ratios greater than 1 indicate excessive revisions. (Impact ratio is called *accuracy ratio* in the literature; however, it seems peculiar that as accuracy ratios above 1 increase, accuracy decreases; thus, I suggest the alternative term.)

Once we know that Ss' probability revisions are not described perfectly by Bayes' formula, a host of experiments becomes possible to determine the influences of various factors on the actual revision, for example:

Size of Sampling Unit. Peterson, Schneider, and Miller (1965) determined the effect of size of sampling unit on impact ratio; i.e., instead of drawing the samples one ball at a time, we might draw 2 at a time, 4 at a time, etc. They used sampling units of 1, 4, 12, or 48 balls, in each case drawing 48 balls altogether. (The urns contained a very large number of balls—approximately 1000—so that the Bayesian theory for sampling 1 ball at a time with replacement would hold to a reasonable approximation for larger sampling units.) A total of 48 balls was finally drawn for each sampling unit (for example, if the sampling unit was 4, 12 drawings were used), and the impact ratio was compared as a function of sampling unit. The impact ratio was highest when the sampling unit was smallest—1 ball at a time—and decreased to a low asymptote when the sampling unit reached 12. The mean impact ratios between these points varied from about 0.47 to 0.26.

Proportion of Predominant Balls. The proportion p of Equation 8.6 has a strong effect on impact ratio. The smaller p, the greater the impact ratio (but p, the predominant proportion, is, of course, always greater than 0.5). Impact ratios greater than 1 were observed for small p values (Phillips & Edwards, 1966; Peterson & Miller, 1965).

Magnitude of Prior Odds. Impact ratios were higher when the prior odds were extreme (9/1 or 1/9) than when prior odds were intermediate (Peterson & Miller, 1965).

Method of Estimating Posterior Odds. Phillips and Edwards (1966) compared four methods of reporting subjective posterior odds. One group ("probability") piled 100 discs into two troughs to represent relative probabilities. Another group ("verbal odds") gave verbal statements of the estimated odds. A third group ("log odds") estimated odds by setting a sliding pointer on a scale of odds spaced logarithmically. A fourth group ("log probability") used a sliding pointer scaled with probabilities, with scale markers spaced according to log odds. Accuracy was greatest for "verbal odds" and "log odds" groups, and least for the "probability" group.

Payment for Accuracy. Are Ss giving their "true" subjective probabilities? One way to investigate this question is to use a payoff scheme so that subjectively expected value decreases as S's stated estimates deviate from his true estimates. Payoffs decreased the amount of conservatism (Phillips & Edwards, 1966).

Size of Likelihoods. As we have seen (Equations 8.4 and 8.5), $L(E)$ is a ratio of two likelihoods of the form $p(E|H_j)$. A likelihood ratio of a specific magnitude, say 4.0, could be the ratio of two fairly small likelihoods, say 0.08/0.02, or of two larger magnitudes, say 0.4/0.1. According to Bayes' formula, it makes no difference—the impact on prior odds should be the same. However, as we have seen, people are not slavish in adhering to Bayes' formula, and it might matter to them. Such was the hypothesis of Vlek (1965), and such were the results found by Beach (1968). For the same likelihood ratios, larger likelihoods resulted in more accurate estimates than small likelihoods.

Detection theory assumes that information is processed via Bayes' formula, and Ss in detection experiments are often required to give subjective probability estimates. Thus one would think that the detection theory literature would contain information on Bayesian probability revision for the case of a normal distribution of samples rather than a binomial. In a detection task, however, the sample location cannot be observed by the experimenter—indeed, the normal distribution is itself hypothetical—so the true Bayesian posterior probability on a trial cannot be calculated. However, with the externally distributed stimulus analogue of the detection task (Section 7.9), the Bayesian posteriors can be calculated by the experimenter, and "conservatism" was observed in such a study (Lee, 1963).

Given that Ss do not follow Bayes' formula, we might ask, where do they "go wrong." Ss are made or induced to start out with the correct prior odds, so they are fine at that point. Then they are presented with a sample (E) of data. A "Bayesian processor," at this point, would calculate the likelihoods of this data for the two hypotheses. S could go wrong here. Then the Bayesian processor would calculate $L(E)$, and then calculate Ω_1. S could go wrong at either of these steps also. Alternately, the processor could bypass the likelihood ratio and calculate the two posterior probabilities, then transform these to odds if need be. We might ask, do people go wrong mainly at one of these stages, or do they "foul up" at every opportunity. Beach (1966) argued that people relate $p(H|E)$ and $p(E|H)$ (posterior probability and likelihood) in accordance with Bayes' formula, but that they misjudge the likelihoods. Peterson, DuCharme, and Edwards (1968) found support for this assertion. They required Ss to estimate likelihoods as well as posterior odds. They found that the deviations of the likelihood estimations from the mathematical values could largely account for the conservatism of the posterior odds estimates.

There is a possible source of conservatism not considered in the experimental psychology literature: S may be suspicious of the experimenter and the whole experimental setup; after all, ruses are often used in experiments, and mistakes are possible. S might then tend to "sit tight" with his initial odds (he might even doubt these). Of course Ss do typically revise their odds in the appropriate direction, but their estimates may, in some cases, be tempered by skepticism. There is further discussion on this issue in Section 8.10.

The Central Tendency Effect in Psychophysics

The conservatism effect in Bayesian probability revision would appear to be a special case of the general finding with psychophysical judgments that when a spread of stimuli are to be judged, the larger stimuli are underestimated and the smaller ones are overestimated. Suppose, for example, that either red (H_1) or black (H_2) balls predominate with a probability $p = 2/3$, and that $\Omega_0 = 1$. If a red ball is drawn, the posterior probability for red, $p(H_1|E)$, would equal $2/3$. A real S would estimate the probability at, say, 0.6, an underestimation. If, on the next trial H_1 or H_2 is chosen anew so that Ω_0 is still 1, a black ball would, by Bayes' formula, lead to a posterior $p(H_1|E)$ of $1/3$, but a real S would, say, estimate 0.4, an overestimation of the smaller probability.

As we saw (Section 3.5), the *central tendency effect* is well-established for probability estimates, but it also occurs for estimations of time, length, rate of work—you name it (Helson, 1964, pp. 94–102). It is important to emphasize that when, in the context of this effect, we refer to stimuli as "large" or "small," we mean large or small relative to the set of stimuli under consideration. For example, 15 seconds would be a "large stimulus" and underestimated when other time intervals for the task are smaller, but it would be a "small stimulus" and overestimated in the context of generally longer time intervals. It follows that the "intermediate stimulus values" that are accurately estimated cannot be specified in absolute terms, for example, 7 seconds, 10 seconds, or whatever. Extrapolation of this knowledge to probability estimates tells us that it is futile to try to find, in an absolute sense, the value of objective probability that is neither over- nor underestimated, i.e., the *indifference point*. Nonetheless, it sometimes seems to me that authors are puzzled or troubled over the failure to find such an absolute indifference point for probability.

Helson (1964) interprets the central tendency effect with his adaptation-level theory—the indifference point is identified with an adaptation level. Wiesen and Shuford (1961), however, feel that a Bayesian approach can account for the central tendency. The *indifference point* relates to a prior distribution of a parameter (it is the mode for an example of theirs). Because prior probabilities as well as current data affect Bayesian estimates, judgments above the indifference point tend to be underestimates, whereas judgments below the indifference point tend to be overestimates. The prior distribution of a parameter would be determined by the S's experience prior to the experiment as well as by information gained in the experiment up to the current trial.

8.6 SEQUENTIAL ANALYSIS

In the usual manner of conducting an experimental investigation, the experimenter decides to take a set number of observations, he makes these observations, and then he performs statistical tests to determine whether to accept or reject various null hypotheses. An alternative method, known as *sequential testing* or *sequential analysis,* requires that the number of observations not be set in advance, but rather that data analysis be conducted after each observation (or set of observations) to determine whether to form a conclusion at that point or to collect more data. The basic idea of the sequential test appeared in the "double-sampling" quality inspection procedure of Dodge and Romig (1929). A full-fledged exposition of sequential testing was presented in a book by Abraham Wald (1947) called *Sequential Analysis.* A merit of the sequential procedures is that they require, on the average, substantially fewer observations than methods based on a predetermined number of observations. In other words, they require less information-gathering than the usual techniques, and this is a good thing, since collecting data (information) is usually thought to be a chore and an expense rather than a joy.

Sequential analysis is of concern to us in this chapter since we are interested in the use of information-gathering in decision making. Since information is costly, the sequential approach to information-gathering would appear to be very appealing from the decision-theoretic point of view. Nonetheless, let us recognize that as originally developed, sequential testing was an outgrowth of the "classical" or "traditional" statistical methods for hypothesis testing, and, as such, the philosophy differed considerably from a decision-theoretic point of view, as embodied in Bayesian statistics (see Section 8.9). In particular, the original developments in sequential testing did not take explicit account of payoffs and prior probabilities. (We discuss such extensions of sequential testing in Section 8.7.)

We must clearly distinguish between an experimenter (not necessarily a psychologist) who uses sequential testing in an objective manner, making explicit calculations as required by the theory, and a laboratory subject (S) whose behavior is compared with the theory. Experimental psychologists have shown some interest in the use of sequential testing in planning their experiments, particularly in psychophysics (for example, Taylor & Creelman, 1967; Levitt & Rabiner, 1967). Our discussion, however, is not aimed at such applications; we are instead concerned with the use of sequential testing (and sequential decision making) as a model for human inference and decision making in general.

Let us illustrate sequential analysis for a specific situation. In the present context, we call the "experimenter" P^A. For simplicity, imagine that P^A is faced with an urn containing red and black balls. There are two possible conditions for the urn: (1) the proportion of red balls is p_1 (hypothesis H_1), or (2) the proportion of red balls is p_2 (hypothesis H_2; $p_1 > p_2$). P^A samples the balls from the urn one at a time (we assume that he samples with replacement, or that the number of balls in the urn is so large that non-replacement does not affect the probabilities). After observing each sample (ball), P^A must do one of three things: (1) conclude that H_1 is true (the proportion of red balls is p_1); (2) conclude that H_2 is true (the proportion of red balls is p_2); or, (3) decide to take another sample. If he forms a conclusion, the test ends. If he decides to take another sample, he observes this sample, and again does (1), (2), or (3). He continues until he reaches a conclusion.

How does he know when to reach a conclusion? The analysis is closely related to Bayesian probability revision (Section 8.5). At each stage a likelihood ratio, $p(E|H_2)/p(E|H_1)$, is formed based on the data collected do far. If $L(E)$ becomes larger than a critical value, P^A accepts H_2. If $L(E)$ becomes smaller than another critical value, P^A accepts H_1. For intermediate values of $L(E)$, P^A decides to make another observation. If the prior odds for H_2 to H_1 equals 1, then the likelihood ratio equals the posterior odds (Equation 8.5). It is as if, then, P^A wishes to see the posterior odds favoring H_1 or H_2 reach some limit, and then he will conclude that one is true.

The critical values of likelihood ratio are determined by the probabilities α and β.[6] α is the probability of accepting H_2 if H_1 were true, and β is the probability of accepting H_1 if H_2 were true. If at any stage $L(E)$ exceeds $(1 - \beta)/\alpha$, P^A accepts H_2, and if at any time $L(E)$ becomes less than $\beta/(1 - \alpha)$, P^A accepts H_1. P^A can set his "risks" α and β as small as he wishes. The smaller the risks, however, the larger the number of observations P^A will need on the average before he can reach a conclusion.

For the problem at hand it is convenient and enlightening to use a graphical

---

[6] α and β are the probabilities for type I and type II errors in the "hypothesis testing" procedure of traditional statistics. In the example, H_1 is arbitrarily considered to be the "null hypothesis."

aid. At any stage in the sampling process P^A has observed a number of red balls r and a number of black balls b. These numbers can be plotted on a graph step by step as the data accumulates, as in Figure 8.1. P^A starts at $(0, 0)$ and each sample leads the graph one step to the right or one step up. Sampling continues until the graph passes one of the two parallel lines. The slopes of these lines are determined by p_1 and p_2, but their locations depend on α and β as well. The smaller α and β, the greater the separation of the lines.

The analysis we have discussed concerns the procedure recommended to experimenters by (some) statisticians as a "best" way of coming to a conclusion

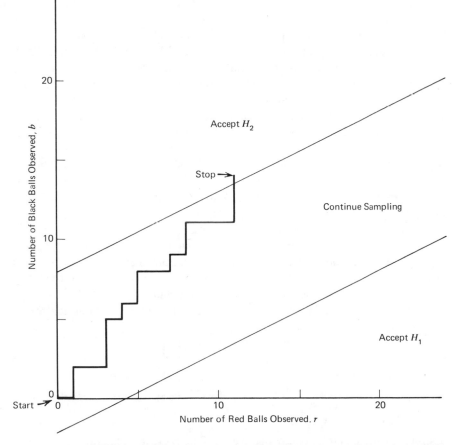

Figure 8.1. Chart for sequential test of a binomial population. H_1 and H_2 are the two possible hypotheses for the probability of a red ball. Testing starts at $(0, 0)$ and proceeds one sample at a time until the graph enters one of the two *stopping regions*. For the particular sequence of observations illustrated, P^A stopped sampling after observing 14 black balls and 11 red balls, and accepted H_2.

in a specific context. Any experimenter who wants to use the procedure would carefully tabulate his data and perform objective calculations. We can ask, however, whether naive Ss form conclusions from incoming data according to similar principles, even though they lack an awareness of the theory and do no objective tabulations or calculations.

Gordon Becker (1958) studied human behavior in a sequential testing situation such as we discussed. Ss were given samples from a binomial (two-valued) population. They were told that the samples came from one of two (or more) populations which were specified. They were allowed to collect as many samples as they wished before reaching a conclusion concerning which population they were sampling from. They repeated the same problem many times. The data available at each conclusion were plotted as a point on coordinates similar to those of Figure 8.1. Each point might be considered to be the upper end of a data-accumulation graph such as the one of Figure 8.1. According to Wald's model, these termination points should fall along two parallel lines with slopes determined by p_1 and p_2. Ss were not told to use particular values for α and β, but one might assume that Ss should at least keep these values constant. The values they used could be determined from the separation between the lines. Becker concluded that Wald's model was a reasonable first approximation to the behavior observed. The decision lines of the Ss, however, were not always parallel, nor did they always agree with the slope required by the theory. One S of eight did not even have straight lines. Generally speaking, Ss appeared to operate more like Wald's model when the problem was difficult, i.e., when the discrimination was between very similar populations, than when the problem was easy. Ss required relatively more samples on easy problems and relatively fewer on the difficult, as if they set α and β lower for the easy problems. Ss differed in the amount of risk and size of sample they preferred. It should be pointed out that Becker used an unusual payoff scheme to motivate Ss, and it isn't clear what strategic effects this may have had.

Francis Irwin and W. A. S. Smith (1956) studied "sequential testing" by Ss for a different problem. S was shown a succession of samples from a normal distribution with a mean and standard deviation unknown to S. He received as many samples as he wished until he was ready to say whether the distribution had a mean greater or less than zero. Distributions were used with means of −1.5, −0.5, 0, +0.5, and +1.5; standard deviations for each mean were 2.0 and 7.5. Presumably S would stop and give his conclusion when he received enough data to reach a desired level of significance (α). In other words, the assumption was that S would behave as if he were a "machine" for performing a classical type of statistical test at each stage (in particular, a t-test). If so, Ss should require more samples to reach a conclusion the greater the standard deviation and the closer the mean to zero, and, indeed, such was the case. (Of course, this does not prove that Ss perform in complete agreement with the statistical model.)

I might mention here a related study, though it didn't involve a sequential test. Irwin, Smith, and Mayfield (1956) presented a fixed number of samples to S from a normal distribution. S then had to state whether the population mean was larger or smaller than zero. Here again, Ss responded to the same factors that would affect the test of a statistical hypothesis; for example, confidence in the conclusions was directly related to sample size and deviation of the population mean from zero, and was inversely related the standard deviation of the population. Similar results obtained when Ss were presented samples from two distributions simultaneously and had to state which pile of samples came from the population with the larger mean.

8.7 SEQUENTIAL DECISION MAKING

The type of sequential analysis that we discussed in Section 8.6 was an outgrowth of "classical" statistical methodology, and thus the end product of the test was a "conclusion" about some fact of nature, rather than a "decision." The conclusion could be "right" or "wrong," but classical hypothesis testing attempted no exact quantitative analysis of the possible payoffs for being "right" or "wrong." If, however, the end product of experimentation is not a conclusion, but a decision leading to a consequence, sequential analysis is incomplete. Spurred on by the contributions of von Neumann and Morgenstern to decision theory, Abraham Wald followed up his work on sequential analysis with a book on *Statistical Decision Functions* (1950) which combined the sequential experimentation and decision-payoff approaches into a unified treatment. A similar approach was taken by Blackwell and Girshick (1954) in *Theory of Games and Statistical Decisions.*

The resulting *sequential decision making* theory requires, as did sequential analysis, that the amount of information-gathering not be settled in advance; instead, P^A must determine at each stage whether to make a decision or to gather more information. He will gather more information not because he wishes to be more sure per se about the true hypothesis, but because he feels that an expected gain in payoff from having more information would more than compensate for the cost involved in gathering it. The "decision" to gather more information is, indeed, a kind of decision, but it is worthwhile to distinguish between information-gathering decisions and what Wald (1950, p. 2) called terminal decisions. Usually, by "decision" we mean the *terminal decision,* which, in conjunction with the state of nature, leads to a payoff for P^A. It would be possible to avoid the distinction between information-gathering and terminal decisions by conceiving a unified set of decisions which would include all possible strategies, terminal or information-gathering, for all possible sequences of observations and terminal decisions. Such a conception would be cumbersome, however, and is just as well avoided.

Let us consider a very simple example to illustrate sequential decision making. Suppose P^A confronts the following payoff matrix:

$$
\begin{array}{c|c|c|}
& b_1 & b_2 \\
\hline
a_1 & 8 & -4 \\
\hline
a_2 & -5 & 7 \\
\hline
\end{array}
$$

Suppose the "state of nature" will be determined by drawing a ball from an urn; b_1 is a red ball, and b_2 is a black ball. To start out simply, let us assume in addition that the urn contains only one ball, black or red. Initially $p(b_1) = p(b_2) = 0.5$, so $EV_1 = 2$ and $EV_2 = 1$. We assume that without additional information P^A would choose a_1 and would have an EV of 2. Now suppose P^A has an opportunity to gain some information; specifically, he is allowed to draw the ball from the urn, note its color and replace it. If the ball is red he will choose a_1 and receive 8; if the ball is black he will choose a_2 and receive 7. Before observing, however, he doesn't know which choice he will make. But based on his current probabilities for $p(b_1)$ and $p(b_2)$ (0.5 each), he can calculate an expected value for his decision, contingent on observing the ball.

$$EV = p(b_1)7 + p(b_2)8 = 7.5$$

That is, with probability 0.5 he will observe red, choose a_1, and receive 8, and with probability 0.5 he will observe black, choose a_2, and receive 7. His EV then is 7.5 (before the observation is made; afterwards it will be either 7 or 8—P^A doesn't know which). Since, as we noted, the EV for this game without the observation is 2, the observation, before it is made, can be valued at $7.5 - 2 = 5.5$. According to the EV principle, then, P^A should be willing to pay up to 5.5 in order to make the observation. If the information costs 5.5 or more, however, P^A would not wish to obtain it. In this very simple example P^A would not wish in any case to make more than one observation, since he learns all that he possibly can with one observation.

Typically an observation merely allows P^A to make more accurate estimates of the probabilities, with additional observations allowing greater accuracy yet. Depending on the situation, as the number of observations increases, the probability estimate for one state of nature can approach 1, or the probability can approach a value less than 1. Let us consider an example of the latter type, using the payoff matrix of the preceding example.

We now assume that the state of nature is to be determined by a random draw of a ball from an urn containing three balls. The urn either has two red balls and one black ball (H_1), or one red ball and two black balls (H_2). Initially P^A has subjective probabilities for $p(H_1)$ and $p(H_2)$ of 0.5.

In order to calculate the EVs for the choices, we need $p(b_1)$ and $p(b_2)$. Given the compositions for H_1 and H_2, and given $p(H_1)$ and $p(H_2)$, we find $p(b_1)$

and $p(b_2)$ by using Equation 3.3:

$$p(b_1) = p(b_1|H_1)p(H_1) + p(b_1|H_2)p(H_2) \qquad (8.8)$$
$$p(b_2) = p(b_2|H_1)p(H_1) + p(b_2|H_2)p(H_2) \qquad (8.9)$$

Substituting,

$$p(b_1) = \left(\frac{2}{3}\right)\left(\frac{1}{2}\right) + \left(\frac{1}{3}\right)\left(\frac{1}{2}\right) = \frac{1}{2}$$

$$p(b_2) = \left(\frac{1}{3}\right)\left(\frac{1}{2}\right) + \left(\frac{2}{3}\right)\left(\frac{1}{2}\right) = \frac{1}{2}$$

Thus, initially

$$EV_1 = \left(\frac{1}{2}\right)8 + \left(\frac{1}{2}\right)(-4) = 2$$

$$EV_2 = \left(\frac{1}{2}\right)(-5) + \left(\frac{1}{2}\right)7 = 1$$

Now if P^A has the opportunity to observe a ball drawn randomly from the urn, the color of the ball (the datum) will alter the subjective probabilities $p(H_1)$ and $p(H_2)$ via Bayes' formula (Equation 8.1). Then these posterior probabilities can be used to calculate posterior values of $p(b_1)$ and $p(b_2)$, which would lead to posterior EV_1 and EV_2. There are two possible observations (data): black or red. The posterior probabilities for H_1 and H_2 depend on which datum occurs, and thus the final EV_i's depend on the datum observed. If the red datum occurs, the reader may verify that the string of calculations outlined leads to posterior $p(H_1) = 2/3$, posterior $p(b_1) = 5/9$, $EV_1 = 8/3$, $EV_2 = 1/3$; thus, if a red datum occurs P^A would then prefer a_1 which would have an EV of 8/3. If, however, a black ball is sampled, this would lead to $EV_1 = 4/3$ and $EV_2 = 5/3$, in which case P^A would prefer a_2 which would have an EV of 5/3. (Note that an observation, black in this case, can lead to a lowering of the EV for the better choice.) We have already calculated that before any observations are made the probability for observing a red or black ball is 0.5. Thus, before making an observation, P^A can calculate an EV in case he chooses to make an observation. This would be

$$EV = (EV|\text{red})p(\text{red}) + (EV|\text{black})p(\text{black})$$

$$= \left(\frac{8}{3}\right)\left(\frac{1}{2}\right) + \left(\frac{5}{3}\right)\left(\frac{1}{2}\right)$$

$$= 2\frac{1}{6}$$

The EV|red and EV|black values were based on P^A's better choice for each possible datum. Without making any observation, P^A's EV is 2, so in this case, by EV theory, P^A would wish to purchase an observation only if it costs less than 1/6.

It is possible for information to provide no average increase in EV, even though it changes the probabilities for the states of nature. Suppose in the preceding example that the revision of $p(b_1)$ and $p(b_2)$ after observation had been smaller (this would be the case if, say, the predominant proportion in each urn had been closer to 0.5, say, 0.6). Then, the EVs for a_1 and a_2 would change very little after observation of a ball. Thus a_1 would be the decision called for regardless of the observation. For a red ball EV_1 would be slightly greater than 2, and for a black ball EV_1 would be slightly less than 2; for our example they would average out to exactly 2, just where we began. The reader might wish to confirm this mathematically.

Analysis of the preceding example was based on the assumption that P^A can make at most one observation, i.e., that P^A faces the simplest sort of truncated sequential procedure. An analysis assuming that P^A can continue making observations would not be as "simple," since an infinite number of possibilities are involved. We cannot, in general, assume that just because it would not be worthwhile to buy one more observation and then make a decision, that it would not be worthwhile to make two or more observations and then make a decision.

If the reader surmises that the optimal strategy for a sequential decision task may be difficult to determine, he is correct. Suppose that in the preceding example H_1 and H_2 were the two states of nature for the decision instead of b_1 and b_2, and suppose the cost for each observation were a constant. The optimal strategy, in EV terms, has been found for the problem (Blackwell & Girshick, 1954, pp. 278–282; Edwards, 1965). It involves testing the likelihood ratio after each observation, and stopping only if the likelihood ratio exceeds some critical lower or upper bound. Indeed, this is the solution for sequential analysis (Section 8.6). In the present case, however, the critical bounds are dependent on the prior probabilities and payoffs.

A number of experiments have been performed on sequential decision making by naive Ss. Dean Pruitt (1961) required Ss to sample from a binomial population until they were willing to decide whether the predominant color was red or green. They received 101 points minus the number of observations for a correct decision, and zero points for an incorrect decision. For his conditions, Pruitt reasoned that the optimal strategy would be to observe samples until one color exceeded the other by four, though he had no proof of this. Indeed, the mean excess of one color over another for the terminal decision was close to 4. One wonders about Pruitt's solution, however, particularly since he told Ss the predominant proportion was 0.6 though he actually used 0.7.

Ward Edwards and Paul Slovic (1965) utilized another sequential task. One cell of 16 in a matrix was "unique." This unique cell might be at any location with equal probabilities. S got one free guess but was charged for any other guesses. After making his free guess S had to go to another matrix, whether he found the unique cell or not. Before making his guess he could purchase as many looks as he wished. The more such looks S used, the higher the probability that he could guess successfully, since there were fewer possibilities left.

The optimal strategy is to take up to L looks, and if the unique cell is not found by then to guess. The maximum number of looks to take depends on the reward for finding the unique cell and the costs for looking. Note that this situation is rather different from what we have been assuming, because the set of possible terminal decisions decreases with each observation; in addition, one can't always distinguish between information-gathering and terminal decisions; the "observation" one pays to make may turn out to be the "terminal decision."

Different sessions required different strategies. Although Ss by no means settled on exactly the optimal strategy, they did make reasonable adjustments in mean strategy from session to session in accordance with the payoffs and costs.

Irwin and Smith (1957) performed a sequential experiment much like the one discussed in Section 8.6; S was shown a sequence of samples from a normal distribution until he could conclude that the population had a mean greater or smaller than zero. In this case, however, S had to pay for each sample ($\frac{1}{2}\phi$ or 1ϕ), and received $0.50 or $1.00 for a correct decision. Though no mathematical solution is available for the task, it seems reasonable that Ss would be willing to pay for more information the greater the reward for being correct, and would be willing to buy less information the more it cost. The data confirmed these expectations, though the differences were not large: the mean numbers of cards for the greater and smaller prizes were 19.5 and 17.7; for the two costs of information the mean numbers of cards were 20.6 and 16.6. As before, the number of samples required varied indirectly with the distance of the population mean from zero and directly with the standard deviation of the population. Smith (1964) essentially replicated the preceding experiment, but by placing greater instructional emphasis on the prize to be won he induced a greater effect for that variable.

Richard Kaplan and Robert Newman (1966) investigated the use of a computer aid in sequential decision making. The basic idea is due to Edwards (1962), who reasoned that a computer might assist P^A with the Bayesian information processing involved in decision making. The processing system is called PIP (Probabilistic Information Processing). In the experiment, a PIP S bought information and estimated the likelihoods that such information derived from each of two possible hypotheses; then a computer calculated the posterior probabilities. S could buy as many samples of information as he wished before making a terminal decision. In the non-PIP group, an S had to make likelihood and posterior probability judgments without a computer or any instruction on Bayes' formula. There was no notable difference between the two groups in amount of money won or in the posterior probability estimates.

The detection theorists have also taken an interest in the deferred-decision procedures, as they call sequential decision making. For example, instead of presenting the signal (or noise) once, it is presented as many times as the S wishes. For each presentation he receives an observation from the signal (or noise) distribution. (If "signal" is the true hypothesis, signal is presented each time S requests an observation, and noise each time if "noise" is the true hypothesis.) The more observations he has, the surer he will be, on the average, about signal or noise; this translates into higher d' measures. References include: Birdsall and Roberts (1965), Swets and Green (1961), and Swets and Birdsall (1967).

The preceding discussion has concerned the gathering of information from a single source. More generally, the protagonist must determine which information source to use.

8.8 INFORMATION THEORY AND INFORMATION GATHERING

We have seen how information-gathering can lead to an improvement in the EV of a game for P^A. In recent years, "information" itself has been the subject of extensive theoretical treatment. I refer, in particular, to the Shannon's (1948) mathematical theory of communication plus subsequent related work. Shannon was concerned with the quantity of information passing through a communication system, and showed how this could be measured. Since, as we have seen, information is highly relevant to decision making, it might be worthwhile to consider briefly the information-gathering process in terms of the technical "information theory" considered by Shannon. First we present an introduction to information theory.

Assume the existence of a set of mutually exclusive, exhaustive events, each with a specified probability. By definition, the *entropy* or *uncertainty* of that set of probabilities is

$$U = - \sum_i p_i \log_2 p_i \tag{8.10}$$

Note: By definition, when $p = 0$, $p \log p = 0$. This special definition is necessary because $\log 0$ does not exist. The 2 in $\log_2$ is the *base*. Outside of information theory, the base is more usually 10 or e (a special number in mathematics).

Within information theory, a "message" is said to convey information from a "source" to a "destination," say P^A, if the message causes P^A to revise his estimates for any p_i. One can calculate a new uncertainty based on the new probabilities. Call the posterior uncertainty U'. Then the information transmitted to P^A by the message (which we could also call an observation or datum) is defined to be

$$I = U - U' \tag{8.11}$$

The unit of measurement for uncertainty and information is the *bit*.

Let us illustrate. A coin is to be flipped and will land heads or tails with equal probabilities. A message relating the result is to be sent to P^A. Before receiving the message P^A's prior uncertainty is

$$U = - \left[\frac{1}{2} \log_2 \frac{1}{2} + \frac{1}{2} \log_2 \frac{1}{2} \right] = 1$$

Note: Since $\log_2 [1/X] = -\log_2 X$, $\log_2 [1/2] = -\log_2 2$. $\text{Log}_2 2 = 1$.

After reception of the message, P^A knows, let us say, that the result was heads, i.e., that $p_h = 1$ and $p_t = 0$. Then

$$U' = - [1 \log_2 1 + 0 \log_2 0] = 0$$

Note: $\log 1 = 0$ for any base.

$I = U - U' = 1 - 0 = 1$. *A message leading to certainty about two originally equally probable events conveys 1 bit of information.*

The posterior uncertainty needn't be 0. For one thing, there might be *noise* in the communications channel which would distort the message, i.e., cause P^A to receive a message other than the one which was sent. Suppose, for example, that the probability of distortion from heads to tails or vice versa is 0.1. This would leave $U = 1$, but U' would no longer be zero, since after receiving "heads" P^A's probabilities would not be 1 and 0—they would be 0.9 and 0.1. U' would be 0.469 and I would be 0.531. Thus probability of distortion of only 0.1 can reduce the information by almost half.

If there are more than two possible events the prior uncertainty can be greater than 1. If, for example, there were four equally probable events, U would be 2; more generally, *for n equally probable events,*

$$U_{max} = \log_2 n \tag{8.12}$$

This follows from Equation 8.10 by substituting $1/n$ for each p_i. *For n events, the uncertainty is greatest when all events are equally probable,* so Equation 8.12 gives the upper limit for n events across all possible probabilities. Hence the designation U_{max}. The minimum uncertainty for any set of events is 0, which would obtain if and only if one p_i were 1 (and all others, of course, were zero).

In our example we calculated the information transmitted by a particular message, namely, "heads." The other possible message, "tails," would convey the same quantity of information, 1 bit. However, in general, the different possible messages convey different amounts of information. Thus we must distinguish between the amount of information that would be conveyed by a particular message and the *average* (or *expected*) *information.*

Let I_j be the information conveyed by received message j, and let $p(j)$ be the prior probability for message j. Then the *expected information* is

$$\hat{I} = \sum_j I_j p(j) \tag{8.13}$$

I_j may be negative, but I must be non-negative. If all messages are equally informative, Equation 8.13 reduces to

$$\bar{I} = I_j \text{ (for any } j) \tag{8.14}$$

It is apparent that an information theory analysis of a communications system requires that relevant source and receiver probabilities be available. For our purposes in the present section we take these to be the "subjective probabilities" of some ideal P^A who receives the messages. In the usual information theory analysis of a communications system, it is assumed that the receiver (P^A) knows the probabilistic characteristics of the communications system and that these are constant. Thus, on each trial the only thing P^A can learn is the particular message he receives on that trial. The expected information $\bar{I}$ remains constant from trial to trial.

For some decision situations employing information, $\bar{I}$ remains constant from trial to trial, and for others it does not. Consider the latter case first, and for this purpose let us return to an example from Section 8.7. The state of nature, b_1 or b_2, is determined by drawing a ball randomly from an urn; the urn is either H_1 or H_2 (two red and one black, or vice versa), but P^A doesn't know which. P^A is allowed to observe the color of a single ball drawn at random. Furthermore, he can make as many such observations as he is willing to pay for, but the last ball observed is always replaced after being observed, so the objective probabilities for red and black don't change.

How much information does P^A receive by making an observation? First we consider the prior uncertainty. But there are several prior uncertainties, since there are several sets of mutually exclusive and exhaustive sets which interest P^A: (1) the color of the sample P^A will observe has a prior uncertainty of 1 bit, since each color is equally likely initially (to P^A); (2) there is a prior uncertainty of 1 bit concerning the hypotheses H_1 and H_2; (3) there is a prior uncertainty of 1 bit concerning the state of nature that will prevail for the terminal decision. The message, i.e., the color of the ball drawn, yields a different amount of information for each set of events.

Initially, the expected information $\bar{I}$ equals I_j in each of three cases, since red and black observations are initially equally informative (see Equation 8.14). Thus we can simply assume, at first, that the observed ball was red. Then the posterior uncertainties and information transmissions for the three cases are: (1) $U' = 0$, as we assume P^A observes the color without error (noise); then $I = 1$ bit; (2) posterior $p(H_1)$ is 2/3 (from Bayes' formula), thus $U' = 0.92$, $I = 0.08$ bits; (3) posterior $p(b_1)$ for the terminal state of nature is 5/9, thus $U' = 0.99$, $I = 0.01$ bits. Well, in terms of bits the observation would appear to provide a meager amount of information about the terminal state of nature. Nonetheless, as we saw in Section 8.7, that meager information does increase the EV of the game for P^A.

If a second observation were made, the uncertainties and information measures would all change. The posterior probabilities for the states of nature from the first observation would now be the basis for the prior uncertainties for (1) and (3). Regardless of the color of the first observation, the new probabilities for red and black would not be equal—they would be 5/9 and 4/9 (not necessarily respectively), and $U = 0.99$. For (2), the new prior probabilities would be 2/3 and 1/3, and the new $U = 0.92$.

In brief, for our decision-making situation, P^A uses the messages to learn about the system; the expected information (in the technical sense) conveyed by successive observations varies according colors observed in the past. The accumulated observations will finally favor the true hypothesis with probability approaching 1; i.e., if H_1 is true, $p(H_1) \rightarrow 1$ as $n \rightarrow \infty$. In the limit, then, P^A will have learned about the system, and as in the typical communications channel, the message will only convey information about the particular ball sampled on a trial, which, under present assumptions. has no value to P^A for decision making.

Now let us revise our assumptions to illustrate a situation of constant expected information and of constant expected value for each trial. Suppose the same two urns H_1 and H_2 are now states of nature occurring with equal probabilities over a series of decisions with the same payoff matrix. On each trial the experimenter randomly chooses H_1 or H_2 as the state of nature for that trial and presents a randomly sampled ball to P^A from the chosen urn. $U = 1$, $U' = 0.92$, and $I = 0.08$ bits, regardless of color. The analysis is largely the same as before, except subjective $p(H_1)$ does not change over trials, so the expected information (or simply I_j in this case) remains the same before each message. (After making his decision P^A may receive conclusive information concerning the true hypothesis, H_1 or H_2, for that trial; however, under present assumptions we are interested only in information coming before the decision and thus possibly affecting it.)

Signal detection, according to "detection theory," is similar to the preceding case (see Chapter 7). Let H_1 and H_2 be "signal" and "no signal." In the case of detection, the sample presented comes from a normal instead of binomial distribution; i.e., the received message j is a value along a continuum. When received messages with different I_j's are lumped together into a single message category, information is lost. If a communications system has a "detector" who responds "signal" or "no signal," and a different "decision maker" who acts on the basis of the detector's conclusion, then the lumping by the detector of a continuum of received messages into "signal" or "no signal" causes a loss of possibly valuable information to the decision maker (Pollack & Decker, 1958). I have analyzed the theoretical amount of the loss as a function of d' (unpublished). The information loss in bits is greatest for intermediate values of d', but the *percentage* loss becomes greater and greater as d' decreases.

Because of the obvious importance of information in decision making, one might expect to find considerable synthetic work bridging information theory and decision theory. There doesn't appear to be much however; for example, the books by Garner (1962) and Attneave (1959) on information theory in psychology do not index "decision," "expected value," "utility," "optimal," or "rational." The work on information-gathering in decision making apparently finds no need or use for technical information measures; instead, the theory requires probabilities directly so that EVs can be gauged. When reference is made to "amount of information" this is more apt to mean number of samples observed rather than information in bits (for example, Pruitt, 1961; Fried & Peterson, 1969). For further discussion of decision making in the context of communication theory, see Toda (1956).

8.9 BAYESIAN AND CLASSICAL STATISTICS

Beginning in the late 1950's there has been considerable discussion within the field of statistics concerning the "traditional" or "classical" methods versus an alternative approached called "Bayesian statistics." By the classical statistical methods we refer to those methods presented in most introductory statistics books for testing hypotheses and estimating parameters, for example, the t-test for accepting or rejecting a "null hypothesis" with a significance level α. The basic ideas for the classical methodology were formulated in the first three decades of the century by Ronald Fisher, Jerzy Neyman, and Egon Pearson.

The Bayesian movement is more recent, having crystallized late in the 1950's. The movement can be characterized by the following four features:

1. Liberal use of prior probabilities and Bayes' formula to derive posterior probabilities from data.
2. "Personalistic" interpretation of probabilities (see Chapter 3).
3. Explicit recognition of the role of payoffs on any terminal actions or "conclusions" resulting from observations.
4. Adherence to the *likelihood principle* (discussed below).

The willingness to use Bayes' formula in statistical practice is not exclusively a feature of the Bayesian school as opposed to the classical school. Fisher (1956, p. 17), for example, asserted that prior probabilities can be used provided they can be deduced from previous data. The Bayesians, however, with their personalistic interpretation of probability, don't feel constrained in this manner. Recall from Chapter 3 that the liberal use of Bayes' formula in the early days of probability theory fell into disrepute over this very issue—the validity of subjective prior probabilities.

The importance of the payoffs contingent on actions resulting from hypothesis testing was well recognized by the classical statisticians; for example, Neyman and Pearson (1933) considered the assignment of weights to various possible wrong decisions. Wald (1947, p. 17) mentioned that the choice of α and β

(type I and type II error probabilities) would be "greatly influenced" by the costs resulting from the two types of errors. If the loss due to a type I error were much greater than the loss due to a type II error, then one would tend to set α relatively small and β relatively large.

From a Bayesian viewpoint, however, such informal adjustments of α and β appear, at best, to be highly arbitrary, and, in truth, even such informal adjustments are seldom seen. On the other hand, we have already noted that Wald (1950), under the influence of von Neumann and Morgenstern, provided a formal analysis of costs in his treatment of statistical decision functions.

According to Savage (1962) the *likelihood principle* was first put forward by Barnard (1947) and Fisher (1955)—no Bayesians. The principle conflicts with Neyman-Pearson theory, which illustrates again that the division of statistics into classical and Bayesian oversimplifies things a bit. In brief, the likelihood principle states that the likelihood of the data observed, conditional on a parameter and considered as a function of the parameter, contains all the information available from an experiment. In particular, given the likelihood, it makes no difference which of a variety of possible sampling schemes was employed. The typical illustrative example for this principle assumes a binomial population—we may as well use our trusty urn with red and black balls. The urn has some probability for red, p. Consider a sample of 10 balls (drawn with replacement, or else assume a very large population of balls), 7 red and 3 black. We might have decided ahead of time to draw 10 balls, or we might have decided to stop when we got the 7th red ball. Consider now the likelihood of the sample as a function of p. For the first sampling method it would be $120p^7(1-p)^3$; for the second sampling method it would be $84p^7(1-p)^3$. Except for the constant multipliers, the two formulas are the same; in Bayesian statistics likelihood formulas which differ only by this constant multiplier are said to be the same. The irrelevance of the constants can be illustrated by reference to Equation 8.5; the posterior odds for two hypotheses depends on the prior odds and on the likelihood ratio. Suppose the two hypotheses are: $p = p_1$, and $p = p_2$. Then the likelihood ratio for the first sampling method would be

$$\frac{120p_2{}^7(1-p_2)^3}{120p_1{}^7(1-p_1)^3}$$

For the second method it would be

$$\frac{84p_2{}^7(1-p_2)^3}{84p_1{}^7(1-p_1)^3}$$

The constants would cancel out in both cases, and the likelihood ratio in both cases becomes $p_2{}^7(1-p_2)^3/p_1{}^7(1-p_1)^3$. In short, the effect of the data on the relative posterior probabilities (odds) is independent of the sampling scheme.

In the Neyman-Pearson approach, however, the sampling scheme does make a difference. An estimate of p from the data which is unbiased for one sampling scheme would be biased for the alternative one. Classical statisticians have worried about the persistent experimenter who continues to collect data until he can reject his null hypothesis; then he stops. The persistent experimenter can indeed come to a rejection of the null hypothesis, even if the null hypothesis is true and regardless of the significance level. The persistent experimenter poses no problem for the Bayesian, however, who will simply want to know the final likelihood ratio (Savage, 1962, pp. 17–18).

It is curious that Savage's (1954) book, *The Foundations of Statistics,* which was so important in crystallizing the Bayesian movement by promoting the concept of personal probability, was not written with a view to altering statistical practice; instead, Savage believed he could give a better justification to current practice (Savage, 1962, p. 9). He later changed his mind, and Bayesians today evince great interest in altering statistical practice. Exemplifying this practical bent are Bayesian tomes *Probability and Statistics for Business Decisions* by Schlaifer (1959), *Analysis of Decisions Under Uncertainty* by Schlaifer (1969), and *Applied Statistical Decision Theory* by Raiffa and Schlaifer (1961).

The first major introduction to Bayesian statistics for psychologists was written by Edwards, Lindman, and Savage (1963), proponents of the Bayesian approach. They set out to compare "such procedures as a Bayesian would employ in an article submitted to the *Journal of Experimental Psychology,* say, [with] those now typically found in that journal." Arnold Binder (1964) reviewed the Bayesian controversy from the sidelines. He found the Bayesian ideas extremely interesting and potentially of practical importance, but felt that actual current offerings to the practical scientist were slim, and, in view of this, he took umbrage at "Bayesian grandiosity." Indeed, it would be useful to have, in addition to Bayesian theory, some real-life examples of Bayesian methodology. (The examples provided by Bayesians may be in a "scientific" or "business" setting, but they seldom actually include the complexities encountered in real scientific investigations or business decisions.)

Since Edwards *et al.* compared Bayesian and classical methodology for *Journal of Experimental Psychology,* I thought it might be helpful to observe the statistical methodology employed by Edwards in his subsequent articles in *Journal of Experimental Psychology.* I hoped to learn thereby how Bayesian theory affects the treatment of experimental data in psychology. If the treatment seemed convincing and not unduly complex I would be interested in using the methodology in my own work. So what did I find? In Tversky and Edwards (1966) there were two standard analyses of variance, with one asterisk for the 0.05 significance level and two asterisks for the 0.01 level. Nothing particularly Bayesian was apparent. Phillips and Edwards (1966) and Peterson, DuCharme, and Edwards (1968) concerned Bayesian probability revisions by Ss (see Section 8.5); there were no particularly Bayesian methods in the statistical treatment of the data, however. On the other hand, there was no sign of t-tests, F-tests, significance levels, confidence intervals, or any of the usual arma-

mentarium of classical statistics. The authors used means, medians, and inter-
quartile ranges. The authors made verbal statements about the differences between conditions; it is not clear whether these statements refer to differences
for the particular data at hand or to intuitive inferences; if the latter, the relation
of these intuitive inferences to Bayesian theory is not obvious, though one might
assume that subjective prior probabilities could affect such intuitive inferences.
It would not appear, however, that such procedures support the Bayesian contention that their methods are *more,* not less objective than the classical ones.

Perhaps we should have been forewarned, when Edwards *et al.* (1963, p.
240), in conclusion, stated: "Adoption of the Bayesian outlook should discourage parading statistical procedures, Bayesian or other . . . " Indeed, the
subsequent articles by Edwards presented no such parade, and certainly a parade
for the sake of ostentation should be frowned on in scientific circles. But a
parade for the sake of teaching and demonstration is much needed and should
be encouraged.

8.10 MOSTELLER-WALLACE STUDY OF *THE FEDERALIST* PAPERS

In this regard, a Bayesian treatment of a real-life historical question by Frederick Mosteller and David Wallace (1964) is most welcome and helpful. Their
problem was to settle the disputed authorship of several of *The Federalist*
papers. These papers were written by Alexander Hamilton, James Madison, and
John Jay to convince New York State to accept the Constitution. For twelve
of the papers there has been uncertainty whether the author was Hamilton or
Madison. Mosteller and Wallace began with prior odds of 1 favoring Madison
over Hamilton for each paper (i.e., authorship by each man was considered
equally likely), though they were not insistent on these odds. They then collected
observations leading to a likelihood ratio for each paper based on the likelihoods
that their observations would have occurred if Hamilton had written the paper
and if Madison had. The likelihood ratio and prior odds then led to a posterior
odds (Equation 8.5) for authorship.

The likelihoods were based on stylistic features differentiating the two authors,
as determined from the papers of undisputed authorship. Mosteller and Wallace
found that although in some respects the styles of the two authors were highly
similar (for example, sentence length), frequency of usage of certain *function
words* (for example, a, an, by, to, and that) as well as other words differed
between the authors. Table 8.1 gives the distribution of occurrence per thousand
words of "by" for Hamilton and Madison. A great many words were examined,
but an attempt was made to use only words which would characterize the styles
of the men rather than the context; for example, the word "trade" might have
been used more frequently by one author because it was his assigned topic; yet

TABLE 8.1
Frequency Distribution for "by" for Hamilton and Madison*

Rate per 1000 words	Hamilton	Madison
1–3	2	
3–5	7	
5–7	12	5
7–9	18	7
9–11	4	8
11–13	5	16
13–15		6
15–17		5
17–19		3

* From Mosteller and Wallace (1964, p. 17).

the other author might have written on the topic occasionally. Though such contextual words do provide evidence, proper treatment of these words involved more difficulties, so they were not used.

Given that various stylistic data differentiating the authors were available, it still remained to calculate the likelihoods of the data for "by" and other words for each disputed paper. The data for each word for each paper led to a likelihood for Hamilton and a likelihood for Madison. In examples up to now we have assumed a very simple model for the data; in particular, we have assumed an urn with two colors of balls for which the binomial distribution could describe the likelihoods. Such a model might, a priori, apply to the use of a word such as "by," but this cannot be assumed—it would have to be demonstrated. The model would be suspect, for it implies that the probability of the word "by" is constant at each word position, regardless of which words preceded a position. If this turned out to be true, it would be remarkable—but it didn't.

Counts for frequency of occurrence of 51 function words were made for each of 247 blocks of 200 words in papers known to be by Hamilton; i.e., for each block, each of the 51 words was observed to occur 0, 1, 2, 3, 4, . . . times. These distributions were compared with distributions predicted from the binomial model (actually the Poisson distribution[7] approximation to the binomial was used). While the model and data agreed fairly well for some words, large discrepancies appeared for others. In particular there were too many blocks with large number of word occurrences (say, 4 or more) for some words, for example, "his" and "may." To gain a better model for the likelihoods, the *negative binomial* family of distributions was fit to the data. Whereas the Poisson distribution involves only one parameter (i.e., the exact distribution is a function of

---

[7] See Feller (1950, pp. 110–115).

mean number of occurrences per block), the negative binomial involves a second parameter as well, κ.[8] When κ is very large, the negative binomial approaches the Poisson, thus the negative binomial can be fit to data well-described by the Poisson distribution; with smaller κ values, it can fit a larger class of empirical distributions as well.

In a hypothetical example we can say that the p for a binomial population is, say, either 2/3 (H_1) or 1/3 (H_2). In real problems these values may have to be estimated; for the problem at hand one parameter for each author must be estimated for the Poisson distribution and two for each author for the negative binomial distribution. Estimation itself is a major problem of statistics amenable to Bayesian and classical treatments. Attempting to use Bayesian theory whenever possible, Mosteller and Wallace had to consider prior distributions of the parameters as well as posterior distributions based on papers of known authorship.

According to the Bayesian analysis, Madison appears, with very high probability, to have authored all 12 disputed papers. The strength of the posterior odds is astonishing; the paper with the greatest posterior uncertainty had odds favoring Madison of 240 to 1; some other odds favored Madison by over a million to 1. Mosteller and Wallace admit that such odds seem "scary," and wonder if they can be believed. Due to the possibility of "outrageous events," they believe the odds are extreme. Outrageous events include possible errors in collecting and handling the data as well as possible fraud or hoax by the authors. Although serious errors or a hoax may be unlikely, even small probabilities for these outrageous events can seriously alter the posterior odds. If Mosteller and Wallace are reluctant to accept the extreme odds resulting from Bayesian theory, should we be harsh on laboratory Ss who show the same "conservatism" in experiments on Bayesian probability revision (Section 8.5), though they lack the rationale considered by Wallace and Mosteller? Perhaps Ss are concerned over "outrageous events" or hoax in the experiment.

The study by Mosteller and Wallace provided much useful insight into the difficulties involved in the utilization of Bayesian theory, and they are considerable. One difficulty they encountered, as we saw, was in the choice a model for the likelihood function. They carried through their analysis with both the Poisson and the negative binomial distributions, and found that the effects on the conclusions were enormous. They conclude that before Bayesian analysis can become routine, extensive new studies of theoretical and empirical distributions will be required.

Mosteller and Wallace were open-minded about the prior odds of 1. A convenient feature of the Bayesian approach which they illustrated is that someone else can easily plug in his own preferred prior odds. Chances are that such prior odds would be less than 10 to 1, however, and even with such relatively strong

---

[8] κ is Greek kappa.

prior odds favoring Hamilton, the evidence would lead to strong posterior odds favoring Madison.

One major aspect of Bayesian statistics was not apparent in the study—payoffs. Many authorities are skeptical about the inclusion of payoffs in the Bayesian analysis of scientific experiments, even though they admit that inclusion of such payoffs may be reasonable for business applications. After all, what are the payoffs and losses for concluding correctly or incorrectly that Madison or Hamilton wrote a particular paper; for that matter, if the absolute truth determines the state of nature for the payoff, how could the true state of nature for the decision ever be determined? It may be that Bayesian analyses in science will find little application of payoffs and decision theory; instead, there will perhaps be an emphasis on probabilities as an end point, as in the Mosteller and Wallace study.

8.11 A MULTISTAGE DECISION SITUATION

In most of the decision situations that have concerned us up to now, P^A's decision affected the consequence for the current situation, but it had no bearing on which decision situation would occur next. In fact, however, real-life decisions are usually of the latter type. P^A must not only consider the immediate consequence, but the consequences apt to result from the future decision situations his decision may lead to. For example, a bank employee could maximize his immediate financial rewards by embezzling. This, however, would lead to a decision situation requiring a choice between waiting for the auditor and the judge, fleeing to Brazil, etc. The prospects in the latter decision situation do not appear promising, so the employee has to forgo the instant wealth. (Of course, not all bank employees agree with this analysis.)

To illustrate some theory and experimental results in this area, we shall follow a paper by Amnon Rapoport (1968). He dealt with a situation he called a *multistage decision* (or *dynamic programming*) *problem*,[9] which he defined as follows: P^A has to make a series of decisions, each of which will lead to some payoff. The decision situation for each trial can be any of a set; each situation is said to constitute a *state*. The probabilities for the possible states on trial $n + 1$ depend jointly on the state and the decision for trial n. A reward (or cost) is associated with each possible transition from state s_j to state $s_{j'}$. In other words, for a given decision situation (state s_j), P^A makes a choice from a set of possibilities (a_i's); for each a_i, there are different probabilities for going to the next state. (This is a contingent choice situation: see Chapter 6.) The "next state" can also be considered a "state of nature," in that it deter-

[9] Some mathematical references on multistage decisions and dynamic programming are: Bellman (1957), Bellman and Dryfus (1962), and Howard (1960).

mines, with the choice a_i, the payoff; however, it is more than a state of nature for trial n—it is the decision situation for trial $n + 1$.

To be specific, we consider a concrete example of such a problem presented to Ss. (The example was based on one presented by Howard (1960), who also discusses the theory employed by Rapoport.) S is to imagine he is a taxi driver operating within and between three "cities": Bronx (B), Manhattan (M), and Queens (Q). These are the three possible "states." At the beginning, he happens to be in one of these "states," say B. There are three cab stands he can drive to (bus station, train station, or airport). These are his possible decisions, given state B. (There are comparable possible decisions for M and Q.) Given state B, and given decision a_i, there are probabilities that his passenger will request a ride to a location in B, in M, or in Q; these probabilities sum to 1 since the taxi driver is allowed no other destinations. The probabilities differ, however, depending on his choice of a_i (taxi stand). The payoff is taken to be the profit after all necessary expenses have been deducted, and this is assumed to depend only on initial state, choice a_i, and destination (next state). For example, if P^A starts in B, chooses stand 2, and happens to get a passenger going to M, his payoff is 9, and would be 9 each time the same conjunction of occurrences happens. This is, of course, a simplification. Another simplifying assumption is that the time needed to complete any single trip, regardless of starting point and destination, is the same.

The probabilities and payoffs are shown in Table 8.2. The right-hand column gives the expected values for given starting cities and choices. One might think, based on our earlier discussions, that the optimal strategy would require P^A

TABLE 8.2
Transition Probabilities, Payoffs, and Expected Immediate Rewards for Rapoport's Multistage Decision Problem

Starting City	a_i	Transition Probabilities Target City			Payoffs Target City			EV_i
		B	M	Q	B	M	Q	
B	1	.00	.90	.10	6	10	30	12.00
	2	.25	.10	.65	16	9	18	16.60
	3	.20	.30	.50	10	13	15	13.40
M	1	.40	.10	.50	30	16	38	32.60
	2	.25	.70	.05	18	31	24	27.40
	3	.60	.25	.15	32	31	22	30.25
Q	1	.40	.20	.40	3	15	9	7.80
	2	.20	.60	.20	6	7	5	6.40
	3	.25	.10	.65	8	4	11	9.55

to make the choice with the highest EV for whichever city he finds himself in. However, some cities ("states") are more favorable than others; for example, if in Manhattan, P^A can make a choice with an EV of 32.60, whereas if in Queens, his best choice only has an EV of 9.55. Instead of thinking of the payoff for the forthcoming trip alone, wouldn't P^A do better to think about future trips; for example, shouldn't he try to get to Manhattan where the payoffs are higher?

The dynamic programming solution requires that the total expected profit be maximized, and the solution, in this case at least, requires that P^A forgo the highest expected payoff for the forthcoming trip. A strategy ("policy") for P^A can be specified by stating a choice for P^A for each state. For the example there are $3 \times 3 \times 3 = 27$ possible strategies (mixed strategies are not called for in this task). For the particular entries of Table 8.2, the dynamic programming solution is: $a_i = 1$ for B, $a_i = 2$ for M, $a_i = 2$ for Q. This strategy can be abbreviated as $(1, 2, 2)$. The long-run EV of this strategy is 22.9. From Table 8.2 it can be seen that the strategy, remarkably, always requires P^A to choose the a_i with the *lowest* immediate EV. If P^A always chose the a_i with the highest immediate EV $\big($strategy $(2, 1, 3)\big)$, the long-run EV would be only 13.7.

S was given a table with the payoffs and an explanation of its relation to the various conditions. He was not, however, shown the probabilities; it was, instead, assumed that he would gain information about the probabilities from experience in the task (i.e., for each decision they learned the passenger's destination). The task was dynamic in two senses, then: the decisions affected the future states, and information relevant to the decisions was gained with experience.

The 18 Ss made a total of 180 decisions each. S was instructed to maximize his total payoff, but was not told the total number of decisions. (This makes a difference; for example, if S knew a decision was his last, he should maximize EV for that trip alone.)

In the final block of trials Ss gained an average payoff per decision of 19.8 (compared with 22.9 for dynamic programming and 13.7 for immediate EV maximization). The last decisions made for each S matched the dynamic programming solution for 6 of 18 Ss. Table 8.2 shows that the mean payoffs starting from state M were much higher than the payoffs starting from the other two states; thus, S might have simply followed the rule, "choose that a_i for any state which would lead to state M with highest probability." It so happened that for the specifications employed, this strategy would be $(1, 2, 2)$, the same as the dynamic programming strategy. Thus, one cannot differentiate between the two approaches on the basis of Ss' responses.

The dynamic programming solution requires specification of the state-change probabilities. These were not given to Ss, though Ss might be expected to learn them to a good approximation through experience. Rapoport required Ss to give estimates for these probabilities at the end of the experiment. Ss underestimated the higher probabilities and overestimated the lower ones (a common finding; see Section 3.5). The estimates did not accord well with a Bayesian learning model proposed by Rapoport. The last choices for 8 of 18 Ss matched a dynamic programming solution based on the estimated probabilities.

Is an optimal strategy one that requires P^A to maximize expected payoff in the long run? As we noted in Section 4.8, P^A may have a "time perspective" implying smaller valuation of a consequence the further in the future it occurs. If so, he should pay relatively greater heed to payoffs in the near future and relatively less to payoffs in the far future. A requirement of this type can be included in multistage decision theory. If β is the discount factor, i.e., the proportion of the original value which remains after a unit of time, the dynamic programming approach can incorporate this constant into the solution (Howard, 1960). When $\beta = 0$ the dynamic programming and immediate EV maximization strategies are the same. β may be equivalently interpreted as the probability that the process will continue; i.e., with probability $1 - \beta$ the present decision will be the last. The greater the probability that the process will end soon, the more P^A's strategy should emphasize immediate gain. (If the decisions were generally costly to P^A, the more likely the process was to end soon, the more he would emphasize minimization of immediate losses.)

Other studies of multistage decision making include Rapoport (1966) and Rapoport (1967).

8.12 SUMMARY

Before making a decision P^A may be presented with information relevant to his decision. By affecting the probabilities for the states of nature, this information can affect P^A's choice. P^A may gain relevant information by observing the states of nature which occur in a series of decisions, or from an auxiliary information-gathering process. The amount of information that can be gained from this auxiliary process may be specified by an experimenter or some other power, or it may be under P^A's control. If the latter, P^A's best strategy is to determine after each observation, and on the basis of all observations made so far, whether to make a terminal decision or to make another observation. Bayes' formula is the theoretical mechanism for calculating the effect of an observation on P^A's probabilities for the states of nature. The impact of data on the subjective probabilities is generally less, however, than the impact required by Bayes' formula; i.e., Ss are generally "conservative." Theories developed within the field of statistics for sequential analysis and sequential decision making have been applied to real Ss in a number of experiments. The impression is that Ss' conclusions and decisions are at least roughly comparable to the theories. Although the information-gathering process in decision making can be described in terms of the "bits" of information theory, it is not clear that this is helpful. Several trends in statistics have culminated into "Bayesian statistics" which proponents claim should revolutionize statistical practice. Mosteller and Wallace exemplified the Bayesian approach in a study of the disputed authorship of *The Federalist* papers; it is clear that Bayesian techniques require further development before they can be widely and routinely employed. In the "multistage decision problem" P^A's decision affects not only his immediate payoff but his future decision situations (and thus future payoffs). In one experiment, at least, Ss showed awareness of the strategic requirements for large long-term payoffs. Although "dynamic decision theory" can involve difficult mathematics, it makes decision theory more relevant to many real-life situations.

REFERENCES

Attneave, F. *Applications of Information Theory to Psychology*. New York: Holt, 1959.

Barnard, G. A. "The Meaning of a Significance Level," *Biometrika* (1947), **34,** 179–182.

Beach, L. R. "Probability Magnitudes and Conservative Revision of Subjective Probabilities," *Journal of Experimental Psychology* (1968), **77,** 57–63.

Becker, G. M. "Sequential Decision Making: Wald's Model and Estimates of Parameters," *Journal of Experimental Psychology* (1958), **55,** 628–636.

Bellman, R. E. *Dynamic Programming.* Princeton, N. J.: Princeton University Press, 1957.

Bellman, R. E., & Dreyfus, S. E. *Applied Dynamic Programming.* Princeton, N.J.: Princeton University Press, 1962.

Binder, A. "Statistical Theory," in P. R. Farnsworth (ed.), *Annual Review of Psychology,* Vol. 15. Palo Alto, Calif.: Annual Reviews, Inc., 1964, pp. 277–310.

Birdsall, T. G., & Roberts, R. A. "Theory of Signal Detectability: Deferred-Decision Theory," *Journal of the Acoustical Society of America* (1965), **37,** 1064–1074.

Blackwell, D., & Girshick, M. A. *Theory of Games and Statistical Decisions.* New York: Wiley, 1954.

Dodge, H. F., & Romig, H. G. "A Method of Sampling Inspection," *Bell System Technical Journal* (1929), **8,** 613–631.

Edwards, W. "Behavioral Decision Theory," in P. R. Farnsworth (ed.), *Annual Review of Psychology,* Vol. 12. Palo Alto, Calif.: Annual Reviews, Inc., 1961, pp. 473–498.

Edwards, W. "Dynamic Decision Theory and Probabilistic Information Processing," *Human Factors* (1962), **4,** 59–73.

Edwards, W. "Optimal Strategies for Seeking Information: Models for Statistics, Choice Reaction Times, and Human Information Processing," *Journal of Mathematical Psychology* (1965), **2,** 312–329.

Edwards, W., Lindman, H., & Savage, L. J. "Bayesian Statistical Inference for Psychological Research," *Psychological Review* (1963), **70,** 193–242.

Edwards, W., & Slovic, P. "Seeking Information to Reduce the Risk of Decisions," *American Journal of Psychology* (1965), **78,** 188–197.

Feller, W. *An Introduction to Probability Theory and Its Applications,* Vol. 1. New York: Wiley, 1950.

Fishburn, P. C. *Decision and Value Theory*. New York: Wiley, 1964.

Fisher, R. A. "Statistical Methods and Scientific Induction," *Journal of the Royal Statistical Society, B* (1955), **17,** 69–78.

Fisher, R. A. *Statistical Methods and Scientific Inference.* Edinburgh: Oliver and Boyd, 1956.

Fried, L. S., & Peterson, C. R. "Information Seeking: Optional versus Fixed Stopping," *Journal of Experimental Psychology* (1969), **80,** 525–529.

Garner, W. R. *Uncertainty and Structure as Psychological Concepts.* New York: Wiley, 1962.

Helson, H. *Adaptation-Level Theory,* New York: Harper, 1964.

Howard, R. A. *Dynamic Programming and Markov Processes,* New York: Wiley, 1960.

Irwin, F. W., & Smith, W. A. S. "Further Tests of Theories of Decision in an 'Expanded Judgment' Situation," *Journal of Experimental Psychology* (1956), **52,** 345–348.

Irwin, F. W., & Smith, W. A. S. "Value, Cost, and Information as Determiners of Decision," *Journal of Experimental Psychology* (1957), **54,** 229–232.

Irwin, F. W., Smith, W. A. S., & Mayfield, J. F. "Tests of Two Theories of Decision in an 'Expanded Judgment' Situation," *Journal of Experimental Psychology* (1956), **51,** 261–268.

Kaplan, R. J., & Newman, J. R. "Studies in Probabilistic Information Processing," *IEEE Transactions on Human Factors in Electronics* (1966), **7,** 49–63.

Lee, W. "Choosing among Confusably Distributed Stimuli with Specified Likelihood Ratios," *Perceptual and Motor Skills* (1963), **16,** 445–467.

Levitt, H., & Rabiner, L. R. "Use of a Sequential Strategy in Intelligibility Testing," *Journal of the Acoustical Society of America* (1967), **42,** 609–612.

Mosteller, F., & Wallace, D. L. *Inference and Disputed Authorship: The Federalist.* Reading, Mass.: Addison-Wesley, 1964.

Neyman, J., & Pearson, E. S. "The Testing of Statistical Hypotheses in Relation to Probabilities *a priori,*" *Proceedings of the Cambridge Philosophical Society* (1933), **29,** 492–510.

Peterson, C. R., DuCharme, W. M., & Edwards, W. "Sampling Distributions and Probability Revisions," *Journal of Experimental Psychology* (1968), **76,** 236–243.

Peterson, C. R., & Miller, A. J. "Sensitivity of Subjective Probability Revision," *Journal of Experimental Psychology* (1965), **70,** 117–121.

Peterson, C. R., Schneider, R. J., & Miller, A. J. "Sample Size and the Revision of Subjective Probabilities," *Journal of Experimental Psychology* (1965), **69,** 522–527.

Phillips, L. D., & Edwards, W. "Conservatism in a Simple Probability Inference Task," *Journal of Experimental Psychology* (1966), **72,** 346–354.

Pollack, I., & Decker, L. R. "Confidence Ratings, Message Reception, and the Receiver Operating Characteristic," *Journal of the Acoustical Society of America* (1958), **30,** 286–292.

Pruitt, D. G. "Informational Requirements in Making Decisions," *American Journal of Psychology* (1961), **74,** 433–439.

Raiffa, H. *Decision Analysis.* Reading, Mass.: Addison-Wesley, 1968.

Raiffa, H., & Schlaifer, R. *Applied Statistical Decision Theory.* Boston: Harvard University, 1961.

Rapoport, Amnon. "A Study of Human Control in a Stochastic Multistage Decision Task," *Behavioral Science* (1966), **11,** 18–32.

Rapoport, Amnon. "Dynamic Programming Models for Multistage Decision-Making Tasks," *Journal of Mathematical Psychology* (1967), **4,** 48–71.

Rapoport, Amnon. "Choice Behavior in a Markovian Decision Task," *Journal of Mathematical Psychology* (1968), **5,** 163–181.

Savage, L. J. *The Foundations of Statistics.* New York: Wiley, 1954.

Savage, L. J., *et al. The Foundations of Statistical Inference: A Discussion.* New York: Wiley, 1962.

Schlaifer, R. *Probability and Statistics for Business Decisions.* New York: McGraw-Hill, 1959.

Schlaifer, R. *Analysis of Decisions under Uncertainty.* New York: McGraw-Hill, 1969.

Shannon, C. E. "A Mathematical Theory of Communication," *Bell System Technical Journal* (1948), **27,** 379–423, 623–656.

Smith, W. A. S. "Effects of Differential Instructions on Value and Cost as Determiners of Decision," *Perceptual and Motor Skills* (1964), **18,** 321–324.

Swets, J. A., & Birdsall, T. G. "Deferred Decision in Human Signal Detection: A Preliminary Experiment," *Perception and Psychophysics* (1967), **2,** 15–28.

Swets, J. A., & Green, D. M. "Sequential Observations by Human Observers of Signals in Noise," in C. Cherry (ed.), *Information Theory.* London: Butterworths, 1961, pp. 196–211.

Taylor, M. M., & Creelman, C. D. "PEST: Efficient Estimates on Probability Functions," *Journal of the Acoustical Society of America* (1967), **41,** 782–787.

Toda, M. "Information-Receiving Behavior of Man," *Psychological Review* (1956), **63,** 204–212.

Tversky, A., & Edwards, W. "Information versus Reward in Binary Choices," *Journal of Experimental Psychology* (1966), **71,** 680–683.

Vlek, C. "The Use of Probabilistic Information in Decision Making," Psychological Institute (Rep. No. 009-65), The Netherlands: University of Leiden, 1965.

Wald, A. *Sequential Analysis.* New York: Wiley, 1947.

Wald, A. *Statistical Decision Functions.* New York: Wiley, 1950.

Wendt, D. "Value of Information for Decisions," *Journal of Mathematical Psychology* (1969), **6,** 430–443.

Wiesen, R. A., & Shuford, E. H. "Bayes Strategies as Adaptive Behavior," Chapel Hill, N. C.: The Psychometric Laboratory (Rep. No. 30), University of North Carolina, 1961.

Wilks, S. S. *Mathematical Statistics.* New York: Wiley, 1962.

CHAPTER 9

Game Theory and Experiments

9.1 INTRODUCTION

Whereas previous chapters have largely concerned "games against nature," we now turn to games involving more than one "rational" player or "interest." The term "theory of games" is often restricted to such situations, hence our chapter title; but the term is also used more broadly to apply to decision theory as a whole.

An important distinction in game theory is between two-person games and N-person games $(N > 2)$. Another distinction is between *pure-conflict games,* *co-ordination games,* and *mixed-motive games* (Schelling, 1958). In *pure-conflict games* any gain by one player in going from one consequence to another implies a loss for at least one of the others. These games are also called *zero-sum,* but it need not be strictly true that the utilities for the players sum to zero in a "zero-sum" game. There need only be linear transformations for the utilities for each player which will make the game literally zero-sum. Thus, a *constant-sum* game is one of pure-conflict, and the terms constant-sum and zero-sum are strategically equivalent (for the *theories* that concern us, at least). In a *co-ordination game* the players have no conflict concerning the desired consequence, but they might have a strategic problem in arriving at that consequence. *Mixed-motive games* involve some conflict in that the consequence most desired by one player is not the consequence most desired by other players, even though the game is not one of pure conflict. Mixed-motive games involve both elements of cooperation and competition. Since most social interaction appears to be of the mixed-motive type, psychologists and other social scientists have concentrated their attention on this type.

We begin with two-person games. The theory for two-person zero-sum games was discussed in Chapter 2, but in Sections 9.2 and 9.3 we consider experimental results. The largest part of this chapter concerns two-person mixed-motive games (Sections 9.5 to 9.10), both the theory and experimental results. Finally, we consider N-person theory and results, concentrating on the formation of coalitions (alliances).

We by no means intend to give a comprehensive or current survey of the mathematical theory of games. That could not be done in one chapter in any case. Instead, we concentrate on the psychological experiments, and provide, in general, only that amount of theoretical discussion required as background to the experiments.

Stochastic models related to those we discussed in Chapter 6 have been applied to interpersonal interaction as well. The motivation is descriptive rather than normative. We shall not discuss these, but the interested reader may refer to the following sources: Suppes and Atkinson, 1960; Suppes and Carlsmith, 1962; Rapoport and Chammah, 1965; Rosenberg and Schoeffler, 1965. Neither can we allow ourselves the luxury of discussing game theory approaches to the concept of "social power." The reader will find relevant readings for this topic in *Game Theory and Related Approaches to Social Behavior* edited by Martin Shubik (1964).

Although in principle the payoff matrix entries should be utilities, and we shall often call them by that name, experimenters seldom measure utilities and use these for their analyses. Instead, they compare S's behavior with game theory solutions derived from objective payoffs (cents or points or whatever).

In an experimental study of, say, a two-person game, the experimenter may have two Ss play each other for a series of trials. Often, however, one player, say P^B, is not a real S, but an accomplice of the experimenter, usually called a "stooge." The stooge plays according to a pre-planned strategy. This technique allows the behavior of an S to be studied as a function of the controlled behavior of the coplayer.

9.2   TWO-PERSON ZERO-SUM GAMES WITH SADDLE POINTS

As stated in Section 2.9, N–M theory specifies a solution for all two-person zero-sum games. If the game has a saddle point o_{ij}, the solution is for P^A to choose a_i and P^B to choose b_j; i.e., a pure-strategy solution is specified. The strategy is maximin. If the game has no saddle point, a randomized mixed strategy solution can always be found which is also maximin—in this case in the sense of maximizing the minimum *expected* payoff rather than the payoff per se. The solutions for both cases are based on the assumption that the coplayer (P^B) is "rational" and is guided by N–M strategy considerations. If the protagonist (P^A) has good reason to believe that his coplayer is not so guided, then the logic of the N–M solution loses much of its appeal. Regardless of the coplayer's deviation from N–M strategy, however, he cannot reduce P^A's security level; if P^A stays with the N–M strategy, P^B's deviation must yield P^A an expected payoff at least as good as he would have against a "rational" P^B.

In this section we consider some experimental results for games with saddle points. The experiments involved repeated decisions over a series of trials. Although in some decision situations multiple trials may lead to new strategic considerations, N–M theory requires P^A (and P^B) to use the same maximin strategy on each trial.

Bernhardt Lieberman (1960) mentioned a study using a 2×2 game matrix. He found that 10 of 14 Ss adopted a maximin strategy, and the others came close. The situation was so simple, however, that one could not conclude that Ss generally adopt the maximin strategy. Lieberman therefore studied behavior in the following 3×3 payoff matrix (payoffs listed are the values in cents of the consequences to P^A—payoffs to P^B are the negatives of these).

	b_1	b_2	b_3
a_1	$+15$	0	-2
a_2	0	-15	-1
a_3	$+1$	$+2$	0

The matrix has one saddle point, at o_{33}, so the maximin solution is $a_3 b_3$. The maximin solution for each player dominates a second option, a_2 or b_1. The possible payoffs for the third option for each player, a_1 or b_2, include the highest entry in the matrix, 15. The possible payoffs for this third option also have the highest arithmetic average.

In the first 10 trials about 69% of the choices were maximin. In trials 101–110 about 92% were maximin, and for trials 191–200, about 93%. The choice percentages for the high-average option were 28, 5, and 4 for the same sets of trials, respectively. Choice of the dominated option remained at about 3% throughout. (This is of particular interest, since axiomatists and other experts typically assume that a dominated option will *never* be chosen; Sections 9.5 and 9.6 are also relevant in this respect.) About half of the 30 Ss came to use the maximin solution exclusively, but the other half continued to make some non-optimal choices throughout the 200 trials (about 15% toward the end). Ss, in post-experimental interviews, were able to give a variety of "reasonable" explanations for deviations from the maximin. These included: (a) a desire to avoid boredom; (b) a feeling that experimenter expected or wanted some variation in the responses; (c) a desire to entice the opponent away from his optimal choice.

Alvin Scodel (1961) also observed behavior for a 3×3 game with a saddle point. There were only 50 trials, but the number of maximin choices increased during this period of time, reaching about 52% for the second 25 trials. (The figure for Lieberman's Ss for the same trials was considerably higher, about 85%.) Scodel differentiated Ss on the basis of their "values" as determined from the Allport-Vernon-Lindzey Study of Values test. Ss who used the maximin strategy relatively more scored higher on the Religious scale and lower on the Theoretical scale than the other Ss.

Richard Brayer (1964) likewise investigated play in a 3 × 3 matrix with a saddle point. Besides the maximin choice, there was a "high average" choice and a "highest payoff" choice. In this experiment Ss played against the experimenter rather than against another S. When P^B (experimenter) played a maximin strategy exclusively, Ss responded in the first 30 trials with about 60% maximin choices, and after 150 trials with about 97% maximin choices.

For some Ss, the experimenter played a randomized strategy with equal probabilities for all choices. For this case Ss chose the option with the highest average payoff most often. The arithmetic average and the EV would be the same for P^B's randomized mixed strategy; thus Ss chose the highest EV option most often, which has also been the general rule for experiments in "gambling." Such a finding does not conflict with N–M theory, since, as we pointed out, N–M assumes a rational opponent; under such circumstances, the maximin strategy would have the highest EV.

In summary, in 3 × 3 zero-sum games with saddle points, Ss commence with a relatively small percentage choice of the maximin option, but this percentage increases over trials. It seems reasonable to interpret the increase in terms of learned subjectively expected values for the various choices.

9.3   TWO-PERSON ZERO-SUM GAMES WITHOUT SADDLE POINTS

As noted, for zero-sum games without a saddle point, N–M theory requires a randomized mixed strategy, one which is maximin with respect to expected values. Discussion of this solution was presented in Section 2.9; the reader may wish to review the material given there.

Lieberman (1962) observed the behavior of Ss in a 2 × 2 zero-sum game without a saddle point. The following payoff matrix was used:

	b_1	b_2
a_1	+3	−1
a_2	−9	+3

The maximin mixed strategies for P^A and P^B are $(\frac{3}{4}a_1, \frac{1}{4}a_2)$ and $(\frac{1}{4}b_1, \frac{3}{4}b_2)$.

For one group of Ss, P^B (the experimenter) used his maximin strategy for 300 trials. The Ss came to respond a_1 about 40% of the time rather than 75%, as the theory requires. A peculiar feature of the matrix, however, is that when P^B plays his maximin, the EV to P^A is the same for each choice, and thus for any randomized strategy. In EV terms, then, there was no reason for P^A to do one thing rather than another. However, as a precautionary measure, the maximin strategy might be preferred since it would protect P^A from any decrease in his EV if P^B changed strategies.

For another group of Ss, P^B changed after 100 trials from his maximin strategy to $(\frac{1}{2}b_1, \frac{1}{2}b_2)$. This group of Ss approached the maximin choice percentage, though choice of a_1 did remain somewhat below the maximin percentage. But the maximin cannot be justified against P^B, since he clearly was not playing his maximin. Under the conditions, Ss would have done better to play a_1 all the time, since against $(\frac{1}{2}b_1, \frac{1}{2}b_2)$, a_1 has a higher EV than a_2. Of course, Ss saw P^B change his strategy once, and might wish to play close to the maximin as a precaution, but since the first group did not take such a precaution, this reasoning seems unconvincing.

A post-experimental questionnaire indicated that most Ss thought that the experimenter's choices were responsive to their own, as in a battle of wits. Actually, as we noted, P^B simply made choices randomly without regard to past choices by P^A or himself. Again we witness the difficulty people have in recognizing randomness.

Malcolm and Lieberman (1965) studied the same game, except that two Ss played each other for 200 trials. For the last 100 trials, 10 of the 18 Ss appeared to conform reasonably well to the maximin choice percentages. The Ss did not describe their strategies in anything like decision-theoretic terms; instead Ss said they simply tried to predict what the opponent would play by observing patterns or by other means, and to choose accordingly. Because Ss could not verbalize their strategies in decision-theoretic terms, the authors concluded that Ss were not following a randomized strategy. I believe, however, that most psychologists would prefer to judge S's strategy in terms of his behavior rather than his verbalizations. In this regard I should point out that conclusions about a randomized mixed strategy depend on more than choice percentages. The sequence of choices must be random, and, as we have seen, response sequences are typically nonrandom, even when Ss attempt to respond randomly (Section 6.8).

Herbert Kaufman and Gordon Becker (1961) used an entirely different technique to study mixed strategies. Instead of observing the proportion of choices, they requested S to state a proportion for a_1 (versus a_2) he would wish to use for the next 100 trials. The experimenter then stated a payoff to S, based on a strategy for P^B that would take advantage of S's deviation from his maximin strategy. (This departs from the usual assumption for the normal form of the game that each player chooses in ignorance of the opponent's choice.) On the next trial S again stated a proportion and received a payoff based on

100 imaginary plays. The expected payoff for a trial was linearly related to the distance from the maximin strategy. Each S participated in five different games, with 50 trials per game. The number of Ss reaching maximin within 50 trials increased from 10% to 65% through the five positions of play. Thus, with experience, more and more Ss were learning to choose the maximin strategy. However, I would judge their task as simpler than reaching the maximin strategy in choice-by-choice situation.

9.4   MIXED-MOTIVE GAMES: INTRODUCTION

The zero-sum game does not appear to model real-life interactions very well. If there is a war in which the two antagonists play their "nuclear strategies," then P^A's loss is not P^B's gain. In business transactions, the choices by P^A and P^B may be profitable for both. Thus, extensions of game theory to non-zero-sum games, and in particular to mixed-motive games, are of obvious importance; indeed, psychologists have shown much more interest in mixed-motive than in zero-sum games. It is perhaps unfortunate, then, that the theory for mixed-motive games is less satisfactory than for zero-sum theory. The present section introduces the theory. Consideration of two-person non-zero-sum games continues in subsequent sections.

Negotiable and Non-Negotiable Games

The non-zero-sum games have been idealized into two types, *negotiable* and *non-negotiable,* which differ not in the payoff matrices but in the manner of play. In a negotiable game, preplay communication between P^A and P^B is allowed, and the players may come to an agreement concerning which act each will choose; the agreement is then binding. Such games are also called *cooperative.* The agreement is comparable to a business contract or a treaty, except, of course, that in real life such agreements are broken with varying degrees of hazard.

In *non-negotiable* (or *non-cooperative*) games, a player must make his decision without prior agreement with the coplayer or prior knowledge of the coplayer's intentions. The zero-sum games discussed in Section 9.3 were conducted under these circumstances; there is, in principle, no need to consider the cooperative case for zero-sum games, since any final agreement could only yield each player his game security level, which he can guarantee to himself anyway.

Strategy Pair Diagram

The *strategy pair diagram* is useful for illustrating two-person non-zero-sum games. Each pair of strategies, $a_i b_j$, can be plotted as a point on the diagram. The abscissa of each point gives the payoff (or expected payoff) to P^A for the

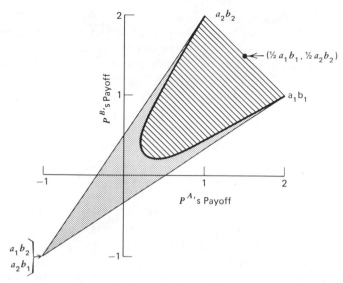

Figure 9.1. Strategy pair diagram for the Battle of the Sexes. (After Luce & Raiffa, 1957.)

strategy pair, and the ordinate gives the payoff to P^B. (The *strategy set diagram* of Chapter 2 is different; each point of the strategy set diagram represents a strategy for only one player, and the payoffs on the two axes are for the same player.) Figure 9.1 gives the strategy pair diagram for the following payoff matrix:

	b_1	b_2
a_1	2, 1	−1, −1
a_2	−1, −1	1, 2

The matrix is taken from Luce and Raiffa (1957, p. 90), who exemplify it as the "Battle of the Sexes." P^A and P^B are taken to be a man and a woman who each have the choice of going to a prize fight or ballet. The man prefers the fight, the woman prefers the ballet; however, either would prefer to attend the less desirable event together than the more desirable event alone.

Strategy pairs a_1b_2 and a_2b_1 yield the same payoffs, thus these two pairs occupy the same position on the diagram. Such pairs are called *equivalent*. Pairs of randomized mixed strategies can be shown on the diagram, but the set need not be convex. The stippled region of Figure 9.1 with its boundary lines contains all the pure and randomized mixed strategy pairs available to P^A and P^B in a non-negotiable game.

Any mixed strategy available in a non-negotiable game is also available in a negotiable game; i.e., the players may agree to play any pure or mixed strategy pair they might have played without agreement. In addition, negotiation allows consideration of strategy pairs unavailable under the non-negotiation conditions. These new strategy pairs are *correlated mixed strategies.* They are mixed in that a player's strategy includes the possible use of more than one act, but they are correlated in that the acts chosen by the two players for a trial are not independently determined. In our illustrative game, for example, the joint randomized mixed strategy $[(\frac{1}{2}a_1, \frac{1}{2}a_2), (\frac{1}{2}b_1, \frac{1}{2}b_2)]$ gives each player an EV of 1/4 (all four outcomes would occur with equal probability). Suppose, on the other hand, that P^A still uses $(\frac{1}{2}a_1, \frac{1}{2}a_2)$, but whenever P^A uses a_1, P^B uses b_1, and whenever P^A uses a_2, P^B uses b_2. Then only consequences o_{11} and o_{22} could occur, and the EVs for both players would be 1.5. Other, lesser degrees of correlation would be possible, as well as other probabilities for a_1 and b_1. The region of Figure 9.1 set off by parallel lines delineates pairs of expected payoffs available only through the use of correlated mixed strategies. The two regions together, showing all available strategy pairs for negotiation, is convex.

Joint Dominance and Admissibility

Dominance, as discussed in Chapter 2, is a relation between two acts or strategies of one player. Act a_i may or may not dominate a_i'. *Joint dominance,* however, is a relation between *pairs* of strategies; specifically, a_ib_j is said to *jointly dominate* $a_i'b_j'$ if the expected payoffs for both players are at least as high for a_ib_j as for $a_i'b_j'$ (higher for at least one player). Just as one strategy dominates another if it is to the "northeast" on the strategy set diagram, one strategy pair dominates another if it is to the "northeast" on the strategy pair diagram. Figure 9.1 illustrates that a_2b_2 and a_1b_1 both jointly dominate a_1b_2 and a_2b_1.

Strategy pairs which are not jointly dominated are said to be *jointly admissible.* From Figure 9.1 one can see that the jointly admissible strategy pairs— sometimes called the *Pareto optimal set*—are a_2b_2, a_1b_1, plus the strategy pairs represented by the line joining them. These pairs are the perfectly correlated strategies with various choice probabilities for a_1 (and b_1). It seems reasonable that a solution for the negotiable game should be jointly admissible; otherwise, another available strategy pair could yield higher expected payoffs to *both* players.

The Problem with Mixed-Motive Games

Recall from Chapter 2 that a_ib_j is said to be an *equilibrium pair* if neither player can improve his expected payoff by playing a different strategy when his opponent stays with his present one. The maximin strategies of P^A and P^B for zero-sum games are equilibrium pairs and conversely; this is vital to the justification of the maximin strategies as game solutions. Non-zero-sum games always have a mixed strategy equilibrium pair, but the equilibrium and maximin strategies need not coincide. Suppose then that P^A thinks it is reasonable to play his maximin. P^B, having the same thought processes, realizes P^A's intentions, but P^B will not then wish to play his own maximin strategy; instead he will figure his optimal strategy against P^A's maximin. P^A will anticipate P^B's plan, will abandon the maximin for another strategy, P^B will anticipate this, etc. *ad infinitum*. In brief, the trouble with non-zero-sum games is that the maximin strategies need not form an equilibrium pair, so the maximin strategies do not have the appeal they had for zero-sum games.

Though various "solutions" have been proposed for non-zero-sum non-negotiable games, these solutions are generally not very convincing, and a "solution" may apply only to some payoff matrices rather than to all. They do not lead to any convincing advice to P^A or P^B for the non-negotiable game of Figure 9.1. Discussion of such "solutions" is provided by Luce and Raiffa (1957, Chapter 5).

We continue discussion of negotiable games in Section 9.9. For now we rest content with the conclusion that negotiation broadens the set of possible strategy pairs and that the strategy pair agreed upon should be jointly admissible (Pareto optimal).

9.5 PRISONER'S DILEMMA GAME: INTRODUCTION

The mixed-motive game which has received the most attention and experimental investigation is called the Prisoner's Dilemma Game (PDG), which, in its two-person symmetric form, is exemplified by the following payoff matrix:

	b_1	b_2
a_1	5, 5	$-3, 7$
a_2	7, -3	0, 0

The symmetric game has these characteristics: (1) act a_2 dominates act a_1, and act b_2 dominates act b_1: (2) the sum of the payoffs for a_1b_1 is greater than for any other strategy pair.[1] According to the *dominance principle* of Section 2.7, a dominated act should not be chosen. This implies that the appropriate strategy pair for the PDG is a_2b_2. Yet this "solution" is unpalatable to many

---

[1] This specification assumes that different arbitrary linear payoff transformations are not allowable for P^A and P^B, for, say, if P^B's "utilities" were multiplied by 10 whereas P^A's were left unchanged, the sum for a_1b_2 would be highest. The payoffs might best be thought of as amounts of a commodity, such as money.

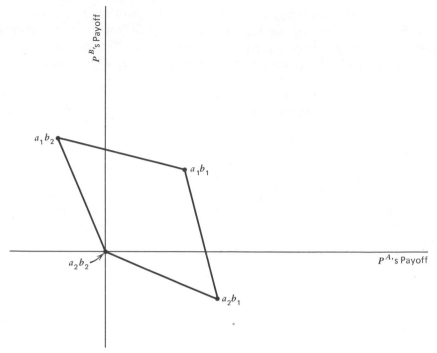

Figure 9.2. Strategy pair diagram for the Prisoner's Dilemma Game.

people, since two "nonrational" players could do better than two "rational" players. Somehow, that doesn't make sense. Thus the dominance principle, which on its face seems hardly open to question, has been questioned by many in the context of the PDG.

The dilemma only occurs for the non-negotiable game. Indeed, the name Prisoner's Dilemma comes from an exemplification of the matrix featuring two criminal suspects who must, without consulting each other, confess (a_2 or b_2) or deny (a_1 or b_1) a crime. The strategy pair diagram is shown in Figure 9.2, from which it is clear that a_2b_2 is not Pareto optimal. It is difficult to believe that a negotiated agreement would or should be anything other than a_1b_1.

The discussions of proper strategy in the PDG hinge largely on whether there is to be one trial or repeated trials. For one play, a_2b_2 seems hard to refute, since P^A, say, due to the dominance of a_2 over a_1, would be better off with a_2 regardless of the choice of P^B. However, with repeated plays, even though no explicit communication is allowed, could not P^A make it clear by his choices that he will come to play a_1 with regularity if P^B will play b_1? Strategy a_1b_1 is not an equilibrium pair, and either player could increase his payoff for a forthcoming trial by defecting to act 2. But then his opponent could punish him by defecting also. If one player sets out to teach the other to cooperate, however, there are dangers. The opponent might "play dumb" and earn himself a nice scholarship at the "teacher's" expense.

Another problem: If both players realize that the "supergame" will have 100 trials, perhaps P^A should play a_1 for 99 trials to avoid retaliation, but why shouldn't he increase his payoff on trial 100 by defecting to strategy a_2? The supergame would then end and P^B couldn't retaliate. But if P^A can so reason, P^B could decide to "beat P^A to the punch" by playing b_2 on trial 99, but P^A, anticipating this could plan to defect on trial 98, etc., down to trial 1. Thus, if logic leads to a_2b_2 for a single trial, it would seem to lead to a_2b_2 for each trial of a supergame of fixed and known length. If, however, the supergame has a stochastic stopping point so that neither player knows exactly when the supergame will end, the cooperative strategy pair can sometimes be justified logically, i.e., a_1b_1 can be an equilibrium pair.

The reader desiring a more extensive discussion of PDG theory should consult Luce and Raiffa (1957, Chapter 5) and Rapoport (1966, pp. 128–144). We now turn our attention to experimental studies of the PDG and related games.

9.6 PRISONER'S DILEMMA GAME: EXPERIMENTS

The logical difficulties involved in determining a rational solution for the PDG hardly constitute a difficulty for use of the game in laboratory experiments. Two Ss can be asked to take the parts of P^A and P^B and to play the game. Even if we can't decide what is rational, we can learn what choices real Ss make. The PDG has caught the fancy of many psychologists. The experimental literature is voluminous, and we will not attempt to survey all of it. The results, in general, concern (1) the effects of experimental variations, and (2) the effects of personality traits. The use of stooges is commonplace so that S's behavior can be determined as a function of various possible strategies an opponent might use.

In the experimental literature, a_1 or b_1 is called the *cooperative* or *collaborative* choice, whereas a_2 or b_2 is called the *competitive* choice. Some experimenters discuss results in terms of percentage of competitive choices, some in terms of percentage of collaborative choices. These figures are complementary, but it will be easier for us if we always report results in terms of the competitive choices. It should by no means be inferred that the S with the higher percentage of "cooperative" choices is more "cooperative" in general. The PDG is not presumed to measure any such personality trait. Indeed, it is doubtful that any useful general measure of the bipolar trait "cooperativeness-competitiveness" could be devised. A basketball player, for example, is both highly cooperative and highly competitive: he is highly cooperative with his teammates, but highly competitive in relation to the opposing team.

First Studies

Scodel, Minas, Ratoosh, and Lipetz (1959) required pairs of Ss to play 50 trials of the following PDG:

$$
\begin{array}{c|c|c|}
 & b_1 & b_2 \\
\hline
a_1 & 3, 3 & 0, 5 \\
\hline
a_2 & 5, 0 & 1, 1 \\
\hline
\end{array}
$$

Payoffs were in cents. Ss learned the consequence (both payoffs) after each trial. For 20 of 22 pairs of Ss, the joint competitive strategy $a_2 b_2$ occurred more frequently than the joint collaborative strategy. The percentage of competitive choices increased over trials.

Another group of Ss was run on the same matrix under the same conditions, except that after 25 trials they were allowed to discuss the game in any way they pleased, though they were not required to come to any formal agreement. This resulted in some decrease in competitive choice, but competitive choices still predominated. In discussion Ss appeared more interested in discovering the opponent's intentions rather than forming an agreement.

Minas, Scodel, Marlowe, and Rawson (1960) observed the choices for pairs of Ss in the following three games differing by degrees from the symmetric PDG as we described it:

$$
\begin{array}{c}
G_{\mathrm{I}} \\
\begin{array}{c|c|c|}
 & b_1 & b_2 \\
\hline
a_1 & 6, 6 & 4, 7 \\
\hline
a_2 & 7, 4 & -1, -1 \\
\hline
\end{array}
\end{array}
\qquad
\begin{array}{c}
G_{\mathrm{II}} \\
\begin{array}{c|c|c|}
 & b_1 & b_2 \\
\hline
a_1 & 3, 3 & 1, 3 \\
\hline
a_2 & 3, 1 & 0, 0 \\
\hline
\end{array}
\end{array}
\qquad
\begin{array}{c}
G_{\mathrm{III}} \\
\begin{array}{c|c|c|}
 & b_1 & b_2 \\
\hline
a_1 & 4, 4 & 1, 3 \\
\hline
a_2 & 3, 1 & 0, 0 \\
\hline
\end{array}
\end{array}
$$

In game G_{I} the dominance principle is not applicable, since against b_2 P^A is better off with a_1. Thus if it is dominance that led Ss to prefer the competitive choice, that motivation is not applicable for G_{I}. Still, $a_1 b_1$ is not an equilibrium pair, so either player might be tempted to defect. But the gain would be small—7¢ versus 6¢ for staying. In G_{II} the dominance relations are reversed—a_1 weakly dominates a_2 in G_{II}, and in G_{III} a_1 strongly dominates a_2. The dilemma is gone. The dominance principle would require $a_1 b_1$, and this would yield P^A and P^B the highest possible payoffs.

Ss were females, knew in advance that there would be 30 trials, and knew they could keep all the money they won. The results were remarkable. The percentage of "competitive" choices (a_2 or b_2) for the three games were 50, 52, and 47, respectively! For all three games, percentage of competitive choices increased over trials.

The authors suggested that S may be primarily motivated to maximize the difference between his gain and the opponent's gain rather than by his own total payoff. For the PDG as well as G_I, G_{II}, and G_{III}, a matrix with the differences between P^A's payoffs and P^B's payoffs would look like this:

$$
\begin{array}{c|c|c|}
 & b_1 & b_2 \\
\hline
a_1 & 0 & -x \\
\hline
a_1 & x & 0 \\
\hline
\end{array}
$$

The *difference game* is zero-sum and has the solution a_2 for P^A and b_2 for P^B, even when a_1 dominates a_2 as in G_{III}.

Effect of Number of Trials

Subsequent research has verified the finding of the initial studies that percentage of competitive choices increases over trials. The initial studies, however, typically employed 30 to 50 trials. Subsequent research has revealed that for a larger number of trials the percentage of competitive choices reaches a maximum and begins to decline. Radlow (1965) found that after about 100 trials the percentage of competitive choices had declined to the starting level. Rapoport and Chammah (1965) used several hundred trials and found that competitive choices declined to well under 50%.

Effect of Opponent's Strategy

In order to study systematically the effects of various P^B strategies upon the choices of P^A, a stooge (accomplice) is used as P^B. The stooge plays different specified strategies against different groups of Ss. Various types of strategies have been used by P^B, including: (1) random play of b_1 and b_2 in set proportions or varying proportions over blocks of trials; (2) strategies making P^B's choices dependent on the current or past choices of P^A.

Vello Sermat (1964) had P^B play randomly with different percentages of b_2 (against different Ss) ranging from 20 to 80 for the first 50 trials, then switched P^B to a 10% or 90% schedule. (He used a game like G_I above, with no dominance, rather than the standard PDG.) Amazingly, these variations in percentages of random play had no detectable effects upon the percentage of competitive choices played by the Ss. As against real opponents, percentage of competitive choices increased in early trials to a level somewhat above 50%. On each trial the Ss also had to predict the choice of the opponent. As we have seen (Chapter 6), the predictions for a series of random binary outcomes are usually probabilistic and roughly match the outcome probabilities. Sermat found for his game, however, that the predictions of b_2 by S (P^A) averaged about 45% and varied around that only very slightly for actual percentages ranging from 20 to 80! Note that the 45% figure is less than the S's own percentage of competitive choices. In a further experiment Sermat found that if P^B played 100% or 0% competitive choices, an effect on S's behavior was noted. Ss played fewer competitive choices (about 30%) against the totally competitive opponent than against the totally cooperative opponent (about 60%).

McClintock, Harrison, Strand, and Gallo (1963) also utilized a stooge who played a randomized strategy of 85%, 50%, or 15% competitive choices, without effect on the percentage of competitive choices played by the Ss. Minas *et al.* (1960) had a stooge play 100% cooperative choices and Ss still played only 61% competitive choices. Bixenstine and Wilson (1963) had the stooge's percentage of competitive choices start very high, go very low, and then go high again, or it went low-high-low. Ss seemed to decrease their own percentage of competitive play as the stooge's percentage decreased, but they still couldn't be induced to make predominantly cooperative choices.

Another line of research has the stooge's choice depend on the play of S. Presumably, if one player were trying to teach or induce his opponent into cooperative play, he would use some such strategy. The "tit-for-tat" strategy has the stooge play the same choice on trial n—competitive or cooperative—that the S played on trial $n - 1$. Such a strategy seems to be of some value in inducing cooperation, but the average effect is not large. Sermat (1964) concluded that "tit-for-tat" tends to divide Ss into two groups—competitive or cooperative. The mean percentage of competitive choices in the last 10 trials for all Ss was still 51%, however. This would not seem to be much different from play against a random strategy.

Although, in principle, the opponent could not match the choice of the S on the same trial for each trial, a stooge in a rigged game can match S's choice. Minas *et al.* (1960) observed behavior against such matching for 50 trials in a PDG. The only strategy pairs ever played were a_1b_1 or a_2b_2. Under these circumstances, S *always* receives a higher payoff for his cooperative choice than for his competitive choice. Nonetheless, 64% of the Ss' choices were competitive! Some Ss thought the matching highly coincidental, but none seemed to think the game was rigged.

Variations in the Payoff Matrix

We have seen how some variations in the payoff matrix changing the dominance relations of the PDG had remarkably little effect on choice. It is also possible to change the payoffs while leaving the basic features intact or to alter the symmetry of the game.

As we saw, the general predominance of competitive choices has been interpreted as an attempt by Ss to win more than their opponents. If the monetary payoffs were made large enough, might not Ss be more concerned with the amount that they could win rather than with beating the opponent? Robert Radlow (1965) studied behavior in the following game having payoffs in *dollars:*

	b_1	b_2
a_1	4, 4	2, 5
a_2	5, 2	3, 3

There were 98 trials, so Ss could not be paid the total winnings; however, they were told that they would be paid for one trial, selected at random, but unknown to them during play. Ss still used about 60% competitive choices.

Suppose the payoffs for the joint competitive strategy were negative rather than positive. Wouldn't this make Ss cooperate more? Oskamp and Perlman (1965) compared behavior for two PDGs. For one game the joint competitive choice yielded — 1¢; for the second game all payoffs were 3¢ larger, so joint competitive strategies would not result in losses. Contrary to the authors' expectations, Ss cooperated more when the joint competitive payoffs were positive.

Rapoport and Orwant (1962) proposed that frequency of competitive play might be affected by the "relative advantage" of defecting from joint cooperation, i.e., by the difference between the defector's payoff and the cooperator's. For the two following games, the *indices of competitive advantage* are 5 and 8:

	b_1	b_2			b_1	b_2
a_1	8, 8	4, 9		a_1	8, 8	3, 11
a_2	9, 4	5, 5		a_2	11, 3	5, 5

Rapoport and Chammah (1965) found that percentage of competitive choices increased directly with the index of competitive advantage. They also found that increasing the payoffs for joint cooperation or increasing the amount of loss for joint competition resulted in fewer competitive choices.

Interesting variations in the PDG are possible by dropping symmetry and the requirement that the greatest total payoff must occur for the joint collaborative strategy. Schellenberg (1964) effected both changes by multiplying P^A's payoffs by 2. The original and transformed matrices were:

	b_1	b_2			b_1	b_2
a_1	3, 3	0, 5		a_1	6, 3	0, 5
a_2	5, 0	1, 1		a_2	10, 0	2, 1

S had three possible positions to fill. He could be in the standard PDG, or he could be P^A or P^B in the transformed game. Against other *S*s the transformation had no effect on percentage of competitive choices. Against a stooge, however, *S* made fewer competitive choices when he had the superior rewards than when he had inferior rewards. This difference appeared particularly when the stooge used predominantly collaborative choices. Other *S*s are not predominantly collaborative, however, and this may explain the lack of an effect for *S* versus *S*.

Instructional, Social, and Personality Factors

Deutsch (1960a) found that amount of cooperative play depended on the orientation given to *S*s by instructions: cooperative, individualistic, or competitive. The cooperative instructions produced a large majority of cooperative choices, the competitive instructions produced a small minority of cooperative choices, and the individualistic instructions produced intermediate results. Radlow (1965) found that instructions emphasizing the maximum sum aspect of the joint cooperative strategy produced predominantly cooperative play. Oskamp and Perlman (1965) used several stooges in a pre-play discussion, but group pressure favoring cooperation or competition did not affect play. The authors also reported that degree of friendship between the pair of *S*s did not affect level of cooperative play. McClintock, Nuttin, and McNeel (1970), however, using a G_{III} game, found that friendship, or, to a lesser degree, mere prior acquaintanceship, decreased the percentage of competitive choices.

Deutsch (1958) reported research by J. Farr showing that the presence of an obnoxious third party induced increased cooperative play. The effect was greater if it was understood that the obnoxious stooge would obtain the money lost through non-cooperation than if the stooge was merely a score-keeper. Sampson and Kardush (1965) studied the behavior of children in the PDG as affected by age, sex, class, and race. For all groups, the competitive choice was predominant.

A number of studies have attempted to correlate personality trait measures with level of cooperative play. Deutsch (1960b) found that *S*s scoring high on the *F* scale (authoritarianism) were less trusting and less trustworthy than other *S*s in a PDG-like situation. Rapoport and Chammah (1965) conclude that personality differences will generally not show up if *S*s are paired randomly, since, over trials, the play of the two *S*s becomes similar, i.e., level of cooperative play is so heavily dependent on the play of the other that the effect of an individual's own personality may be hard to discern. If only a few trials are used, an effect might appear (as for Deutsch, 1960b), or one can pair similar *S*s and then contrast the level of cooperative play across pairs. Using this latter technique, Lutzker (1960) found that level of cooperative play correlated with scores on a scale of internationism he developed. McClintock *et al.* (1963) reported a similar effect, but even the "internationalists" played more than 50% competitive choices.

A number of studies have reported that male pairs play more cooperatively than female pairs; one study showed that with mixed pairs, a common, intermediate level of cooperative play is used (Rapoport & Chammah, 1965).

Summary

In multiple-trial PDG experiments, Ss use both competitive and collaborative choices, but the competitive choices typically predominate. Even in a game restructured so that "individual" and "social" rationality coincide, Ss use the "competitive" choice about half the time. Perhaps Ss are largely motivated by a desire to outscore the opponent regardless of the absolute levels of the payoffs to each. Percentage of competitive choices appears to be remarkably resistant to variations in the opponent's strategy. In fact, Ss have difficulty in understanding the opponent's strategy; they don't recognize random play and are relatively unaffected by variations choice probabilities by P^B. It does not appear that the opportunity to win significant amounts of money can induce a high percentage of joint cooperative play, though payoff matrix variations do have some effects. The effect of personality variables on percentage of random play may be hard to detect with random pairings of Ss, but they may appear if similar Ss are paired.

Experimentation with the PDG is proceeding apace. For a recent review and additional references, consult Vinacke (1969).

9.7 BLOCKING GAMES

There are a variety of two-person mixed-motive games which cannot be described in simple normal form, but which have been used to study cooperation and competition. The games which we describe in this section all involve the possibility that the two players will block each other from reaching their goals; thus we might call these *blocking games*.

The prototype is the *trucking game* used by Morton Deutsch and Robert Krauss (1960, 1962). The two players are "truckers." At the beginning of a trial each attempts to move his truck from his "starting point" to his "destination." (See Figure 9.3.) There are two routes possible for each player: a "slow route" and a "fast route." On each trial the payoff for each player is inversely related to the time he takes to reach his destination. Each player would prefer to take the fast route, but it has only one lane, so if both players attempt to use it at the same time, they will meet "head-on" and neither can continue until the other backs up out of the lane. Each player has a separate slow route on which he can't be blocked, but this route takes longer so the payoff is less (in the Deutsch and Krauss studies it involved a loss).

In some conditions one or both players may control a gate on the fast route.

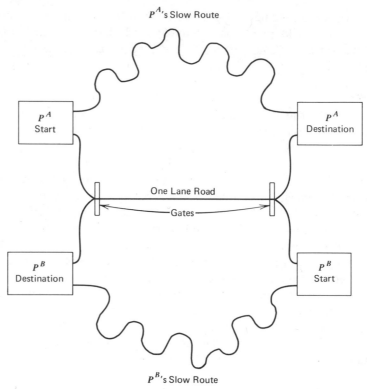

Figure 9.3. Schematization of the trucking game. (After Deutsch & Krauss, 1960.)

Deutsch and Krauss interpreted the gates as *threats:* if only one player has control of a gate it is a *unilateral threat* condition; if both players have control of a gate it is a *bilateral threat* condition. The gate can only be closed by a player while he is on the short route himself. After closing the gate, however, a player may back off the short route and take the long route, leaving his opponent blocked from the short route by the gate. A player knows at any time if he is blocked by a gate; i.e., he doesn't have to reach the gate to find out. At any time during a trial a player knows only his own position, unless he and the coplayer are head-on in the short route. Each trial starts anew with each player at his starting point.

The trucking game is analogous to the Battle of the Sexes game of Section 9.4. As in that game, each player has a favorite consequence (going through the short route with no blocking), but on a single trial both players cannot have what they want. If each player attempts to get what he wants, regardless of the desires of the coplayer, neither succeeds, for in the Battle of the Sexes the strategy pair is a_1b_2, yielding -1 to each player instead of 2, and in the trucking game the result is a standoff on the short route which has both players losing money.

If the Battle of the Sexes were to be played as a negotiable game, a reasonable solution would be an alternation between a_1b_1 and a_2b_2. In the trucking game the comparable solution is for P^A, say, to wait until P^B has taken the short route, then to go through himself (this is better than taking the long route). Then on the next trial, P^B should wait for P^A to go through, etc., alternating (or "taking turns") on successive trials. Though the trucking game has not been used, to my knowledge, under negotiation conditions, players could come to this solution over trials through tacit bargaining or through discussions, if allowed.

Using this experimental game with imaginary money payoffs, Deutsch and Krauss (1960) found that Ss got the most total payoff under the no-threat condition and least under the bilateral threat conditions. In the unilateral condition, the player with gate control did better than his opponent, but not as well as he would have done without a gate. Ss appeared to be improving in payoff over trials, but only 20 trials were used.

Deutsch and Krauss (1962) investigated the effect of communication. Ss could converse over an intercom (bilateral communication), or only one player could talk (unilateral). When communication was only permissive, it had little effect; but when it was compulsory, it seemed helpful in the unilateral threat condition.

Other experimenters have used the trucking game or some variant of it. Borah (1963) used a gameboard and a chess pawn for a "truck," but had the two "routes." Borah used electric shocks as "threats," but these appeared to have no effect. Shomer used a game with no "long route" and fines as threats (Kelley, 1965). All male dyads made more profit than all-female dyads. Gallo (1966), using still another version of the game, found results generally similar to Deutsch and Krauss', but, using real money for payoffs, found that Ss made a profit under real-money conditions, whereas they sustained a loss under the comparable imaginary money conditions.

Deutsch (1969) reviewed the work on blocking games, replied to criticism of his experiments and conclusions, and considered the possible relevance of such research to real-world affairs.

9.8   PANIC BEHAVIOR

Alexander Mintz (1951) was interested in panic behavior in groups and studied an analogue of panic in the laboratory. Just as the trucking game resembles the Battle of the Sexes but does not have a simple normal form representation, Mintz's "cones-in-the-bottle" experiment resembles the PDG, but has no simple normal-form representation. Mintz's experiment concerned a group of N persons (fifteen to twenty-one) instead of two persons. Each player held a string which went from the player, through the neck of a large bottle, to a cone of wood or metal. The task was for each player to draw his cone out of the bottle. Due to the size of the cone, only one could be drawn through the bottle neck at a time. In one condition, there was a fine or reward for any individual, depending on how fast he got his cone out. In another condition, there were no fines or rewards, and the instructions emphasized group cooperation in drawing out all the cones as quickly as possible. In other words, team performance was emphasized instead of individual performance.

The differences across conditions were startling. The reward-and-fine condition was characterized by "traffic jams" at the bottleneck; for some groups, no cones were removed within the time period allowed. Discussion facilitated the solution. No serious traffic jams occurred for the "team" condition. Using a comparable task, Kelley, Condry, Dahlke, and Hill (1965) found that the more dire the punishment for non-escape within the time limit, the smaller the percentage of Ss who escaped.

Mintz related his findings to such panic behavior as occurs when someone yells "fire" in a theatre. Many times in such circumstances, many people are injured, even though all might have escaped unhurt in an orderly withdrawal. Although the PDG per se was not appreciated at the time Mintz wrote, comparable dilemmas in social behavior have long been recognized. Essentially, as Mintz pointed out, panic behavior occurs where the "orderly" joint strategy is not in equilibrium, since, assuming that others will be orderly, one's best chance of escape is to be disorderly and to rush to the exit. The situation is thus unstable. Once panic starts, it is problematical whether one is better off in the mass of people or waiting near the advancing fire while the exit remains hopelessly clogged. As Mintz pointed out, it is not danger per se which turns a group of people into an "irrational crowd," since trapped miners or submariners seem not to panic. This can be explained strategically, for there is no desperate action available to the individuals which will save them at the group's expense.

Many social dilemmas appear to be of the prisoner's dilemma type: during the Depression, bank panics caused otherwise viable banks to fail; an army that might hold a defensive position can collapse if individual soldiers have tempting escape routes.[2] PDG-like social dilemmas need not involve danger. Selfish behavior may simply be more profitable than cooperative behavior. It is often more profitable to dump industrial wastes in a river than to recycle them. An important function of law and government is to change the structure of situations so that individual and social rationality do not conflict. Thus, government-insured bank accounts deprive the panic-prone individual of a motive for closing his account. A combination of tax incentives and fines can make recycling more profitable than dumping.

---

[2] Schelling (1966) points out that Xenophon recognized this principle and chose defensive positions accordingly.

9.9 SOLUTIONS FOR NEGOTIABLE GAMES

The experimental games we have discussed up to now have not been strictly either negotiable or non-negotiable. Since Ss were not urged or required to reach binding contracts, the games were not negotiable; yet, with multiple trials, a kind of tacit communication is possible, as we have noted. For example, with a tit-for-tat strategy in the PDG, P^A can inform P^B of his intentions. In some experiments explicit discussion or notes were allowed, but these did not result in binding contracts. We now turn to the negotiable game in the strict sense. In this section we discuss some theory, and in the next section some experiments.

In the negotiable game there is presumed to be a preplay discussion, usually called *bargaining,* the purpose of which is to reach an agreement or *contract.* (The term "bargaining" is also used in reference to multiple-trial PDGs and other multiple-trial games involving jockeying for advantage.) We wish to determine what contract, i.e., agreed joint strategy, might or should be reached. What a theory specifies for the agreement is called the *solution.* As we shall see, a variety of theories exist, and they lead, in general, to conflicting solutions. These solutions are not strategies that can be played by a single player—they require the consent of two players, each of whom would in general prefer another joint strategy. Thus the solutions depend on notions of *fairness* as much as individual maximizing. Because of this, the solutions might be thought of as attempts to specify what a "fair" arbiter would suggest as a settlement. In this light, most of the theories we discuss are sometimes said to be *arbitration schemes* which cannot be defended in terms of individual strategy considerations.

In Section 9.4 we concluded that the contract should be Pareto optimal (jointly admissible). However, each player has a game security level which he can assure to himself by his maximin strategy. Pareto optimal contracts may exist which would yield a player less than his security level. Presumably the players are bargaining so that each may end up better off than he would be otherwise. Therefore, it seems neither reasonable nor likely that a player would consider a contract offering him less than his security level. The subset of Pareto optimal joint strategies offering *each* player at least his security level is called the *negotiation set.* On the strategy pair diagram it is that subset of the Pareto optimal set north of P^B's security level and east of P^A's security level. (See Figure 9.4.) Von Neumann and Morgenstern considered the negotiation set to be the game solution and did not feel that they could further delimit the contract that should or would result.

John Nash (1950, 1953) proposed a solution which yields a specific strategy pair. The solution depends on a utility for P^A, $u_0{}^A$, and a utility for P^B, $u_0{}^B$, which can be plotted on the strategy pair diagram as a point $(u_0{}^A, u_0{}^B)$, called that *status quo point.* Let us postpone interpretation of the status quo point and state *Nash's solution,* which is that joint strategy which maximizes the product $(u^A - u_0{}^A)(u^B - u_0{}^B)$ for $u^A \geq u_0{}^A$ and $u^B \geq u_0{}^B$.

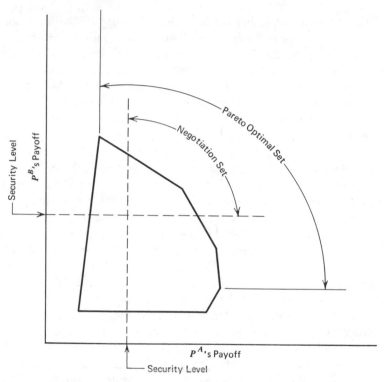

Figure 9.4. Illustration of the Pareto optimal and negotiation sets on the strategy pair diagram.

The solution has a number of appealing properties: (a) the solution is Pareto optimal; (b) players in a symmetric game, i.e., one that "looks" the same whether played as P^A or P^B, receive equal payoffs; (c) the solution is independent of irrelevant alternatives, i.e., if new strategy pairs are added (without changing the status quo point), the solution to the new game either remains unchanged it is one of the added strategy pairs; (d) the solution allows arbitrary and different positive linear transformations to the utilities of P^A and P^B without changing the solution; i.e., in utilities, the new solution would be related to the old one by the same transformations.

The status quo point has received varying interpretations. Usually, once we "set" players into a game, they are forced to choose an alternative; but for the bargaining situation a "no-deal" consequence is sometimes allowed which is not among the strategy pairs considered for the game. For this case, the status quo point is typically taken to be the utilities for P^A and P^B if no contract is reached and, thus, if the game is not played.

If, as usual, the players must choose a strategy from the game, the status quo point might be the security levels for the two players. The Nash solution with the security levels as status quo is called the *Shapley procedure*. Nash (1953) has suggested another possible status quo based on threat strategies.

Two other proposed solutions differ from the Nash solution by requiring, in effect, interpersonal comparisons of utility. Howard Raiffa (1953) noted that if the differences between payoffs to P^A and P^B are considered, the differences constitute a zero-sum game. Suppose P^A, say, has an advantage in the zero-sum game, i.e., his security level is positive. Then, since he could assure himself this much advantage over P^B without cooperation, might it not be reasonable to let him have this advantage in the contract. This, then, is *Raiffa's solution:* The contract should be the Pareto optimal strategy pair offering P^A the advantage over P^B he could assure himself in a zero-sum relative advantage game. (If there is no such strategy, the solution offers P^A that Pareto optimal strategy pair most nearly giving him his assured advantage.) Raiffa's solution, as given, is not invariant to arbitrary and different linear utility transformations for the two players. Thus, unless the utility scales for P^A and P^B can be standardized, the solution is meaningless. Raiffa proposed that the highest utility in the matrix for each player should be 1 and the lowest 0. With the understanding that such a normalization of the utility matrix must precede calculation of the Raiffa solution, the solution is now meaningful. The normalization suggested is not compelling, however, and another procedure could yield a different solution. Braithwaite's (1955) procedure differs from Raiffa's only in the normalization of utilities. Neither solution is independent from irrelevant alternatives.

For symmetric games such as the Battle of the Sexes or the symmetric PDG, the various theories we have mentioned all lead to the same strategy pair. For the Battle of the Sexes (see Figure 9.1), the solution lies midway along the Pareto optimal set: $(\frac{1}{2}a_1b_1, \frac{1}{2}a_2b_2)$. This yields each player an EV of 1.5. If there is to be but one play, a coin flip could decide between a_1b_1 and a_2b_2. For the symmetric PDG, all solutions specify a_1b_1, the joint collaborative strategy. For asymmetric games, however, the solutions go their separate ways, and none of them is entirely compelling. For a more detailed discussion of the proposed solutions to negotiable games, see Luce and Raiffa (1957) and Rapoport (1966).

9.10 EXPERIMENTS IN BARGAINING

Equal Strength

Sidney Siegel and Lawrence Fouraker (1960) had pairs of Ss bargain for a contract in a simulated bilateral monopoly situation. One S of a pair played the part of the sole manufacturer of a product, and the other S played the part of the sole distributor. Thus, to do business and make money both players had to deal with each other. Bargaining concerned the quantity of goods the distributor would take and the price he would pay per unit.

Siegel and Fouraker assumed that the cost per unit increases with the quantity manufactured (for quantities of interest) and that the demand from the distributor's customers goes down as quantity increases. The manufacturer has a minimum unit price for any quantity—namely, his average cost for production; below that he would lose money. The distributor likewise has a maximum price that he can pay; otherwise, he would have to sell at a loss. As the quantity increases these two limit prices become closer and they finally meet; at this point neither man can make a profit.

A Pareto optimal solution requires a contract with a specific quantity of goods, calculable from the economic model. This is the quantity which maximizes joint profit. The joint profit is the money remaining from the distributor's sales after his costs and the manufacturer's costs have been paid. Suppose the maximum joint profit is $100; then only contracts allowing $100 joint profit can be Pareto optimal. For if the joint profit were $98, say, any contract with the $100 profit would allow the same division of money as before plus $1 more for each man. The maximum joint profit contract always jointly dominates other contracts.

Assuming that both players agree on the Pareto optimal quantity of goods, there remains the division of the joint profit between the players. This is determined by the price agreement. The unit price in a Pareto optimal contract can vary anywhere between the two limiting prices, the higher of which would give all the joint profit to the manufacturer, and the lower of which would give all the joint profit to the distributor.

Siegel and Fouraker's experiment was designed to see what sort of contracts real Ss would arrive at. Would they be Pareto optimal? How would joint profits be divided? Each S of a bargaining pair had a paper showing his profit for each possible contract, where a contract consisted of a quantity of goods and a unit price. Although the Pareto optimal set of contracts seems like a good place to start the bargaining as well as to end it, recognition of the Pareto optimal contracts requires that a player know the joint profit for a contract, not simply his own profit. In real-life bargaining, a bargainer may not know his opponent's profits for different possible contracts. This is considered a private matter which the company has no desire to reveal. For one thing, such revelations could be strategically harmful. Suppose the distributor, for example, has lower costs than the manufacturer would guess, and thus makes a greater profit. If the manufacturer knew this, he could say: "Look here. With my expenses I'm making only a modest profit while you're getting rich from selling my product. You can very well afford to pay me a higher price." What can the distributor reply: "But I'm greedier than you"?

Thus, the amount of information available about the coplayer's profits would seem to be an important factor in bargaining. Accordingly, the pairs of Ss differed in the amount of information available to them. Ss in the "incomplete-incomplete" condition had only their own profit tables. Ss in the "complete-complete" condition had both profit tables. In the "complete-incomplete" condition one S had both profit tables and one had only his own.

Although theorists generally concede that a contract will or should be Pareto optimal on rational grounds, they often demur in specifying a specific contract in the set on rational grounds. Instead, the specific contract is often said to be determined by subjective factors such as "bargaining skill." In order to keep subjective factors to a minimum, the Ss were not allowed to discuss contracts verbally, and, in fact, never saw each other. Instead, contract suggestions were passed back and forth by note. The session ended when one player accepted the latest proposal by his coplayer. The profits listed in the profit table were then paid to the Ss; each was actually bargaining for his own pay for participating.

Pairs were almost always able to reach a contract within the two hour limit. The contract quantity varied around the Pareto optimum; the more complete the information, the less the variability of different pairs of Ss around the Pareto optimum. Even in the incomplete-incomplete condition, 9 of 11 pairs reached a contract quantity within 10% of the Pareto optimum.

The mean tendency was to split the joint profit evenly between the buyer and the seller. This seems to agree with all proposed theories yielding a specific Pareto optimal strategy pair (when utility is linear with money). For example, the only reasonable status quo point would seem to be no-deal, in which case the Nash solution requires a 50–50 split of the profits. Neither player can enforce a relative advantage over the other, so Raiffa's procedure would also require an even split.

Differences in payoff within bargaining pairs were greatest when the information available for the pair was the least and vice versa. A bargainer with complete information seemed to have no advantage over his partner who had incomplete information. In fact, there was a tendency for a bargainer with incomplete information (say, P^A) to have a higher profit than P^B. P^B knew of P^A's relative ignorance, and thus perhaps did not resent P^A's overambitious requests as much as he would in a complete-complete condition.

For one group of Ss, P^A was told he would have a chance to double his money if he won a profit of at least $6.10, and P^B was told he would have a chance to double his money if he won a profit of at least $2.10. (Maximum joint profit was $9.60, which would allow $4.80 each in an even split.) These Ss were run under incomplete-incomplete conditions. Mean profit won by P^A was $6.25, and mean profit won by P^B was $3.25. The authors interpreted the effect in terms of level of aspiration induced by the instructions. The bargaining sessions tended to be longer than for the preceding experiments. The difference in payoffs for P^A and P^B would undoubtedly have been less if there had been complete information.

Kelley (1965) used the Siegel-Fouraker bargaining game, but added the possibility of threats. In some conditions, an S could threaten to impose a fine on his coplayer, or actually impose the fine (at some cost to himself). The threats appeared not to affect the results of the bargaining so much as the attitudes towards oneself and the coplayer.

There has been much conjecture concerning the manner in which a bargainer should make concessions. Should he begin bargaining with extremely ambitious conditions, expecting to make generous concessions, or should his initial position be close to his minimal acceptable one? Should he reciprocate a generous concession by his opponent, or should he stand his ground and exploit the apparent weakening of his opponent's position. The effect of different bargaining strategies on the final result can be studied in the laboratory by letting one S of a bargaining pair be a stooge who uses a preplanned strategy. A few such experiments have been completed. Komorita and Brenner (1968) found that a bargainer could get a better result by being tough rather than by matching his opponent's concessions. Pruitt and Drews (1969) found that high time-pressure on the negotiations decreased the initial demands, but not the rate of change of the demands over trials.

Price Leadership

In a second monograph entitled *Bargaining Behavior,* Fouraker and Siegel (1963) studied bilateral monopoly under conditions of *price leadership.* The manufacturer, P^A, as price leader, announced a unit price at which he would sell his product. The distributor, P^B, then stated the quantity he would buy, and the transaction was complete. The stated price and quantity were not subject to further revision. For one transaction, the situation would appear to be a type of non-negotiable non-zero-sum game in which P^B chooses under the condition of certainty; i.e., P^B knows P^A's choice before he makes his, and knowing his own profits, he might be assumed to choose the quantity giving him highest profit. Price leadership by P^A, then, might seem to be an advantage for P^B, but it is not. For if P^A knows P^B's profits and assumes that P^B will optimize his own profit, then P^A, to maximize his own profits will choose a price that, after P^B's choice, may give P^A the majority of the joint profit, and, indeed, more than he could get by an equal-split of payoff. The point on the strategy pair diagram, by this reasoning, will be Pareto optimal. It is called the *Bowley point.* With repeated transactions, the distributor, P^B, might try to "teach" P^A to choose a price allowing a more equitable split of the joint profit, much as "teaching" can take place in repetitions of the PDG.

Fouraker and Siegel found that the experimental results depended on the amount of information available to P^A and P^B and the number of trials. Single trials yielded solutions close to the Bowley point, as did repeated trials with incomplete information. With complete information and repeated trials many distributors were able to force the transactions away from the Bowley point toward an equal-split Pareto optimal point. Ss experienced in business produced about the same results as college students.

9.11   CO-ORDINATION OF CHOICES

As we noted, Thomas Schelling (1958) differentiated between *pure-conflict, mixed-motive,* and *co-ordination games.* The co-ordination game is the polar opposite of the pure-conflict (zero-sum) game, in that any possible gain to one player in going from one consequence to another would also entail a gain to the other players, and losses would be related likewise. Thus, there is no conflict of interest at all. We exemplify:

	b_1	b_2	b_3
a_1	1, 1	0, 0	0, 0
a_2	0, 0	0, 0	0, 0
a_3	0, 0	0, 0	0, 0

There is no conflict at all in this game because both players desire the same consequence, o_{11}. It is nice to know that decision situations can exist that don't involve conflict between the players, but the preceding matrix is strategically uninteresting. The obvious solution is the strategy pair a_1b_1, and neither player should have any difficulty in making a choice.

The following co-ordination game has greater interest:

	b_1	b_2	b_3
a_1	1, 1	0, 0	0, 0
a_2	0, 0	1, 1	0, 0
a_3	0, 0	0, 0	1, 1

There is no conflict in this game either, in the sense that if one player suggests that they should mutually aim toward a particular cell, o_{ij}, the other player would have no reason to object.

If, as we assume, no preplay discussion is allowed, the players do have a problem of co-ordination even if they have no conflict. Though both players are indifferent between o_{11}, o_{22}, and o_{33}, they could easily end up in an off-diagonal cell if they can't communicate.

Schelling proposed that for many such co-ordination games, the players can co-ordinate their choices for one play without communication. Of course, with multiple-trials, a kind of communication takes place, and players can come to co-ordinate their choices, as they (often) do, for example, in blocking games (Section 9.7). Schelling proposed, however, that such co-ordination of choices is often possible on a single play due to an ability of players to name a "prominent" choice.

To test his notion, Schelling gave a group of people a series of decision problems. In each problem, each person had the same set of possible choices. Ss were instructed that to win they must all make the same choice (without communication), but that it could be any one of the possible choices. One problem was to name "heads" or "tails." Thirty-six of 42 Ss named "heads." A difficulty with such experiments, from the viewpoint of Schelling's theory, is that people tend to predict heads more often than tails on a single trial anyway. In a problem requiring Ss to name the same number from a set, Ss tend to give the same number or numbers, but there are similar biases in just picking numbers, with no requirement to co-ordinate. I don't think that Schelling would want to equate such biases with "co-ordination," and I believe that in controlled experiments an ability to co-ordinate would become evident.

It is interesting to analyze such co-ordination from one player's viewpoint, assuming, for simplicity, that there are only two players. We might at first think that the problem for P^A is to guess what P^B will choose and name the same thing. But such an analysis should account for the fact that P^B is trying to guess what P^A will choose. Should not P^A then really be trying to choose what he thinks P^B thinks that he, P^A, will choose? But such an approach, applied to both players, leads to an infinite regress.

Schelling argues that the ability to co-ordinate choices is of importance in mixed-motive games as well. He considers the 50–50 split of profit to be such a prominent result. If two players had to agree on a split without communication, the prominence of 50–50 would assist them.

9.12   *N*-PERSON GAME THEORY: INTRODUCTION

Up to this point, the chapter has dealt entirely with two-person games. For many situations, however, from card games, to board of director meetings, to international diplomatic conferences, the payoffs to each player depend on the choices of more than two players. Thus game theory, to be complete, must include the *N*-person condition.

As might be expected, the addition of more players vastly complicates the theory. And, unfortunately, the difficulties involved in *N*-person theory do not appear to bring sufficiently compensating rewards. Most of *N*-person game theory seems to strike most people as neither convincing nor esthetic; nor, relative to two-person games, have psychologists taken much interest in the use of *N*-person games as experimental paradigms. Thus, our motivation for discussion of *N*-person games is not large. We will only attempt to sketch an outline of the field, to illustrate some of the difficulties with the theory, and to describe some experimental results. In the present section we concentrate on the basic concepts of the theory of games as formulated by von Neumann and Morgenstern (1953).

It is possible to extend any of the two-person games we have discussed to more than two persons, obtaining an *N*-person generalization of each. For example, one could have a three-person zero-sum or non-zero-sum game without pre-play communication. In particular, one could have a three-person PDG in which the sum of payoffs to all players would be greatest for $a_1b_1c_1$, but in which the dominance principle would require each player to choose act 2 (Rapoport, Chammah, Dwyer, & Gyr, 1962). One could generalize negotiable games to three or more persons (or interests).

Coalitions and Side Payments

Major interest has focused on a feature of games with three or more persons missing entirely in two-person games—namely, the possibility for the aggregation of the players into *alliances* or *coalitions*. For example, in a three-person game, two players can form a coalition and decide on a correlated strategy. In this way, each may be better off than by playing alone. The questions then arise for an *N*-person game: how many different coalitions will (or should) form, which players will belong to each, and what joint strategy will each coalition adopt?

It is conceivable that P^A could do very well by correlating his strategy with P^B, but that P^B has no reason to correlate his strategy with P^A. In such circumstances, it is conceivable that P^A may try to buy P^B's cooperation, i.e., P^A may offer P^B an *inducement* (or *bribe,* or *side payment*) to entice P^B into an alliance. P^A can afford to pay such an inducement because of the larger payoff he will receive he has P^B's cooperation. Assuming that the rules of the game allow such side payments, the questions arise: which players will (or should) offer which other players side payments, how much will they be willing to offer to whom, and how much will a player demand as a side payment before entering a coalition?

Transferable Utility

Suppose two allies act in concert; P^A receives u_{ij}^A and P^B receives u_{ij}^B. After P^A gives P^B an agreed side payment, however, he will not be as well off as u_{ij}^A, but P^B will be better off than u_{ij}^B. P^A does not give P^B part of his utility, per se; instead, we assume he gives P^B some commodity, money, for instance, after which P^A's resultant utility is less than before. It constitutes a considerable simplification in game theory, however, if after the transfer or any possible transfer between any two players, the sum of utilities for the two players is the same as before transfer. If so, we speak of *transferable utility,* even though, strictly, it is a commodity that is transferred. (In reality, P^A's side payment to P^B might be a service, such as shoe-shining or flattery, but for now let us assume it is commodity.) Since the theory considers that any quantity of utility might be transferred, the commodity, ideally, should be infinitely divisible.

If money were the commodity for payoffs and side payments, then utility could be transferable if every person in the game had a utility scale linear with money, at least for the range of payoffs in the game, and if the utility scales for all persons had a common origin and unit. In short, let us assume henceforth that our payoffs are dollars and that dollars measure utility. Money is not infinitely divisible, but let us not demean ourselves by squabbling over fractions of a cent.

Characteristic Functions

Henceforth, then, we assume that the payoffs are dollars. Furthermore, we assume that the game is constant-sum in dollars. The sum of dollars across all players in the game (but not necessarily for the members of a coalition) is the same (possibly zero) for any consequence, before side payments are made and afterwards. Suppose a coalition T forms in a game with constant sum C. The best way for the other players to limit the winnings of T to a minimum, and therefore to make their total payments maximum, is for all of them to band together in a counter-coalition. Then, if the coalitions are considered to be "persons," the situation comes down to a two-person constant-sum game to which the maximin solution applies. Let the value to T of the game, assuming a maximin strategy, be $v(T)$. Then the value for the counter-coalition $v(-T) = C - v(T)$. There is a value v for each possible coalition, i.e., v is a function of the coalition and is known as the *characteristic function* of the constant-sum game to which it applies.

If it doesn't pay for any of the players to form a coalition, i.e., if each member of a possible coalition could do as well by choosing independently, the game is called *inessential.* Otherwise, the game is *essential.* We concern ourselves only with essential games.

It is possible to *normalize* the characteristic function of a game without affecting strategic considerations. For the 0,1 normalization, the value for the coalition of all the players (call this the *universal coalition*)—the largest possible value of the characteristic function—is set at 1. The value for each "coalition" of one player only (call these *solitary coalitions*) is set at 0.

Imputations

The strength of different possible coalitions is given by the characteristic function. The payments to individual players should also be important for coalition theory. The following two conditions (restrictions) are thought to be reasonable in this regard. One is that each player should receive at least as much as his security level for individual play. The second, *Pareto optimality,* is that the sum of payoffs to all players should equal the sum that the universal coalition could get (it could not possibly be more). Otherwise, the players could form the universal coalition instead and divide the additional profit among themselves, improving the payoffs to everyone. Any set of possible payoffs in a game satisfying the above two conditions is called an *imputation*.

von Neumann-Morgenstern Solution for Triads

We now consider the von Neumann-Morgenstern "solution" for the three-person constant-sum game allowing side payments. There is only one 0,1 normalized essential constant-sum three-person game. By the definition of 0,1 normalization, the value of the universal coalition is 1, and the value of each solitary coalition is 0. The only other possible coalitions consist of two players. The value to any coalition of two players must be 1, since the excluded player has a value of 0, and the sum across all players is constant at 1.

Suppose the three-person game were the following: There is $1 available. The three players may form a universal coalition and divide the money among themselves, or two players may form a coalition and divide the dollar. This game has an easily described characteristic function. Let T_1 be any solitary coalition, T_2 be any coalition of two players, and T_3 be the universal coalition. Then $v(T_1) = 0$, $v(T_2) = 1$, and $v(T_3) = 1$ describes the characteristic function of the constant-sum game. We are assured that a normal-form realization for this game can be constructed, but we can skip that.

If P^A and P^B ally, it seems reasonable for them to split the $1 payoff equally. This would yield the imputation $(1/2, 1/2, 0)$. This is an imputation because each player gets at least his security level for solitary play (0), and because the sum of the payoffs equals the total that the universal coalition could get. But on the basis of symmetry, a like split between P^A and P^C or P^B and P^C seems as reasonable and as likely. Can we at least propose that one of these three symmetric results will or should occur? Well, no. For suppose P^C notes the incipient formation of coalition $\{P^A, P^B\}$. Won't P^C reason: "I'd better act fast and not worry about the niceties of an even split. I can't offer either P^A or P^B an even split since they already can get that. So I'll offer P^A 3/4 and take 1/4 myself. Compared to coalition $\{P^A, P^B\}$ both P^A and I will benefit by 1/4." So P^C makes the offer to P^A. How can P^A refuse, rational lover of money that he is? Thus P^A and P^C agree to enter into coalition with the imputation $(3/4, 0, 1/4)$. But before they can, P^B thinks, "I'll make P^A or P^C a better offer, so I can at least get something," and we go on and on.

The von Neumann-Morgenstern definition of a solution is a set of imputations stable with respect to one another in this sense: given that one imputation in a set is about to be agreed on, there is not sufficient motivation to shift to another imputation in the same set. The original three imputations we discussed form such a solution. They are: $(1/2, 1/2, 0)$, $(1/2, 0, 1/2)$, and $(0, 1/2, 1/2)$. Given that one of these is about to be effected, only one player is motivated to change—the one who is left out. A second player would lose nothing by changing, but he is not motivated to change. Since it takes two to agree to a change, a change cannot be motivated.

But there are an infinity of such solutions, i.e., stable sets. Furthermore, some solutions include an infinity of imputations. What's more, every possible imputation is included in at least one solution! The nature of the solution is not limited to "split-the-dollar." Any essential three-person constant-sum game comes to the same end. Needless to say, the von Neumann-Morgenstern solution does not seem to offer much to either descriptive or normative decision theory. But as a mathematical opus, it is admired, and von Neumann and Morgenstern are certainly not to be denigrated because they did not complete the theory they created. Indeed, their pioneering efforts are much appreciated and other workers developed the theory further. But this further work has its limitations as well. The reader is referred to Luce and Raiffa (1957) and Rapoport (1970) for a more extensive introduction to von Neumann-Morgenstern game theory and related work.

Kalisch, Milnor, Nash, and Nering (1954) presented four-, five-, and seven-person games in characteristic function form to Ss, and required them to come to agreements concerning coalitions and division of payoffs. The experimental paradigm proved to be of interest for studying coalition formation, though, for reasons that should be clear, such experiments can hardly be expected to confirm or deny the descriptive accuracy von Neumann-Morgenstern game theory—for what does that theory predict?

The same people participated in a series of games. Coalitions of more than two persons were typically built up from smaller coalitions rather than coming together at once. There was a tendency for members of a coalition to split the payoff evenly, but if the coalition had been built from an original pair, the original pair tended to demand a greater amount of money than the new members of the coalition. The coalition most likely to form was a two-person coalition with the largest payoff, even though other arrangements might have given the participants more payoff. Although for four-person games the geometrical arrangement of the players seemed to have no effect, this was not true for five- and seven-person games. As the number of Ss increased, bargaining became hectic and confused. In spite of instructions designed to instill a completely selfish attitude in the players, they frequently took a fairly cooperative attitude. This was apparently motivated, in part at least, by a desire to keep in the good graces of other Ss so they could get in coalitions over a series of games. Informal agreements, though not binding, were honored.

Other experiments on coalition formation will be considered in the next section.

9.13   OTHER COALITION THEORIES
AND EXPERIMENTS

In sociology there is a tradition of interest in coalition formation, a tradition usually traced to Georg Simmel,[3] who wrote on coalitions of persons as well as of larger units such as nations. The meaning of "coalition" is more general and more vague in sociology than in game theory. It might mean only joint activity, as two children playing together, or two persons attempting to influence the opinion of a third person (Mills, 1953; Borgatta & Borgatta, 1963). Due to this conception, one area of research has concerned the analysis of group discussions. Mills (1953), for example, analyzed the conversational interaction in three-man problem solving groups, and concluded that a triad tends to break into a *pair* and an *other*. He stated that his finding supported Simmel's contention that triads generally so segregate. This generalization has not been universally supported, however (Borgatta & Borgatta, 1962).

Based on the writings of Simmel and the more recent findings of Mills and others, Theodore Caplow (1956) formulated a theory for coalition formation in the triad based on the relative *power* (or *strength*) of the players. He assumed that any player of the triad wishes to "control" the others, and will do so without allying himself, if possible. If alliance is necessary, however, he would prefer to form an alliance with a player weaker than himself than with an equal or stronger player. No alliance is formed unless the summed power of the coalition assures control over the third player. It is assumed that the power of the alliance equals the sum of the powers of the allies. Caplow's theory does not allow for an alliance between all three members since no one could thereby gain control of anyone else.

Figure 9.5 illustrates six types of relative powers for three players and indicates which players would be motivated to ally with which other players. There are three possible pairwise coalitions, $\{P^A P^B\}$, $\{P^B P^C\}$, and $\{P^A P^C\}$. Depending on the relative powers, no pair may be motivated to ally (Types 4 and 6), one pair may be motivated (Type 2), two pairs (Types 3 and 5), or three pairs (Type 1). If one or no pair is motivated, the prediction of the theory is unique. If more than one pair is motivated, the theory simply says that any of the motivated coalitions might occur. Note in particular that for Type 5, P^C can choose between a stronger and a weaker ally. The theory states that either might form. P^C will end up being controlled in either case.

Edgar Vinacke and Abe Arkoff (1957) devised an experimental situation to compare Caplow's theory with a "rational" analysis. The rational analysis agrees that no coalition would form for Type 4 and Type 6 triads, but that for all other types, every possible pairwise coalition can win, and no one can win by himself. Thus, rationally, the players are equivalent and the initial

---

[3] Georg Simmel (1858–1918), German philosopher and sociologist.

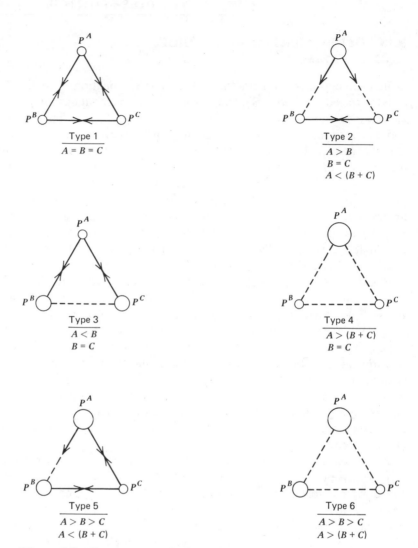

Figure 9.5. The six types of triads discussed by Caplow (1956). *A, B,* and *C* are the "powers" of P^A, P^B, and P^C, respectively. An arrow away from one player toward a second indicates that the first player is motivated to ally with the second. According to Caplow, a coalition will form only if the motivation is mutual (double arrow). (After Caplow, 1956.)

"power distributions" are meaningless. In terms of game theory, all essential constant-sum three-person games are strategically the same, as we saw, and the coalition of any two players is equally reasonable.

To compare these theories, Vinacke and Arkoff had triads play a game on a modified parchisi board. Players had tokens which went 67 steps from start to finish. The first player or coalition to finish received 100 points. A player could move his token the number of steps equal to the outcome of a rolled die times his "power." His power was a small integer determined randomly. Thus for a Type 5 triad, the powers of 4, 3, and 2 were randomly assigned to the players. At any time in the game two players could agree to form a coalition, and this agreement had to include how many of the 100 points each player was to get. Since the same die throw applied to each player in the game, the powers strictly determined who would reach the finish first, unless there was a coalition. The rules were such that any coalition with a greater power than the isolate would win, regardless of when in the game the coalition was formed. Logically, then, it was not necessary to throw the die at all, since the powers and the coalitions completely determined the results.

Each triad of Ss played each type of game three times. There were 30 triads, so each type of game was played 90 times. The number of coalitions of each kind that occurred is shown in Table 9.1. For Type 1, the possible coalitions occurred about equally often, which would accord with either Caplow's theory or the rational theory. For 10 trials no coalition occurred. Caplow's theory only allows one coalition for Type 2, $\{P^B P^C\}$; indeed, that coalition clearly predominated, although other coalitions sometimes occurred. Caplow's theory allows two possible coalitions for Type 3 and Type 5, and these predominated. It is curious that for all the "essential" games the weakest player is better off than the strongest, both in Caplow's theory and in the results. "Weakness is strength." The most "powerful" player only had an advantage in the non-essential games where he needed no allies to win. The strongest player was even worse off for

TABLE 9.1
Frequency of Coalition Formation by Allies and Type*

Coalition	Type 1 (1–1–1)	Type 2 (3–2–2)	Type 3 (1–2–2)	Type 4 (3–1–1)	Type 5 (4–3–2)	Type 6 (4–2–1)
$\{P^A P^B\}$	33	13	24	11	9	9
$\{P^A P^C\}$	17	12	40	10	20	13
$\{P^B P^C\}$	30	64	15	7	59	8
Total Coalitions	80	89	79	28	88	30
No Coalition	10	1	11	62	2	60

* From Vinacke and Arkoff (1957).

Type 5 in the results than in Caplow's theory, for P^C preferred to ally with middle-strength P^B.

The majority of point splits were 50–50 for Types 1 and 2 where the predominant coalitions were between players with equal weights. For other types, however, where coalitions were between members of unequal power, the player with the greater power generally received more points. The most extreme splits occurred for Type 4 and Type 6 when the most powerful player had no need to ally at all, but sometimes did.

Caplow (1959) elaborated his theory to differentiate between three reward conditions: continuous, episodic, and terminal. In the *continuous* case reward is inherent in the interaction. The theory as already described is said to apply to the continuous case. In the *episodic* case, reward occurs periodically. The "rational" analysis applies to this case, since the rewards in game theory come only at set times and are not inherent in the interaction. In the *terminal* case, the controlled isolate is eliminated and his resources are distributed. After this, however, the stronger member of the coalition can eliminate the weaker. Any contract between the two can be broken by the stronger with impunity, since the weaker player has no place to turn for assistance. Thus, in the terminal case, the only coalitions that can form are between equals.

The Vinacke and Arkoff experiment would seem to be "episodic"; however, the results match the "continuous" case predictions. Thus Caplow (1959) suggested that the Ss regarded the game as "continuous" and therefore acted "rationally." Again we see effort to rationalize observed human behavior.

Caplow reported an analysis of sibling coalitions, identifying age with power. As it turned out, however, alliances were based on similarity of sex, age, and interest rather than relative strength in the triad.

Vinacke and his co-workers have performed a series of related experiments on coalition formation in triads, investigating the effects of various experimental conditions. In particular they have been interested in the differences in behavior for male and female triads. They have called the female strategy "accommodative" and the male strategy "exploitative" (Vinacke, 1959, 1964, 1969; Uesugi & Vinacke, 1963; Vinacke & Gullickson, 1964; Vinacke, Lichtman & Cherulnik, 1967).

William Gamson (1961b) developed a theory of coalition formation based on the work of Caplow and Vinacke which he calls *minimum resource theory*. Gamson assumes that players come into a game with different amounts of *resources,* where resources play a role comparable to Caplow's power. It is assumed that a critical amount of resources is necessary to gain control of a situation, and that a coalition which gains control gets to divide a payoff among its members. Gamson assumes that no player has veto power; i.e., there is no member who must be included in the winning coalition. He hypothesizes that the payoff will be divided among the winning coalition members in proportion to the resources brought to the coalition by its members. Of the various winning coalitions possible, the one that forms, according to Gamson, is the one that wins by the smallest margin. Suppose, for example, that in a convention 51 votes are needed to win, and that P^A has 30 votes. If he joins with P^B, say, who has 30 votes also, he would get 1/2 the winning payoff. If he joins with P^C, however, who has 40 votes, he would get only 3/7 of the total payoff. Thus, the more the winning coalition exceeds the resources needed for winning, the less any given amount of resources is worth to a coalition member.

Gamson's theory differs from Caplow's for the Type 5 coalition. Gamson would predict formation of $\{P^BP^C\}$ but not of $\{P^AP^C\}$, since the former is a minimal winning coalition and the latter is not. As already noted, Vinacke and Arkoff found that $\{P^BP^C\}$ predominates.

Gamson (1961a) tested his theory for a make-believe convention with five players controlling different numbers of votes. The winning coalition members had "jobs" to divide among themselves. The theory had some success. Payoff was positively related to resources, even when, from the game theory point of view, this was not necessary. Gamson (1962) analyzed presidential nominating conventions since 1900 to test his theory for a real-life situation. The theory appeared to have modest success, though there are difficulties in applying the theory. For one thing, backers of a nominee can't be sure they will get their prize, since the nominee has to win an election first.

Richard Willis (1962) extended Caplow's coalition theory to the tetrad (four-person group). Though it is often remarked that the triad is radically different from the dyad because it is the smallest group in which a coalition can form, the tetrad, too, has its unique feature, for it is the smallest group in which a counter-coalition can form. The theory was tested in a game similar to Vinacke's, except that the die was rolled *separately* for each coalition or individual, and coalitions could not be formed or changed once play began. The results were not very encouraging to Caplow's theory (or to minimum resource theory either, though Willis did not discuss the latter).

The procedural differences could have been very important. When the die is thrown separately for each sub-group, the most powerful coalition need not win—with luck, a less powerful coalition might win. As insurance, a player might want to form a stronger alliance than he otherwise would. The procedural variation is worth pursuing, since in real life, the consequence of a clash between alliances only slightly different in "power" is difficult to predict.

9.14 SUMMARY

The three major areas covered were zero-sum games, mixed-motive games, and coalition formation. In zero-sum games with saddle points, Ss do not start with the "rational" maximin strategy, but they use the maximin strategy more and more over successive trials. This trend reflects the greater success experienced with the maximin than with other choices; if, due to the strategy of the opponent, *S* is more successful with a non-maximin choice, he favors that alternative. In zero-sum games without saddle points, rational analysis calls for a mixed strategy. Though evidence is slight, *S*s generally do not adhere to the mixed strategy required, nor do they appear to appreciate the principles behind the maximin mixed strategy.

The vast majority of psychological research on two-person games has concerned mixed-motive games. The "rational" analysis of mixed-motive games does not, in general, lead to a clear-cut strategy prescription; this has been no hindrance, however, to the use of the two-person game for the study of factors affecting cooperation and competition. The Prisoner's Dilemma Game has received most interest. The two players in this game each have two choices, "cooperative" (socially rational) and "competitive" (individually rational). The competitive choice has been predominant in most experiments. *S*s are apparently more concerned about receiving more payoff than the coplayer than with the absolute amount of the payoffs.

*S*s in bargaining experiments tended to reach contracts in which the bargaining pair split the maximum possible joint profit equally between them. The less the information available to the pair, the more they deviated from the result.

The major interest in *N*-person game theory has concerned coalition formation. The von Neumann-Morgenstern theory for the three-person constant-sum essential game does not specify which coalition will form; indeed, all of the infinite number of imputations occur in some "solution." Sociologists have devised alternate coalition theories based on the "power" or "resources" of the players. Though such theories may not stand up to a "game theory" analysis, they have had quite good success in predicting the results from coalition formation experiments for triads. These experiments have demonstrated that, oftentimes, "weakness is strength."

REFERENCES

Bixenstine, V. E., & Wilson, K. V. "Effects of Level of Cooperative Choice by the Other Player on Choices in a Prisoner's Dilemma Game, Part II," *Journal of Abnormal and Social Psychology* (1963), **67,** 139–147.

Borah, L. A. "The Effects of Threat in Bargaining: Critical and Experimental Analysis," *Journal of Abnormal and Social Psychology* (1963), **66,** 37–44.

Borgatta, E. F., & Borgatta, M. L. "Coalitions and Interaction Concepts of Support in Three Person Groups," *Social Forces* (1962), **41,** 68–75.

Borgatta, M. L., & Borgatta, E. F. "Coalitions in Three-Person Groups," *Journal of Social Psychology* (1963), **60,** 319–326.

Braithwaite, R. B. *Theory of Games as a Tool for the Moral Philosopher.* London: Cambridge University Press, 1955.

Brayer, A. R. "An Experimental Analysis of Some Variables of Minimax Theory," *Behavioral Science* (1964), **9,** 33–44.

Caplow, T. "A Theory of Coalitions in the Triad," *American Sociological Review* (1956), **21,** 489–493.

Caplow, T. "Further Development of a Theory of Coalitions in the Triad," *American Journal of Sociology* (1959), **64,** 488–493.

Deutsch, M. "Trust and Suspicion," *Journal of Conflict Resolution* (1958), **2,** 265–279.

Deutsch, M. "The Effect of Motivational Orientation upon Trust and Suspicion," *Human Relations* (1960a), **13,** 123–139.

Deutsch, M. "Trust, Trustworthiness, and the *F* Scale," *Journal of Abnormal and Social Psychology* (1960b), **61,** 138–140.

Deutsch, M. "Socially Relevant Science: Reflections on Some Studies of Interpersonal Conflict," *American Psychologist* (1969), **24,** 1076–1092.

Deutsch, M., & Krauss, R. M. "The Effect of Threat upon Interpersonal Bargaining," *Journal of Abnormal and Social Psychology* (1960), **61,** 181–189.

Deutsch, M., & Krauss, R. M. "Studies of Interpersonal Bargaining," *Journal of Conflict Resolution* (1962), **6,** 52–76.

Fouraker, L. E., & Siegel, S. *Bargaining Behavior.* New York: McGraw-Hill, 1963.

Gallo, P. S. "Effects of Increased Incentive upon the Use of Threat in Bargaining," *Journal of Personality and Social Psychology* (1966), **4,** 14–20.

Gamson, W. A. "An Experimental Test of a Theory of Coalition Formation," *American Sociological Review* (1961a), **26,** 565–573.

Gamson, W. A. "A Theory of Coalition Formation," *American Sociological Review* (1961b), **26,** 373–382.

Gamson, W. A. "Coalition Formation at Presidential Nominating Conventions," *American Journal of Sociology* (1962), **68,** 157–171.

Kalisch, G., Milnor, J. W., Nash, J., & Nering, E. D. "Some Experimental *n*-Person Games," in R. M. Thrall, C. H. Coombs, & R. L. Davis (eds.), *Decision Processes.* New York: Wiley, 1954, pp. 301–327.

Kaufman, H., & Becker, G. M. "The Empirical Determination of Game-Theoretical Strategies," *Journal of Experimental Psychology* (1961), **61,** 462–468.

Kelley, H. H. "Experimental Studies of Threats in Interpersonal Negotiations," *Journal of Conflict Resolution* (1965), **9,** 79–105.

Kelley, H. H., Condry, J. C., Jr., Dahlke, A. E., & Hill, A. H. "Collective Behavior in a Simulated Panic Situation," *Journal of Experimental Social Psychology* (1965), **1,** 20–54.

Komorita, S. S., & Brenner, A. R. "Bargaining and Concession Making under Bilateral Monopoly," *Journal of Personality and Social Psychology* (1968), **9,** 15–20.

Lieberman, B. "Human Behavior in a Strictly Determined 3 × 3 Matrix Game," *Behavioral Science* (1960), **5,** 317–322.

Lieberman, B. "Experimental Studies of Conflict in Some Two-Person and Three-Person Games," in J. H. Criswell, H. Solomon, & P. Suppes (eds.), *Mathematical Methods in Small Group Processes.* Stanford, Calif.: Stanford University Press, 1962, pp. 203–220.

Luce, R. D., & Raiffa, H. *Games and Decisions.* New York: Wiley, 1957.

Lutzker, D. R. "Internationalism as a Predictor of Cooperative Behavior," *Journal of Conflict Resolution* (1960), **4,** 426–430.

Malcolm, D., & Lieberman, B. "The Behavior of Responsive Individuals Playing a Two-Person, Zero-Sum Game Requiring the Use of Mixed Strategies," *Psychonomic Science* (1965), **2**, 373–374.

McClintock, C. G., Harrison, A. A., Strand, S., & Gallo, P. "Internationalism-Isolationism, Strategy of the Other Player, and Two-Person Game Behavior," *Journal of Abnormal and Social Psychology* (1963), **67**, 631–636.

McClintock, C. G., Nuttin, J. M., Jr., & McNeel, S. P. "Sociometric Choice, Visual Presence, and Game-Playing Behavior," *Behavioral Science* (1970), **15**, 124–140.

Mills, T. M. "Power Relations in Three-Person Groups," *American Sociological Review* (1953), **18**, 351–357.

Minas, J. S., Scodel, A., Marlowe, D., & Rawson, H. "Some Descriptive Aspects of Two-Person Non-Zero-Sum Games, II," *Journal of Conflict Resolution* (1960), **4**, 193–197.

Mintz, A. "Non-Adaptive Group Behavior," *Journal of Abnormal and Social Psychology* (1951), **46**, 150–159.

Nash, J. F. "The Bargaining Problem," *Econometrica* (1950), **18**, 155–162.

Nash, J. F. "Two-Person Cooperative Games," *Econometrica* (1953), **21**, 128–140.

Oskamp, S., & Perlman, D. "Factors Affecting Cooperation in a Prisoner's Dilemma Game," *Journal of Conflict Resolution* (1965), **9**, 359–374.

Pruitt, D. G., & Drews, J. L. "The Effect of Time Pressure, Time Elapsed, and the Opponent's Concession Rate on Behavior in Negotiation," *Journal of Experimental Social Psychology* (1969), **5**, 43–60.

Radlow, R. "An Experimental Study of 'Cooperation' in the Prisoner's Dilemma Game," *Journal of Conflict Resolution* (1965), **9**, 221–227.

Raiffa, H. "Arbitration Schemes for Generalized Two-Person Games," in H. W. Kuhn & A. W. Tucker (eds.), *Contributions to the Theory of Games,* II. (Annals of Mathematics Studies, 28), Princeton, N. J.: Princeton University Press, 1953, pp. 361–387.

Rapoport, Anatol. *Two-Person Game Theory.* Ann Arbor, Mich.: University of Michigan Press, 1966.

Rapoport, Anatol. *N-Person Game Theory: Concepts and Applications.* Ann Arbor, Mich.: University of Michigan, 1970.

Rapoport, Anatol, & Chammah, A. M. *Prisoner's Dilemma.* Ann Arbor, Mich.: University of Michigan Press, 1965.

Rapoport, Anatol, Chammah, A., Dwyer, J., & Gyr, J. "Three-Person Non-Zero-Sum Nonnegotiable Games," *Behavioral Science* (1962), **7**, 38–58.

Rapoport, Anatol, & Orwant, C. "Experimental Games: A Review," *Behavioral Science* (1962), **7**, 1–37.

Rosenberg, S., & Schoeffler, M. S. "Stochastic Learning Models for Social Competition," *Journal of Mathematical Psychology* (1965), **2**, 219–241.

Sampson, E. E., & Kardush, M. "Age, Sex, Class, and Race Differences in Response to a Two-Person Non-Zero-Sum Game," *Journal of Conflict Resolution* (1965), **9**, 212–220.

Schellenberg, J. A. "Distributive Justice and Collaboration in Non-Zero-Sum Games," *Journal of Conflict Resolution* (1964), **8**, 147–150.

Schelling, T. C. "The Strategy of Conflict: Prospectus for a Reorientation of Game Theory," *Journal of Conflict Resolution* (1958), **2**, 203–264.

Schelling, T. "Strategy, Tactics, and Non-Zero-Sum Theory," in A. Mensch (ed.),

Theory of Games. New York: American Elsevier Publishing Comp., 1966, pp. 469–480.

Scodel, A. "Value Orientations and Preference for a Minimax Strategy," *Journal of Psychology* (1961), **52**, 55–61.

Scodel, A., Minas, J. S., Ratoosh, P., & Lipetz, M. "Some Descriptive Aspects of Two-Person Non-Zero-Sum Games," *Journal of Conflict Resolution* (1959), **3**, 114–119.

Sermat, V. "Cooperative Behavior in a Mixed-Motive Game," *Journal of Social Psychology* (1964), **62**, 217–239.

Shubik, M. (ed.) *Game Theory and Related Approaches to Social Behavior.* New York: Wiley, 1964.

Shubik, M. "Game Theory, Behavior, and the Paradox of the Prisoner's Dilemma: Three Solutions," *Journal of Conflict Resolution* (1970), **14**, 181–193.

Siegel, S., & Fouraker, L. E. *Bargaining and Group Decision Making.* New York: McGraw-Hill, 1960.

Suppes, P., & Atkinson, R. C. *Markov Learning Models for Multiperson Interactions.* Stanford, Calif.: Stanford University Press, 1960.

Suppes, P., & Carlsmith, J. M. "Experimental Analysis of a Duopoly Situation from the Standpoint of Mathematical Learning Theory," *International Economic Review* (1962), **3**, 60–78.

Uesugi, T. K., & Vinacke, W. E. "Strategy in a Feminine Game," *Sociometry* (1963), **26**, 75–88.

Vinacke, W. E. "Sex Roles in a Three-Person Game," *Sociometry* (1959), **22**, 343–360.

Vinacke, W. E. "Intra-Group Power Relations, Strategy, and Decisions in Inter-Triad Competition," *Sociometry* (1964), **27**, 25–39.

Vinacke, W. E. "Variables in Experimental Games: Toward a Field Theory," *Psychological Bulletin* (1969), **71**, 293–318.

Vinacke, W. E., & Arkoff, A. "An Experimental Study of Coalitions in the Triad," *American Sociological Review* (1957), **22**, 406–414.

Vinacke, W. E., & Gullickson, G. R. "Age and Sex Differences in the Formation of Coalitions," *Child Development* (1964), **35**, 1217–1231.

Vinacke, W. E., Lichtman, C. M., & Cherulnik, P. D. "Coalition Formation under Different Conditions of Play in a Three-Person Competitive Game," *Journal of General Psychology* (1967), **77**, 165–176.

von Neumann, J., & Morgenstern, O. *Theory of Games and Economic Behavior,* 3rd ed. Princeton, N. J.: Princeton University Press, 1953.

Willis, R. H. "Coalitions in the Tetrad," *Sociometry* (1962), **25**, 358–376.

CHAPTER 10

Finale

10.1 RETROSPECTION

In the first chapter of this book we discussed the concept of rationality. It should be clear by now that the body of concepts and research results known as "behavioral decision theory" has not answered any of the basic philosophical questions about reason summarized in Section 1.2.

The concept of reason and its role in human affairs remain elusive. Nonetheless, it seems to me that the work summarized in this book has a contribution to make to these questions. For one thing, we can now better understand the difficulties involved in asserting whether a choice is rational or not. An intellectual's call for a rational approach to public policy, for example, may cause righteous stirrings within us, but are the Neanderthals who advocate policy contrary to our desires really irrational, or do they merely have contrary beliefs and interests?

There is a trend these days among the educated young people to reject the life and the dictates of "reason," and to advocate instead feeling, confrontation, and self-expression. As we noted, such "back-to-nature" movements have appeared throughout history. Of course, "reason" has usually been requisitioned by the "Establishment." The citizens of all modern societies are told from childhood that the political, religious, and economic ideologies of the state are based on "reason." Nonconformists, then, tend to reject "reason" along with the ideologies. It is not at all clear, however, that the prevailing ideologies of any modern state are "reasonable," nor is it clear that feeling, confrontation, and self-expression are "unreasonable." Rioting, burning, and looting are "clearly unreasonable," but many participants in the racial riots of the 1960's reasoned that these riots would impel Whitey to improve the lot of ghetto dwellers.

Even for the simplest laboratory situation, it is difficult to determine which option is rational. Time after time we have seen that if one scientist thinks he has demonstrated "irrational" decision making, another is sure to dispute the experimental techniques and/or the definition of rationality used by the first.

When all is said and done, the differences between descriptive and normative decision theory become blurred (Section 1.5). Descriptive and normative theories are like reluctant lovers, whom the behavioral scientist pushes toward matrimony like a spinster aunt. To the degree and extent to which a match is made—which, indeed, has not been great—the final result is apt to appear as much like a straightforward empirical fitting of data to a mathematical model as a demonstration of "human rationality" per se.

The attempt to align normative theory with observed behavior will undoubtedly continue. This is not to imply, however, that all investigators are concerned with effecting such an alignment. Most published papers in the areas we have reviewed concern only the descriptive aspects of decision making. It may very well be that most investigators don't give a hoot whether man is "rational" or not. I really don't know. But many obviously do, and the notion of rational man is the theoretical core around which a behavioral decision theory forms. Without this core, I don't believe that a relatively cohesive subject matter known as behavioral decision theory could exist. Instead, the empirical investigations that have concerned us would become aligned with other theories, as indeed, they have to some extent, for "decision theory" has no exclusive rights to empirical results in any area of investigation. Therefore, we have had to attend to the theoretical core of behavioral decision theory—the idea of a rational man.

It appears that absolute assertions that man is rational or not are meaningless. There are too many options and ambiguities in defining rationality. In a tautological sense, all decisions might be considered to be rational. It seems to me that if we want to have a theory which states that men make rational decisions, we may do so, but let us accept the assertion as a tautology. To do so would merely be to follow the course set down by Jeremy Bentham, the man who, perhaps more than any other, might claim to be the founder of behavioral decision theory. The task of understanding the rationality of individual decisions in terms of individual beliefs, wants, information-processing capacities, etc., would, of course, still be with us, to offer us a worthy challenge. This approach seems much more palatable to me than the rather confusing series of "demonstrations" and "counter-demonstrations" of human rationality.

10.2   RELATIONSHIPS TO OTHER PSYCHOLOGICAL THEORIES

In this section we will briefly consider some relationships between behavioral decision theory and other psychological theories. It may be surprising, but basically decision theory is not so different from many other better-known theories. We can by no means discuss decision theory as it relates to all major theoretical positions in psychology. In order to consider a wide spectrum of theories, we select the positions of Tolman, Lewin, and Freud for comparison and contrast with decision theory.

Of course, as we saw in Chapters 6 and 7, mathematical learning theory has constituted the major theoretical competitor to decision theory. Mathematical learning theory is largely an outgrowth and development of stimulus-response theory, and since we have already had opportunities to compare decision theory with mathematical learning theory, we forgo discussion of stimulus-response theory at this point.

Tolman

If the mathematics is left aside, the decision theory formulation of learning sounds very much like Edward Tolman's (1932, 1959) *expectancy theory*. Tolman felt that the facts of learning are best conceived as the learning of "what leads to what," i.e., what act leads to what goal. The expectancies the organism learns would be called probabilities in decision theory. The probabilities for states of nature give the "expectancies" that an act will lead to a consequence (goal). Both decision theory and expectancy theory assume that the organism attempts to reach desirable consequences (goals) and to avoid undesirable ones.

Tolman also discussed the learning of values. Before a child touches a flame, he might expect that the result would be pleasant. With experience, his expectation changes, and he avoids flame. Behavioral decision theory has paid scant heed to the learning of utilities (values). It has mostly been concerned with the utilities for different amounts of money, a commodity with which Ss have considerable experience. However, in real life, people often have to make decisions when they have little basis on which to evaluate a possible consequence.

Lewin

Kurt Lewin's (1936) *field theory* may also be usefully compared with decision theory. Lewin's concept of valence is very similar to the concept of utility. A person moves toward a region of positive valence because a force (vector) acts on him moving him in that direction. Negative valences give rise to forces tending to move a person away from this region. Lewin's vectors are actually unobservable, so basically his theory, like decision theory, assumes that people are attracted to "desirable" and repelled from "undesirable" consequences.

It might seem that the idea of subjective probability is somewhat alien to Lewin's basic notion that behavior results from the action of "forces." Nonetheless, Lewin and his colleagues did use the idea of subjective probability in an analysis of level of aspiration (Lewin, Dembo, Festinger, & Sears, 1944). It was hypothesized that S chooses the level of aspiration that maximizes his expected payoff. This indeed sounds very much like decision theory. (For more recent discussions of the level of aspiration in relation to decision theory, see Siegel (1957) and Starbuck (1963).)

Kurt Lewin is well-known for his analysis of different types of intrapersonal conflict: *approach-approach conflict, approach-avoidance conflict,* and *avoidance-avoidance conflict*. These conflict situations have greatly interested psychologists, and it is worthwhile to examine them in terms of decision theory.

In the *approach-approach conflict*, at least two alternatives will yield the individual desirable consequences, but by making one choice he loses the rewards that the other choice would offer him. Such conflict is evident in the child who must choose a candy bar from among several kinds. This type of conflict is not thought to be as painful as the other two. The child finally chooses one candy bar and usually manages to be content with it.

According to Leon Festinger's (1962) *theory of cognitive dissonance,* after the approach-approach decision is made, an individual unconsciously decreases the valuation of the rejected consequence and increases the valuation of the chosen consequence, thereby decreasing his discomfiture resulting from the unavailability of the rejected consequence. Such unconscious post-decisional changes in utility, if they occur, should be of great importance to behavioral decision theory. To mathematical decision theory, the approach-approach conflict is a trivially simple decision situation under the condition of certainty.

In *approach-avoidance conflict,* the individual is both attracted and repelled by the same consequence. Such conflict is often studied in the laboratory by putting a hungry rat in an alley which has food at the end; however, if the rat goes to the food to eat he will be electrically shocked. The rat is presumably conflicted because he would like to approach the food and eat, but wants to avoid the shock. A decision theory formalization of this situation might be two possible choices under the condition of certainty: one leading to the consequence no food-no shock, and the other leading to the consequence food-shock. We might consider this latter consequence to be multidimensional, and wonder whether it can be adequately represented by a single-valued utility. Such a two-alternative conceptualization would miss that aspect of the situation which has been of greatest interest to psychologists: the behavior or the organism in the alley. He tends to approach to within a certain distance of the goal and to vacillate around this point, the distance being a function of various experimental parameters. Neal Miller (1944, 1959) has interpreted this behavior in terms of goal gradients. The attraction of the food is presumed to become greater the more the organism approaches the goal. The fear of the shock is likewise presumed to become greater as the organism approaches the goal, but at a faster rate. The two gradients cross at the point of vacillation. If, indeed, the attraction or fear of a consequence (or component thereof) varies with the distance from the goal, it should be of great interest to behavioral decision theorists, for one might infer that the utility of a consequence is greatly influenced by the distance of the protagonist from the goal. The "distance," in general, would presumably not be simply inches, yards, etc., but some more general measure of remoteness, which might include distance in time. Indeed, as we discussed in Section 4.8, time to consumption presumably affects utility, though behavioral decision theorists have evinced little interest in the consideration. Perhaps we cannot simply equate goal gradient with utility. In any case, the approach-avoidance conflict and behavior observed therein provides a challenge to the decision theorist.

A third type of conflict considered by Lewin is the *avoidance-avoidance conflict*. In this case, the organism must choose between two undesirable consequences. For example, a rat might have to proceed down one of two arms of a maze—one leading to a shock, and one to a loud, fearful noise. In such a situation, an organism might prefer to avoid making a choice, which might be conceived as a third alternative, except that circumstances (the experimenter) may arrange to force a choice after some time limit.

One could imagine many other kinds of intrapersonal conflict situations, in particular, those involving probabilistic determination of the consequences. It would appear that decision-theoretic analysis of such intrapersonal conflict situations and the behaviors they give rise to would enrich decision theory.

Freud

It might be thought that no psychological theory could differ more from decision theory than Sigmund Freud's. After all, decision theory views—or aspires to view—human behavior as rational, whereas one of Freud's great contributions was to point out how much of human behavior was "irrational." In spite of the differences in concepts and methods between the theories, however, Freud's basic motivational assumptions are remarkably similar to the utilitarian-hedonistic assumptions of decision theory. Just as Bentham postulated that men attempt to maximize pleasure and minimize pain, so Freud, at least in the earlier formulations, assumed man to be dominated by the attempt to maximize his pleasure. The *id,* granted, is dominated by the *pleasure principle,* but does not the ego operate to oppose the impulsive desires of the id and hold them in check? It does, but only so that ultimate total pleasure can be maximized under the constraints of reality. The ego prohibits or delays instinctual gratifications only to the extent required to avoid the dire consequences to the person entailed by attempts to gain immediate and direct gratification.

Although Freud's theory did emphasize the "irrational" in man, the type of irrationality he emphasized is not the opposite of the rationality of decision theory. The sort of irrationality emphasized by Freud concerned the failure of men to recognize their own true motives. It is incumbent upon a theory postulating that a man cannot recognize the true motives to provide a theory of true motives and a methodology for deriving the true motives for given behaviors. As far as I am aware, a satisfactory scientific program of this sort remains to be effected. The most that can be said for the moment is that psychotherapists and their vocational kin often deny the motives offered by a man for his behavior; each practitioner may have his own motivational hypothesis to offer instead, but expert analysis often differs between practitioners. Of course, men may be well motivated to lie about their own motivations; if a child spills his spinach on the floor, the consequences may depend on whether his reason is "It was an accident," or "I dislike spinach and refuse to eat it." The offering of consciously false motives would not be "irrational" in Freudian theory.

It does not appear to me that decision theorists have been much concerned with the degree of consciousness of human motivations. They have, instead, usually judged the optimality of human decisions by observing human decisions. This being the case, the motivational irrationality of Freudian theory is not very pertinent; i.e., a "rational man" need not account for his motives.

Freud considered frustration and conflict to be essential elements of neurosis. The neurotic symptom was thought to be a source of substitute satisfaction for the thwarted instinct. Although the patient may view his neurotic symptom as painful, it may be in truth less painful than open recognition of the situation the symptom masks. John Dollard and Neal Miller (1950) extended this idea; they considered a neurotic symptom to be learned by the *positive* reinforcement it entails. In other words, even though a neurotic may not understand the origin of his symptom, it may be thought of as an unconscious strategy for minimizing his sufferings. This certainly does not appear to be theoretically irreconcilable with decision theory.

Although a neurotic may not understand the basis of his symptoms, some authorities apparently suspect that many inmates of mental hospitals cultivate "irrational" aberrations with various degrees of awareness, for "aberrations" can actually be advantageous in some situations. For example, if an inmate has a reputation for losing self-control, his keepers will be wary of upsetting or offending him. "Unreasonable" behavior by children may likewise have strategic advantages (Schelling, 1963). A child subject to "tantrums" must be handled with care, especially if there is company. The reader may recall that Polonius saw "method" in Hamlet's feigned (?) "madness," so the notion of a "mad" strategy is not new.

Although "aberrations" and "unreasonable" behavior may be seen, at times, as strategically advantageous, this is not the only view that decision theory can suggest. "Neurotic individuals too often behave as though they have only one choice—a self-defeating one—and all too often accept this choice. The psychotherapeutic process for these people is to allow them to gain understanding of alternative choices measured in terms of risks and gains." (Alexander and Selesnick, 1966, p. 316).

10.3 APPLICATIONS OF DECISION THEORY

Each of us must, throughout our lives, make many serious and difficult decisions, so there is a natural interest concerning the assistance that "decision theory" might provide for "real-life" decision making. In a sense, mathematical decision theory has been "applied" in the development of a behavioral decision theory. Interest in "applied" decision theory, however, usually concerns the possibility of using decision theory for improving the profitability of business decisions, for increasing the effectiveness of a military force, or for enhancing the financial success and/or general well-being of the individual in his personal affairs.

Let us distinguish between applications of mathematical decision theory and applications of behavioral decision theory per se. Mathematical decision theory has certainly found applications but particular mathematical techniques may be classified under more than one field of mathematics, so use of a technique might be said to exemplify the use of some other field as well as decision theory. For example, we saw in Section 5.7 that Thorp profited handsomely from his expected value calculations for the game of twenty-one. His technique, however, would more likely be classified as "applied probability theory" than "applied decision theory." Many mathematical optimization techniques are applied by people who call their field "operations research," not decision theory. Whatever the name used, there have been many applications of mathematical optimization techniques in business and the military.

The emphasis of the present book, however, has been on human behavior, and in this section we are primarily interested in application of the techniques and findings of behavioral decision theorists. Nonetheless, it does seem worthwhile to briefly consider the controversy that has surrounded the reputed military applications of game theory. In brief, during the past decade there has been a series of articles by respected intellectuals attacking the reputed undue influence of "game theory" upon American military strategy. The authors of these articles have been particularly disturbed that game theory was determining America's nuclear strategy. In fact, however, there seems to be little or no reason to believe that game theory either is or could be applied to determine military strategy. There seem to be several factors behind the rumor that "the sky is falling." For one thing, "war games" do exist, and have existed throughout history, an early example being chess. Currently war games are played on computers. (The term "war games" is also applied to training and practice exercises involving the movement of real military units.) Second, military and diplomatic conflicts have been discussed in game-theoretic terms by authorities such as Schelling (1963). Apparently, the distinction between war games and the game theory of von Neumann and Morgenstern is not well understood. As we saw in Chapter 9, game theory is really not very useful, especially for non-zero-sum "games" like nuclear war. Considerable publicity has been given to calculations of how many millions of people would die for a first nuclear strike, a second, etc. Many persons took offense that such figures could be discussed in such an apparent cold and calculating manner. Such calculations and the strategic planning in relation to them, however, are not the result of game theory. There seems to be a good deal of indignation about the use of the term game in relation to war; people apparently feel that nuclear war, if not all war, is more than a "game." They fear that militarists, not fully appreciating the difference between a "game" and real war may be too ready and willing to commit nuclear war. That may be. But, American military strategy can hardly have been formulated through the "theory of games." For a review and discussion of the controversy see Wohlstetter (1964). For a review and critical analysis of war gaming in general, see Wilson (1968).

We mentioned "war games" using computers. In recent years these have apparently been very popular with the military as training devices. Computer-based "management games" and "political games" have also come into vogue (Graham & Gray, 1969). In all these games, the player or players make their choices, enter these into the computer, and the computer determines the results in terms of profits, battle losses and gains, election results, or whatnot. The reader might interpret the use of these games as an application of "game theory."

As pointed out above, however, the field of computer gaming should be distinguished from the mathematical theory of games. Whereas mathematical game theory concerns the definition and specification of optimal strategy, computer-based gaming is used to expose people to simulated environments for the purpose of education and research. There may be no specified optimal strategy for a computerized game, but this doesn't concern the people who use these games, since the point is not to define optimal strategy in any case. To give an example, one might program the game of "Monopoly" so that the computer takes the part of one or more players. The computer would be given rules for buying property, investing in houses, etc. A subject could then play against the computer and see what results. One could compare different Ss to see how they played, and to see the relative financial gains of the different Ss. But there is no implication that the computer's strategy is optimal. Nor need one specify an optimal strategy for S, although in some cases this may be possible. Of course, much of the research discussed in Chapter 9 proceeded quite apart from a definition of optimal strategy. For example, the abundant research on the Prisoner's Dilemma Game has not been based on any clear-cut understanding of optimal strategy for the game. Quite often the "opponent" in the PDG plays a preplanned strategy which could be readily programmed for a computer, and, indeed, such computerized games are being used. In addition, one can use the computer to play an optimal strategy where this is known so there is no clear dividing line between computerized games and the game theory that concerned us in Chapter 9. Nonetheless, computerized gaming and the mathematical theory of games should not be considered to be synonymous.

While being open-minded and receptive to new educational techniques, I am skeptical concerning the reputed great educational value of computerized gaming. I expect that I could argue cogently that students of business could benefit from playing "Monopoly," and that chess playing could sharpen the strategic thinking of officer candidates. In addition, one could demonstrate how students show much greater avidity towards playing "Monopoly" or chess than attending to the usual lectures. Of course, "Monopoly" and chess are classified as recreational games in our society, and educators would have a hard time convincing students, parents, or taxpayers that such games can substitute for the usual classroom learning. But when a computer is used and the game is billed as educational from its inception, people are more impressed.

Although the game environment (computer rules) is designed for realism, in actuality the real environment is going to differ from the simulated one, so the habits and expectations learned may not be entirely appropriate in the real situation. Furthermore, even if the simulation were perfect and S's optimal strategy were known, S, even with long experience in the game, would probably come to misapprehend that environment and fail to reach the optimal strategy. Certainly we have seen much evidence to suggest this in Chapter 6 and elsewhere. If the environment is really well-understood, and if the optimal strategy is known, there is something to be said for explaining these in a straightforward manner.

So far in this section we have pointed out that mathematical techniques of optimization have been used to advantage in business and the military, though these techniques might not be called decision theory. In addition, we noted that one should not identify computer-based "war games," "management games," etc., with the mathematical theory of games, though there are points of contact between them. Although computerized games may have some educational values, the limitations of such games are apt to be overlooked.

Now we consider applications of behavioral decision theory per se. Such applications are largely for the future. Here I will simply outline how the techniques and findings of behavioral decision theorists might be applied.

First let us dispose of a "paradox." If, indeed, man is a "rational" being, is he not already making rational decisions? If so, how can any improvement be realized from application of any techniques or findings of decision theory? Actually, as we have seen, "rational" can be used in many senses. In one sense, all men are always rational (Section 10.1). But in other senses, they are not. It may be possible to convince somebody to use a new method for decision making, by convincing him that the new method will help him to realize greater gains. For example, behavioral decision theorists have amassed considerable evidence that people are very poor at perceiving the properties of statistical sequences. In a game situation, for instance (Chapter 9), people often perceive a perfectly random sequence as the canny and purposeful play of a "diabolical" coplayer. Even in a non-game situation (Chapter 6), random sequences are perceived to have structure. Although in lieu of anything better, people give considerable weight to "intuition," if they were shown careful scientific evidence that such intuitions are unsound, many would readily accept better methods.

What might the better method be? Objective analysis of the data. For example, sequences could be analyzed by hand or on a computer for sequential dependencies. Of course, objective analysis comes at a price. It takes time and effort, if not money per se. Due to increasing availability of computer facilities and the decreasing cost per computation, the justification for objective analyses becomes greater and greater. In general, the following approach is suggested whenever it appears that objective analysis could improve the payoffs to be received over those to be expected from subjective analysis and decision making. Estimate the expected gain from objective analysis over subjective approach. If this gain exceeds the "cost" of the objective analysis (where "cost" includes time taken and "costs" of delaying the decision, if this is required), take the objective route. Estimating the losses involved in decision making based on subjective analysis may not be easy, but the behavioral decision theorist can, in principle, make a unique contribution here.

The increasing importance of Bayesian statistics implies an important role for the behavioral decision theorists, for, according to this movement, subjective probability judgments can, indeed, should be part probabilistic inference. But a variety of methods are possible for taking subjective estimates. Which methods should be used? The answer to this question must be based, in part, at least, on experimental comparison of different methods.

We mentioned that the increasing availability of computers together with the decreasing per computation costs are affecting the extent to which objective analysis of decision situations can replace off-the-cuff judgments. The computer will also have a profound effect on decision making for other reasons. First, recall that optimal decisions can be made and so judged only in relation to a set of possible decisions. Many decisions fall short of what they might be because feasible alternatives were not considered. Indeed, in the so-called "problem-solving" tasks used by psychologists, S's "problem" is to "think of" the alternative which leads to the desired consequence; once this is known, "decision making," in the sense of deciding among alternatives from a known decision matrix, is a trivial task. A computer can supply a list of alternatives having desirable properties. For example, there is now a computer-based service for suggesting lists of colleges meeting a student's requirements. The student can therefore choose a college well-suited to him—one, perhaps, that he previously knew nothing about. When a person is needed to fill a job, lists of qualified personnel can be obtained from a computer file. These persons might have been overlooked otherwise. There are many similar matching systems, such as computerized dating services, computerized real estate listings, hotel reservations—the possibilities are endless.

The computer and communication revolution also promises to change decision making in organizations by allowing top management to receive information from lower echelons much more quickly than previously. Whereas information about activities at lower echelons normally reaches top management only through a painstaking process of data collection, tabulation, report writing, revision, etc., data can now be collected and analyzed by computer, and be available on cathode ray tube displays almost immediately whenever top management desires. Such "management information systems" have yet to prove their worth, and skeptics believe that such systems are being oversold, but they appear to be the coming thing.

10.4 PROSPECTION

What may we expect of decision theory in the future? In spite of the considerable research performed so far, our understanding of human decision making is still very tenuous. Anyone interested in researching human decision making will find ample opportunities, both for empirical and theoretical research.

It is clear that the limitations on human information-processing capabilities must limit a man's decision-making capacities. This has been recognized particularly by the signal detection theorists, but no definitive conception of what these capabilities are exists. Decision theorists must enlist the assistance and knowledge of experts in such fields as short-term memory, sensory processes, and learning to understand the limitations.

Particularly because of the Bayesian philosophy there will be more research aimed at finding the best methods for obtaining subjective probability estimates. At present, as we have seen, there are a variety of methods yielding similar but sometimes different results.

In the future, decisions theorists will pay more attention to the temporal aspects of decision making, including time discounting of utility and scheduling. In real life, a consequence is not only some immediate payoff; it also constrains the decisions available to a person henceforth (Section 8.11). When decision theorists understand such temporal considerations better, perhaps they will begin to have some worthwhile contributions to make about such important areas as vocational choice, educational motivation, and crime.

Because of the computer-communications revolution, subjective analysis will increasingly give way to objective analysis. The behavioral decision theorist will become increasingly competent concerning which tasks to assign to the human and which to the computer.

But even if subjective probabilities are effectively assessed and data analysis is accurately and rapidly performed by computer, decision theory can be of little value if the consequences cannot be assessed adequately. Of course, if amount of money is the only type of consequence of interest to us, the problem is simplified, but far from solved, for as we saw in Chapter 4, the attempts to measure the utility of money ended in no really satisfactory resolution. But if decision theory is to be applied to our personal decisions, we surely will have to evaluate nonmonetary consequences as well. Otherwise, behavioral decision theory can be no more than the experimental arm of economic decision theory. But men obviously value social status, personal affiliation, autonomy, and many other considerations besides money per se.

Such factors have been largely ignored in the studies we reviewed in this book, but human decision making in general can be understood and properly guided only if they are recognized and accepted. At the present time human wants are poorly understood. If all possible futures for a person were imagined, how could he know which to choose, or how would anyone else be able to guide him? How do I know that I wouldn't be happiest as a Trappist monk, as a hippy, or as a policeman? Indeed, the best solution might be to alternate between these occupations on a weekly basis. Utility theory, at best, can only quantify current desires for various consequences. But the adult differs only by degree from the young child who reaches out to touch fire and who has a phobia against rabbits; the adult is also attracted to consequences that would, in practice, be disillusioning, and is repelled from consequences that might work out very well. A decision maker who carefully calculates probabilities but who is confused about what consequences would really satisfy him may be on a fool's errand.

But philosophers have been trying to figure out what people want for centuries, and psychologists have been working on the problem for a shorter time without very much success. The question is not really being attacked by behavioral decision theorists; for the answers, we must look to personality theorists, clinicians, social psychologists, and general psychologists. Of course, they don't have the answers today, and it doesn't look like they soon will, but some of them are at least concerned with the question. Perhaps non-psychologists will contribute more than psychologists.

The competition existing between decision theory and stochastic theory, which we have noted for several areas of investigation, will result in no clear-cut victory for one or the other. It can't be said that either approach has been remarkably successful in accounting for observed behavior, in spite of the flexibility of both approaches. Both decision theory and stochastic theory will continue to thrive for the foreseeable future.

The seemingly large differences between decision theory and stochastic theory are more apparent than real. Decision theory is a kind of mathematized cognitive theory, akin to Tolman's (Section 10.2). Stochastic theory, on the other hand, can be thought of as a mathematized kind of stimulus-response theory. After cognitive and stimulus-response theories vied for many years without resolution, it was recognized that except for terminology, the theories were very similar (Tolman, 1959). Although decision theory seems to be very different from stochastic theory, such differences can, in many cases at least, be attributed to the terminology. For example, if a stochastic model proves successful, decision theorists can interpret the model in terms of "information processing" instead of the "conditioning of elements."

Using stochastic models where necessary, behavioral decision theory in the future will produce increasingly accurate descriptive models of human decision making. These models will draw freely upon terminology and metaphors of the computer-communications sciences. As repugnant as computer metaphors are to many people, the lure will be irresistible. The resulting conception of a man might more accurately be called an information-processing-decision-making theory of man, but that term will never be the rage. "Humanistic" psychologists will worry about this conception of man, and will deny that man is "nothing but" a computer. While it will often appear that these "humanists" misunderstand the science that they criticize, and while alternative humanistic programs will be sketched with annoying ambiguity, they will serve a useful purpose if they help us remember that rational man is not the same as economic man.

REFERENCES

Alexander, F. G., & Selesnick, S. T. *The History of Psychiatry.* New York: Harper, 1966.

Dollard, J., & Miller, N. E. *Personality and Psychotherapy.* New York: McGraw-Hill, 1950.

Festinger, L. "Cognitive Dissonance," *Scientific American* (1962), **207,** 93–102.

Graham, R. G., & Gray, C. F. *Business Games Handbook.* New York: American Management Association, 1969.

Lewin, K. *Principles of Topological Psychology.* New York: McGraw-Hill, 1936.

Lewin, K., Dembo, T., Festinger, L., & Sears, P. S. "Level of Aspiration," in J. McV. Hunt (ed.), *Personality and the Behavior Disorders.* New York: Ronald, 1944, pp. 333–378.

Miller, N. E. "Experimental Studies of Conflict," in J. McV. Hunt (ed.), *Personality and the Behavior Disorders.* New York: Ronald, 1944, pp. 431–465.

Miller, N. E. "Liberalization of Basic S-R Concepts: Extensions to Conflict Behavior, Motivation, and Social Learning," in S. Koch (ed.), *Psychology: A Study of a Science,* Vol. 2. *General Systematic Formulations, Learning, and Special Processes.* New York: McGraw-Hill, 1959, pp. 196–292.

Schelling, T. C. *The Strategy of Conflict.* Cambridge, Mass.: Harvard University, 1963.

Schrenk, L. P. "Aiding the Decision Maker: A Decision Process Model," *Ergonomics* (1969), **12,** 543–557.

Siegel, S. "Level of Aspiration and Decision Making," *Psychological Review* (1957), **64,** 253–262.

Starbuck, W. H. "Level of Aspiration," *Psychological Review* (1963), **70,** 51–60.

Tolman, E. C. *Purposive Behavior in Animals and Men.* New York: Century, 1932.

Tolman, E. C. "Principles of Purposive Behavior," in S. Koch (ed.), *Psychology: A Study of a Science,* Vol. 2. *General Systematic Formulations, Learning, and Special Processes.* New York: McGraw-Hill, 1959, pp. 92–157.

Wilson, A. *The Bomb and the Computer.* New York: Delacorte, 1968.

Wohlstetter, A. "Sin and Games in America," in M. Shubik (ed.), *Game Theory and Related Approaches to Social Behavior.* New York: Wiley, 1964, pp. 209–225.

NAME INDEX

Italicized page numbers concern entries in reference sections.

SUBJECT INDEX

Roman letter symbols and abbreviations appear in alphabetical order. Greek and special symbols appear at the end. The index omits many symbols or special uses of symbols defined within and limited to one or a few pages.